P9-DBY-678

Praise for *All That Is Bitter & Sweet*

"On paper she is sensitive, thoughtful, devoid of narcissism or unnecessary drama, and shows superb judgment in collaborating with Vollers."
—*Publishers Weekly*

"I can honestly say it's the best memoir of a famous person I've ever read (and I read them guiltily and somewhat obsessively). Because Judd has done something extremely rare—taken her personal story and interwoven it with the suffering others have experienced, and made her story relevant to theirs, rather than the other way around."
—*Psychology Today*

"A keenly felt memoir of a dysfunctional upbringing twined with an adult life of progressive social advocacy."
—*Kirkus Reviews*

"In this deeply moving and unforgettable memoir, Ashley Judd describes her odyssey, as a left-behind lost child attains international prominence as a fiercely dedicated advocate. Her story ranges from anger to forgiveness, isolation to interdependence, depression to activism. In telling it, she resoundingly answers the ineffable question about the relationship between healing oneself and service to others."
—*SheKnows*

"Ashley Judd has written a deeply moving story—amazingly, searingly *frank*. It is her life story, warts and all. As I read her account of her childhood, I asked 'How could one so traumatized, so abused in childhood, become the woman we know: so caring, so altruistic, so compassionate, so concerned for others, and so joyful?'"
—Archbishop Desmond Tutu

"Ashley Judd has lived an extraordinary life. She has learned from it and turned it into a blessing and a call to action for others. Her journey is both moving and inspiring, unique and universal. Reading about it makes your own life make more sense."

—MARIANNE WILLIAMSON

"This lovely woman, this movie star, this determined dreamer will be familiar to you, assuming you have struggled to resolve your childhood, carve out a career, and make greater use of yourself. Ashley Judd's story reminds us to work harder and on more important tasks, and promises that if we do, contentedness awaits."

—KELLY CORRIGAN, *New York Times* bestselling author of
The Middle Place and *Lift*

"Ashley Judd has given us magnetic and searingly honest portrayals of diverse women on screen. Now with the same honesty and magnetism, she brings us her true self on the page. From her childhood to her revolutionary empathy with women and girls living very different lives, her path will inspire readers on journeys of their own."

—GLORIA STEINEM

"Judd's hauntingly beautiful memoir reflects upon her life as actress, wife, daughter, sister, woman of faith, and ultimately, as friend of the world's forgotten. *All That Is Bitter & Sweet* is engaging as a narrative—I could not put it down—but this is not your typical 'celebrity memoir.' *All That Is Bitter & Sweet* is written with uncommon depth and uncommon love. It has the power to transport you not only into the mind and spirit of a true activist, but into the elusive meaning of our shared humanity, and even into unexpected places in your own soul. Prepare to have your eyes opened and your heart jolted."

—SUE MONK KIDD

"Over the last decade I have watched my gifted, brilliant friend grow as an artist, but more important, as a wise, deeply empathetic woman. I have read the diaries that are the heart of this memoir since she began traveling the world, fearing for her safety and sanity, baffled why she chooses these grueling missions. *All That Is Bitter & Sweet* will be a revelation to readers, exposing Ashley Judd for what I have known for years, that she is an amazing woman doing extraordinary work."

—MORGAN FREEMAN

"There are certain books that stay with you long after the last page—Ashley Judd's *All That Is Bitter & Sweet* is that very type of book. With her sincere honesty, her commitment to servant leadership, and her intense passion for everything that she is involved with, Ashley Judd presents a multilayered portrait of how one person—committed, caring, and conscientious—can truly make a difference. She may be our program's No. 1 fan, but after reading this, you can count me as one of her top fans."

—JOHN CALIPARI, head coach, University of Kentucky

"Rarely has such a heart been twinned with such a head, analytical of every troubled corner of the world as well as her own soul. I've worked with Ashley Judd as an activist, and she's a force of nature who can take on any disasters put in her way. Her grace is her not-so-secret weapon."

—BONO

"*All That Is Bitter and Sweet* is, at its heart, the story of Ashley Judd's awakening. In sharing the secrets of a childhood fraught with neglect, abuse, and debilitating depression, she confronts the stigma of mental illness and celebrates the serenity that comes with the hard work of recovery. The reward is a new role on a new stage—global advocate for HIV/AIDS sufferers. The humanitarian pursuit of social justice and gender equality is gritty work, but the people she meets in the slums, brothels, sex-slave markets, clinics, and orphanages reinforce her faithful contention that every life has value. Judd's search for justice and peace—for herself, and for the millions without a voice—is testament to the adage that when we help one person, we help the whole world."

—GREG MORTENSON, *New York Times* bestselling author of
Three Cups of Tea

All That Is Bitter & Sweet

ASHLEY
All That Is Bitter & Sweet
JUDD

WITH
MARYANNE VOLLERS

A Memoir

FOREWORD BY
NICHOLAS D. KRISTOF

BALLANTINE BOOKS TRADE PAPERBACKS
NEW YORK

2012 Ballantine Books Trade Paperback Edition

Published in the United States by Ballantine Books,
an imprint of The Random House Publishing Group,
a division of Random House, Inc., New York.

BALLANTINE and colophon are registered trademarks of Random House, Inc.

Originally published in hardcover in the United States by Ballantine Books, an imprint of The Random House Publishing Group, a division of Random House, Inc., in 2011.

Library of Congress Cataloging-in-Publication Data

Judd, Ashley.
All that is bitter & sweet : a memoir / by Ashley Judd with Maryanne Vollers.
p. cm.
Includes bibliographical references.
ISBN 978-0-345-52362-4 (hardcover : alk. paper)—ISBN 978-0-345-52482-9 (ebook)
1. Judd, Ashley. 2. Motion picture actors and actresses—United States—Biography.
I. Vollers, Maryanne. II. Title.
PN2287.J83A3 2011
791.4302'8092—dc22
[B]   2011002939

Printed in the United States of America

www.ballantinebooks.com

2 4 6 8 9 7 5 3 1

Book design by Diane Hobbing

For my beloved grandparents

~ ~ ~

"You are the bows from which your children as living arrows
    are sent forth.
The archer sees the mark upon the path of the infinite
    and He bends with you His might that
His arrows may go swift and far.
Let your bending in the archer's hand be for gladness;
For even as He loves the arrow that flies,
So he loves also the bow that is stable."

—*KAHLIL GIBRAN, The Prophet*

Love is a great thing, yea, a great and thorough good; by itself it makes everything that is heavy, light; and it bears evenly all that is uneven. For love carries a burden that is no burden, and makes everything that is bitter sweet and tasteful.

—*THOMAS À KEMPIS*, *The Imitation of Christ*

CONTENTS

FOREWORD

NICHOLAS D. KRISTOF

The essence of being a famous Hollywood actor is that you have cameras constantly pursuing you. It's a law as fundamental as gravity: A lens seeks a star. To those in the crosshairs, the paparazzi are as annoying as they are inescapable—like a swarm of mosquitoes by a lake. Some stars simply go into hiding. Instead, Ashley Judd invites the cameras to join her as she tackles AIDS in Madagascar or sex trafficking in India. She uses her fame to focus attention on issues of vital importance to all of us, while giving voice to the voiceless around the world.

After college, she almost entered the Peace Corps—in which case, she might today be working for, say, Population Services International in Cambodia. These days, what do you know, she *is* working for PSI in Cambodia—and in Nicaragua, South Africa, and everywhere in between, as a board member and global ambassador. This isn't just a photo op, but a calling. She advocates for more than a dozen groups, ranging from Equality Now to Defenders of Wildlife, and has spoken out passionately on topics from coal mining to family planning. In 2010, she put her Hollywood career on hold and earned a mid-career degree at the Harvard Kennedy School of Government. That's serious.

A solid chunk of *All That Is Bitter & Sweet* is Ashley's recounting of the stories she has heard from the front lines in the struggle to improve reproductive health and fight poverty and injustice around the world. Those survivors are some of the world's greatest experts on these issues, and she gives them the microphone.

Ashley's cause is a monumental struggle. The central moral challenge of the nineteenth century was slavery, and in the twentieth century it was totalitarianism. In this century, the equivalent moral challenge is to address the oppression that is the lot of so many women and girls around the world—the millions of girls trafficked into brothels, the tens of millions who are kept out of school, the hundreds of thousands of young women who die in childbirth each year, the millions whose genitals are mutilated, and so on. And quite apart from the injustices, addressing these issues is a practical imperative: The best way to bring stability to fractured societies such as Afghanistan and Pakistan, and the most effective way to fight poverty worldwide, is to educate girls and bring those educated women out of the margins of society and into the formal economy. That's the work that Ashley bears witness to in this memoir.

When I opened the book, I expected to encounter descriptions of neglect and sexual abuse in Africa and Asia. What surprised me was that some of the abuse and neglect described is closer to home, swirling around Ashley herself as a young girl. That abuse, including a rape while Ashley was a fifteen-year-old trying to pursue life as a fashion model halfway around the world, left deep emotional scars that she has had to deal with as an adult. So this book intertwines tales of personal abuse with examination of mass abuses—they are not just parallel, but also complementary. After reading her personal story, I think I understand better why Ashley has been so committed to addressing injustices afflicting girls in Guatemala, Cambodia, Kenya: Her own legacy of abuse left her emotionally fragile, yes, but it also left her armed with unusual empathy. Her antennae were always out for other little Ashleys, some in far more dire circumstances.

There's a tendency to tune out these kinds of global problems, seeing them as sad but inevitable. Prostitution, after all, is often described as "the world's oldest profession." And if babies die of diarrhea or measles in Africa, if women die in childbirth there, that's seen as tragic but also the bleak reality of the world we live in. Humanitarians may have inadvertently fed this fatalism by focusing relentlessly on the world's problems and ignoring the successes, for the truth is that there has been huge progress. In 1960, there were about 20 million children dying annually before the age of five. With today's increased world population, that's equivalent to 55 million children. Instead, because of new clinics and hospitals, vaccinations and malaria medicines, bed nets and sanitation, the toll has dipped to about 8 million each year. That's still far too many children dying needlessly, but it also means that more than 40 million children's lives are being saved annually—a stunning achievement.

Cynics sometimes say that saving lives just leads to population explosions and more Malthusian tragedies ahead. But in fact when parents see that their children will survive, they have fewer. Family sizes are coming down sharply in poor countries around the world. We're also getting smarter about what interventions are cost-effective. And microsavings (helping the poor save money effectively) seems to be even more effective than microlending in lifting people out of penury. In short, this war on global poverty is one that we're winning. It's not depressing, but encouraging. For the first time in the history of the world, all human beings may have an opportunity to make something of themselves.

And that's what this book is: an ultimately encouraging exploration of some grim topics. Ashley plumbs the depths of depression—her own struggles with her mental health, and her painful encounters with global ill health—but it's also a story of resiliency and triumph. Ashley persevered and worked out her traumas. And she also is spending her life chipping away at injustices and poverty around the world. So beat the drums. Sound the trumpets. This is a tale that is not melancholic but inspiring. It deserves the spotlight that Ashley brings to it—and, yes, the pesky cameras, too.

Listening.

If I am not for myself, who will be for me?
If I am only for myself, what am I?
If not now, when?

— *RABBI HILLEL*

PROLOGUE

Forcibly Displaced Persons Camp, Kiwanja, Rutshuru,
Democratic Republic of the Congo, September 2, 2010.

A patch of raw earth, carved out of the forest: dried mud ribbed with ditches, tiny dwellings fashioned from plastic, sticks, fabric, some thatching. The residents are mostly women and children, victims of a relentless civil war. Everyone is dead tired and dirty. The scene offers snapshots of the horrors of eastern DRC: displacement, malaria, AIDS, malnutrition, and an epidemic of extreme violence and rape that defies the imagination. A week ago, in the village of Luvungi, rebels fighting for control of the vast mineral wealth in the region attacked a small village and raped 240 women of all ages. UN peacekeepers eleven miles away had been prodigiously warned and did nothing to prevent or intervene in the atrocities. Rape is a weapon of war here.

This camp is a small oasis of security, if not hope, for a handful of Congolese. I spot a young, sweaty child named Durika, wearing a piece of a black garbage bag. She extends her arms to me, and I scoop her up. She is limp and frail. I rock her and sing to her, pour water in my hand and wipe her face; she is blazing hot. Her mama, Muntuzu Angel, lives in a minuscule, tidy makeshift shelter, the only home she and her seven children have known for the past two years. When I ask where they sleep, she uses her hand to gesture to the bare dirt floor. She tells me she had been gang-raped by soldiers, more than once. She fled to the forest after the first gang rape and then to this camp after her mother, father, and husband were all murdered by militia. While we visit she nurses a toddler named Naomi. I tell her that is a lovely name, also my mother's name. Muntuzu

Angel has a beautiful, soft presence. She tells her story gently. She confides that she doesn't usually let on that the baby was conceived in rape; she does not want Naomi to be stigmatized. This child is as cherished as her babies conceived in love, she tells me.

Once again, I am staggered and humbled by the human capacity for suffering, resilience, and compassion that I experience in this hellhole, and all the other hellholes I have visited in the past seven years. I thank Muntuzu Angel for our time together. She whispers, while I am still holding her child, that I am a woman just like her, that I am no different. We both cry, something transcendent passing between us. I tell her that I will never forget her, and I will tell her story. It is a promise I have made, and kept, dozens, maybe hundreds, of times in Southeast Asia, Central America, India, Africa. Mere days after meeting Muntuzu Angel, I, with famed human rights activist John Prendergrast, would solemnly carry her narrative directly to President Paul Kagame of Rwanda, spending three hours with him strategizing on ways to extinguish militias in eastern DRC.

~ ~ ~

As I walk to the next hut, children swarm around my legs. I feel an unseen hand stroke my forearm. And I freeze. This is the moment that kills me, that will haunt my sleep. The unseen child, touching my arm, too shy to be held, perhaps not up for the struggle to reach me through the clamoring throng, but wanting to connect, to touch me.

Who was she?

There are other snapshots:

A boy who looks no more than three but may be older, stunted from malnutrition, lumbering under the weight of a heavy jerrican filled with water and a large bundle of wood lashed to his back. He falters up a steep, loose dirt path in the mountains. I catch his eye. He stares at me with something that looks like rage.

A smiling girl in her too large, dirty yellow dress; the moment we begin to hold hands, she shines. My heart sings alleluia.

A miner missing a front tooth who, thrilled to be photographed, throws off his hat with joy, wanting his face to be as close to mine as possible. I love him.

A Congolese senator, traveling with our group, explaining to me that in his country "we take care of ladies, believe they should be protected." I decide that this is not a conversation worth pursuing.

~ ~ ~

The only safe place for us to stay is in Goma, a gritty, filthy town on the shores of Lake Kivu. I buckle down for the night in my threadbare hotel room. I sleep well at first, then somewhere along two in the morning I inevitably wake up. Faces float by; tormented distant eyes pin me to the bed. I write in my journal, process the events of the day, call Tennie, my adopted grandmother and spiritual mentor, to try to make sense out of the insensible. I fight off giving in to anger and despair.

I guiltily turn on my iPod, which ironically, appallingly, contains some of the bloodstained conflict minerals from the mines over which multiple armed militias and the national army are fighting. Raping the very old, the very young, everyone in between, militias terrorize and destabilize communities, eliminating resistance. The UN and International Rescue Committee estimate that hundreds of thousands have been raped in eastern DRC, five million have died since 1996. Two million are displaced in North and South Kivu alone.

I listen to the *Wisdom of Forgiveness* written by His Holiness the Dalai Lama and my friend, Victor Chan. In it, the Dalai Lama speaks with a fellow lama who had been tortured by the Chinese for years.

"Were you ever afraid?" His Holiness asks.

"No," replies the man.

"Really? You never felt fear?" presses the great spiritual leader.

Pause.

"Yes. I was afraid I would lose compassion for the Chinese."

It takes my breath away.

I am asked by my spiritual practice to examine the violence in my own thoughts, where all violence starts. I am asked to regard even "justified anger" as a dubious luxury. I am asked to remember I have no idea what I am capable of, under such circumstances. I am asked to love my enemies.

What is this grace, that allows me to feel mercy for the murderer, love for the perpetrator? It is a question I have pursued across continents and scrutinized in my own heart and soul.

I am often asked why I regularly leave behind my comfortable life, my beautiful farm, my incredible husband, to visit squalid and often dangerous places, advocating sustainable grassroots programs that improve the lives of the world's most vulnerable people, bringing attention to the core causes and conditions of their suffering. I go because I must. I go because I love it. But why do I love it? Why do I eagerly, even as I know I induce my own grief, lean into gender equality, human rights, and social justice work with such zeal? I am, by the grace of God, slowly learning that piece of my own story. My values spring from my deep belief that there is no separation between myself and women like Muntuzu Angel, or the politician who dismissed her, or even the soldiers who raped her repeatedly. I have an unshakable conviction that we are all One Being, created by a loving God. It is sometimes all that sustains me through each wrenching encounter. My emotions play a crucial role, too, for as I feel, those very feelings teach me precisely what my values are.

Since I began this work in 2003 as the global ambassador for Population Services International, a public health nonprofit, and the partner organizations I have enthusiastically joined along the way, I have been on the front lines of the battle against preventable diseases like malaria and HIV/ AIDS; traveled into the depraved world of human trafficking, sex slavery and labor slavery; visited the palaces and corridors of power, engaging the decision makers who can improve public policies.

My aim, when I began this journey, was to make my life an act of worship, to be useful to my fellows. To do this, I would witness firsthand the stories of the poorest of the poor and carry their narratives like treasure home to the richest country in the world, America. I hoped it might be possible that I could help change, and perhaps even save, lives.

What I did not expect was that one life I would change and save would be my own.

All That Is Bitter & Sweet

Chapter 1

FAMILY OF CHANCE, FAMILY OF CHOICE

COURTESY OF THE AUTHOR

Mamaw and my mother. Before seeing this snapshot, I had not known they had shared lighthearted moments.

Say not, "I have found the truth," but rather, "I have found a truth."

—*KAHLIL GIBRAN*

*M*y favorite author, Edith Wharton, wrote in her autobiography, "My last page is always latent in my first, but the intervening windings of the way become clear only as I write." So it has been with me as I have undertaken to make sense of my own past.

Although the home of my heart is in the Appalachian Mountains, I always considered it auspicious that I was born in Southern California, one of the most transitory places in the world, during one of the most turbulent springs in American history. When I arrived by cesarean section at Granada Hills Hospital on April 19, 1968, California was the epicenter of a society in the throes of a cultural and spiritual upheaval. The Vietnam War was raging. The nation was still reeling from the assassination of Martin Luther King Jr., and Bobby Kennedy would soon be gunned down at the Ambassador Hotel in Los Angeles, leaving a generation of idealists lost in a tide of grief and regret. Some of the flower children who had flocked to San Francisco for the Summer of Love were now panhandling for loose change along Hollywood's Sunset Strip—a place I would soon know well.

My parents, Michael and Diana Ciminella, were small-town kids from rural eastern Kentucky. Like most everyone else in the Los Angeles basin, they had moved to California looking for a fresh start in what Joan Didion described as "the golden land where every day the world is born anew." In 1967, my parents bought a tract house on a cul-de-sac in Sylmar, a suburb carved out of olive groves in the San Fernando Valley, about twenty miles north and a world away from Hollywood. My dad sold electronic components for the aerospace industry; my mom stayed home and seethed with boredom. They had dreams, just different ones. And they had secrets.

They had married too young and for the "wrong" reason—namely, the unplanned pregnancy that produced my older sister, Christina (you know her as Wynonna), when Mom was only seventeen. It was a typical story of the time: high school girl becomes pregnant and "has" to marry her teenage boyfriend. But there was a twist: Michael wasn't the father of Diana's baby—something he didn't know at the time of the wedding, and something my sister and I wouldn't learn for decades. When I came into the world four years later, my family's troubled and remarkable course had already been set in motion, powerfully shaped by my mother's desperate teenage lie and the incredible energy she dedicated to protecting it.

I began to understand the dynamics of my past, and how we are only as sick as our secrets, when I was thirty-seven years old and started on a simple and practical path of personal recovery. It was then that I discovered we all belong to two families: our family of choice and our family of origin. My family of choice is a colorful assortment of surrogate grandparents, aunts, uncles, and friends who infuse me with love, belonging, and acceptance. My family of origin, the one into which I was born, was also brimming with love but was not a healthy family system. There was too much trauma, abandonment, addiction, and shame. My mother, while she was transforming herself into the country legend Naomi Judd, created an origin myth for the Judds that did not match my reality. She and my sister have been quoted as saying that our family put the "fun" in dysfunction. I wondered: Who, exactly, was having all the fun? What was I missing?

As I write these words, I am happy to say that each of us has embarked on a personal process of healing, and my family is healthier than it has ever been. We have come far. In our individual and collective recoveries, we have learned that mental illness and addiction are *family* diseases, spanning and affecting generations. There are robust strains of each on both sides of my family—manifested in just about everything from depression, suicide, alcoholism, and compulsive gambling to incest and suspected murder—and these conditions have shaped my parents' stories (even if some of the events did not happen directly to them) as well as my sister's and my own. Fortunately, along with the dysfunction is a legacy of love, resiliency, creativity, and faith in a family whose roots I can trace back at least eight generations in the mountains of Kentucky and about 350 years in America, and as far as the shores of Sicily. That history is as much a part of my DNA as the arch of my eyebrows or the color of my hair. It's imprinted in the soft r's and long vowels that well up in my voice when I'm speaking about my home place or the way I whoop for my dogs from the doorway, barefoot, in a nightgown, assuming my mountain woman stance with a hand on one hip, a way of being as natural to me as breathing.

Although I now make my home in rural middle Tennessee, eastern Kentucky still calls to me. Kentuckians have a deeply ingrained, almost mystical sense of place—a sense of belonging that defines us. As a teenager, I took a friend to see my great-aunt Pauline's farm. She passed away when I was in the fourth grade. Nevertheless, although I had not been there since I was ten years old, I navigated my car deep into the countryside, to her homestead on Little Cat Creek, without making a single wrong turn. More recently, after flying over catastrophic mountaintop removal coal-mining sites in Pike County, I drove to Black Log Hollow in Martin County, where my paternal grandmother was raised. When I pulled onto Black Log, something ineffable—without words and deeper than memory, from a place so primal that it transcends thought and conscious action— tugged at my soul. I went unhesitatingly to the first mailbox on the right. The stenciled name read "Dalton," which was my paternal grandmother's maiden name; I had found my great-grandparents' home and realized that folks to whom I am kin lived there yet. I called on the residents, and like a cliché, the old woman inside accused me of being the law or a tax collector. The only thing missing was a rifle across her lap.

These mountains can hold dark secrets. Mary Bernadine Dalton, who became my Mamaw Ciminella, never talked to me much about her family or her years growing up. Her mother, Effie, was married at least five times. The husband who fathered Mamaw and her two sisters disappeared from the scene—she never said why, at least to me, although Papaw Ciminella, who loved family dearly and was a devoted reminiscer, told me that my great-granddaddy had hit Effie and she'd ended that marriage on the spot. Mostly, what I knew was that Mamaw was a gorgeous mountain girl with a luscious figure who, like the Kim Novak character in *Picnic,* fell for a charming, exotic outsider who loved adventure.

Michael Lawrence Ciminella (Papaw) was the son of Sicilian immigrants who had settled in western New York, on the shores of Lake Erie. His mother was a classic homemaker in the Italian tradition, his father had a good job making wine for Welch's, and they were surrounded by a vibrant extended family. They raised five children together, including Papaw. But, according to my cousins, there was a dark side to this quintessential American story. A family member had raped Papaw's mother, and his oldest brother was conceived in incest. I can only imagine the suffering that created in Papaw's family as he grew up, and it may explain why he developed ulcers that kept him out of military service during World War II. As a young man, Papaw, after his exciting tenure in the Civilian Conservation Corps in the western states, which allowed him to discover his love of rambling, installed copper roofing and gutters up and down the Appalachian Mountains. It was on one of these trips that he met the beautiful Billie Dalton at a clandestine juke joint in Inez, Kentucky. He swept her away from the local hero she was dating and married her in 1944, after a six-week courtship. They moved to Erie, Pennsylvania, where he found a good job with General Electric building locomotives during the war. My father, Michael Charles Ciminella, who came along, was their only child.

After the war, Papaw and Mamaw briefly owned a diner in Erie until Papaw, who used to play some serious poker, lost the business to one of the local "hard guys" in a card game. His gambling days over (for a while, at least), Papaw moved his young family back to eastern Kentucky, where he worked as a brakeman for the C&O Railroad. He was a wizard with all kinds of metalwork, and he eventually turned a part-time business building and installing gutters and siding into the successful Ashland Aluminum Products Company.

Dad idolized his father, whom he remembers as outgoing, immensely competitive, hardworking, and honest. Papaw never lied or cheated to make a sale, and he expected people to pay him when and what they owed him. Mamaw, in her early years, was as outgoing as Papaw. They were a beautiful and stylish couple, accomplished dancers who enjoyed socializing and golfing at the country club. But Dad's memory is that Mamaw grew more eccentric as she got older. She liked her house to be perfectly clean, neat, and orderly. She also tended to fret, particularly about the health of her only child.

Dad had come down with a bad case of rheumatic fever as a young boy. It took him years to recuperate, and the family moved to Florida during the winters to help him heal. Mamaw must have been terrified of losing him, because she nearly smothered him trying to keep him safe. He chafed at her vigilance, and when it came time for high school, he asked to go to Fork Union Military Academy in Virginia to slip out from under her watchful eye. Dad thrived there, academically and athletically. The once sickly kid had turned into an outstanding baseball player, whose achievements were chronicled in the local paper and who briefly considered going pro. When he was sixteen, his parents bought him a Corvair Monza so that he could drive himself back and forth to Ashland.

As soon as he received the car, Wendell Lyon, his best friend back home, enlisted him to drive him and his girlfriend, Linda McDonald, who would eventually become my godmother, to the movie theater over in Huntington, West Virginia. To seal the deal, Linda arranged a blind date for Michael with her pretty, fourteen-year-old across-the-street neighbor and friend, Diana Judd.

Michael and Diana dated on and off for the next three years, and she has said that he first proposed marriage when she was only fifteen. She also claims she never loved him, but she enjoyed being taken on dates to the country club, and she was impressed by the comfortable lifestyle of the Ciminella family, which seemed luxurious compared with her family's humbler circumstances.

Charles Glen Judd, my maternal papaw, came from a family that didn't have much money, but they had laughter, stability, and love. He was born on Shirt Tail Fork of Little Blainecreek, alongside a farm that had been in the family for generations. Papaw Judd and his folks moved to Ashland because the job options in Lawrence County were coal mines or nothing. When he was a senior in high school, he fell for a fourteen-year-old strawberry blonde cashier named Pauline "Polly" Oliver.

Polly, my maternal grandmother, whom we call "Nana," came from a strange and troubled background. Her paternal grandfather, David Oliver, had turned on the gas oven and then hanged himself in front of his sons, aged only six and four, apparently because he was distraught that my great-great grandmother had left him. Howard, Nana's father, managed to save himself and his younger brother by breaking out a window. Howard, in turn, married a flophouse alcoholic party girl named Edie Mae Burton, who repeatedly cheated on him. When Nana was nine years old, her dad was found in the bathroom with a bullet in his head; it looked like suicide, but everyone suspected Edie and her boyfriend. Edie took off soon after the funeral, dumping Nana and her two younger siblings with her rigid, intimidating grandmother, Cora Lee Burton. Nana raised herself and her brother and sister among a collection of maladjusted grown aunts and uncles who were still living at home, and she went to work at her grandmommy Cora Lee's restaurant, the locally loved Hamburger Inn.

She was just fifteen when she married Glen Judd, and it must have seemed like a good deal. Glen bought his own treasure of a gas station and called it Judd's Friendly Ashland Service. When he and Nana started having children, they bought his parents' big wood frame house at 2237 Montgomery Avenue. Diana was the firstborn, followed two years later by Brian, then Mark, then Margaret.

My mother has always described her early childhood as idealized, happy, and secure, like a Norman Rockwell fantasy, with a stay-at-home mother who cooked wonderfully and a father she adored, who was hardworking and popular in the community. For Nana, though, the marriage was no picnic. Papaw Judd was a decent man who made a good living at the filling station, but he was as tight with money as two coats of paint. Nana never had new clothes and didn't have a washer and dryer until the youngest of their four children was out of diapers. When the furnace quit, Papaw Judd told Nana to fetch plastic from the dry cleaner's to insulate the windows. It was the only time Mom remembered her mother standing up to him about household finances. Papaw also worked long hours, often staying late to drink whiskey.

My mother describes herself as wildly imaginative and a perfectionist as a child, the kind of kid who always had her hand in the air at school, earned good grades, and kept her room immaculate. She had neighborhood friends to play with in the humid summer evenings and siblings she loved, especially her gentle and funny younger brother Brian. Like all children, Mom must have absorbed the tension in the household, but she says the only thing she missed as a child was the attention of her elusive father. While she yearned for his affection, she learned to be noticed in other ways. Mom was a born extrovert who used her babysitting money to take tap-dancing lessons. And folks around Ashland all say how popular and beautiful she was.

By the time Mom was a junior in high school, Dad had graduated from Fork Union seventh in his class and was enrolled at Georgia Tech. He flunked out after only one year—he said he was having too much fun fooling around to go to class. In the summer of 1963, he and Mom were still dating sporadically, but neither of them was about to marry. He had pulled his act together and was on his way to earning a 4.0 during summer school at Transylvania University in Lexington, Kentucky. Mom was thinking about college applications and dreaming of the future when suddenly her idyllic world, her parents' marriage, and all of the Judd children's childhoods were shattered.

Her beloved brother Brian had been concealing a strange, painful lump on his shoulder that had been bothering him for weeks. He feared something was wrong with him, but he was more afraid of missing a much-desired vacation with a school friend. Soon, though, my grandmother noticed the lump and took him to our local doctor. Dr. Franz immediately knew it was grave and recommended seeing a specialist in Columbus, Ohio, where Brian was diagnosed with a deadly form of Hodgkin's lymphoma.

While her parents were in Ohio with Brian, Mom stayed behind to start her first day of classes as a high school senior. It was the first time she had ever been left alone in the house, and Charlie Jordan, a boy from Ashland (who interestingly was often mentioned alongside my dad in the local newspaper's coverage of baseball) whom she had also been dating, came over for a visit. She later wrote in her memoirs that she was "too emotionally spent to put up her usual defense," and they had sex for the first time. It was not the tender, romantic experience she had dreamed about. She woke up the next morning racked with shame and told no one what had happened.

The experience cost her dearly. She missed first one and then another period, and with growing panic, she realized she was pregnant. Because she didn't have a driver's license, my mom took some money from her piggy bank and secretly hired a cab to drive her to Dr. Franz's. Upon confirming her pregnancy, he put his head in his hands and wept. He knew well what her family was already facing with Brian, and with abortion both unthinkable and illegal, there was nothing he could do to help her.

If I trace the story back to what is a crucial moment, the first time my mom missed her period, I am left to use my imagination to fill in blanks, guided by what I know about small-town America in 1963, the social expectations of "good girls," and the excruciating grief that was unfolding in my grandparent's home while my uncle Brian lay dying of childhood cancer. Papaw spent his life savings trying to save his son. According to Mom's letters to Dad, Nana was "beside herself, about to have a nervous breakdown." I know from my aunt Margaret and uncle Mark what a lost, emotionally punishing time it was for them, too. As a result, I now have nothing but empathy for my young, vulnerable mother as I picture her in her sweet childhood room, engulfed in the profound loneliness and terror of those awful months. Mom has told me she let Charlie know she was pregnant. It did not go well. He asked Mom to return his class ring and informed her he would be leaving soon to join the armed services. Even though he knew he was her biological father, Charlie never tried to contact my sister. Upon his death, his family members, whom I have gratefully come to know, told us he had newspaper clippings about my sister in a drawer. It seems he was proud of her.

My mother was now living under a pressure for which she was wholly unprepared. Until then, her greatest concerns in life were limited to things like forgetting to set her damp hair in rollers on a Saturday night and thus rushing to ready herself for Sunday school the next morning. In a moment to which only she is privy, and based on a sense of despair and urgency I can only imagine, she determined to identify Michael Ciminella, instead of Charlie Jordan, as the baby's father. Once she set this narrative in motion, she would commit to it completely. She took total ownership of the story and would not vary from it one iota, promulgating and defending it as if her life depended on it.

The letters she sent to my dad during this time give me a precious glimpse of the girl who told this lie. "Sheez," she wrote. "One day, my whole life is ahead of me, and then . . ." She trailed off. According to Dad, he was baffled when she told him she was pregnant. Although they had once, as he later told me, "hopped in the sack and almost had sex," the act had never been fully consummated. Still, he figured, a girl could easily become pregnant. Besides, he loved my mother, and he simply could not fathom that she would lie about something so enormously consequential. He accepted her word and wrote a letter telling her they should marry. He couldn't think of any option other than doing the right thing.

When Nana found Dad's letter tucked under Mom's mattress, she confronted her daughter, screaming hysterically. But according to Mom, Papaw Judd's reaction was more painful. He stood quietly in the doorway, looking dazed and crushed and small. He rarely hugged her, but somehow he managed to on this inauspicious occasion. She could smell whiskey on his breath.

On January 3, 1964, Mom and Dad were married in a sad ceremony in a Baptist church in Virginia, where nobody knew them, so shamefully regarded was the occasion. Mom borrowed a navy blue suit from her mother. The only guests in attendance were both sets of parents, who were barely on speaking terms, blaming each other's children for ruining their dreams. The photograph from that day is one I can bear to look at only briefly; it is steeped in melancholy.

After the wedding, Nana rather mercilessly told Mom to move in with the Ciminellas, because she wouldn't be able to handle a crying baby in the house along with her own sick child. So Mom carried her little suitcase up to Dad's attic bedroom, with its junior high school pennants and trophies, where she would stay by herself while Dad continued his education in Lexington. It must have been the loneliest winter imaginable. After having rarely slept outside her own home, and then only to spend the night at a girlfriend's house, she was a scandalously knocked-up teen living with adults she barely knew, knowing their son was not really the father of her baby. Her girlfriends were wrapped up in Ashland High Tomcats basketball and prom dates, but Mom had dropped out of high school when her pregnancy started to show and finished her courses with a tutor.

Mom gave birth to my sister, Christina Claire Ciminella, on May 30, 1964, the week her high school class graduated. She received her diploma in the mail. Back at school in the fall, Dad wrote Mamaw and Papaw letters, thanking them for taking such good care of "Honey and the baby," whom they often drove to Lexington on weekends to visit him, telling them how much he loved them for it. The writing is touching and sweet.

My sister's birth was the only happy coda in a grim year. Brian's cancer treatments weren't working, no matter how many specialists he saw, Finally, after months of deep yet brave suffering, Mom's beloved brother died, leaving a gaping wound in her and her family's heart and soul that I doubt has ever truly healed.

~ ~ ~

Mom and Dad continued to raise their new daughter with tons of help from both sets of grandparents. To help make ends meet while still a student, Dad worked delivering newspapers and loading a UPS truck. Eventually Mom and the baby joined Dad in a small apartment where married students could live at Transylvania University. After several months of living with Mom, and more experience in the methods of creating babies (and how pregnancies are prevented), Dad began to wonder whether Christina was really his child. He can't remember the exact moment the light went on, or when he figured out that Diana's ex-boyfriend, Charlie Jordan, was the biological father. All he knew was that he loved my sister and accepted her as his own, he was in love with his wife, and he was perfectly content to be a family. He decided not to confront Mom with his suspicions and moved on with their life together.

In 1967, Dad graduated and was offered a job with Amphenol, an electronics company based in Chicago that sold airplane parts. The little family of three lived there while Dad went through his training as a sales engineer. When he was finished, the company offered him a position at its plum office in Los Angeles. Both Mom and Dad jumped at the chance to move to exciting California. I was conceived right after they heard the news and born the following April.

My sister, who was four, thought I was a gift just for her. In photographs, I am lying on my belly while she powders my back, or she is sitting in a small rocker holding the little bundle that was infant me. She would rock away, pausing only to pat my cheek. I'm told I was a happy, easy baby with hugely chubby cheeks, deep dark eyes, and olive skin inherited from my father's Sicilian side of the gene pool. As I started to walk and talk, my dad nicknamed me "Ashley Famous"—which, if you ask me, was an improvement over "Fat Ashley," another early nickname from my folks, or what my first best friend later called me: "Chipmunk Cheeks."

I don't remember much about those early years in Sylmar, in the San Fernando Valley, when Dad was busy building his career in the aerospace industry. Mom says she longed to get out of the boring valley, and my first memories are of the two-story house they rented in 1970 in West Hollywood on Larrabee Street, just off Sunset Strip and around the corner from the Whisky a Go Go. It was a marginal neighborhood, and my parents' lifestyle was typical for the "anything goes" era. Mom and Dad had started experimenting with pot while we lived in Sylmar, and by now Mom smoked regularly to escape her suburban blues. The habit stuck with her after we moved to Larrabee Street. I remember there was always marijuana inside the house, and I heard about the smack dealers out on Sunset Strip, where Christina walked by the bars on her way to elementary school. Dad was prone to taking hallucinogenics with friends on Saturday nights

Dad lived with us there for a year, but the marriage had begun to deteriorate. Mom was working part-time as a model and a secretary in a production company, with hopes of breaking into show business somehow. She also started running around with a would-be actor who lived in the neighborhood, and Dad knew about it. I have a vague but aching memory from that time, when I was about three years old: I was alone in the backyard, sitting in the swing—probably because my parents were fighting inside the house—when Dad came out and knelt in front of me. He was moving out, and he'd come to say goodbye. I don't remember the words, just the feeling of a silent hole opening in my young life.

Dad moved in with a buddy from work who had a place in Manhattan Beach. I used to stay with him once in a while. I remember sleeping there on strange, dark sheets and sucking the life out of my thumb.

The would-be actor Mom had been dating moved in with us after Dad left. He made our lunches and babysat for Chris and me while Mom worked as a receptionist in a Century City law office. I was too young to know what "normal" was supposed to be, but I felt very uneasy around this man. He gave Gabrielle, my friend who lived across the street, and me the creeps. Another character peopling my young world was Joanna Cole, who rented space in our basement. I used to love escaping down into her "lair." I would screw up my courage to pick my way down the dark, narrow stairs, from where I could see her twin bed pushed in the corner of the basement. She always welcomed me warmly and began reading to me, especially *The Lion the Witch and the Wardrobe*, which initiated my intense wonder with stories. In 1972, Mom's younger sister, Margaret, moved in with us, too. As Mom put it, she had eloped as a young teen with the wrong man back in Kentucky to escape their parents' worsening marriage and just as quickly divorced the boy. She had a sweet baby daughter, Erin, who was four years younger and like a sister to me.

Aunt Margaret didn't like Mom's live-in boyfriend one bit, and she was adamant that she would not tolerate being around physical abuse, which was happening in the house. She told Mom she had to choose between her or the boyfriend, and Mom, for a period of time, chose the man. After Aunt Margaret left, things went downhill fast. According to Mom, he turned out to be a full-blown heroin addict with a criminal record (although others maintain he just dealt pot for which he did time). I have only hazy memories of it, but I do recall that he used to knock us girls around. I remember in particular the time he threw my sister up the stairs, seeing her crumple as she hit the landing. After Mom finally tossed him out, he broke into the house and assaulted her badly enough that she grabbed us and moved to a motel for the night. When a police officer friend of Mom's showed up at the house to pick him up for parole violation, the boyfriend had vanished for good.

During all this drama, Dad tried moving back in for a while, but the marriage was irreparably shattered. Their divorce was finalized in 1974. Dad decided to move to Chicago for a better job at the home office. He arranged to travel on business to Los Angeles as often as he could, and would spend long weekends with us at the house while Mom stayed elsewhere. Like many bitter ex-spouses, she never missed the chance to run him down in front of us. She began a campaign of character assassination, telling us she never really loved Dad, trying to make him seem pathetic and weak for loving her when it was not reciprocated. He says he was trying to support us, but she told us he'd abandoned the family with no money. Mom denigrated him incessantly, trying to make him sound dangerous and untrustworthy. "He's a liar, he's a cheater, he's no good," she'd say. "He never loved you girls." Mom always told me that dad didn't want me, that he even had pressured her to have an abortion. She also called me a "foam baby," indicating her birth control had failed her.

In the sadness and confusion that followed their final break up, I withdrew into myself, my imagination, and my friendship with Gabrielle, with whom I played games in which we imagined being rescued (her parents were divorced, too, and her mom was an active alcoholic). Christina expressed her anxieties in other ways. It was clear at an early age that Sister (that's what we call each other in the South) had a special musical gift. She could hear a tune on a television cartoon, then immediately go over to the piano and pick out the melody, or imitate Woody Woodpecker uncannily, making us laugh. I also remember that when she was still very young, grown-ups starting treating her as if there were something wrong with her. She began wetting the bed when she was eight, when Mom and Dad split up. She also walked in her sleep—once, a friend identified her in her footie pajamas walking on Sunset Strip in the middle of the night—and suffered frightening asthma attacks. She was also strong-willed, truculent, and acting out with rage. They started talking about her in hushed tones, labeling her as a "troubled kid." I'm sure they meant well, but that label incensed me because I could see her as the little girl she actually was. Those adult voices seemed, to my child's mind, so condescending and patronizing, and their attitude certainly didn't seem to help her any. I think it was my first personal exposure to real unfairness, and I suspect that it's where I began to develop an extreme sensitivity to any kind of injustice and rage at my impotence to protect a vulnerable child who couldn't protect herself.

Even though she sometimes teased me mercilessly or tickled me until I wet my pants, I loved my big sister madly. She was my protector. I remember jumping into bed with her while our house on Larrabee Street rattled during a big earthquake. When I was still too little to be in school all day, I would play in my sister's room to feel closer to her. I was so eager to learn to read and write and count, and I would sit at her tiny table pretending to study, doing what I imagined she was doing in big-girl school. I remember trying to write, making little peaks and valleys in a straight line, and calling Mom in. "Yes, they do look like m's and n's," she said, and when she left, I floated through the rest of my self-administered studies, so proud that I was fit to be tied.

I so wanted to fit in with the grown-ups that it was frustrating when I couldn't keep up. I hated to be left out of a conversation. I remember sitting at the supper table when I was about four, listening to the adults discuss the spiritual nature of God. With inspired timing, I picked up my sparerib and declared, "God is a sparerib!" Spirit, sparerib—it all sounded the same. My mother and her friends started laughing—for them it was one of those cute *Kids Say the Darndest Things* moments. But I took it badly. I felt ridiculed and humiliated. It felt as if every time I mixed up a word my mother would laugh and tell everybody, and I never thought it was funny. It was shaming and it hurt, especially because they didn't seem to realize how sensitive I was, and they only laughed harder when they saw my embarrassment.

Another time I was sitting up on the kitchen counter when my favorite song came on the radio, "You're So Vain." The lyrics were so weird and wonderful that they captured my imagination: clouds in my coffee? I loved it. I was very expressive, and it didn't take much encouragement from my sister and mother to really get me going, belting it out with abandon at the top of my lungs, crazily off-key, while they egged me on. But eventually I realized that I wasn't being celebrated for my animated performance, with my chubby cheeks and elastic face: I was being laughed at. It was confusing, and it broke my spirit. I never sang again. It was several years before my mother and sister began to sing together, but it was clear from the outset that I was not going to be included.

~ ~ ~

Not long after he moved back to Chicago in 1974, Dad decided he'd had enough of his nine-to-five job in the aerospace industry. He'd been working to support a family since he was nineteen, and now he did what a lot of people his age had already done: He dropped out. He packed a couple of pairs of jeans and a raincoat, and with $2,000 in his pocket and $8,000 in the bank, he took off in his MGB to find himself. He wandered around the country for a few months, eventually moving back to Lexington, Kentucky, where he learned a new skill as a leather craftsman. When he wasn't sleeping in the back room of the leather shop where he worked, he stayed at an old fishing camp he had rented right on the Kentucky River called "Camp Wig."

Meanwhile, whatever dreams Mom had of making it big in Hollywood weren't working out. Right before I was ready to enter the first grade, she decided to give up on Los Angeles and head back to Kentucky to study for a nursing degree. She felt a calling to become a nurse, possibly because she had been helpless to ease her brother Brian's suffering. She looked around for the right school and decided on the RN program in Eastern Kentucky University in Richmond.

This was the beginning of our vagabond years. Mom was a restless gypsy at heart, never satisfied to stay in one place, full of dreams of bigger things. I would attend thirteen schools between the ages of five and eighteen, as I was bounced around from town to town, household to household, from Los Angeles to Kentucky to Northern California and back again, while Mom roamed, developing her lofty dreams. Along the way, I was taught to believe that our lifestyle was normal and never to question it or complain, even when I was left alone for hours, sometimes days at a time, or when I was passed without warning to yet another relative. During these years I largely looked after myself—for example, learning to cook my own meals for myself when I was eight. Of course, I loved my mother, but at the same time I dreaded the mayhem and uncertainty that followed her everywhere. The consistent nurturing seemed to end when I was still very young, and I never knew what to expect next, whether I'd be tucked in by her, left alone to do the task myself, or left with a complete stranger. I often felt like an outsider observing my mom's life as she followed her own dreams. Sometimes I was allowed momentarily into her inner sanctum—the bedroom while she studied or where I was occasionally permitted to sit beside her as she applied her makeup. I spent a lot of time waiting and watching, hoping for my turn with her. It rarely came.

Chapter 2

THE SAFEST PLACE IN THE WORLD

At my beloved great-aunt Pauline's farm on Little Cat Creek in
Lawrence County, Kentucky.

You can judge the moral stature of a nation by the way
it treats its animals.

—*MAHATMA GANDHI*

After Dad found out that Mom was moving us back to Kentucky, he offered to put us all up at Camp Wig while she studied for her degree. Mom decided to declare a temporary truce in her war against Dad in order to score a place for us to live, and Dad put aside his simmering resentments to have us girls back in his life. So for several tense months in 1974 and 1975, we were more or less living together again as a family.

Camp Wig could be amazing for exploring, being half-naked and wild, kept company by tomcats and playing in the fecund river mud, but it was not practical. It was buggy and hot in the summer and freezing cold in the winter. We did have indoor plumbing, which some of our neighbors did not: a toilet and a small, funky shower. (When a neighbor friend of Sister's was over playing with us, she wanted to try taking a shower. It was her first, and she was so scared, we crowded in there with her.) I had the pervading sense that we were living without direction or structure, although I was unable to articulate the chronic, low-grade feeling of *something* being not quite right. There was a classic seventies hippie vibe at the camp: the Stones and Joni Mitchell playing on the stereo, grown-ups smoking pot. Although today I know they thought they were simply trying to correct the taboo around bodies and sexuality that had warped their parents' generation's attitudes, I was exposed to adult nudity (skinny-dipping in the river, grown-ups coming in and out of the bathroom naked), and it felt icky. Dad kept a copy of *The Joy of Sex* in plain view. (Well, plain view when Sister retrieved it from his bedside and showed it to me!)

Sister and I were quite feral, and in good weather it could be fun, even the time she pushed the lawn mower over a nest of yellow jackets. We made the best of it, sitting on the screened-in back porch eating graham crackers and drinking milk, with me commiserating while I carefully observed the backs of her knees swell up. But mowing was a rarity at Camp Wig, which at times bore a strong resemblance to an abandoned property—at least, compared with our grandparents' homes and what I thought was normal and safe. Thick vines hung from trees in the undulating front yard, and I remember wandering around in grass taller than my head, eating blackberries off the bushes, chasing fireflies, swimming across the wide, powerful river, bravely climbing fences from which to leap onto any bareback horse I came across, gripping a section of mane, and squeezing my tiny legs till I fell off and got the wind knocked out of me again.

We were always well clothed thanks to our grandparents, and there was enough to eat. I have the most special memories of Mamaw and Papaw taking us to the shops in Ashland or fancy department stores in Lexington like Shillito's for our back-to-school gear. They were so careful picking out and buying each item, making sure it was quality made, would last, and that we had "room to grow." I also know they put cash in my parents' hands. To supplement our meals, Dad would hunt rabbits and catch catfish for dinner, and I flinched in bed in the early morning at the sound of his hammer coming down on their heads after he'd picked the lines. In the winter, he would take me deer hunting with him. I remember the old-growth woods being so beautiful, with ice frozen in patterns over the creeks, the meadows covered in curtains of mist. Those were good times. Memories of shivering and huddling under cotton quilts with my mother and sister on frigid mornings were not as pleasant. And the river kept flooding that spring, threatening to ruin our sparse belongings and prompting several frightening middle-of-the-night evacuations. I don't recall the moments of being awakened, grabbed in my nightgown, but I wish I could forget watching, petrified, as water began to seep through the floor and under the door of the MGB as we fled the rapidly rising river.

Every morning we rode the yellow school bus out of our backwoods enclave and past the elegant, beautifully maintained horse farms that ringed Lexington. I loved school and was an eager student, even though on the first report card I remember, my teacher wrote, "Talks too much." It wouldn't be the last time. But I was as much a reader as I was a talker and had been for quite a while. When I was a kindergartner in West Hollywood, I had been reading aloud to the class when something magical happened.

"Try reading to yourself, Ashley," said the teacher.

"But I don't know how," I said.

"Sure you do."

So I looked down at the page . . . and *it happened.* The words became a voice in my head, and something shifted forever. I was an explorer making landfall in a vibrant new world.

Now that I was in first grade, I had already outgrown the remedial books, like the Dick and Jane series. I thought they were pointless. They were so stark, and the supersaturated primary colors bored me, as did the simplistic world they painted. I already knew life was more nuanced than that. I didn't relate. And I didn't like how Jane always seemed to be trailing behind Dick and the dog. I preferred something with guts, intrigue, and magic. I was soon devouring the Little House on the Prairie series and especially fairy tales with moral complexities. Someone gave me a child's version of Genesis that fascinated me. I literally wore the pages out with my thumb. And on my own I learned the order of the books of the Bible.

There was a cinder-block Holy Roller church just down the road from us along the river, and one week while they were having a revival, I got saved. As with so many of my childhood memories, I don't have any idea how I arrived there, why I had gone to the meeting with one of my little friends from up the river, where the grown-ups were, what the evangelist said, or what it was that compelled me up the aisle for a full immersion baptism. My memory resumes when I am sitting at the foot of my bed, still damp, crying softly, frightened I was going to be in big trouble for having done something momentous in secret. First my mother entered the room and knelt in front of me, looking concerned, and then my father came in. I wondered if they thought I'd fallen in the river or some such.

"I got saved," I whimpered.

They weren't mad at all. In fact, they both hugged me, were happy and supportive, which really surprised me. It was one of the few times that I can remember them agreeing on anything and the last cooperative effort they made on my behalf for many, many years.

Mostly, they fought. Dad wanted to spend more time with us, and Mom did her best to drive him away from Camp Wig, back to his room behind the leather shop in Lexington. When Mom and I passed him in town once, I was transfixed by the sight of him, but she ignored him. Eventually he decided that as long as he was paying the rent, he was going to move back to Camp Wig full-time. At that point Mom moved out, telling us she couldn't stand him anymore. She rented a converted garage apartment out in the country near Berea, an idyllic and creative college town about forty minutes across the river from Camp Wig. Sister and I finished the school year living alone with Dad. Mom would occasionally come to pick us up for weekends. During one of those visits, on the most beautiful spring day I still have ever seen, we floated over the swollen Kentucky River on a rickety ferry and drove through lush, rolling land to visit her apartment. I recall looking out the window at redbud, dogwood, daffodils, irises, and pom-pom bushes, knowing exactly what heaven must look like: a spring day in Kentucky.

~ ~ ~

At the end of that next summer, during which Sister and I had continued our routine of living with our grandparents, Mom came by and swooped us up without warning and took us to a new home. She had befriended a kindly music professor from Berea College, who for a small rent let us live in a beautiful house on her rural estate in the hamlet of Morrill. The house was so lovely that it had its own name: Chanticleer. It was filled with Appalachian crafts such as hand-hooked rugs and Early American antiques and was surrounded by lawns and woods. I was enchanted by the new place and didn't even mind starting second grade in a new school. I suppose I was mystified that Dad had suddenly disappeared without any explanation from Mom. I don't remember the precise moments of asking her where he was, what had happened, and if he still loved me, but I know I did, and my memory picks up as I am standing in front of her and she won't answer me directly, instead saying vitriolic, gruesome things about him. Mom had kept a briefcase of his, with what seemed to me like important grown-up papers, including check stubs. What I remember most is that after her tirades about Dad, I would hide with his briefcase and look through its mysterious contents, wondering who, and where, he was. It was all I had of him.

During this time Mom was busy with school and a boyfriend, and I have long successive memories of nothing but time, endless time, spent on my own. A pattern of isolating myself, having secret, unacknowledged feelings of deep pain and anger, and especially stultifying loneliness, began in earnest. I guess it was a reaction to being alone so much, and perhaps as an adaptation, a response to relationships in which my needs were not being met. Sometimes I would lie in bed for long stretches of time, staring at the knotty pine wall in my bedroom, or color the same images incessantly (a log cabin under a rainbow—no humans; or a lone old man). I realize now that this was my first bout of childhood depression. My distracted mother and sister saw only what they needed to see: an intelligent, charming child who was eager to please. Nobody saw a depressed seven-year-old who needed attention and possibly treatment. Thus my journey with the disease of depression began and progressed as I grew older and many times nearly killed me. Just the first hint of what was to come.

Chanticleer's lonely legacy did include one enduring gift, what is perhaps my best memory of my mother. My relatives tell me I always had an entourage of imaginary friends I had invented to keep me company, and that I believed in them wholeheartedly. I spoke to my unseen friends with unself-consciousness, even in public places. At Chanticleer, I went further, and began to create a whole community of fairies and set about immersing myself utterly in their world. I spent days and days crafting tiny, elaborate houses for them out of grass, leaves, moss, and acorns among the roots of giant trees and along the rocky-edged creeks deep in the woods that surrounded us.

Mom was always busy with school. When she was home, she would be squirreled away in her room studying, and I suppose I missed her terribly. But when I had her attention, she could be wonderful, and she was clearly charmed by my heartfelt devotion to my fairies. At dusk one autumn afternoon, we were getting out of her red Volkswagen Beetle and I noticed a piece of paper blowing across the yard.

"Go get that, Ashley," said Mom.

"Why do I have to pick it up? I didn't leave it there!"

"Just go get it."

Finally I gave in and fetched the piece of paper. When I looked at it closely, my jaw dropped—it was a letter addressed to me from the fairies! Mom had made up a language for them, along with a hieroglyphic alphabet, which I had to translate. In my room alone, I read how they told me how hard it was to write, because the pen was so big and they had to stand on one another's shoulders to hold it upright. I was enthralled. All I wanted to do for the rest of the school year was commune with the fairies. They helped me through some very rough and lonely days. I have no memories of friends from school, except playing one cold winter afternoon on an empty playground with a girl I didn't know, discovering she was still there, too, because her parents were divorced and there was no one to pick her up on time. Fairies helped distract me from such painful disappointments and feelings of insecurity.

When Mom was home from school, she would sometimes give me a dime or quarter to rub her feet while she worked on her nursing studies. I am sure we did some other things together, but those aren't the memories that stuck. I learned to cook my own breakfast, and that expanded into another dimension of my autonomy in the household. I guess she needed me to be able to look after myself to a large degree.

My mother and sister were beginning to fool around with singing, learning old mountain songs and discovering their uncanny harmonies. Berea is a mecca for traditional craftspeople, artists, writers, and musicians and home to an American treasure of a college whose mission is to educate Appalachians. My sister, who was by then in the sixth grade, flourished in the environment. Dad had given her his Gibson Classic guitar, and he had already taught her a few chords while we were at Camp Wig. Now she practiced on it constantly (as well as our baby grand piano), and Mom definitely recognized her incredible potential. But they were also starting to go at each other, and I found myself cringing on the sidelines of increasingly bitter fights that began to characterize life in our household.

My sister would be banished to her room, which was above mine, and we would pass each other notes in a basket we rigged on a pulley system outside between our windows. Once she included a toenail that had fallen off in one of our basket emissaries, just to gross me out. It bothered me that Mom was so hard on her. It still seemed I was the only one who realized she was just a kid.

While Mom was at school and Sister was off playing music or hustling games at the billiard parlor (she had become an accomplished little pool player), a hippie couple who lived down the hill used to let me hang out with them. One evening, they took me to town with them. While they were helping a friend do some remodeling on a storefront, they let me wander around, alone. An old man everyone knew beckoned me into a dark, empty corner of the business and offered me a quarter for the pinball machine at the pizza place if I'd sit on his lap. He opened his arms, I climbed up, and I was shocked when he suddenly cinched his arms around me, squeezing me and smothering my mouth with his, jabbing his tongue deep into my mouth. Somehow I twisted out of his grip and ran away.

When I told the couple what he did, they didn't believe me. "Oh, that's *not* what happened, Ashley," I was told. "He's a nice man, and that's not what he meant."

It never occurred to me to tell my mother, but I tried to tell Uncle Mark, my mother's younger brother, who was visiting us from college. I adore Uncle Mark and always felt safe with him. He would hold a hand mirror for me after I bathed, so I could see myself to comb my hair, and he read to me every evening we spent together. When I returned home that night, Uncle Mark was sitting on the floor next to the stereo, listening to a record through headphones. I sat down slightly behind him, where I could see his profile, and practiced telling him what had happened with the old man. I remember so clearly saying the words out loud and then looking carefully to see if he heard me. He never did. And I never tried to tell him, or anybody, again. I had lost my voice, my power to speak, and it would be a long, long time before I gained it back. This inability to express what was happening inside would be a hallmark of my future depression.

~ ~ ~

While we were living in Berea, Nana filed for divorce from Papaw Judd. She had finally had enough after a marriage darkened by drinking, the death of one child, and her two daughters becoming pregnant as teens. To make matters even more unbearable for her, Papaw Judd had been having a love affair with a feisty and colorful woman, Cynthia, for the past seven years of their marriage, and it was driving Nana nuts with grief and jealousy. Mom was backed into a corner, put in an impossible position by Nana, who asked her to testify against her daddy in the divorce proceedings. Instead, she chose to take the geographic route and flee. So at the end of my second-grade summer with my grandparents, Mom moved us back to California, where she would finish her nursing school studies in Marin County.

We moved into a one-bedroom apartment over the post office in Lagunitas, a rural hamlet on the edge of a state forest. It was a real step down from Chanticleer, cramped and noisy because of a bar next door. Mom went to school all day and worked as a waitress at night. I resumed spending a lot of time alone. I explored the redwood groves in Samuel P. Taylor State Park and played in the creek that filled with salmon during the spawning season. I made myself meals like Chef Boyardee pizza from a box and baked my own chocolate-chip cookies from scratch and walked myself to the school bus, even on the first day of school, although I wasn't entirely sure where I was supposed to go. At school I made friends easily, and everyone thought I was outgoing, never seeing the loneliness that was normal to me by now.

One day, our third-grade teacher asked us to fill out forms that included emergency contact information. In a moment that has become an iconic snapshot of my childhood, I couldn't turn in my card, because I had no idea whose name to put down. I wrestled with my terrible dilemma on the school bus, completely at a loss. Mom and her boyfriend at the time were at the apartment when I returned home, and I decided to ask him if he'd be my emergency person. They looked at me and started to laugh. I was completely serious, as only a nine-year-old can be, and their laughter crushed me. To this day, whenever I go to the doctor and fill out my forms, my pen hesitates for a second over the blank line for my emergency contact.

While I was in the fourth grade we moved again, to a duplex a few miles up the road, in Forest Knolls. By this point, with all the moves and all the upheaval, what I suspected at age eight during my first depression I now knew for certain: Something was terribly lacking in my life, an aching, unverifiable awareness that something wasn't right. I was at times feeling angry about my perpetual latchkey status—particularly when I invited friends home from school and couldn't find the dang latchkey! Once I had to break a window to enter the house. Even though a lot of other kids were in the same predicament—this was California in the 1970s, after all—I started comparing myself with peers who had houses and horses and what

I imagined were much better lives and longing for the day we might have more stability—or even reliable heating and cooling.

There were so many people missing in my life. Mom's decision to run to California triggered an estrangement with Nana that would last a full seven years, when they finally buried the hatchet. We rarely saw her, even when Sister and I visited Kentucky, and almost never heard from her. I missed her, I loved her, and I loved her home. When we were living in Forest Knolls, Sister and I received a small box from her, full of mismatched pieces of costume jewelry that had been leftover inventory at Pollock's, the jewelry store in Ashland where Nana now worked. I sat on the floor in the closet, holding one earring that said "Aquarius" and another that said "Sagittarius," marveling, "She knows I am alive, she sent me mail, what is she trying to tell me?" Maybe, just maybe, she was letting me know she loved me, too.

We stayed in Marin County for two years, and I honestly don't have any memories of my dad from that time. I don't recall receiving a birthday gift from him or sending him a card on his birthday; I wasn't even confident of the date. I did not have a photograph of him. There were no calls, no Christmas presents (Dad later claimed that he had sent us presents and checks—that Mom had signed and cashed—but we certainly never saw any of them). I only recall snippets of secretive sharing with other kids whose parents were divorced, whispering, "My mom and dad hate each other." Otherwise, I guess I made myself stop thinking about him because it was too painful. Other than as a figure my mother loathed, he disappeared from my life.

Meanwhile, Mom and Sister were starting to be serious about becoming a musical duo—or at least Mom was. My sister just loved to play; with a guitar in her hands, her sense of peace was palpable. The broken and ever-changing home and troubled relationships around her faded, enabling a talented, funny, endearing young teen to emerge. It was when she could shine, be fully herself, perhaps with a rose placed behind her ear or a garland of flowers on her head, without all the other crap going on around her to distort things. But Mom had bigger dreams, and she required my sister's cooperation. Mom began accusing my sister of being lazy, and she was always after her to practice. She gave her lists of things to work on, lyrics to learn, chords to master by their next at-home rehearsal.

Whenever they were practicing together in the bedroom, I was sternly instructed never to interrupt on pain of severe grounding, no matter what the reason. It was a pattern that would continue as they built their musical careers. Sometimes I needed help with something, maybe homework, or had a question that felt important. Sometimes my ride was waiting, some kid whose family has agreed to take me for the weekend or the week, and I needed $5, because I was so ashamed of not bringing money when I went over to a friend's house. Instead of knocking, I would stand at the doorway, listening to their ethereal harmonies with my arms limp by my sides, unsure what to do.

My mother and sister's increasing enmeshment only reinforced the feeling that I was a stranger in my own family. I remember so clearly sitting on a plane with Sister, bound for a summer with my grandparents in Kentucky. Sister was weeping, forlorn, looking out the window at Mom, who was waving goodbye from the tarmac below.

"Yeah, I'll miss her, too," I said.

Without taking her eyes off Mom, she snapped, "You have no idea what it's like for Mom and me."

I thought to myself: *Apparently not. And I don't want to know. I am going to stay one hundred percent out of that deal.*

~ ~ ~

I spent every summer of my otherwise chaotic childhood with our grandparents in Ashland, and I believe they are the reason I am alive today.

Sister and I visited together until she was about ten, when Mamaw decided it was too much to handle both of us at once; after that we would switch between the Judds and the Ciminellas. But the summers we spent together when we were little are my most precious memories with my big sister.

Mamaw and Papaw's house at 1515 Morningside Drive is an address I still equate with peace and stability. It was the safest, most fun place in all the world. After living all year with a sense of dislocation, a haunting tentativeness and uncertainty, often unsure where my mother and my sister were, always scrounging for a meal, I found the gentle routine at the Ciminella house intensely comforting. In the mornings Mamaw fixed us buttered toast with raspberry jam, cut into squares, and cranberry juice served in elegant little glasses with stems. Papaw was already at work, out early to beat the heat, and I loved to look at his newspaper and see his print on the crossword puzzle, which he left for Mamaw to finish. I considered it my job to read the comics and Dear Abby and ask Mamaw about any interesting dreams she may have had.

After breakfast, I would play outside and maybe sweep the walk while Mamaw dressed for the day. She always looked simple and utterly beautiful. After errands or shopping for school clothes, we'd often have lunch at the Chimney Corner downtown or at the country club. Papaw would pop out of the men's grill (there was a lot of card playing going on!) to greet us with big hugs and kisses. After the interminable fifteen minutes to allow lunch to safely digest, we would be carefree and in the pool—it was total and complete heaven. I would do daring dives off the high board, and Papaw would wave to me from the golf course as I sought to impress him. We could even order treats at the poolside snack hut and simply sign our grandparents' club membership for payment! Afterward, Sister and I would shower and compare the sizes of our mosquito bites and the deepness of our tans: Sister was a golden brown; I was the color of Papaw's morning coffee.

Mamaw served supper at home every night at five fifteen sharp—fresh summer food, much of it grown in the back garden, served by candlelight, on good china with a beautifully set table. Papaw washed up, and everyone looked and smelled so fresh and clean. Having played hard all day, and feeling so wonderfully safe, I was usually famished; my appetite was enormous for my size, and I was always given my fill, serving after serving, to admiring statements about the hollow leg I was surely trying to fill. Supper was followed by the greatest dessert in the world: chocolate pudding, which I still love; and I'd snack before bed, too, just as I do today, often using Mamaw's china and having what we would share in the small booth in their wonderful kitchen. After we were allowed to snuff out the candles, the magic hour began. We'd play in the yard with sparklers or bat pitches Papaw tossed. Or sometimes Sister and I did elaborate dances wrapped in floral towels we imagined were exotic fabrics from faraway lands, performing in the sunken living room to a rapt, captive audience of two. Often when there was a Cincinnati Reds game on television, I'd lie in bed with Papaw, watching it on a black-and-white TV with the sound turned down so we could listen to the radio broadcast, while also perusing yesterday's box score in the evening paper. At bedtime we would be slyly told to "skin a rat," and our adoring grandmother would devotedly bathe, dry, powder, swaddle, comb, and pamper us.

Best of all was when Mamaw and I would gather up all the soft pillows from the bedrooms and make a nest on her bed. She would cut off the air-conditioning and open all the windows—mountain all the way, she despised air-conditioning, as do I today. Cuddling on her bed, we would play cards, giggle, sing ditties, or just listen to the katydids chirping in the Kentucky twilight. That downy, soft bed was the high altar of my childhood.

~ ~ ~

Until Nana and Papaw Judd divorced when I was eight, they lived together in the beautiful, classic American house that was filled with generations of smells, love, and comfort. It was roomy and broad, with a front porch complete with a swing I loved, beveled glass windows, a fascinating attic, an alluring basement, and secret places for imaginative children to play. The drawers were still filled with report cards, marbles, toys, and drawings belonging to Mom and her siblings, their books on the shelves. The yard was enthralling, and I often spent hours under the low-hanging limbs of soft evergreens, making a world under there. There was an air of sadness in the house as well, because of the lingering memory of Uncle Brian and the terrible wound his death left in the family, a wound that Nana and Papaw Judd's marriage ultimately did not survive. Nevertheless, I have wonderful memories of that house, which I regard practically as a member of the family.

The most fun was when Papaw Judd took us way out to the country to visit his family's home place or to spend time with his sister, Pauline. I worshipped Great-Aunt Pauline, who was a sophisticated, educated woman with a sensitive nature who chose, for love, to live an old-fashioned lifestyle on a poor farm in rural Kentucky. She and Great-Uncle Landon lived in what was to me a gorgeous mountain farmhouse filled with practical furniture that today would be rustic collectibles and decorated with delightful old flowered wallpaper. By the 1970s they had some electricity and one big black telephone in the kitchen, but they still used an outhouse and drew water from a well that had to be boiled on an iron wood-burning stove for cooking and bathing. (It is this home that the press has often conflated with my other homes, writing that I grew up dirt poor without electricity and plumbing.) Great-Aunt Pauline always had at least a dozen dogs on the property, all named after Democrats. She was an amazing cook; everything was raised on the farm or traded for. I remember the oilcloth tablecloth on her kitchen table and the incredible dinners (that's the noon meal) she would put out. If I could magically have any meal in the world, it would be her fried chicken dinner, buttermilk biscuits, and homemade blackberry jam. She worked from sunup until sundown, completely present in the life she chose. I spent my afternoons on her screened-in porch, just watching, and content by proxy, seeing how much Papaw Judd clearly loved being there, using his pocketknife to cut fresh cucumbers into slices he would salt and share with me.

These are my most precious memories, and I have dreams about them to this day. All children deserve to be cherished in this way. I was lucky to have this reserve of memories to cling to during the rest of the year, of a place where there was no neglect, no fighting, no drug and alcohol abuse to witness, no worries about being anything but a child, where it was okay to be vulnerable and have little-girl needs. Those recollections sustained me and probably saved my life when I was in so much despair that, even as a young child, the only way I could think to make the ache in my heart lessen was to die. They are also why I understand profoundly that every child needs a safe person and a haven. I continue to draw on the unconditional love I was given during those times, both as an essential resource for myself and as a source of love that I am able, when I am at my best, to give away in incredible abundance.

Chapter 3

BUTTERMILK AND MORNING GLORIES

Our wedding day at Skibo Castle in the Scottish Highlands.

I never spoke with God,
Nor visited in heaven;
Yet certain am I of the spot
As if the chart were given.

—*EMILY DICKINSON*, "Time and Eternity, XVII"

The two-hundred-year-old farmhouse where my husband and I live in rural Williamson County, Tennessee, pays homage to the spirit of safety and graceful domesticity that I remember from the beloved sanctuaries of my childhood. The countryside where we live is impossibly lovely, with green rolling hills, open pastures, creek-cut hollows, artesian springs, and beguiling examples of American farm and cottage architecture set along the winding roads. It's real, not kitschy and packaged, with old farming families and hillbillies living alongside music-business money, poverty mixed with comfort.

When I began to dream of making myself a home I could live in for the rest of my life, a home that would shelter me longer than anywhere I had ever lived before, this was the place the fates seemed to choose for me. In 1993, after the house I was renting in Malibu was destroyed in a wildfire, leaving me stranded, my sister gave me a fabulous fixer-upper of a farmhouse on a piece of her land. I was grateful for her kindness and thought nothing of forgoing Los Angeles to settle into the rural, bucolic life I so dearly love. The property was the original homestead of the Meacham family, who once owned the large farm from which my mother and my sister bought acreage whenever they could afford it. My sister and her kids live within walking distance of my back door, while our mother and her husband of twenty-five years, Larry Strickland, whom we call Pop, live down the road. My father now comes for long visits with his creative, lovely wife, Mollie Whitelaw. Even though I'd spent so much time apart from my family when I was growing up—the chaotic, painful separations of my childhood continued long after the Judds settled in Nashville and became stars—we're still in one another's lives, for better or worse. Mostly better. Along the way, these bountiful Tennessee hills have seeped into my soul and given me a home where my heart can finally be safe and find some rest.

~ ~ ~

It took years to restore the old Meacham place to its former beauty. I pulled from deep memories of comfort, associations of unconditional love, rural living, and elegance. To begin, I jotted down simple notes that became my guiding document, things like "Great-Aunt Pauline and Great-Uncle Landon's farm; the old home place on South Shore; Nana's small print floral sheets; quilts; soft, faded velvet, old-fashioned flowery wallpaper; chenille blankets; Mamaw and Papaw's dining room table; beautiful trims; crafts from Berea." I had my work cut out for me. The house had only one small bathroom, put in during the 1960s by a local vocational school's student project. I uncovered and restored five fireplaces and other old-fashioned features that made it so wonderfully period. I salvaged beaded board, leaving splotchy layers of beautiful old hand-painted wallpaper exposed. The onetime smokehouse was converted into a ridiculously charming guesthouse.

My other guiding principle was to make the house completely open to the outdoors. Windows were enlarged, skylights installed. I added floor-to-ceiling glass to the screened sleeping porch, the most lived-in room in the house, from which we look out on wooded hills folding into pastures of native grasses (which I constantly battle my sister's farm manager to keep from mowing!).

All of my life I've drawn solace and inspiration both from wild spaces and lovingly tended gardens. Fern-shaded creeks, fields of Queen Anne's lace, hills covered with bluegrass, dogwoods, and redbuds—a childhood landscape that imprinted on me as a pastoral ideal and stirs in me the most bittersweet longing.

In restoring the land around my farmhouse, I wanted to re-create my own memories while honoring the history of the place. I replanted the gardens with what I knew various Meachams across the generations had grown, which meant native species that flourish. Morning glories and moon vine cover my porches. Old varieties of hollyhock lean against columns, fences, and gates. Salvia, hostas, zinnias, and pretty much everything else you could think of grow somewhere in my garden, offering riots of color. I went rose mad in London filming *De-Lovely* and have dozens of bushes to prove it. I planted over thirty thousand daffodils—my ongoing gift for two-year-old me, my child's eyes filled with shy wonder in a faded photograph, admiring a daffodil in Nana and Papaw Judd's garden forty years ago.

I named my home Chanticleer after the lovely hilltop home in Berea where I had lived during second grade. In spite of the many painful memories associated with it, it was where, out of sheer necessity and a will to survive, my imagination took flight.

When my husband, Dario Franchitti, and I married in Scotland in 2001, I re-created wooded scenes inspired by Chanticleer as the theme of our wedding: Moss, rock, branches dripping with lichen, daffodils, and other fragrant bulbs were our decorations. We met on a blind date in 1999, having been set up at the wedding of mutual friends. We count that date, May 17, as our anniversary. Buttermilk, my beloved hound, was with me that night, so my future husband landed both his wife and his dog in one fell swoop. I had no idea what he did. He had no idea what I did. But we sure knew we were wild about each other right away. I loved the little boy that I glimpsed in Dario, and his wholesome values, especially his kindness and fairness. I knew my soul would be safe with him. My husband is a race car driver, and of his many accomplishments, perhaps most notable is winning the Indianapolis 500 twice, and the IndyCar championships in 2007, 2009, and 2010. But in spite of our clearly public professions, we have enjoyed, by exceedingly careful intention, a discreet life together. We support each other at public appearances, such as races and red carpet events, but we do our best to keep our private lives separate. Our marriage is sacred.

Some of Dario's grandparents emigrated from Italy to Scotland, while other ancestors trace very old Scottish lines. He loves the Italian part of his heritage and is a Scot through and through. He muses that the passion of the Italians and the canniness of the Scots have yielded his particular character as a race car driver. We live in an eighteenth-century house in Scotland part of the year, where I especially love our time spent in the Highlands. When he's on this side of the pond, Dario's home is at Chanticleer. Every special occasion, he gives me trees for the farm (an especially cleverly done wedding anniversary was our seventh, for which the metal is copper, so he gave me seven copper beech trees). Our best moments are spent outdoors, walking the hills with our dogs, lying in the grass, and watching dozens of species of birds, especially the herons and hawks. Our life together here is as nourishing and restorative as any I could imagine. It is a balm.

On summer evenings Dario and I will often sit on the back stone steps, still warm from the sun, spooning ice cream, listening to the crickets, cicadas, and frogs as they tune up for their entertaining nightly symphony. The fireflies come out, proving there is a gracious God who has made a magical, beautiful world. The cats join us, either scanning the gardens, hillsides, and valley for interesting attractions or weaving about us, wanting to be brushed. Our cockapoos, Buttermilk and Shug, engage in their nightly ritual, which we call "harassing the defenseless nocturnal creatures," and we futilely attempt to restrain them from bounding up the hills and running the valleys. We leave food out for the feral cats we have named (having briefly trapped them to spay/neuter/inoculate and return), and I pretend I am their mama, even though they claim me only for their daily bowls of wet and dry. When one adopts us, we rejoice.

Like many folks, I have a wonderfully deep relationship with animals. They anchor and structure my world. Their unconditional love and four-legged wisdom enriches my life and helps me heal. They provide the connection, the spirit of play and rest, and the acceptance that transcends all doing, all circumstance. My animal companions give me the gift of needing my love—and I have love in abundance. Percy, for example, was a stunning gray point kitty with whom I shared my pillow each night for years. We held hands as we slept (Dario would take pictures, showing me in the morning) and ate off the same plate. Percy never took his eyes off me, thereby giving me at long last what my parents had been unable to sustain during my childhood, that invaluable feeling of being the center of somebody's world. The animals provide my routine, keep my moorings, and keep me in relationship with other beings at all times. It's not possible to isolate myself for long or stay caught up in either the vainglories or morbid reflections of life when animals are nearby. And that is one of the reasons animals are often prescribed by doctors for emotional support.

We had dogs and cats growing up, but I moved around so much that I hardly remember many by name. There was Mule the hound dog when we lived in Berea, and Cotton, my beloved little tomcat who sprayed my cheerleader pom-poms in high school. The first dog I ever loved with tender devotion was Banjo (we called him a Heinz 57 mix), whom Mom and Pop, my stepfather, bought when I was in college and let me share as if he were my own. He was the greatest dog ever, until the King, aka Buttermilk, came along.

After wrapping *Double Jeopardy* in 1998 following a long spell in Vancouver, British Columbia, I came home to my newly restored farmhouse, and one afternoon Mom materialized at the door, standing there with a bright, sly smile on her face.

"I have a wrap gift for you!" she sang out.

I rolled my eyes. "How much does it weigh?" I knew it was a dog, and I was unsure this would suit me. I'd never had a dog as an adult, and cats were really my thing. She began to gush and presented me with a beautiful fluffy yellow cockapoo puppy, without a doubt the sweetest, most adorable, easy-to-make-the-center-of-my-life animal imaginable. Although I didn't want to show her how pleased I was, I was smitten.

I named him for his creamy yellow curls that reminded me of the foamy bubbles that collect at the edges of a milk pail, and because buttermilk with a skillet of cornbread is, as far as I am concerned, a staple of life, as he has become for me. We were inseparable from the start, and he was forgiving and patient with me as I struggled to learn the art of raising a canine. I was aghast when he peed on my bed while we were playing. A cat would *never do that*! We tried crate training, but it was agony. He howled so plaintively, so relentlessly, when separated from me that there was no doubt he would be sleeping in the bed.

Dario understands when I say that Buttermilk is the great love of my life. I know Buttermilk better than I have known any human, and he surely knows me better than anyone. I call him my thighbone; we sleep alongside each other every night, with him positioned alongside my leg so that my hand rests upon him throughout the night. His baby sister, Shug, came along, and little did I know I had the capacity, the space, inside of me to love that way again. But I did, and she expands my soul. Shug falls asleep stretched out on her back, placed down the middle of me, the back of her head tucked under my chin, her little tail lined up with my belly button. Heaven for us both.

When I meet new people at parties, I am often asked if I have any children. Most folks consider it a harmless small-talk opener, and rather than be rude or get too personal, I usually give a laugh and say, "No, we have pets." This is the truth—in our household animals are full family members—but the whole story is far more complicated. The fact is that I have chosen not to have children because I believe the children who are already here are really mine, too. I do not need to go making "my own" babies when there are so many orphaned or abandoned children who need love, attention, time, and care. I have felt this way since I was at least eighteen and I had an argument about it with a childhood friend. He maintained that people with "our genes and opportunities are the very people who should have kids;" I countered that folks with our awareness and ability to contribute should instead focus on the children already born and suffering so needlessly. I figured it was selfish for us to pour our resources into making our "own" babies when those very resources and energy could not only help children already here, but through advocacy and service transform the world into a place where no child ever needs to be born into poverty and abuse again. My belief has not changed. It is a big part of who I am.

Over the years I have quietly "adopted" many children in America and in different parts of the global South—a better term for the developing world—sending money for health care, food, schooling, and shelter in ways that are appropriate for the places where they live and which improve their chances for better lives. But it wasn't until 2002, when a stranger named Kate Roberts contacted me at just the right time, asking me to join just the right campaign, that I saw an opportunity to impact—beyond donations—the lives of millions of children and young people I already considered part of my own family.

The letter was an appeal for me to become the global ambassador for YouthAIDS, the HIV/AIDS prevention programs at Population Services International, a nonprofit public health organization. My job would be to raise awareness and funds for PSI's programs, which target the most poor and vulnerable populations in the world. Would I consider traveling around the world, representing the organization?

This seemed like an enormous request, but I was intrigued. What I could not yet know was that this letter would not only begin a rich, life-changing education, but would also launch me on the path toward my own healing.

Chapter 4

THROUGH THE TRAPDOOR

LUCA GHIDONI/FILMMAGIC

Pursued by paparazzi, I nonetheless stop to befriend a dog.

Where I came from, the nights I had wandered
and survived, scared them, and where
I would go they never imagined.

—*MARGE PIERCY,* "Always Unsuitable"

The invitation from Population Services International arrived at what seemed to be a very inconvenient time. My acting career was at such a frenzied peak that I had starred in six movies in the past four years and I felt as if I were being pulled in ten directions at once. In the summer of 2002, when I began filming a noir thriller called *Twisted* in and around San Francisco, I was as successful, and as sick and tired, as I had ever been in my life.

Twisted should have been an enjoyable movie to make. I was excited to be working with director Phil Kaufman, a remarkable auteur who had directed *The Unbearable Lightness of Being*. I had wonderful support from my costars Andy Garcia and Sam Jackson—both of whom happen to be among the kindest, funniest, and most generous artists in show business. But it turned out to be a difficult shoot, with seemingly endless night scenes, and as the weeks wore on, I grew more miserable. It probably didn't help that my character was a depressed homicide inspector with a nasty temper; a lonely woman who was consumed by unresolved trauma from her past. She medicated herself with alcohol while—and here's the thriller part—her casual sex partners were murdered one after the other.

The role was physically demanding and draining, as were the logistics of the locations all over the Bay Area. One frigid morning I would be clambering over rocks to stare at a waxy corpse bobbing in the bay; that night I'd be in a police gym, training to fight like a cop. The length of the shoot precluded me from finding a rental property for the duration. The constant shuttling between sets and temporary dwellings left me feeling continually nervous and adrift. I was disconcerted by a sensation of always being in transition, always on the threshold of something else. It was disturbingly familiar. Without realizing it, I was reprising the pain and uncertainty of my dysfunctional childhood living arrangements, where I never knew what to expect next. This unwelcome déjà vu was fueled by the fact that my rental homes were in Marin County, just north of San Francisco, where I had spent those two soul-destroying years in third and fourth grade.

My anxiety that summer was compounded by the added stress of being apart from my husband for a few weeks at a time. I typically spend a lot of time with Dario during his racing seasons on the IndyCar circuit. I unabashedly regard my husband as one of the greatest open-wheel racers in history, and having grown up with remarkably gifted people, I find it perfectly natural to passionately support his talent and the rigors that racing at his level demands. I love the rhythm and repetition of going to the same events year after year, the arc each race weekend entails, from preparation to practice to qualifying to racing. But film schedules are rigid, like the racing calendar. Dario often flew thousands of miles to be with me between his races, and I cheered up when he was around: We would hike the Marin headlands or he would take long rides on his bicycle, and we often had company when both local friends and family came to visit. However, I was relying on him too much to stabilize my moods, and I found his comings and goings between races to be very hard.

I was plagued by insomnia, a condition I have lived with since childhood, which used to worsen when I was unsettled. Eventually my anxiety kept ratcheting up even when Dario was with me. I tried to make everything perfect for him: the right turkey for his sandwiches, the latest video games in my trailer, as if somehow that would make him happier, and if he were happier, maybe he'd magically be able to stay longer, and if he stayed longer, maybe I wouldn't have anxiety. Follow? On the set, I was obsessing about my shooting schedule, making myself a nuisance to the hardworking production staff by constantly bargaining for later call times because I was so exhausted. I kept telling myself I would feel better *if I could just . . .* get fifteen minutes more sleep, come to work later, squeeze in this personal appointment, or whatever.

This pattern of trying to control my environment is an old coping mechanism that I developed during my chaotic childhood. By trying to arrange everything outside of me to be "just so," I could occasionally secure a modicum of emotional and mental relief from the pain inside. And because it worked sometimes, and I had no other tools, I continued attempting to manage everything more and more, in pursuit of the ephemeral relief. By 2002, these survival skills were working against me. My emotional life was increasingly unmanageable. I was sick and tired of being so tired—I fought it all the time—but I had no idea what was really wrong with me, and I didn't know how to change the cycle, even though I desperately wanted to.

~ ~ ~

I was never treated for the "spells," as I called them, that had started when I was about eight years old, and I would lie in bed for hours on end, day after day. Nobody in my family seemed to notice, and I never mentioned it to anyone because I was being taught that my needs and wants were too much, that they were not okay. I had no idea there might be help for a child like me. The episodes continued as I grew older. I never knew when I would "fall through the trapdoor," as I have come to characterize my episodes of depression, and what might trigger my free fall, and my stays in the lonely hell of depression were of unpredictable duration. I might rally in a day or two, or I might be down for three months. During an especially despondent stretch of time, when I was in grades six through ten and living with Mom, Pop, and Sister in an old farmhouse south of Nashville that I used to refer to simply as "the Hell Hole," my young heart was in so much pain that when Mom wasn't periodically pulling out the gun she kept under the bed to threaten Pop, I often played with it, trying to summon the courage to shoot myself. On into my twenties and thirties, I had periods of falling through the trapdoor, and I tried to lift my moods and self-soothe with alternative regimens like breathwork (therapeutic controlled breathing), meditation, and yoga.

I was first exposed to yoga when I was a little girl. Mamaw loved taking yoga classes at the YWCA in Ashland, Kentucky. She gave me a book I still have and treasure, with pictures of an animal on one page and a child doing the yoga posture named for that animal on the companion page. I would practice the poses because it was fun, especially on rainy days when she did not take me to the pool, and I dabbled in it over the years. I started a regular practice in 1994, while I was living alone in New York and performing in *Picnic* on Broadway. It was a bad time for me. I couldn't sleep, I couldn't shake the relentless despair, I was eaten alive with anxiety, and I was desperately groping for some kind of psychic relief. I intuitively took myself to a yoga class. In the practice, I was seeking restorative poses, the ones in Mamaw's book, like the child's pose, turtle, and rabbit. They soothe, nurture, and hold the body safe; they are calming to the nervous system—things I surely needed.

The yoga was indeed wonderful for my body and spirit, and the meditation was momentarily calming, but neither was the panacea I'd hoped for. Once more, in the fall of 1996, depression took me down a dangerous path. This time, instead of insomnia, I couldn't seem to sleep enough. My mood was desolate, and I couldn't stop losing weight, no matter how much I ate. I attributed most of the exhaustion I felt to a busy work schedule. After the Broadway show, I'd been filming steadily, often working back to back on productions that, however exciting, were also wearing. *A Time to Kill* opened in the summer of 1996, I had gone straight into *Norma Jean and Marilyn*, and *Kiss the Girls* had just wrapped when my baseline mood deteriorated so badly I could do nothing to hold ground.

I was going out with Michael Bolton that fall. Although we dated for only about six weeks, he made a poignant impression on my life. In October I accompanied him to Austria, where he was performing at the Vienna State Opera. I had some clothes fitted before the trip, and by the end of the short stay, they were hanging off me. I slept all day long in the gilded hotel room. Michael would go to rehearsal in the mornings, and I would be waking up when it was time for dinner. I attributed my lethargy to jet lag. Michael proved to be a compassionate and gentle friend. He never tried to push me or shame me; he just left me to my own process. Days later, I began to wonder, *Why can't I get out of bed? Where does the time go?* Then, by the grace of God, I somehow remembered a questionnaire I had seen in a doctor's office waiting room. It was a checklist for depression. Things like "Persistent, sad, anxious, or 'empty' mood. Unexplained weight loss. Feelings of hopelessness, guilt, worthlessness. Thoughts of harming oneself. Hyper- or hyposomnia . . ." I didn't know if I identified with everything, but I identified with enough.

At last, here was an explanation, a name, an actionable thing: depression!

Inspired, I moved faster than I had in days. I practically clawed my way to the telephone to call a therapist I casually knew in Franklin, Tennessee, to suggest a doctor who could prescribe medication. Franklin was the closest thing I had to a fixed address. I had been essentially homeless for the past three years, after the house I'd been renting in Malibu burned to the ground in a wildfire, with all my possessions inside (except Mamaw's pearls, which I had thankfully been wearing at the time), while I was on the *Ruby in Paradise* press tour. Because I was constantly working at the time, I was living out of hotel rooms, rented homes on locations; and between jobs, because my farmhouse restoration was a long-term project, squatting either at Mom and Pop's or at Sister's.

As soon as I returned home and dropped my bags in my mom's guest room, I went to see the psychiatrist my therapist friend had recommended. I remember feeling incredibly vulnerable in this strange new setting as I shared what I knew then of my story. I waited expectantly to hear her verdict.

"You have mild, anxious depression."

My first thought was, *If this is mild, I cannot even imagine what major is. I am nonfunctional, and this is mild?*

"Where does it come from?" I asked.

"Unresolved childhood grief."

Silence.

"Okay, what do I take for that?"

I wanted medication. I had suffered enough that I was willing to try it. I was radically grateful for anything that resembled a viable solution to the problem I had lived with for so long, which until now had not even had a name. She gave me a prescription, and I went home and read the molecular formula and studied the insert. Would it work faster if I took it in the morning? Or at night? On an empty stomach? Or a full stomach? Following the doctor's suggestion, I started a mood journal to keep track of things so I could give her clear data during our check-ins. Then I just lay in bed, waiting to see if I felt different.

A few days later, I started feeling wildly restless and insatiably hungry. I needed so much food during this time, I would eat raw tofu straight from the package (I was a vegetarian then). In spite of eating like a horse, I continued to lose weight, and I eventually bottomed at 112 pounds, which is

far too thin for my five-foot-seven-inch frame (a healthy weight for me is
130 pounds). In the middle of one night, I heard a distinct, piercing cry and
bolted straight up from a dead sleep before realizing the noise was coming
from me. I had started wailing like a banshee. Mom and Pop's dog, Banjo,
who was asleep next to me, went flying off the bed in a panic—I nearly
scared him to death. I probably would have terrified myself if I could have
considered that disturbing stream of anguish, what it was and where it was
coming from. I was purging grief. It lasted over an hour. Confusing words
erupted out of me unbidden, things like "I was just a little girl, it wasn't
my fault"and "Why did you leave me at school? I was so little, I couldn't get
home!" and the plaintive refrain of my childhood, "Where is everybody?"

I told my doctor about it the next day, and she said that was something
called "freeing of the affect." Apparently, with the medication beginning
to work, emotions that I hadn't felt because I was depressed were beginning to be released. She said it was normal, and that I would continue to
have these episodes, although they would be shorter and less intense over
time. Indeed, I started feeling a bit better. But I was by no means out of the
woods. There was no way I could start to recover while I was living under
my mother's roof.

Mom loved having me stay with her, and there were some good times.
She still shows the guest bedroom to people and says it's my room. But
it was not healthy for me to be there while I was so depressed. I was constantly exposed to the same family dynamics, which I have learned had set
up the underlying causes and conditions of my disease in the first place.
And nobody could seem to understand. I was accused of being a "wound
addict" if I tried to express my feelings of grief. I was being traumatized all
over again, reenacting the childhood in which my reality was denied. The
situation was not only painful, but downright dangerous.

When my family went away for New Year's, I stayed home alone. I had
been running a low-grade fever for weeks, which for me was a telltale
physical symptom of depression, and I was not in any mood to celebrate
the holidays. I lay in bed or outside under trees by the creek for days, ru-
minating about ways to ease the pain I felt with every heartbeat. Mom and
Pop have always interpreted the Second Amendment in a particular way,
and they kept a lot of guns in this house, just as they did in the Hell Hole.

One night, after another crappy day of feeling lousy, when I was rummaging for yet another late-night snack, I opened a drawer and found a loaded shotgun. I thought, *These people have absolutely no idea the kind of distress I'm in; they are unable to see me as I am right now.* It was a long, shaky, cannot-stop-crying, fetal-position kind of night.

Later, I learned that many depressed people are so inert before starting medication that they can't even kill themselves—but once the meds kick in, they can begin to muster just enough energy to take action. Self-harm was an idea that lived rent-free in my head during my worst depressions, that in the absence of healthy tools gave me essential emotional relief. Next morning, I phoned the therapist I knew as soon as her office opened. She told me to come in, and I lay listlessly on her sofa while she and my general practitioner figured out what to do with me. My GP told me the obvious choice: The Vanderbilt Psychiatric Hospital in Nashville was an option, but she warned in hushed tones that it would go on "my record." Influenced by his own stigmatized view of depression, I chose simply to check into the county hospital under the guise of some vague ailment. (My GP is a great guy, but he still whispers in his office when he asks me how my recovery from depression is going.) That day was an interesting turning point in my life. I have wondered what would have happened if I'd gone to the psychiatric hospital and received proper treatment for depression, which I clearly needed, beyond simply taking antidepressants. It might have saved me years of further grief, or it might have done further damage if I had been given the wrong kind of treatment. Ultimately, God had something very special in mind for me, but that would be *ten years* down the road.

In the short term, my brief stay in the hospital was a salve. As soon as an IV was in my arm, my fever came down and I started feeling better—although I think my relief was related more to being out of what was for me a toxic environment and having my mental illness acknowledged without judgment. The nurturing care the nurses gave me was profoundly moving. They weren't treating me as if I were crazy; they were just doing what nurses do—running the bath, checking on me, being kind. I needed that. But I did continue to have spells while in the hospital: emotional meltdowns and impulses to self-harm. I kept them secret from the nurses, because I wasn't in the habit of identifying and talking about these things with anyone yet, and I was scared they would reject me if I seemed too crazy for them. I was afraid of being in trouble for having an emotional problem.

During all this, I was still hoping to attend President Clinton's second inauguration in January 1997, to which I was invited because I had campaigned for him and introduced him when he spoke in Kentucky. I even tried on Armani gowns in the hospital while still attached to an IV pole. It was an unrealistic wish.

When I felt well enough to leave the hospital, I took the advice of the therapist friend and moved out of my mom's house. I rented a beautiful cottage on a farm near Franklin and started taking better care of myself. I had a lot of massages, practiced yoga and breathwork and meditation. One particularly special girlfriend called from L.A. every night at bedtime, knowing that was always the hardest time of day for me. Although I didn't yet have all the tools I have today, I was instinctively working through my anger to access the pain and grief that was beneath it. And very slowly I began to heal.

In March I made my first trip to Los Angeles in many months. My interest in the outside world was returning and I felt a little stronger emotionally. Although I was still exceedingly vulnerable, it was time to begin reengaging with my professional life after a long winter of depression-induced hibernation. I accepted an invitation to *Vanity Fair*'s Oscar party, thinking that could be a good way to dip in a toe. Valentino came to my hotel room to tie the sash on my dress, and I felt special as I walked out the door and faced the bank of cameras on the red carpet. But at the party, I soon found myself drinking coffee to stay awake. I felt lonely and isolated in a big, festive crowd and decided to leave early. I was actually trying discreetly to slip out when an exuberant friend led me across the room and sat me down next to an elegant man with a strong presence and a shock of gorgeous wavy black hair: Bobby Shriver.

We sat there a bit and chatted. He was drawing little sailboats on his paper napkin, and I assumed that he was one of the idle rich. So I asked somewhat facetiously, with a little aggression, "So do you have a job?"

Bobby was a lawyer, journalist, businessman, and record producer who made Christmas records with artists like Bono, Madonna, and Stevie Wonder to support the Special Olympics, the spectacular organization founded by his mother, Eunice Kennedy Shriver. (His father, Sargent Shriver, had started the Peace Corps, and his sister, Maria, is a superb journalist.) After he ran down the basic résumé, Bobby asked me, "What's *your* job?"

I said, "Well, acting is my job, but it's not my vocation."

"So what's your vocation?"

I was not up for being coy and could not tolerate what felt like nonsense. Depression can be good for me that way: It helps cut the bull and strips me down to the essence of what matters and what is worth living for—although I sometimes lack the flexibility of choosing the right time and place to share such things. I looked this stranger in the eye and said, "My vocation is to make my life an act of worship."

He pushed back from the table, excused himself, and went to the bathroom.

I was thinking to myself, *How's that for an Oscar party line?* But it was the absolute truth, although perhaps more of an aspiration than a reality at the time. Even if I wasn't doing social justice work, I was always praying, reading, writing, and trying. God was the central fact of my life, the principle around which I tried to organize everything. Bobby later told me he didn't really have to use the bathroom; he had to compose himself because he was so floored by my response, which he thought was the perfect answer. He came back to the table, and we talked some more about what the God of our understanding might be calling us to do, and service as an expression of God's love. By the end of the evening we knew we had made a deep, lifelong connection. We tried dating for a short time but found out we were better at being spiritual siblings. We met at yoga classes, and he took me to his Exeter class reunion. When Papaw Ciminella, who was a lifelong racing enthusiast, was dying, I left the hospital long enough to attend the Kentucky Derby with Bobby. When my grief suddenly poured out of me in between the social events of the day, Bobby ended up sitting with me patiently, holding the space for me as I keened. He proved to be a perfect friend and always encouraged me to give more of myself to the sick and the suffering, emphasizing that such work is not about pity, it's about justice.

Chapter 5

MAKING OF A RABBLE-ROUSER

Making the *Y* in *Kentucky* (with a broken ankle) while watching my alma mater's men's basketball team.

A man wrapped up in himself is a very small man.

—*BENJAMIN FRANKLIN*

I've always had an intense sense of righteous indignation and an urge to speak for the voiceless and oppressed—likely because I felt so invisible and invalidated when I was a child. I could never stand to see anyone being abused, especially my sister, whose childhood was undoubtedly as difficult as mine, although in different ways.

By the time I was in college, I was ready to become a full-fledged social activist. At the University of Kentucky, I completed a major in French, four minors, and the full honors program curriculum—but my undeclared major was rabble-rousing, or at least as much rabble-rousing as one could do and still belong to an old, elite social sorority. Tapping into that legacy grounded me in a meaningful way. And I loved the idea of living in the Kappa Kappa Gamma sorority house, a beautiful southern home with nice furniture and wallpaper, located in a separate, elegant quadrant of the campus. I moved into a four-woman room and relished the sense of camaraderie.

I was a smart kid who loved learning and earned mostly great grades but because I had attended thirteen different schools during my scattered childhood, I was unevenly educated when I arrived at college. At first I was unsure of myself. I had been told I was smart and special, and I was expected to be fairly perfect and to represent my family in and out of school with charm, poise, consistency, and ease. But I was pretty confused about my alleged gifts: Was I smart? Was I gifted? Was I even capable? One of the things that really threw me was that in my little girl's mind I had somehow made up that if one were smart, everything should be effortless. If one were talented, one should not have to try hard. As a result, even when I made good grades in high school, I hid a haunting fear that I was worthless and a fraud. But within the "loco parentis" of the campus and my sorority, I soon felt safe enough to be myself.

I attacked academic life at UK in a way that viscerally sparked my mind, spirit, and emotions. I could feel new thoughts germinate and grow, I could feel areas of my brain expand and crackle with earnest life and confidence where previously there had been only fear, guilt, and debilitating shame. In the most meaningful way, I grew up. I discovered the fearless scholarship of gender studies, the enthralling explorations of anthropology. I was lucky enough to gravitate toward spectacular professors, especially feminist ones, who revolutionized my life with their teaching and revelations. I studied the philosophy of agriculture and discovered that despite famines there was never a food shortage, just problems of distribution, political will, poor governance, and apathy that caused millions to starve. I recall sitting at a table and studying so hard, reaching for new ideas, making intuitive connections, that I could feel things fire in my brain. I was turning my gaze both inward and outward; claiming through deeply personal experience citizenship in a much larger world; and slowly starting to recognize my responsibilities and interconnectedness with suffering people everywhere.

Living away from home and family, I was, for the first time in my life, mostly happy. At the student center, I joined every progressive cause I could find, from Amnesty International to the NAACP. I listened, crying, to LPs, brought out of South Africa by friends, of Archbishop Tutu's Christian antiapartheid message, and I organized demonstrations against my university's ongoing financial association with apartheid. I led a campuswide student walkout of classes to protest a university trustee's use of a racial epithet. I uncomfortably began to face my government's deep enmeshment with dictators and complicity with gross human rights atrocities worldwide, especially in Central America and sub-Saharan Africa.

The driving urgency of songs on U2 albums like *Boy* and *The Unforgettable Fire* fueled these first forays into human rights and peace activism. It was through their liner notes that I discovered Amnesty International and leveraging art and pop culture to protest human rights abuses. When *The Joshua Tree* came out toward the end of my freshman year, I was captivated along with the rest of the world. But I also discovered a tangential personal connection to the band. *Rolling Stone* magazine put U2 on the cover that week, and it was noted in an interview with the band that they were fans of my mother and sister. In particular, drummer Larry Mullen Jr. said he was digging the Judds' music, playing "Rockin' with the Rhythm of the Rain" in his car. I was instantly extremely cool around the Kappa Kappa Gamma house.

I traveled to France the summer after my sophomore year with some classmates and a professor to spend six weeks immersed in language, culture, and history, then stayed on "to find myself," as I told my mother. When I found out that U2 would be playing the Hippodrome de Vincennes, I introduced myself to U2's management as Wynonna's little sister, and they kindly gave me a backstage pass. Even though I was comfortable in that milieu from my upbringing, I was swollen with excitement at being backstage. I was nineteen years old and on my own, and Bono, Larry Mullen, all the band members, their spouses, and the crew embraced me. I look back now and can only thank God for putting these people, who have had such a defining, spiritual impact on me, into my life at such an impressionable age. At President Obama's inauguration, Larry's wife got to reminiscing about what a little girl I was when she met me. That the same girl had since grown up to host the Inaugural Purple Ball and embrace the world is, in part, a testament to my friendship with the U2 family.

My sense of fairness—or more accurately, unfairness—was being keenly developed, both in and outside the classroom, equipping and motivating me for the life of service I now love and that gives my every day such purpose. And it has, without ever having been my intention, helped heal the wounds of my own childhood.

~ ~ ~

As much as I loved college, I was a somewhat erratic student, and still given to spells of depression. More than once, I would petition to take advanced classes, even graduate level, and then drop them. I overloaded my schedule, racking up 143 hours in four years, taking four minors and a separate honors curriculum. After my initial experiment with communal living at the sorority house, I managed to convert a tiny janitor's closet, complete with a deep sink for mops and pails, into a single bedroom. By my senior year I was isolating myself a lot in an off campus apartment I'd unwisely rented. I spent more and more time with a sorority sister I loved, who could be just as socially withdrawn. Once, we decided to throw a party. We decorated my apartment, stocked the bar, and waited. At about eight p.m., we realized that neither of us had invited anyone. We spent the evening playing cards and went to bed early.

In the spring of 1990, I attended my honor's program graduation ceremony, which was held separately from the big class graduation on campus, at a beautiful club for the horsey crowd outside of Lexington. I drove out there alone under a full moon and never thought it was odd that I had no guests in attendance. I was surprised to see the other kids' families at the ceremony. I accepted my honors certificate to the polite applause of a crowd of strangers. Then I packed up and drove home to Tennessee, restless and preoccupied with what to do next with my life.

~ ~ ~

For a time when I was in college I had briefly considered Christian missionary work, knowing I wanted to travel the world and be useful. But I was deeply uncomfortable with the idea that indigenous people were "doing it wrong" and that I would be there to help them "get it right." The Peace Corps seemed like a better fit. I applied and was accepted during my senior year of college, in 1990, and dreamed of going to graduate school in anthropology afterward. But soon I was torn between spending the next two years of my life in Africa and finding the courage to honor the equally deep impulse I had to act.

It was a difficult decision for me. Theater was one of my minors, and I had been doing what I know today is acting—living truthfully under imaginary circumstances—since third grade. I vividly recall one day after school crossing a field of golden grass in Marin County and deciding I want to walk, think, and, most important, feel like the girl in the book I was reading at the time. I closed my eyes, set my intention, conjured her narrative, and opened my eyes again, fully expecting to perceive the world as truly different, for the air on my skin to seem strange! Well, it wasn't quite that dramatic, but I was on to something. My imagination had found a dynamic expression that gave me years of solace and friendship. My books were my best friends; their characters peopled my interior world. Acting in my room or outdoors, where I spent hours and hours, gave me an essential, private, and sanctioned outlet for expressing my feelings, many of which were not welcome in the family. Through acting I could siphon off anger, soothe loneliness, cry out some of the pain, and hide from the shame and confusion that so often dominated my home. Rather than be rejected for feeling, I could create my own safe space and have a modicum of control in an often out-of-control world. Acting helped me survive, and it enriched my life.

The summer after college, I was increasingly conflicted about my commitment to the Peace Corps and the fear that if I didn't pursue acting now, I never would. It didn't help when my sister would tease me about the Peace Corps in front of her friends on the road and at home, commanding me to "pop a squat" to show them how I would be living in Africa. I started avoiding my Peace Corps recruiter's calls. Without telling them—an immature move, to say the least—I decided I could postpone the life of service I hoped to lead. If I didn't give acting a try at twenty-two, I suspected I feared I would carry a regret the rest of my life.

Never one to do things in a small way, I covered my terrific uncertainty with bravado and painted "Hollywood or Bust, Cecil B. DeMille, here I come!" and "I am ready for my close-up" on the BMW 325e my sister had given me for high school graduation. Then I attached a small U-Haul trailer to the back and headed west.

I'd thought I might be able to volunteer at Planned Parenthood and pursue other forms of activism while I took acting lessons and went to auditions in L.A. Before I left, my mother and sister's manager, Ken Stilts, met with me about what kind of plan I had in place for myself upon my arrival in Hollywood. I began to tell him about the activism opportunities I had researched. He scoffed at me, saying, "Are you going out there to save the world, or to act?" Daddy Ken, as we all called him, was a condescending, hard drinking patriarchal figure who always had to be right. Once he shamed my sister for getting a tattoo—even though it was a heart and cross with a banner that said "Mom." He humiliated her in front of her entire organization, refusing to speak with her for days. He bullied me, too, but in the absence of much healthy fathering, I thought that it was normal, and I was intimidated enough to listen to him. I internalized his message that I *had* to choose between a creative life and a life of service.

It is a message I still hear today from some people—many of them in the media—whose imaginations are so limited that they believe I can legitimately be only one or the other, a creative person or an advocate. It's interesting to watch the cunning ways that artists, women in particular, are endlessly discredited, trivialized, and infantilized. The cynics contend that if I were to give up acting to focus exclusively on public service, well, my service would never be valid, because I had once had a career as an actor. (Forgetting, of course, the previous job description of that right-wing icon Ronald Reagan.) Or that when I opt out significantly from acting for a period, as I tend to, it's because my movies are lousy and my career is failing. They can't hold in their minds that perhaps I am both—a serious actor who chooses how much time to spend acting, which has been not a whole lot of time for several years, and a serious advocate who is profoundly committed to pursuing social justice and human rights at home and abroad.

Anyway, within three days of arriving in L.A., I was enrolled in the Playhouse West acting school and began studying under the amazing teacher Bob Carnegie. I began to audition and landed work almost immediately, most auspiciously a bit part in a union show that allowed me to join the Screen Actors Guild, solving a major conundrum for many actors struggling to break in. Next, I landed a recurring role on the NBC hit show *Sisters*, with the theater great Swoosie Kurtz playing my mother, which paid bills while I continued to study faithfully at Playhouse West. My most special moment early in my career was being cast in *Ruby in Paradise*, written and directed by iconic independent filmmaker Victor Nuñez. I loved the script so intuitively that I cried for three days and through all my appointments with Victor. I just knew we were perfect for each other.

In the film my character, Ruby Lee Gissing, arrives in a Florida resort town looking for a fresh start in her young life. I decided to drive to the set in Panama City through East Tennessee, Georgia, and Alabama to work on my accent and see where I was coming from as this character. I took one-lane country roads the whole way (with my pet rabbit, Stinkerbelle, along for company). The poverty I witnessed was shocking. I saw Appalachian folks that even I thought only breathed in books. I sat on a shack front porch with three generations of black women one Sunday afternoon in

Alabama, just drinking in their culture and the music of their voices. Acting was giving me everything I loved to do: being alone and traveling and discovering closeness with strangers.

Ruby won the Sundance Film Festival in 1993, and acting awards poured in. Before I realized what had happened, being a working actor and movie star was my norm. By the time I arrived on the set of *Twisted* in 2002, I had starred and costarred in nineteen movies and two Broadway plays, was one of the highest-paid women in Hollywood, and had lived the red carpet life as full-time as anyone could manage while residing in Tennessee and Scotland.

Although I loved the creative process and those fleeting, magical moments of acting, the righteous indignation, the furious need for social justice, still percolated under the surface. Once I had abandoned that part of myself at twenty-two, I didn't seem know how to reconnect with it.

Then, suddenly, I was shown the way.

~ ~ ~

One dawn, after a grueling night of shooting *Twisted*, instead of settling down for a day of sleeping it off, I sat at my desk and began sorting through mail. At the top of the pile was a letter from Kate Roberts, forwarded by one of my agents. As I read through her proposal to become the YouthAIDS ambassador for Population Services International (from here on lovingly referred to as "PSI"), I realized she was offering me a chance to help save lives and raise public awareness of the most devastating human crisis since the days of the bubonic plague. Could this be what I was looking for, the opportunity to reconnect with my latent passion? A chance to bring a voice to the voiceless, to address the injustices I had witnessed throughout my childhood?

I was well aware of the scourge of AIDS. The virus had already consumed the lives of many of my colleagues in the arts and was particularly cruel and out of control in the developing world. By the end of 2001, more than forty million people were living with HIV and AIDS, and there were twenty million AIDS orphans, creating inevitable future social crises, the vast majority in sub-Saharan Africa and Asia. Three million people were dying each year. Clearly this was a global emergency. But my first reaction to Kate's request to help was that I would also need to investigate Population Services International to verify it wasn't a fly-by-night outfit or, worse, some sort of front for a right-wing group that would use my social capital for a hidden agenda. I didn't want to do harm accidentally or, my ego said, be embarrassed.

Instead of trying to get that elusive daytime rest in between scenes, I scoured the Internet for information, putting my academic hat back on for a bit of research. I liked what I found. I read that PSI was founded in 1970, when it began as an international family planning agency making condoms accessible in hard-to-reach areas. Since then it had grown into one of the most efficient and effective nongovernmental organizations (NGOs) in the world, focusing on maternal and reproductive health, child survival, malaria prevention and treatment, and HIV/AIDS. It had an obsession for measuring its impact, something that made it popular with donors such as the Gates Foundation and the United States Agency for International Development (USAID). Its online brochure said PSI worked with local businesses and citizens' groups in more than sixty developing countries "to deliver lifesaving medical products and services to the most vulnerable populations." For such an international nonprofit with an annual budget of $400 million, its overhead was extremely low—less than 5 percent— and it documented measurable results in lives saved. So far so good.

In 2001, Kate Roberts had launched the YouthAIDS campaign within PSI to reach the fifteen-to-twenty-four-year-old age group that frighteningly accounts for half of new HIV infections worldwide—the majority of those being girls who are most often sexually exploited. A former high-powered advertising executive, Kate had decided to treat the AIDS emergency as a business, employing the same strategies she had once used to sell soda pop, bubble gum, and cigarettes to teenagers. She would use this technique, known as "social marketing," to promote AIDS education, abstinence, and condom use among vulnerable kids. Because young adults, even in the poorest countries, are influenced by mass media and celebrity, YouthAIDS harnessed pop culture and created "edutainment" to make healthy behavior change sexy and cool.

I read that YouthAIDS partnered with grassroots groups and FBOs (faith-based organizations) to provide peer counseling, drop-in centers (safe, relaxed, often entertaining places where lifesaving information is made available), and voluntary and confidential testing services for teenagers, prostituted women, migrant workers—in other words, those most at risk of infection. (I would later learn to add married women to this high-risk group.) YouthAIDS created hip public service announcements for TV and radio using popular local and international celebrities and athletes and was participating in the MTV World AIDS Day "Staying Alive" concerts. Along with other performers, YouthAIDS was supported by rap and hip-hop artists like Snoop Dogg and P. Diddy to spread the message. . . . *um, who?* Those names were a red flag. My feminist instincts flared, and my enthusiasm sputtered.

As far as I am concerned, most rap and hip-hop music—with its rape culture and insanely abusive lyrics and depictions of girls and women as "ho's"—is the contemporary sound track of misogyny. I believe that the social construction of gender—the cultural beliefs and practices that divide the sexes and institutionalize and normalize the unequal treatment of girls and women, privilege the interests of boys and men, and, most nefariously, incessantly sexualize girls and women—is the root cause of poverty and suffering around the world. Gender inequality is implicated in every obstacle to peace and poverty alleviation: lack of access to education, along with early and forced marriage; lack of ability to choose the number of and space the births of one's children; lack of legal rights, including exclusion from inheritance and land tenure; and lack of access to capital and political power. So how could I join a campaign alongside men who make their living reinforcing the exploitation and oppression of women?

I was so fired up, I didn't even consider restraint in my reply, such as: "Dear Kate, How kind of you to think of me. I'm busy right now—could you possibly ask again in a month? And by the way, I do have some concerns I hope you will be open to discussing. . . ." Instead I sat down at my computer and fired off a three-page single-spaced manifesto on gender equality and mass media that my Women's Studies professors would have given an A+. Kate and I laugh about it now, but my language was totally high-handed, as in: "You're undermining your own message if you're using misogynistic pop artists to send empowering messages about healthy behavior to impressionable teens. Wise up, sister."

My ideas haven't changed since then. If anything, I am more radicalized by every trip around the world I take. But thanks to the example of Bono and others, I have greater personal acceptance of and tolerance for—and in some cases deep personal affection for—the people who create music in those genres, even while rejecting their choices. Bono once invited me to a dinner in New York with Bill Gates and P. Diddy, whose real name is Sean Combs, to discuss the HIV/AIDS emergency and to enlist Sean's mass popularity to reach millions of kids who imitate him with the message of prevention. I came to know him as a polite and kind family man—not the P. Diddy persona I would never be able to relate to. Equally, I know the man Curtis Jackson, not the rapper 50 Cent. I have never been more shocked in my life than when Curtis took the stage at an event launching his participation in the RED campaign (the amazing cause-related marketing strategy run by Bobby Shriver to raise money for the Global Fund to Fight AIDS, Tuberculosis, and Malaria) and became 50 Cent onstage. I watched him morph from a thoughtful, soft-spoken young man into a posturing, threatening, "pimping" gangsta, spewing toxic, abusive lyrics. (I was equally surprised to see the crowd go nuts, responding wildly to the performance.) Today, I challenge myself, as Herbert Spencer would put it, to abandon "contempt prior to investigation." I try to hang out longer in that troubling zone known as ambiguity, while still maintaining my principles. It is a tricky but worthwhile pursuit, one I place squarely in the realm of spiritual practice. But I was not there yet when Kate Roberts sent me her letter.

I spilled my guts to Kate. I would not be part of an organization that used artists who objectified, commodified, and sexualized women and normalized male violence. "Take it or leave it, those are my conditions," I wrote. And then I stuck the letter in the mail, never expecting to hear back.

Soon after, I received a lovely, heartfelt reply from Kate. She told me she absolutely agreed with me, reassured me that PSI was not that kind of organization—that it was firmly a feminist organization committed to empowering girls and women and helping to change and improve gender attitudes worldwide. Then she described some of her extraordinary experiences working in the field, including grassroots strategies for reaching disempowered women that help them improve their health, which is the foundation for all sustainability. She lost me when she described market-based solutions that help girls attend and stay in school, and allow women to move into the formal economy, but I was increasingly impressed. Even so, I still hesitated.

~ ~ ~

As fate would have it, the very week I read Kate's letter, I received a call from Bobby Shriver. He asked me—rather, told me—to join him and Bono on a ten-day "Heart of America" bus tour of midwestern states to raise awareness about the African AIDS and extreme poverty emergency. With Bono and Jamie Drummond, he had recently cofounded DATA (Debt, AIDS, Trade, Africa)—a nonprofit group that advocated forgiving Africa's crippling foreign debt so that its people could lift themselves out of disease and poverty (DATA eventually became the revolutionary ONE Campaign).

I thought the bus tour was a great idea, and I would have loved to sign right up, but I felt I had to decline. Dario and I live in his native Scotland for part of the year, and I had made a commitment to our fall departure date. I knew he was keenly looking forward to it; he gets so homesick, and I wanted to keep my word. A few days later the phone rang again, and it was Bono.

It was impossible to resist both Bobby *and* Bono. This was the team that the following January would secure the largest commitment in history from one nation to fight a disease—from, of all people, George W. Bush (to his eternal credit). Because of their efforts, $15 billion over five years would be channeled into the President's Emergency Plan for AIDS Relief (PEPFAR). Now Bono was using the same energy and determination to enlist me to build support for the cause in the American heartland. Like Bobby, Bono knows my heart of hearts *and* will shamelessly call me out on my core values and my faith. I call it being "Bono-ed."

"Africa is literally going up in flames," he said in his fervent Irish brogue. "And we're standing on the sidelines, holding a watering can." I had heard him use this analogy before, and it always pierced my heart. Now he made it personal. "Ashley, our generation will be known for three things—the war on terror, the digital revolution, and what we did or did not do to put the fire out in Africa. This is not a celebrity cause, Ashley. History, like God, is watching what we do."

What could I say?

Over the years the relentless, gentle, brilliant Bono has often sucked me into his ecstatic vortex, stirring me to engage in the pursuit of justice, equality, fairness, and peace. Those who know him for his wraparound blue sunglasses, his intense, glorious performances with U2, and his co-lossal humanitarian efforts may also sense how much fun he is to hang out with. He's a gifted mimic and can tell stories using an arsenal of voices and gestures. Like his equally special wife, Ali, the Irishman is irresistible. And once he's dazzled you, he'll call on your better angels to join him on the front lines of hope.

Now both these uniquely influential men were pressing me to drop everything and spend a couple of weeks showing Americans why they should care about Africans. And this Kate Roberts person, cannily on the same subject, was asking for much, much more.

~ ~ ~

I was still thinking it over when I returned to my apartment after another long night of filming on the gritty San Francisco docks. I limply pulled off my clothes. I was so dead tired that I briefly fell asleep while lean-ing against the shower, waiting for the water to warm up. When I star-tled awake and saw the water running, I automatically stepped into the shower without checking the temperature and, for about the fourth day in a row, was shocked by a frigid blast of Bay Area ice water. Even mice avoid this after a few bad experiences. But this time, instead of bursting into tears and throwing myself another pity party, or calling my husband to whine, or directing my rage at some random thing outside of me (or my own body), something inside me snapped and I was given the abso-lute gift of getting over my little petty dramas and concerns. I had a fierce word with myself about the two billion people a day who do not have ac-cess to safe drinking water, much less the incredible luxury of *piped* water. I matter-of-factly completed the business of my shower and thanked God for my blessings and the unbelievable abundance of my life. And then we began to talk.

As I dried myself off, I finally woke up to what was happening to me. If these diverse, impressive, eminent, committed people were contacting me at the same time to help do something about the world's most urgent health emergency, giving me an extraordinary opportunity to do service on a global scale for the same vulnerable populations who so moved me as a younger woman, shouldn't I take that as a sign? I would be surrounded by experts: epidemiologists, PhDs, policy writers. I was being given a golden chance. Shouldn't I say yes?

When I told Dario that I wanted to join in the fight against AIDS and poverty, to resume the work I had loved so much in college, and that I would like to renegotiate the beginning of our annual stay in Scotland, to my utter delight he was completely supportive. In fact, he wanted to come along with me on the "Heart of America" tour. And Bono still swears Dario was an even better public speaker on the issue than I. The talk Dario gave in Indianapolis was humble, inviting, and true.

I sat down and called Bobby to say, "I'm in." I wrote to Kate Roberts and told her I was ready to discuss becoming the global ambassador for YouthAIDS. I agreed to meet her in Chicago on the third day of the tour. I felt in my soul that I was finally about to realize my true vocation, and I rejoiced. I knew my life was changing. It was exciting, and daunting, too.

~ ~ ~

We started out from Lincoln, Nebraska, on December 1, World AIDS Day. The eleven-city tour would take us across Iowa and Illinois, Indiana, Kentucky, and Tennessee. Bono, Bobby, and Jamie Drummond, DATA's chairman and chief organizer, chose to bypass the media-rich, oh-so-sophisticated East Coast and West Coast and focus on the interior, because, as Bono explained, it's a place of strong communities and families, where the nation's "moral compass resides." He told one newspaper reporter, "We came to the heartland to get at the hearts and minds of America." The plan was to engage people where they worshipped and where they lived, to dispel some of the myths about Africa as a vast, dysfunctional wasteland, and to put a human face on the AIDS catastrophe. We wanted to reach out to unlikely allies, such as blue-collar workers, evangelical Christians, small-town mayors, and regional newspapers, because we believed they would warm to the cause once they understood the depth of the crisis and knew that they could make a difference. As I often said, "It took an Irishman to remind me of President Harry Truman's quote, that if you give Americans the facts, they'll do the right thing."

My job on the "Heart of America" tour was to emcee the events, articulate the problems that needed fixing, recite the grim statistics, and begin to address the issue of faith as the basis for this *cri de coeur*. I would also engage the crowds and make them comfortable with my good old American self before turning them over to the electrifying, hyperverbal Irish rock star who simply blew people's minds as he exhorted them to greatness.

"This isn't about charity, it's about justice!" Bono would say as he took the stage. "We can't fix every problem, but we must fix the ones we can!" He would take out his guitar and experiment with a song the band was thinking about playing at the Super Bowl, thrilling people with this privileged peek at U2 music in the making. By letting us into his world and opening his heart, he made every one of us want to be better.

There were also appearances by other celebrities and notables, such as Lance Armstrong; Chris Tucker; the famous epidemiologist from Harvard, Dr. Jim Kim (now president of Dartmouth College); nutrition expert Dr. Dean Ornish; and even Nebraskan multibillionaire investor Warren Buffett. Our traveling road show included speakers and performances by the Gateway Ambassadors, a mesmerizing Ghanaian children's choir, some of them HIV-positive, with whom we prayed as a group before each rally. But we were all very clear that each evening centered on the testimony of Agnes Nyamayarwo, a Ugandan nurse whom Bono had met on a recent trip to Africa. It was her first time in America. Agnes's story is devastating. She was a devout Catholic who'd had ten children with her husband, an American-trained agronomist. But her husband died of AIDS in 1992, having been infected outside their marriage, and she was left a single mother infected with HIV. In a sadly common African irony, she continued to work as a nurse, caring for others, while she herself had no medications for her HIV-positive status. Her eldest son, Charles, was so stigmatized by his father's disease that he disappeared from boarding school and was never heard from again. This was perhaps the hardest part of her story to share each evening: not knowing where her boy was. Had he been run off, or fled? Had he been killed by bullies, as has been known to happen? Additionally, Agnes had unknowingly infected her youngest son, Christopher, in utero. She nursed him for two years before he died.

"Excruciating pain gripped my heart like a vise during those long hours, days, weeks, and months prior to his death," she told one interviewer. "Looking at his deteriorating condition, tears would just flow from my eyes and it is then that he would say, 'Mummy, why are you crying? I will be okay.' His innocent face and words have always remained with me and filled many of my waking hours. His determination to get better always returns to haunt me, for I knew even then that without proper medication that he needed, Chris was fighting a losing battle."

I listened keenly every time Agnes told her story. It was impossible to witness her grace and see her resilience and remain apathetic. Audience members would come up to us later and tell us that it was Agnes who made the crisis seem real, not like something happening to strangers in an alien world. Meeting this one woman made me realize how little I truly knew about the challenges of life in the global South.

When we reached Wheaton College, a private Christian school outside of Chicago, Jamie was nominated to implore me not to talk about condoms. They were afraid of offending the students. Naturally, I wasn't having any of it.

"These are my people, Jamie," I said. "I am comfortable with evangelicals. I grew up part Pentecostal." So I took the stage and shouted, "They don't want me to talk about correct and consistent condom use! They don't trust Christians to get it!" The kids were cheering. It was great. They let everyone know they could be devout Christians at a sectarian college and still accept the A, the B, *and* the C of HIV prevention: *a*bstinence; *b*eing faithful and delaying onset of sexuality; and *c*orrect and *c*onsistent *c*ondom use with every sexual act. (Eventually, I would add my own D: *d*elay of sexual debut, especially important for girls, who are so often preyed upon by older men.)

~ ~ ~

Kate Roberts joined us in Chicago, as planned. I liked her immediately. She was an elegant Englishwoman in her mid-thirties, with chestnut hair cut in a chic bob and a graceful carriage that radiated energy and purpose. In fact, I liked her so much that I didn't mind that the first thing she said to me in our get-to-know-you moment was, "I have to tell you, I loved you in *Pearl Harbor*." Then, after I pointed out that I was not in that movie, she continued to insist that I was. I thought: *Wow, I think I've met my match in this woman!* It's another thing we still laugh about.

I didn't realize that Kate had actually come to audition me for the job of global ambassador. Just as I had tried to perform due diligence by researching PSI and YouthAIDS, she in turn wanted to observe me in public and see how I handled the material. Kate accompanied me to the next event, which was a meeting in a South Side Apostolic Faith Church where each member of our group was going to talk to the congregation about HIV. After listening from the sidelines to Agnes's story, I confessed to Kate how inadequate I felt. I had so much feeling and intensity, but I felt like a bit of a fraud and was scared I'd do something unhelpful. "I don't have any experience in the field."

"Then let me tell you a story," said Kate. She described Mary, a prostituted woman who made her living in a squalid Kenyan brothel. Mary had been hired by PSI/YouthAIDS to be a peer educator for other exploited women, teaching them how to protect themselves and their clients from the spread of HIV. Kate told me that PSI/YouthAIDS tries to change risky behavior and empower people to use condoms—female condoms for exploited prostitutes and male condoms for their clients. But Mary gave Kate an example of the violence that goes on in the highly dangerous world of forced paid sex and how treacherous it can be to try to be safe. One night Mary was trying to persuade a client to use a condom, but instead he pulled a wrapped piece of candy from his pocket and jammed it into her mouth. "Chew!" he ordered. So she chewed the wrapped candy as he glared at her. "See!" the client hissed. "That's what it's like using a condom."

And then he beat her to a pulp and raped her.

I turned away from Kate and walked to the microphone. I was enraged by what I had heard and a powerful sense of humiliation engulfed me. Time and space dissolved, and somehow Mary was with me as I boldly expressed her righteous indignation in America, an anger Mary, as a disempowered African woman, is denied. These were the first, lurching steps I took toward a purpose I could suddenly feel, even if I couldn't wholly understand it yet: My role was to share the sacred narratives of people who are ignored by this world, to make them real to powerful governments and ordinary citizens who, rightly or wrongly, will listen to me. And it was my own background that modestly qualified me for this newly revealed mission—not just the fame that had accompanied my acting career, but more meaningfully, my very own shame, my very own righteous anger, my very own journey as an abused and neglected girl. While my circumstances were obviously different, I identified powerfully with Mary's *feelings*. It would take several countries and many brothels and slums to piece it together, but in offering myself to my newfound brothers and sisters everywhere, I met an additional, equally precious child: the girl I had once been.

After the meeting, I sat in a pew. I was overwhelmed by the power of being in a charismatic church with a predominantly African-American congregation that was really "getting it"—recognizing that gender inequality, poverty, exploitation, preventable disease, and all the human rights violations inherent in the HIV emergency are connected to their own everyday lives in America. I had been in a fact-finding, making-sense-of-it-all mode since the beginning of the tour. I was being serious and professional and was intent on doing a good job. But now I was in a safe, faith-filled place where I could give in to all my feelings, and I began to feel the presence of the Holy Spirit. I started to sob. The harder I cried, the more strongly I felt the presence of God. This is an experience I always cherish, one that brings down all my walls and affirms and validates my values—it is a time when I feel so vulnerable and raw, yet totally safe and protected, when I seem to become part of an unfathomable whole. I cried and cried. I can never control what happens when the Holy Spirit comes, and it's futile to try! I was sitting near Bono, and he gave me an empathetic look that said, "Oh, there she goes!" Kate saw this, too, but didn't seem concerned. After a while, I pulled myself together and got back on the bus. I was ready for the next step.

"Where do we go first?" I asked Kate.

Chapter 6

OUK SREY LEAK

MARSHALL STOWELL/PSI

Ouk Srey Leak, the orphan who let me love her.

When your face
appeared over my crumpled life
At first I understood
Only the poverty of what I have.
Then its particular light
on woods, on river, on the sea,
became my beginning in the colored world

—*YEVGENY YEVTUSHENKO,* "Colours"

The airplane touched down in Phnom Penh in July of 2004 on a runway shimmering in the heat. As I stepped out of the cabin door, I breathed in a humid concoction of exhaust fumes, garbage, the musky perfume of river water, and the intoxicating smell of jasmine: Summer in Southeast Asia.

Papa Jack was waiting for Kate and me at the gate. As soon as I saw his familiar Irish face and silver hair, I knew it was real, I knew we were here to work. I threw open my arms and hugged his neck.

All business, ever on it, he said, " Let's go," as he led us toward customs.

Jack Driscoll, a former New York City police detective who had worked with the FBI, is a dear friend who also handles my security. There is only one "requirement" Dario has of me on my trips: Please travel with Papa Jack. We first met him in Texas while I was filming *Where the Heart Is*. He was working for Natalie Portman at the time, and his wonderful disposition and clever mind were on ample display. He was also a discreet presence—so discreet, in fact, that when we would play Botticelli to while the time away on set in between shots, he was supplying Natalie with answers. It took me ages to figure out why she kept disappearing and returning with fantastic guesses. (I mean, she's awfully smart, but did she really know, at age eighteen, the names of all three Marx Brothers?) I knew I wanted this man on my team, even more so when he found one of my cats, Buttercup, after someone let her out of my trailer in the dead of night.

"In all the years, I've never lost a pet," Jack will tell you, deadpan, in his Staten Island accent.

Jack and I began to work together when I was on location in New York City shooting *Someone Like You . . .* in 2000. He's a consummate professional, making me feel perfectly safe without smothering me and all the while becoming the crew's favorite person. That works for me, because smothering makes me nuts, and I like to fly under the radar. Once, during the filming, I hopped on the subway and asked Jack to meet me at a stop downtown. When the doors opened, I saw the platform swarming with uniformed police—a woman had just been stabbed in the station. Jack found me in the crowd and shepherded me through the police lines. A sergeant he'd known when he was in the NYPD recognized him (he seems to know everyone).

"I'd like you to meet Ashley Judd," said Jack.

"No kiddin'?" said the sergeant.

"Yeah. We're trying to get to the set on time."

The next thing I knew, I was racing through the streets of New York in the back of a squad car, and he never said, "Told you so," about my wise idea to ride the subway to the set.

Jack got his nickname on another movie we did together, where he took on the rather unpopular responsibility of wrangling everybody (which could include up to five or seven pets) on early mornings, helping us be on time. He was a father figure as well as a watchful presence. From then on, it was "Papa Jack." I have since chosen to significantly scale back my moviemaking and let go of the blockbuster, movie-star life, but I do look back on that stretch of time with Papa Jack and our small, tight-knit crew with a great deal of fondness. He became family to Dario and me, and when he lost his wife to cancer, we flew to Staten Island to be by his side at the funeral.

Papa Jack agreed to work for PSI for a fraction of his usual rate. Despite its size and its reach, the nonprofit runs on a tight budget, which both pleases donors and maximizes our impact, and most of the travel and accommodations for my trips are donated. In this way, almost all of the money raised goes into AIDS prevention programs—a cause, it turned out, that was close to Jack's heart. Jack told us that one of his brothers had died from complications of AIDS. This was his way of honoring his memory and giving back so that others might not suffer.

With Papa Jack riding shotgun, we merged into the Zen chaos of Phnom Penh traffic. Laid out along the branches and tributaries of the Mekong River, the capital city's traffic mirrors the currents and eddies that surround it. Vans, pedicabs, motor scooters, bicycles, and pedestrians all drift along with no regard to right of way, paying no attention to street signs. To make matters more intriguing, people were precariously piled and perched on scooters in remarkable numbers, astride, sidesaddle, on the handlebars, and on the back fender—and holding their young while doing so. As if that weren't enough, many were wearing pajamas. I was told that Cambodians wear their newest, most matched clothing, which often happens to be . . . pajamas. In this totally non-Western swirl, in bright daylight, outfitted in sleep suits, somehow they all survive and eventually reach their destinations. Ours was the InterContinental Hotel, where most folks on NGO and political business stay.

I busied myself organizing my room as I needed it to be—not a small task at the time—put all the flowers and garlands presented to me at the airport and at points along the way in special places of honor and got the Internet going so I could post dispatches from the field to friends, family, and supporters. After cleaning up and ordering a meal that would become my menu for the entire trip (something I have repeated everywhere I go; eating the same thing three times a day helps keep life simple, eliminates unnecessary sensory distractions, and helps to focus my mind and emotions). I settled in to read the briefing materials Kate had handed me. They contained the usual facts and figures, forming a snapshot of the country, plus fascinating details of how our grassroots programs work.

The Kingdom of Cambodia is about the size of Missouri, squeezed like an orange between the Gulf of Thailand, Vietnam, Laos, and Thailand. Once the seat of the ancient Khmer Empire, Cambodia was subsequently colonized by the French, bombed by the Americans, and savaged by a genocidal dictator named Pol Pot and his psychotic Khmer Rouge, until finally returning to self-rule as a constitutional monarchy in 1993. It was then PSI set up its first office in Phnom Penh.

By that time the AIDS epidemic had slipped across Cambodia's strife-torn borders and taken hold in the brothels of Phnom Penh and other population centers. PSI found partners in government agencies, local nonprofits, and private industry to help prevent the epidemic from leaping into the general population. PSI subsidized the manufacture of "Number One" condoms and marketed them specifically for this high-risk group. They showered the brothels with condoms. The campaign seemed to be a big success in reducing infection rates. By 2002, a World Health Organization survey showed HIV rates declining in Cambodia, while the exploitative sex industry accounted for only 21 percent of new HIV infections, down from 80 to 90 percent when the program began. But Cambodia still had the highest percentage of HIV seroprevalence in Southeast Asia. And AIDS was still little understood among the country's fourteen million people, 70 percent of whom live on subsistence farms.

My itinerary was filled with visits to brothels and orphanages, meetings with government officials, and a trip deep into the countryside to visit a program run by Buddhist nuns. My job was to learn intensively about HIV, other preventable diseases, and effective grassroots remedies and not just share this information with the media, but also receive the sacred narratives of affected people and share those narratives with the world.

Because all lives in Cambodia have been touched by the genocide, I had to confront the trauma and loss that still shapes the Cambodian experience; I spent my first morning in Cambodia at the national genocide museum. In the van with Kate and Papa Jack, I looked intently out the window on this fascinating new world as we crawled through traffic until we reached a stark three-story building near the center of the city. Tuol Sleng prison was an ordinary high school before Pol Pot converted it into a torture chamber. It has been preserved as it was during the actual rule of terror and now stands as a monument to lacerating human cruelty—austere, chilling, cautionary. I felt I could sense evil in the dank air; the dark bloodstains on the concrete floors knocked the wind out of me. As many as twenty thousand prisoners passed through these corridors between 1975 and 1979: students, doctors, innocent shopkeepers who were brutalized until they "confessed" to being enemies of the Communist regime. They were forced to name others before they were executed, and those they implicated were also arrested, tortured, and killed. Those who weren't arrested were driven out of the cities and towns and rounded up in forced-labor reeducation camps. The country's infrastructure was devastated in every conceivable way. The social fabric was destroyed. Even the monks were slaughtered. At least 1.7 million people were murdered in the Cambodian genocide, about a fifth of the population, including nearly every person with any form of higher education. Was I absent during the six weeks this was being taught in school? I had known nothing of this slaughter and my country's part in it.

Pol Pot was a meticulous killer who wanted everyone inventoried, so the interrogators at Tuol Sleng kept detailed records. The walls of the museum are covered with stunning photographs of each murdered person, like a perverse high school yearbook. Visitors, most of them Cambodians who had lost family in the genocide, were holding one another, sobbing openly as they stared at the exhibits. I cried with them, totally overwhelmed. Some of the photographs seemed to speak. They were taken the instant mothers were separated from children, as vicious tricks were played, promises of amnesty made, and then torture and murder committed. There was one child who especially disturbed me; sometimes a face is archetypal, and in it I see other faces. This little boy reminded me of Dario. I was shattered. It was a haunting, deeply disturbing experience.

Later that day we visited a clinic, clean though very modestly outfitted, run by one of PSI's partners. I sat with a woman stricken with AIDS, wasting away on her deathbed. When I asked about her family, all she could whisper was "Pol Pot," indicating they had all been murdered.

I was beginning to grasp the intergenerational nature of trauma, how the whole population of Cambodia was scarred. Survivors were haunted; children carried their parents' grief and guilt. A Cambodian doctor I met had survived the Pol Pot regime by pretending to be an illiterate peasant. He worked in a forced labor camp, and for four years, one wrong word, one allusion, one careless gesture, would have betrayed his true identity and led to his execution. He carried on his grueling charade even though it meant watching others die when he knew he could help them. The doctor's desperate strategy worked, and he survived. He was now the head of Cambodia's malaria prevention program.

To me, his story illustrated both the tragedy and the resiliency of the Cambodian people. It was one of many I would hear. The minister of commerce was twenty when Pol Pot came into power. He lost seventy-two relatives to the genocide—his entire extended family from every living generation. He told me they were so desperate for help from America, they would use rocks to spell out S-O-S on the ground, hoping that when the surveillance planes flew over, the pilots would see their message and rescue them. But the Americans had destroyed Cambodia with bombs, then abandoned the country to murderers.

Incrementally, we are making amends. I visited an American–run free hospital for the poor in Phnom Penh called Center of Hope. And USAID has been funding crucial medical projects through NGOs like PSI and its local partners. The years of war, genocide, and mass migration had turned Cambodia into one of the world's poorest countries and a nation of orphans and widows. In 2004, women headed a quarter of households, and most earned less than a dollar a day. Many women, devoid of alternatives, succumbed to prostituted sex work to survive or were lured to the city in search of factory jobs only to be tricked, forced, coerced, and outright kidnapped into brothels, from which there is usually no escape. Desperate parents sometimes knowingly turned their young daughters over to brothels to help work off their debts, to raise money to feed other mouths at home. Some were sold outright to traffickers for international sex slavery.

Our guide into Phnom Penh's netherworld of prostitution and trafficking was the great Mu Sochua, then Cambodia's minister of women's and veterans' affairs and one of the most inspirational people I have met. She is a tiny, delicate woman with high cheekbones and a quiet, implacable resolve. Sochua was a student in 1972 when she was able to flee Cambodia and the war, but her parents were killed in the genocide. After eighteen years of exile in Europe and the United States, where she earned degrees in social work and psychology, Sochua returned to help rebuild her shattered country. She founded Khemara—one of PSI's partners—the first ever homegrown NGO in Cambodia run by women, for women; their mission is to provide comprehensive health, education, and vocational training programs. She went into politics, and as soon as she was appointed minister, she launched a national campaign for gender equality. Politics reinforced her commitment to social justice; I have never met another official who chooses to walk dangerous public parks after dark in order to witness sexual exploitation firsthand, to continue to steel an outrage she forges into a passion for democracy.

The Khmer culture has traditionally been patriarchal, with women expected to obey their fathers, husbands, and elders without question. "Society always treated young boys and men as kings," Sochua explained. Women had few rights to begin with. But after years of war, the social constraints that moderated the exploitation of girls and women fell apart.

Although prostitution had always been present, the industry grew explosively after Pol Pot's regime. Cambodian men flocked to the brothels, and men were paying for sex with younger and younger prostituted women, even children, believing that sex with young children increased their virility. Some even believed that raping a young virgin would cure AIDS and other diseases, a myth that helped create a sickening market for girls ten and younger. "Genocide took the soul of my country," Sochua said. "Men no longer have limits, and the rule of law has broken down." According to numerous human rights reports, the Cambodian police were more likely to be demanding bribes and abusing prostituted people than enforcing the law.

This morning, Mu Sochua guided us into Svay Pak, the most lawless and depraved brothel district in Cambodia; she later told me that she and her associate had grimly and purposefully conspired to take me, "a bright light, to the darkest place." About six miles outside of the capital, we entered an affluent-looking neighborhood of smoothly stuccoed villas painted in pastel colors and perched on stilts. I was about to comment on them, making up something positive in my mind about this domestic expression of relative economic prosperity, when Mu Sochua, in a voice thick with disgust, told us that these houses belonged to pimps and traffickers. The money that built them came from sexual pain and humiliation.

The nice little houses soon gave way to a congested warren of muddy alleys and storefront brothels hidden behind sliding metal grates. I will never forget peering into a gap between houses that afforded a harrowing glimpse of very young children and women in a courtyard. There was a small outdoor fire smoking. They were hanging wash on a line. We heard tinny music playing from a cheap boom box.

"That is Vietnamese music," Sochua told me. "They have been smuggled here from Vietnam for sex."

I thought: *Slaves? This is what slaves look like? They aren't shackled? They light fires? They do wash? They listen to music from their homeland?* This was but the beginning of a series of revelations that would bend my mind and break my heart.

The next bizarre thing for me to grasp was that I could visit slaves, sit intimately with them, hearing details of their realities through open dialogue and sharing, yet when I left they would still be slaves. As public health advocates, we could be tolerated by pimps and madams, who, while not exactly friendly, would accept our presence and medical assistance. The women, girls, and boys had been vilely raped and abused the night before I arrived, and after I left, it would be mere hours before the humiliation and emotional torture began again.

Next was that the expression of stupendous grief and pain from captive people would not move their captors to set them free. The outpouring of anguish I witnessed meant nothing to those who caused and (so it seemed to me) could end it.

The distress was stunning, and I was so emotionally flooded that I shut down a few times. What I had chosen to face simply exceeded my capacity to process, and eventually I would have to develop an effective and safe method for coping in order to endure in this world of human rights atrocities. I look at photographs from that day, and certain moments are crystal clear, hyperlucid, while others make me feel slack, lethargic, fuzzy, much as I did in the moments I became overwhelmed. Eventually, as I learned how to stay present in the brothels, everything would be seared into me: pieces of dirty, floral-printed cotton hanging between filthy mattresses; squares of linoleum meeting the wall; a person's few possessions crumpled in a bucket; the madam relaxing on the landing, watching a black-and-white TV; the eyes of men as they lined up to buy prostituted sex and their eyes as they emerged from paid sex acts.

In a small round room, I met a group of about seventeen sex slaves. They had dressed up for me, as clean as they could be in their circumstances, equal parts excited and shy to have a guest. Mu Sochua offered a few words of introduction, describing me as an American woman, a Hollywood actor, who had traveled from America to meet them. I instinctively sat down and held the hands on either side of me. Then, I must have asked each person to tell me about him- or herself, perhaps inquiring what they wanted me to know about them, because by the end of our time together, I had scooted on my bottom around the circle, reaching out to each person as intimately as I could. I ended up hugging and even cradling each one as they explained how they became a sex slave and what their life was like. I didn't know what else to do. Thank God my faith teaches me that listening is the beginning of empathy and, when followed by action, is a powerful prayer.

The most unforgettable story from that day was told to me by a transgender sex slave who had a frightening scar crisscrossing her face. She told me how, when she realized growing up that she was different from other boys, her family shunned her and she fled to Phnom Penh. She burrowed her head into my chest, sobbing violently, as she told me how she was broken in as a slave by a man who pinned her down and raped her while a dog mauled her face. She had contracted HIV. (In fact, most everyone in the room was HIV-positive, which was why Khemera had been permitted access to them.)

I have a beautiful photograph of her that makes me cry as hard as any ugly story I've heard, any image of despair I've seen. It is taken from behind me, showing a close-up of her face nestled in the crook of my shoulder. Her face is slick with tears, her mouth is open in a wide smile, her eyes are looking directly into the lens. She seems radiant, luminous, joyous—I believe it's because someone listened; someone touched her for the purpose of love rather than harm. I wonder how long this moment of relief lasted for her?

The next thing I remember, I was holding hands with my transgendered friend, surrounded by sex slaves, walking with Mu Sochua out into the sunlight and through the streets of Svay Pak. As we walked, Sochua told me approvingly how radical and magical and defiant this act was, for the local pimps, madams, traffickers, and clients, who were no doubt watching, to see a government minister and a Hollywood star, their heads held high, taking up with human beings they thought they owned.

As I write this in 2010, the grief is as fresh as it was that day, knowing the majority of those I met in that small round room are still sex slaves. Their stories are known to Human Rights Watch, and posted on their website. I read and reread them, wrapping my mind around a reality that should be impossible.

Another iconic story from that day is one I would hear over and over again worldwide, differing only in small details. Later that day, we drove back to Phnom Penh and sat in a small, dirty community center that nonetheless carried a strong message of empowerment and resilience. It was a place where vulnerable, abused women could begin to form female alliances. I watched a session in which prostitutes practiced verbal skills through role-playing. They were learning how to introduce the necessity of a condom with their clients and teaching one another strategies to reduce both resistance and violence.

Each woman in this group, save one, came from impoverished families and worked in prostitution because she had little or no education and no opportunities. ("Prostitution occurs in the absence of choices," Ruchira Gupta, who became a hero to me in India, would teach me.) All of these women sent money home. Some prostituted women were aware of the risks they were running in the midst of an AIDS epidemic, but one told me, "I may be dead in a few years from contracting HIV/AIDS, but I don't have food for tomorrow." I have since had others say to me, "My life is so miserable, I don't want to use a condom. I want to die."

Another of the peer educators told me her story in detail: Poor and rural, struggling to survive, she contemplated a typical migration to an urban area in search of work in a garment factory, where conditions were often harsh. A seemingly kind friend said, "Oh, I can get you a job at the factory where I work." After traveling to the capital, she discovered to her horror that her friend had sold her to a man who locked her for a week in a hotel room, where he abused her obscenely. He threatened to have her gang-raped if she resisted and beat her if she was anything less than fully compliant. At the end of the week, he sold her to a brothel, where she was ordered to work to *pay him back what he had spent on her.* In addition, she was told she had to pay her room and board at the brothel. She had been a virgin. I despairingly puzzled over the economics of this strange math, before I could accept that modern indentured servitude is terribly common.

She was such a gentle young woman; it was hard to reconcile her manner with the brutality she had just recounted. My soft-spoken friend explained how now she was ruined and unable ever to return home. She came to the center to learn vocational skills that might someday allow her to earn enough money on which to live; they offered hairdressing, sewing, and beading training, as well as access to medical information and other services. As a peer educator who helps identify and sensitize other slaves and prostitutes to the health risks that are inherent in sexual exploitation,

PSI paid her a small sum, which allowed her to accept fewer clients to eke out her living.

The name of Sochua's campaign for gender equality was Neary Rattanak, meaning "Women Are Precious Gems." She told me that she had turned an old Khmer saying, "Men are like gold, women are like white cloth," into a motto: "Men are like gold, women are like precious gems." The redemptive message was that unlike white cloth, a gem is a thing of permanent strength and value, and if it is soiled, it can be polished and made to shine even more brightly.

I lost touch with Mu Sochua for a time, but I never forgot her. I kept a news article about her my mother had given me in my bedside drawer for years, a fierce tableau of courage and an exhortation for me never to forget that day or the reality of the modern slave trade, in which more people are trapped than at the height of the slave trade in the nineteenth century. Trafficking in human beings is a $12 billion business, more lucrative than the illegal drug and arms trade, and it is a major factor in the continuing AIDS pandemic.

I was unsurprised when Mu Sochua was nominated for a Nobel Peace Prize in 2005. And in 2008, with the help of international pressure, she was finally able to persuade her government to enact its first antitrafficking law and to shut down the notorious brothels in Svay Pak. Unfortunately, most of the pimps and traffickers simply moved to other locations and went further underground. United with scholars and activists worldwide, I have intensified my antislavery efforts, realizing that as long as there is a demand for prostituted sex, people will find a way to sell girls and women. "Demand abolition" is essential.

~ ~ ~

From a public health perspective, condom distribution and education programs in Cambodian red-light districts had been effective, and most new cases of HIV/AIDS were no longer originating in the brothels. Now HIV was more often spread from husband to wife and between sweethearts who still had unprotected sex. PSI did market research to find out why Cambodians resisted using condoms and what would make them change their attitudes. A survey indicated that most Khmers in romantic relationships believed that using a condom implied you didn't trust your partner. But it was "okay" to use condoms for family planning. So PSI marketed the OK brand condom, and designed a series of television ads showing young couples negotiating their condom use. It was a huge success—and sales of the OK condom went up 7.5 percent in just one year.

PSI also helped produce a popular television soap opera ominously titled *Punishment of Love*, which chronicled a couple's ongoing saga of unsafe sex and its consequences. PSI supports dozens of "edutainment" projects like this throughout the developing world, reaching hundreds of millions of people with healthy behavior change messages.

Because many of those millions have no access to TV or even radio, the organization sends mobile video units stashed in rugged four-wheel-drive trucks to rural outposts. As evening fell, I had the thrill of adventure in my heart while I accompanied one such tricked-out truck deep into the hinterlands of Cambodia. By the end of this one day, I had already seen and done more in Cambodia than I imagined I would in my lifetime. PSI was giving me a window to the world, through the lens of public health, the building block of a sustainability, and as painful as the glimpse often was, I was also loving every minute of it.

My companions were a dynamic team of gregarious kids, many of them HIV-positive (and breaking considerable social taboos by outing themselves in public). They were experienced, energetic, and determined to improve health outcomes among poor people, and proving it by putting on up to twenty-five shows a month in fields, parks, and villages across Cambodia. Taking this show on the road was no act of whimsy—the journey was arduous and difficult. The peer educators were more than professionals: They sang and acted, entertained and engaged their rapt audience as if their lives and the lives of others, depended on it. And they do. Their presence is a fantastic draw for rural folks, some of whom don't even have electricity. From the truck they show episodes of the soap opera, and then perform comedy routines and bring up members of the audience to participate in skits that combine medically accurate sex education with good old-fashioned fun.

After I emceed for a while (they don't necessarily know my specific films, but boy, do they understand "Hollywood star") I snuck off to a field with tall grass from which I could watch the spectacle from a distance. I sat very still on the ground, aware of where I was on the globe, the night sky looking so different than it does from our back porch. I peered through the dark, rich air around me, gazing toward the cone of light and eruptions of laughter that pulsed from the circled-up crowd. It was quite a sight. *Look at me now, Mamaw and Papaw, playing on a summer's night.*

~ ~ ~

The next morning, we drove to another neighborhood on the edge of the city and squeezed through a narrow dirt lane, arriving at a makeshift school for poor kids and AIDS orphans run by Khemara, our partner NGO. The building was no more than a collection of thin straw walls surrounding a clay tile floor with a few woven mats in the middle. The kids did their darling "Oh, here's the grown-up we are supposed to charm with our songs" routine, and I was charmed indeed. Then they scattered.

I sat on a mat and waited patiently. Finally, by ones and twos, and then in a swarm, they surrounded me. They had dirty clothes and runny noses, and some of them were visibly malnourished, with the telltale yellow-tinged hair that comes with vitamin deficiency. They were tiny for their age—some of the five- and six-year-olds looked no bigger than toddlers because of stunting—and their eyes were sad beyond their years. Many of the orphans were already HIV-positive.

After asking permission to hug them—a custom in Cambodia—I cradled them, held their hands, smoothed their hair, and made them giggle. We basically just loved on one another. I spoke in English, trusting that tone and melody would be intuitively understood and felt, giving them my encouragement, prayers, and affirmations. It was difficult to leave, and I struggled to stay on the schedule that had been created.

My next destination was at the end of the dirt road in a peri-urban slum. It was yet another collection of one-room houses on stilts, with ravines ribbing their way underneath. As we got out to walk, an ebullient little girl with long black hair and a short-sleeved blouse with a Peter Pan collar burst out of the crowd. Before any grown-ups could explain, she leaped onto me, wrapping her legs around my waist and flinging her arms around my neck. Introductions were no longer necessary; she was my next appointment. Ouk Srey Leak was an eleven-year-old AIDS orphan who was being cared for with the help of Khemara. Although her delicate face was sad and serious, she greeted me with unusually intense and spontaneous physical warmth.

She jumped down, took my hand, and began to pull me toward her home. I asked if, on the way, she would give me a tour of her neighborhood. An important feature we passed was the well that provided her community's drinking water. It immediately brought to mind the wells on family farms in eastern Kentucky that fascinated me as a child and the deep satisfaction of drinking delicious cold water. Srey Leak's well looked functional, but of course microbes and parasites are not visible to the naked eye; there was no way to ascertain the quality of this drinking water upon which thousands relied. Diarrheal disease is a massive global public health crisis, the second leading killer of children under the age of five worldwide. PSI addresses unsafe drinking water by socially marketing point-of-use water purification solution, which costs pennies to provide safe water for a family of five for a month. We also socially market and give away oral rehydration salts, essential for recuperating from otherwise deadly episodes of diarrhea. Srey Leak was very patient with my keen interest in her well, and I was so glad it was nearby. Girls in Southeast Asia can spend up to six hours a day doing chores, much of that time involved in searching for and carrying water.

Her small hut was where she had lived with her parents until they died of complications of AIDS. She was able to stay here alone with the help of an aunt who lived in the neighborhood and a health care program run by Khemara. I stepped inside her spare, neat wooden hut and felt a shiver of recognition. With a translator seated nearby, I sat on the floor and Srey Leak, whose name means "Perfect Girl," curled into my lap. I was cross-legged, and we fit together perfectly, as if we belonged just this way. As she nestled up against me, my arms completed the circle of holding, fully enveloping her, and I began to rock her. She relaxed against me as she told me how her parents had died one after the other and how much she wanted a mother. If the rocking slowed, she would press into me, wordlessly letting me know she wanted more. She showed me a small photo album with pictures of her beautiful family—mother, father, and grandparents—enshrined in plastic. It was all she had left of them.

I told her about my grandparents and softly shared some of the ways I am able to keep my relationship with them dynamic and alive, even though they had passed on from the physical world. Last night, in fact, I had very auspiciously had one of my deep, beautiful, heart-piercing dreams about Mamaw, the kind that happens on occasion and nearly breaks me in half with its bittersweetness. She had come to me just as she had been in life, appearing so naturally and fully that I could see every eyelash, the exact color and flecks of her irises. She had whispered guidance, direction, and care to me, soaking me in the unconditional love she gave me in such abundance in life. I described the dream to Srey Leak and told her how I could tenderly conjure scenes with such attention to detail that I could re-experience my grandparents' love, walking in my mind's eye through precious memories. I talked with her about praying.

I made a stupid mistake while I was trying to be lighthearted for a moment and had changed the subject to daily chores. When I found out that she did the dishes, I exclaimed, "Oh, I had that chore when I was a kid!" I told her I didn't think that had been fair, as it should have fallen to my older sister, and didn't she agree? "Aren't the dishes for the bigger kids in the family?"

She thought it over and said, "Well, I don't have anybody." I felt ashamed—I had forgotten she had no siblings. I said a silent prayer, asking to be taught how to be more considerate. She handled my gaffe with poise.

We carried on snuggling and talking for the better part of an hour. When it was time to go, Kate and I gave her a wrapped gift box filled with a backpack, clothes, and school and art supplies. I knew her grief transcended being "fixed" by a gift, but I hoped it would keep her mind distracted for a spell.

I told her I would never forget her, and I asked her to show me where she slept so I could picture here there. She led me to a thin mat on the floor, a few feet from where we had been sitting all this time, in the corner of her hut. I found this especially sad, maybe because of those evenings I'd spent on the bed with Mamaw, and I fought back an urge to sweep her up, carry her on my hip, keep her safe, and bring her home with me.

It is wholly unnatural to walk away from a child in need, especially one with outstretched arms. It defies my humanity and is easily the hardest part of this job I have so eagerly taken on. I have often pictured Srey Leak in our home, daydreaming that she and the aunt who looks after her have come to live with us. I have stood in the doorway of the guest room in our house I have imagined would be theirs (she would want her aunt to sleep in the same room with her, at least at first). And in my imagination, Srey Leak goes on to assimilate the best of what America has to offer, and whether she grows up to live a quiet, simple life, or has troubles that stem from her many losses, or overcomes those losses and goes on to be of great service to her fellows, I love and accept her unconditionally.

But she still has a place in Cambodia with her aunt and her people. I know that. And with help from Khemara and PSI, she also has a chance at a better future. I have a picture of her burying herself into me, her eyes a million miles away even as she clings. My chin rests gently on her head. My eyes are closed. I am wearing Mamaw's pearls, a treasured gift from the woman who taught me to love this way, whose lap was the high holy altar of safety and comfort when I was little. Sometimes still, Tennie, the grandmother of choice God has given me, holds me this way. She has a swing on her screened-in porch, and various of us kids and grandkids will on occasion ask her, "Will you please rock me?" We never outgrow our need to be held.

I haven't seen Ouk Srey Leak again, and because of standard personnel changes in our staff in Cambodia, I have sadly lost track of her. Once, though, I received a package from her. She had drawn beautiful pictures for me. One is a pair of hands, reaching up from the bottom of the page as if growing up from the earth. They are cupped. Out of them flows all of creation, all manner of wonderful animals, plants, the sun, moon, and stars. It took my breath away.

I rock her still.

~ ~ ~

That afternoon we flew to Siem Reap, northwest of the capital, where PSI was opening a satellite office to serve Cambodia's rural areas. We stayed at a beautiful, peaceful hotel near the Angkor Wat temple compound, where the magnificent ruins of Cambodia's past are being slowly reclaimed from the jungle. I took advantage of a few hours off to hike barefoot through the tangled forest, but I wasn't fully present. The next morning, I was up early, feeling tight, anxious, and frustrated. After tea, I began recording my daily entry in the video diary I was keeping to be used as part of a documentary for PSI. I set up the camera on my dresser, started to talk about the time I had spent with a tiny orphan the day before, and promptly exploded into tears. *Cut.* Well, that was a clue to my agitated state. I wept bitterly for Ouk Srey Leak and her grief and for something that her story touched deep in my own heart, something I couldn't yet name.

I began to revive during a long drive out through the rural Cambodian countryside. Fresh air, open fields, and gentle farm animals cheered me. The views were lovely, the roads narrow, people few. When we arrived at a *wat*, or temple, I discovered where a lot of the people were: here, waiting for me! There were village children lining the road, and from a distance the monks in their saffron robes and the white-shirted Buddhist nuns looked like a bouquet of marigolds, dahlias, and zinnias scattered on the pagoda steps.

The polished stone floor was cool on my bare feet as I was led out of the blazing sun and into the quiet corridors of the simple stone building with a soaring roofline. The monks came filing in and greeted me in an extraordinary and happy ceremony that had me lying prone before them as they chanted a blessing on me. We all sat cross-legged on mats; even the shoeless Papa Jack in his safari vest and khakis managed a half lotus. The head monk led his charges through the prayers, their resonant singsong voices sometimes echoed, and always affirmed, by the rows of observers on either side of the Buddha's sacred alley. At the end the senior monk spoke special blessings and graced me by gently tossing sprays of jasmine blossoms and lotus flowers. Praying? Flowers? It was a dream come true.

As if that weren't transporting enough, I then went outside, where

I was surrounded by the "*wat* grannies," a posse of five-foot-nothing, shaved-headed Buddhist nuns, mostly toothless women with brown, weathered faces who pawed me into a state of belovedness. Through my translator they murmured beautiful, hopeful things to me about well-being, long life, responsible and giving nature, and future happiness. I instantly adored them. I soaked them up and kissed them and held them while the most toothless of the bunch cheerfully gummed my arm. I showed them a picture of Dario and told them that I hoped to bring my handsome husband for them to meet someday. They laughed and clucked like happy hens as they passed around fresh coconuts to sip the cool, sweet milk.

The *wat* grannies are part of a PSI program funded by USAID that pairs vulnerable, at-risk children from the countryside with surrogate grandmothers. The elderly nuns each take five or six children and basically do to them what they did to me: love them. They mentor the children and help educate mothers (if they haven't migrated to the city for work) about proper child care. Most important, they provide compassion, wisdom, and continuity in a place that is still reeling from the ravages of war and cultural annihilation.

I crossed the yard to a two-walled thatched hut on stilts in which thirty-five women sat with their babies. They were taking a course in mother-child nutrition as well as medically accurate, detailed reproductive health education. I learned that they had never been taught about sex or had any child care instruction before this program. The most schooling any of them had was four years of primary school, so they could barely read. The instructors used colorful, easy-to-identify illustrations to supplement the lessons. Today the women were learning the basics of breast-feeding. Some of the most dynamic of them would be trained as peer leaders, to reach out to those who had not attended the programs—a specialty of PSI and its partners.

When school was over, we had a kaffeeklatsch, hut style. Sisterhood is delicious wherever one finds it. We shot the breeze for more than an hour, sometimes giggling, as the women told me about their lives. When I asked one of them what she called her six-week-old baby, she thought for a minute, then replied, "Naughty." The women howled.

I think the classes were also a welcome break from the grueling routine of rice farming. They rose at four a.m., worked in the fields all day, then prepared the meals—always rice, sometimes seasoned with fish—before going to bed at eight p.m. There was no electricity and not much entertainment. But the women told me they loved to sing, and I cajoled them into a song—a haunting, trilling melody that somehow survived the years of killing. Song, spirit, memory. Some things simply cannot be erased.

So my last day in Cambodia, spent with the poor, illiterate, subsistence rice farmers of a postconflict nation, was glorious.

That night, I unfolded my mat in the hotel room and said a grateful prayer:

Thank you for toothless old women.
Thank you for tender young mothers.
Thank you for jumpy kids who don't trust outsiders but are so quick to
    laugh and play.
Thank you for wide-eyed babies.

Chapter 7

AVENGING ANGEL OF THE SISTERHOOD

Never underestimate the power and love of grandmothers.

Christ has no body now on earth but yours,
No hands, no feet but yours,
Yours are the eyes through which is to look out
Christ's compassion to the world
Yours are the feet with which he is
To go about doing good;
Yours are the hands with which he is to bless us now.

—*SAINT TERESA OF AVILA*

*B*y the end of my first full day in Thailand, I had an idea for my next thriller movie: I was going to play an avenging angel of the sisterhood who rescued women who were trapped in brothels. I would work subtly and quietly in the dark, in ways so covert that my movements would go unnoticed until my sisters were safe in my arms and on their way to freedom. Then, in giant, thunderous strokes, I would overturn the operations that kidnap women and children to sell for sex. For the sequel, I planned a full-on superhero turn, upending poverty, banishing ignorance, leveling the land for the light of equality and dignity to shine across.

It was a tantalizing fantasy, but sometimes there are problems that even superheroes can't fix in a flash. That was the lesson I learned in a grubby, neon-glitzy karaoke bar in Pattaya.

The day had started with a routine visit to the brand-new PSI offices in Bangkok. I was trying to adjust to the modern, high-rise bustle of Thailand's capital, only an hour's flight away but decades removed from the economic stagnation, quiet rice paddies, pagodas, and small huts of Cambodia. The office is situated in a gleaming modern tower in the city center. Vibrant, full-color posters showcasing savvy use of media and pop culture to reach young people lined the walls. Slick PSI-generated commercials with positive behavior change messages were playing on TVs.

I loved meeting the field staff, remarkable, dedicated people whose whole career paths are spent serving people in need. Olivier Le Touze, PSI's then deputy country director in Thailand, at the border with Bangladesh was a young Frenchman whose first job was in Burma, helping refugees fleeing forced sterilization (a form of ethnic control). I had never even heard of such a thing, much less someone whose dream job straight out of college was to tackle this form of human rights abuse. I also met John Hetherington, who was relieved to be stationed in Bangkok after years in Karachi, where he and his family had to be evacuated five times after threats by militant Islamists. Working in the developing world to improve reproductive health, curb the tide of HIV/AIDS, and prevent disease is not for the faint of heart. Sometimes reaching the most at-risk people means putting your own life on the line. It is important to me to spend time with local staff, from the technical teams to marketing specialists, those writing grant applications and those in accounting, the peer educators and the drivers, the demographers, those in research and metrics, all of them, to honor them for their often unnoticed, underrewarded work and indeed the miracles they make happen every day.

Thailand was spared the ravages of war, mass murder, and fanatical leadership that hobbled its neighbors in Southeast Asia during the last century. With its infrastructure intact and an infusion of American cash, Thailand experienced an economic boom during the Vietnam War and continued to thrive in the postconflict era. Despite the current global economic meltdown, its manufacturing sector is strong, and Thailand exports more rice than any other country. But it is probably better known as a tourist destination. Most of the foreign visitors come for the golden pagodas and white-sand beaches, but a sickening percentage of them are here for sex, a readily available and very cheap commodity.

HIV/AIDS first appeared in Thailand in the mid-1980s among the male and female prostituted sex workers and intravenous drug users. From there the virus made its inevitable journey into the general population, as husbands brought it home to their wives, who then gave birth to infected babies. Unlike many governments that denied or ignored the epidemic, the Thai leadership mobilized early with a comprehensive education and prevention program. The authorities required all prostitutes to use condoms, which were manufactured and distributed by an amazingly practical Thai politician and businessman named Mechai Viravaidya, also known as "Mr. Condom." The campaign had astonishing results: After an all-time high of 143,000 new HIV infections in 1991, the number fell to 19,000 in 2003; and overall, HIV was reduced by a jaw-dropping 90 percent. Thailand proved that clever intervention works. Mechai calls condoms "weapons of mass protection."

Still, there were more than 600,000 HIV/AIDS sufferers in Thailand, along with ominous signs that the virus was about to make a comeback. Prevention and education program funding quickly ran dry. A new generation of young people who didn't remember the earlier campaigns was coming of age. PSI decided to open up shop in Thailand in 2003 to help revive and supplement the programs that once worked so well. It might have been just in time: A recent survey sponsored by the United Nations had shown that 95 percent of Thais polled believed that AIDS remains a big problem in Thailand, but 75 percent of those polled—and 80 percent of people aged fifteen to twenty-four—felt that they were not personally at risk.

PSI was launching a new brand of condom called "One." After months of careful and precise social marketing research, they determined that young Thais want to be independent, different from their parents, take what they like from the West, and create individual personalities. The upbeat campaign spoke to that. I loved the television spot that showed the One condom packet pulsing like an eager little heart in the back pockets of jeans and purses of hip young people in shops and discos, ending with the tagline: "Got Your ID?" (We have other campaigns that target businessmen whose nights out invariably end with them purchasing sex.)

Afterward we stopped for lunch at a beautiful, quiet seaside restaurant, a calm moment in the center of the storm. While we ate, a banana tree smiled at my soul. I excused myself and climbed up onto one of her graciously curved branches and turned my back on people for a moment, looking up in her crown of leaves and out at the indigo Gulf of Thailand. I stretched myself out, fully supported by her nurturing branches. "Rest, O beloved, rest in me." Then it was time for the two-hour drive south to the prostitution capital of Asia.

Compared with the more discreet and ambiguous storefront brothels of Cambodia's Svay Pak district, the raucous neon bars that line the streets of Pattaya look like a postapocalyptic Vegas strip for sex tourists. The resort city was a notorious destination during the Vietnam War, where U.S. Navy ships would anchor offshore and spill thousands of troops onto the beach for "rest and relaxation"—nothing more than gross sexual entitlement and exploitation. Although prostitution was and is illegal in Thailand, hundreds of bars sprouted in Pattaya, stocked with cheap liquor and "bar girls" to satisfy the demands of paying customers. After the war ended, the sex trade remained, switching gears effortlessly to service a steady stream of men, mainly from Europe and America, with a preference for young Asian flesh.

Pattaya was among the first places where HIV established a beachhead in Asia. At one point it was estimated that more than 40 percent of the prostitutes here and throughout Thailand were HIV positive. After a concerted effort by the Thai government in the 1990s to contain the epidemic (which was, after all, bad for tourism), the rate went down to less than 12 percent. But with a constant stream of new girls and boys coming in from the rural areas and neighboring countries, public health groups like one of PSI's partners, had to remain vigilant in supplying condoms to the brothels and teaching the prostitutes why and how they had to use them.

We were permitted access to the brothel district, which was blocked off with a wooden sawhorse by a police officer who literally "looked the other way." I became increasingly aghast as we progressed along the streets, where women in hot pants and glittery halter tops sat outside the bars in cheap plastic chairs, legs crossed, or stood posed sadly in postures that approximated provocation against the garish wall, as if they were living prizes in a carnival game. We parked in front of a bar, one of so many crammed onto the manic street where we had arranged to meet with a gaggle of women trapped in prostitution. Papa Jack, Kate, and a PSI staff member who would translate for me were welcomed cheerfully inside by a madam stationed behind the bar.

The women greeted me as their "big sister," so I called them my "little sisters." We nestled like a litter of puppies on the plastic-covered sofas (I tried not to think about why they were wipeable) as they told me about their lives. Their stories were remarkably similar to those we had heard in Cambodia. They all had married at eighteen or nineteen; all were divorced by their husbands soon after. The money they earned having exploited sex was supporting young children, elderly parents, and even a brother's children. Several stood out. One was in full possession of a brazen personality; she seemed to be a ringleader. Another, snuggled on my right, was at the other end of the spectrum, stoic, subdued. She seemed vulnerable. Unlike the others, she wore no makeup and her hair wasn't fixed up, just in a simple ponytail. She held my hand in hers. When I went to hold someone else's hand, trying to spread myself around, she gripped the side seam of my pants.

She told me she grew up on a farm in a province far away, in the northeast, and came to Pattaya desperate for work to support her thirteen-year-old son (her husband had abandoned them, her in-laws disowned her, her own family could not support her and was disgraced by her divorced status). She had no education, no skills, no safety net. For two weeks she wandered the district, approaching businesses, resorts, homes, offering her services as a maid. She found no employment. She earned nothing to send home. Her son, whom she had left on his own in their hut, was running out of food. (The story bluntly demonstrated the cycle of vulnerability that poverty creates. I grieved for her; but, oh, who was grieving for him?)

A woman she didn't know, sensing her plight, suggested she try the bars. She did not know what this meant. However, once told, and seeing scores of other women working in this way, she succumbed to what sociologists call "economically forced prostitution." She endured one hellish month of paid sex with tourists and Thai men before returning home to her son, a small pocket full of money. Denying reality, hoping against hope, she stayed with her child until they were inevitably in the same position once more: penniless, meager rations, no prospects. Today, the very day I was there, was her first day back in the brothel. That was the difference I perceived in her. She was fresh. She could still emotionally articulate her regrets. I could smell the countryside, which lingered on her. I began to call her my "farm friend." The layers of loneliness within her transcended language. She brimmed with quiet despair.

We talked about her first time, the lying down with an alcohol-soaked stranger for money. One of her peers interrupted at this point and said, "You just smile and realize it's business, and do what you have to do." My farm friend smiled at me sadly.

Another of the women told us that she was a very young girl when she was first brought to the brothel. They sold her virginity to a German tourist who had taken Viagra to prolong his erection. In a chilling monotone, she described how he raped her so many times that her vagina was torn apart and she had to be hospitalized immediately after he left. Now, she slept upstairs with the other girls and women on mats on the floor. Each was forced to take as many clients as possible, day and night, and were given one day off a month. I picked up the strong alliances they were able to forge behind the scenes, even in this setting: a woman, for example, giving up her precious day of relief for another who needed it more.

Kate asked, "If you didn't do this job, what job would you like?" It turned out they'd all had dreams, like any other young women. This was what they wanted to be: a policewoman, teacher, singer, doctor, flight attendant. And my farm friend? When I asked her she said, "I want to be like you."

I weep, as if she were still whispering this in my ear.

My new friends wanted to show me their living conditions upstairs, which sounded like hog pens—no furnishings, eight to ten in a room, one bathroom shared by all. But the madam fiercely drew the line when they asked to take us upstairs. She went from the gregarious greeter behind the bar to dangerous disciplinarian in a flash.

It was time to go. As we hugged goodbye, my farm friend clung to me especially. She graced me with kisses on the neck that in local custom signifies respect and deference. Her desperate tears mixed with my own sweat. We clasped our hands in prayer and bade our farewells. I was filled with a nearly debilitating grief and guilt, swooning with panic as we walked out, leaving them behind. I had felt the same toxic emotional cocktail in Svay Pak and in the orphanages. I thought: *I can't leave my sisters in this bar. I am going to get them out.*

I knew I couldn't rescue every woman and child from every bar, karaoke club, beer garden, brothel, and other place of slavery. I couldn't take in every orphan. Yes, I could advocate for them, I could cry out their stories from the mountaintops, I could help protect them from HIV/AIDS, unintended pregnancy, help them make water safe for drinking, prevent and treat other health disasters, and I could agitate for change, but I couldn't personally rescue, educate, and provide for every sex slave, every child at risk of being trafficked.

These six, however, I could. And I would.

On the sidewalk outside, I realized Papa Jack had prevented men from entering the bar so we could visit in a relatively quiet space, devoid of customers. However, outside, men were queuing. The tableau I saw on the sidewalk seared into my brain: A white man was towering over a frightened girl. He seemed to fancy himself James Dean, arm coolly cocked against the wall. She sat under this false wing in a plastic chair. His hair was greasy. He looked down on her. I hated him. Only Papa Jack's presence prevented me from confronting him. I wanted his name. I had a rapid fantasy about shaming him publicly in his home country. I wanted to hurt him.

~ ~ ~

I quickly made a plan to ask Dario to help me. It could not possibly cost that much to send these women back to their homes, to send the one to Denmark who had a cousin there, and pay for them to go to school. We would make a deal with them: We would provide housing, food, and educational funds plus a little petty cash until they graduated and had a way to generate income; PSI could check up on them, make sure they were okay.

I would be the avenging angel of the sisterhood, setting my sisters free.

I told my plan to Kate as we began our drive back to Bangkok. She immediately started talking me down.

"I'm sorry, Ashley," she said. "I understand the urge to rescue everybody, but that's not how it works. PSI is not a rescue organization. We are a public health organization. That is our core competency, and we do it well. We have to stay clear of rescuing, or we would lose all access to slaves and prostitutes."

I felt as if I were in the proverbial rabbit hole as Kate unleashed a bewildering profusion of information. She explained what I had already witnessed: that we could not do our work without the cooperation and, yes, trust of brothel owners. The hard, painful truth was that if the pimps and madams thought we were impeding their business or had other agendas and motives, they would shut down the programs and kick us out.

She explained that we had to walk a fine line to operate within the existing system, as abhorrent as the system was, in order to have privileged access to an underground population. She had to remind me that what we do in brothels is but a thin slice of PSI's work. We are much more: malaria prevention and treatment. Safe drinking water. Child survival. Maternal health. Reproductive health. Family planning. In sixty-five countries worldwide.

"In this setting, we do public health triage, if you will, to protect enslaved prostitutes from disease," said Kate. "However demented it sounds, it is a portal of grace to help people no other organization has the chance to get to. Slaves would have no health care providers *at all* without PSI."

By now I was curled in a ball on the backseat, whimpering. We had reached the end of the brothel district, and the police moved aside sawhorses to let us pass. I realized the police were not there to keep the peace or enforce the law; they simply decided who had access. We pulled onto the main road north and left the world of Pattaya behind, as if it hadn't existed. I couldn't let that happen.

"But Kate, if we don't help them, who will?"

"There are rescue organizations and churches that specialize in this work, Ashley," said Kate. "They could be tipped off based on what we see on our visits, especially when we see and hear about children used in prostitution." She assured me that there were dozens of rescue groups in Thailand and across Southeast Asia that provide shelter, legal counseling, and, most important, education and training for slaves and prostituted sex workers who wanted the chance of a better life. Kate told me about the incredible Somaly Mam, a former sex slave who opened three rehabilitation shelters in Cambodia and has rescued hundreds if not thousands of slaves through her NGO.

"We can ally ourselves with extraordinary partners whose core competency complements our own," said Kate. "And as individuals, we can of course fight like hell with the NGOs that have expertise in the abolition of the modern slave trade."

PSI also has a long-term plan to empower women by providing the structure and the tools they needed to improve their lives within their existing circumstances. ("God will meet me where I am," I began to repeat to myself. "Come as you are," the old hymn says.) We are able to help many prostituted women supplement their incomes, training them as peer educators, allowing them to reduce the number of "clients" they are forced to take. One woman's reproductive health empowerment helps her educate scores of others. We offer them English lessons because so many clients are North American and European tourists and they need our language to insist on condom use, to speak up for themselves in a dynamic in which they are powerless (and to stick to their guns on the condom; men will often pay more for condomless sex). We give them medical checkups, often on the premises (many are not allowed to leave the brothels, others are too ashamed or psychologically disabled to leave), tests, and the medicines to stay healthy and treat disease.

"We're looking out for them in every way short of dragging them away in the middle of the night," said Kate.

By the time we reached the hotel, I was more or less talked out of my naive rescue plan. But rage still roiled inside of me. As I had so many times in my life, I escaped into my imagination. Soaking in the bath, I wrote the avenging angel script in my head. In the satisfying climax, God would descend on those streets of Pattaya and with a great wind of loving rage wipe out the despicable, heinous practice of humans selling humans. Those plastic chairs, charming icons of front porch America, on which hundreds of poor, uneducated, exploited women sit waiting for strange men to defile them, would be picked up and churned through the air, their ugly stories turned into mere songs on a distant wind. The men who trawl, the men who rape, the men who believe they have a gross entitlement to women's sexuality, who privilege their interests and violate over and over our bodily integrity and sexual autonomy, would be washed into the indigo gulf to have their violence and their lust and their hate and their ignorance beaten out of them by turbulent waves. Then they will be left back on shore, desperate not to make the same mistakes again, and again, and again.

What remained would be joyous and at peace, a gentle mirth in the universe.

I toweled myself off and called Dario. I think I talked the entire time. Later, I would realize he had done all sorts of interesting things while I was away, but I never asked.

~ ~ ~

The next day, I met another sister when we were joined by Coco Lee, a young pop superstar from Hong Kong. Kate Roberts had scored a major coup by signing up Coco to join the YouthAIDS campaign. That was her genius: Instead of imposing an American idea of what was hip and sexy, and presuming how people would respond to healthy products and messages, YouthAIDS analyzed what worked in each culture and designed the campaign around it. Coco and I hit it off right away. She was sunny and open, and she was traveling with her sister, something that certainly resonated with me.

We drove a few hours north of Bangkok into some low, verdant mountains to reach our first destination, Wat Phra Bat Nam Phu, an AIDS hospice run by Buddhist monks in the village of Lopburi. As we arrived, I saw a Buddha rising through the trees above a hillside monastery, radiant in his loving, benevolent smile. I figured he must be delighted with the monks who lived and worked in the whitewashed buildings below, because they were the embodiment of kindness, compassion, sympathy, and equanimity—the four tenets of Therevada Buddhism.

We entered through a spired archway and were greeted by the abbot, an energetic, round-faced, middle-aged man in saffron robes whose ordained name is Alongkot Dikkapanyo. His warm, scholarly manner made me think of him as "Professor Monk," and indeed, he was highly educated, with a master's in engineering. Along with him was Father Michael Bassano, a Maryknoll priest from upstate New York who volunteered at the hospice. In 1992, while visiting a local hospital to comfort the sick, the abbot met a man in the last stages of AIDS who had been abandoned by his family. He held the man's hand as he died and in that moment decided to establish a hospice for AIDS victims at his monastery. There was so much need. In Thailand, the stigma of the virus was so great that as soon as a person was diagnosed with HIV/AIDS, he or she was shunned by the whole family and cast into the street. Many made arduous treks across Thailand, hoping to arrive in time not to die alone. Some were so frail and exhausted from the journey, they literally crawled the final mile up the hill to the temple.

The original hospice had eight beds for full-blown AIDS patients. Now it was a four-hundred-bed complex with four floors of patients and a waiting list thousands of names long. The hospice had never received funding from the government. It relied on donations from tourists, corporations, and NGOs like PSI. By 2004, the understanding of AIDS had improved, but the stigma had not abated. Father Michael presided over the cremations of those who died in their care. Afterward, the ashes were scooped into small plastic sacks and marked with the names and dates of death. If they were rejected by the families—and almost all were—the ash sacks were placed alongside an enormous Buddha in an open-air temple on the grounds. I was deeply moved to be invited to sit in prayer and meditation with the monks and Father Michael as we joined in perfect ecumenical observance to pray for the souls of the dead, each of us according to our faith. I placed my hands in prayer at my heart, as I had been taught as a small child in Sunday school, chin lowered. Thousands of sacks of human remains towered before me, a monument to the heartbreak of AIDS.

These days, in addition to compassion and care, the monks were able to provide the sick with a measure of hope. Thailand had defied the international pharmaceutical companies that clung to their proprietary rights and started distributing a powerful antiretroviral cocktail of drugs that were reversing the symptoms of AIDS. Now, instead of crawling to the hospice only to die, a growing number of patients were being given the drugs and regaining their health, staying on the grounds in long-term facilities.

Professor Monk and Father Michael took us through the four-story hospice. At the moment there were no doctors on staff; very few in Thailand were willing to work with HIV/AIDS patients, which made me feel so sad and angry. (Did the Hippocratic oath come with an exception clause?) But there were volunteer nurses to administer drugs and palliative care. The first floor was for the "least" sick patients. They were terribly gaunt and suffering from everything from tuberculosis to thrush, a severe mouth infection. Yet they were beautiful to me. They beamed at their two fathers, the monk and the priest, and greeted me with gladness and appreciation. Having lost their families of origin, patients were told that they belonged to a new family now, one that would care for them and love them unconditionally.

I watched Father Michael glide from bed to bed with a kind word and a loving touch for every patient, as well as the kitchen workers, the cleaning staff, and the nurses. He made people laugh. I loved him, and I emulated his approach as I visited with the patients. Through his exquisite nurturing he was a masterful teacher, and that afternoon has enduringly shaped the way I want to be present in this work. I stroked backs, powdered the freshly bathed (ah, those memories of grandparents, again), massaged heads, held hands. I praised the semiliterate as they practiced writing. I snuggled, kissed, caressed, and prayed. We worked our way up through the four floors, with each story holding progressively sicker patients. We smiled with those who were feeling better, soothed those who were failing.

There was an especially weak and tiny woman who could barely open her eyes, who did not have the energy to move or speak. She was almost gone. Three weeks ago, in the middle of the night, she got on a bus alone in the north of Thailand and came to the temple. She had tapped into a profound resolve to essentially pilgrimage here. She knew where she wanted to die. And I can understand why.

Because this was meant to be a teaching moment as well as an educational opportunity for us, Coco Lee and I were joined at one point by some photographers to document our visit to the ward. I climbed onto a bed with a very sick and emaciated man, whose head was quite swollen, put my arm around him, and kissed him on the cheek as the cameras whirred. The message: If a famous woman isn't afraid of catching HIV from AIDS patients, you shouldn't be, either.

The next day that picture ran in full color on the front pages of Bangkok's five morning newspapers. I was taken aback that the papers had barred out the patient's eyes so that he couldn't be recognized, as if he were a criminal. The positive publicity we generated was a significant step toward destigmatizing AIDS in Thailand, but even as it prepared to host the world's largest AIDS conference, the country clearly had a long way to go.

Chapter 8

DARK NIGHT OF THE SOUL

My soul sister, Seane Corn, and me at a spiritual retreat.

When one is out of touch with oneself, one cannot touch others.

—*ANNE MORROW LINDBERGH*

The time I spent with Father Michael at the AIDS hospice, observing his respectful interaction with Professor Monk and his honoring of the Buddhist iconography, gave me an awful lot to think about.

I am Christian. I practice my faith. To paraphrase Thomas Jefferson, I hold Jesus in the highest regard, in preference to all others. I am also inclined to believe that the deity I know and call Jesus is the same Consciousness others know as the Compassionate Buddha, Sri Krishna, the Creator. I was raised in an array of Protestant churches; because we moved so much, I ended up going to just about every kind, I think, sometimes attending whatever denomination was within walking distance. Papaw Ciminella was Catholic and I loved worshipping with him, though initially his church's ways were strange to me. I wish I could ask him today what he was thinking when he encouraged me to take holy communion with him!

Except for a stretch of time early on at the University of Kentucky—when I was briefly attracted to a form of Christian fundamentalism practiced by a few friends but ultimately rejected it as intolerant and judgmental—I have, encouraged by both my mother and my father, believed the paths are many, the journey is one.

After my spell as a fundamentalist, I began to trust that God was big enough to handle my doubt, my scathing inquiry, my pain over injustice, and that such thoughts did not need to be shamefully repressed in order for me to qualify as faithful. I began to study and respect the Jewish tradition of intellectual probing, closely examining the sacred texts. I gained the confidence to wonder openly, and some of my pastoral counselors might even say harass the clergy, about the flagrant, chronic misogyny that has come to dominate interpretations of nearly all religions and most scholarship. I began to have the courage to identify, and to pray to, a nonpatriarchal God, a God beyond social and cultural constructions of gender. I didn't want just Father God; I needed Mother God, too. I realized that perhaps, just maybe, I could expand my God concept to include a "God who looks like me." And perhaps this God looked not just like me, but maybe like the dirty, poor, wretched, exploited, sick, and abandoned people in all corners of the world.

My God is inclusive. And with wonderful irony, it was some of the more conservative Christians in my life who helped me get there. Turned inside out by some of St. Paul's infamous teachings about women, I was devastated when asked to read from them at a family wedding. Riding in the car with Uncle Mark, I wept bitterly. He is a minister and a chaplain in the Baptist Church, a seminary graduate, fully ordained in that congregation. Rather than using my raw vulnerability as a moment to lecture me about the "right" way to believe, or the superiority of a particular sectarian interpretation of scripture, he simply turned to me and with enormous tenderness said, "Ashley, I love you." That moment has always exemplified grace to me.

I return to the same lessons repeatedly. While the Golden Rule is in the gospel, there are close versions of it in every faith. In the sixth grade I was in a pickle at school; I had some keen social dilemma that I can no longer remember. Mom happened to be home, and I decided to risk running it by her when she was putting me to bed. After listening, she asked me a question.

"What is the Golden Rule?'

I paused; I could not remember it.

"You know it," she said. "Think about it." Then she left.

A few moments later, it came to me: *Do unto others as you would have them do unto you*. I've always thought that was an inspired stroke of parenting on her part. She essentially told me that I have internal wisdom and that I must go inside to find my answers. Using the Golden Rule as the example was especially deft. Rather than encouraging me to rely on her for answers, she helped me see that I had already been endowed with spiritual formulas, applicable to everything in my life, that would lead me to solutions.

Many of my heroes are mystics, such as Thomas Merton, Mechthilde of Magdeburg, St. Teresa of Ávila, and certainly Gandhi. I love Native American ways, too; I have been given my native spirit name by a Cree elder in a powerful ceremony, I follow the cycles of the moon, and I regard all beings as my brothers and sisters. Hinduism makes sense to me: The God I love is so big, it can be helpful to focus on particular aspects of God's personality rather than attempting to have a relationship with the whole of the vast eternal One. Buddhism, well, this I also love: compassion, loving-kindness, meditation, and service. I know that we all love the same God, in spite of our many cultural differences. Meditation, for example: I learned how to sit through yoga with Buddhist friends, yet all I am doing when I sit is *being still,* and my uncle Mark, that beautiful Baptist, is the one who taught me the scripture "Be still and know that I am God."

Yet after a while exploring the realms of ecumenical faith, I'll be inexorably swallowed up by the resiliency of the specific tradition in which I was raised. I never stray too far. I often find myself yearning for the ritual of communion, I long for the little mountain church, icons of Appalachia, and Sunday dinner on the ground. I dream of the third pew on the left in the First United Methodist Church on Winchester Avenue in Ashland, Kentucky, where I learned the doxology. I reach for my own, deepest traditions in times of pain or stress. Which may be why, after an afternoon of witnessing the suffering of so many abandoned hospice patients, I found myself yearning for Jesus. And as I watched Father Michael pay his respects to Professor Monk by bowing slightly in front of him with his hands in the culturally appropriate gesture of respect and deference, I wondered about that commandment that says, "Thou shalt have no other gods before me." Once more, it was conflated in my head. I wondered how Father Michael explained it to his superiors, this easing from mass to Buddhist chants with radiant enthusiasm. I wanted to ask him if he tried to slip in a little Christ chat with patients. Even Mother Teresa of Calcutta qualified which deaths were "beautiful" on the basis of Christian conversation. But then I thought more about all the ineffable things I had seen today, the incontrovertible peace and palpable presence of grace, and how I was inspired by the monk and the priest working side by side in addressing the needs of the sick, rejected, and despised.

Then I remembered.

Sometimes I forget, but it does always come back to me: God is Love. Period.

~ ~ ~

That night I retreated to my hotel room in Bangkok to write up my journals and prepare for a big day tomorrow. Sleep didn't come easily, and my stomach was uncomfortable. I figured I was hungry, as I typically eat a lot but hadn't been doing so here, and I have low blood sugar, which can make me nauseated. Eventually I fell asleep.

A short while later I woke up sick as a dog, erupting from both ends. When I could lift myself off the floor, I'd go back to bed, trembling with aches, listening to my stomach build up for its next maneuver. I was writhing in pain.

I tried to put it in perspective. When Ouk Srey Leak in Phnom Penh gets the trots, she goes to an outside hole toilet. No running water for her, not even to wash her hands. One of the friends I met in the hospice lived at home for seven years, HIV-positive and ill, neglected by his family before he came to the temple. He had no one to comfort him, no one to offer him medicine, no one to help him heal. I figured I shouldn't feel so bad, but I did.

I decided to reach across the international date line and call my friend Mimi in California—she would still be awake. She answered on the first ring, I asked for advice, and she suggested we call one of our yoga teachers, Seane Corn, for reminders about postures that would support and soothe me through this. Seane is an incredibly dynamic instructor who emphasizes the spiritual as well as the physical benefits of the practice. In fact, they are inseparable. The word *yoga* means "to unite" or "to yoke," and teachers like Seane show us how there is a divine connection between mind, body, soul, and all creation. She also teaches that the body absorbs and remembers every experience, good and bad, and these in turn affect our health. The mind-body-spirit phenomenon has been increasingly studied and measured by plain ol' Western doctors and has largely become mainstream. Seane had just returned from a weekend retreat on energy work and was flush with guidance and perspective to share with me.

Speaking through Mimi, who held a phone to each ear, Seane advised me to lie on the floor with my legs placed up a wall and reminded me of the simple, consoling relief of a cold cloth on a fevered forehead. Then she gave me the lesson I really needed.

Seane said what was actually making me sick was the devastation I had witnessed during my trip and not setting and maintaining appropriate boundaries as I did so. I had left myself too open to the suffering of others, extending myself beyond empathy to vicarious trauma. My body was manifesting the emotional pain. She said it was critical that I pray every morning before I left the hotel and pray upon my return, to ground and protect myself. Mimi agreed. They reminded me I could not take on the pain of everyone I met, the HIV-positive prostitutes, the orphans, the sick mothers in their huts, my farm friend trapped in a brothel.

Seane's words flowed through Mimi's voice. It said, "You can carry the message. But you are not *the* message. God's love is the message. Quit taking on people's stuff. Pray for the spiritual wisdom to have discernment between empathy and enmeshment. There is a God, and it's not you."

When I realized what had truly been bothering me, I broke down in sobs. I bawled and bawled until reasonable people would think a body would be dried out to its bones, then I cried some more. I wanted to forget, to go home, be in my yellow kitchen, wearing my great-aunt Pauline's apron, baking a cake. I wanted desperately to lie with our dogs pulled up against me, their bodies running perfectly down my core, all of us breathing and sleeping and loving as one person. I wanted to sit on Squeaker's little grave and fiddle with my roses, accompanied in the garden by our cats Bunny, Amelia, and Albert, and see Agnes on the upstairs porch, waiting in our spot for me to come brush her. I wanted to lie down on soft, old cotton sheets and share my pillow with Percy, who purrs in his sleep while we hold hands. I wanted my husband to hold me and for sex to be all that it is meant to be, beautiful and kind and fun and fascinating and a union between two bodies, characters, and souls.

Seane and Mimi were right. I had been trying to take on the pain of the world without realizing it, making myself sick—physically, emotionally, and spiritually. I had been praying for the exploited, their abusers (well, sometimes), and those who try to help them, but not for myself. I had no mastery over my own trauma and unresolved grief, which was being seriously triggered. (It would be a while before I would even begin to understand what that meant and know what to do about it.) I had even done something genuinely embarrassing, perhaps the most embarrassing thing I have ever done in my life, because of my immaturity in this work. Holding that first HIV-positive, transgender sex slave in Svay Pak, unsure of what to do about her tremendous display of vulnerability, keen to help in any way I could, in my mind I had whispered, *Give your pain to me, I can handle it. Give it to me.* Now my own grandiosity took my breath away. Although it was well-intentioned, it was nothing less than overweening hubris! When I put all of this together, lying on the carpeted floor, words rushed to my mind: *The Lamb of God is the One who takes on our suffering, having chosen to die that we might live. Cast all your care upon Him, for He cares for you.*

I had felt the unmistakable presence of the Holy Spirit a lot on this trip, especially (strangely, perhaps) when I invited Her into the most desolate places. In the Pattaya bar, as I prayed upon entering, the power of the Holy Spirit was so instant, so enormous, characterized inadequately as a rushing wind, that I nearly dropped to my knees right then. I wish I had; it was obviously what I needed. I also saw God in action among the *wat* grannies and the gentle monks of Lopburi. But I hadn't seen a lot of God in my bedroom. There, my self-will had cut me off from the sunlight of the Spirit.

I was reminded of one of my favorite pieces of scripture, an especially powerful series of verses, from Ephesians. It is about how to prepare for spiritual warfare—and make no mistake about it, that is what this was:

> *Wherefore take unto you the whole armor of God . . .*
> *Stand therefore, having your loins girt about with truth, and having on*
>   *the breastplate of righteousness;*
> *And your feet shod with the preparation of the gospel of peace;*
> *Above all, taking the shield of faith . . .*
> *And take the helmet of salvation, and the sword of the Spirit, which is*
>   *the word of God*

I needed God's armor. My thinking had become distorted; pain had tricked my heart into taking on God's work, confusing it with my own.

Seane was right: I could be God's light, *but I could not work out each person's salvation.* I could not rescue each person. I could not heal them. *Only God could.* I repeated it over and over like a mantra, with my legs up the wall, a washcloth over my eyes, as I buckled down to wait out my own dark night of the soul.

~ ~ ~

As soon as the sun was up, I called Kate and told her I needed a doctor to settle my turbulent gut. I had obligations to meet, including an appointment with the prime minister of Thailand that afternoon. By midmorning it appeared that everyone in the hotel knew I was ill. When I called room service for ginger tea, they asked what else they could do to help me feel better. Housekeeping sent me pink lotuses and a get-well card. The hotel sent a Western-style doctor to my room who prescribed a typical round of pills that suppressed symptoms. Meanwhile, Kate tracked down a wonderful Chinese doctor who used acupuncture to calm my stomach. He determined that the heat had done me in, and I had to agree. It had all been a little too hot, too emotional, too intense. But I wouldn't have changed a thing. I started taking his herbs and ignored the other doctor's advice—except for his suggestion to eat warm chocolate pudding, my ultimate comfort food, so associated with Mamaw and Papaw, and those tender, musical summer nights in eastern Kentucky. God, it was delicious, and it was all I could keep down. I put on a clean white cotton nightgown and waited. Healing became merely a matter of time.

In spite of shaky legs, aching hips, the sweats, and the often abrupt need to run to the toilet, I not only got through the day, but with my PSI/YouthAIDS team ran a very successful afternoon meeting with Thaksin Shinawatra, the prime minister of Thailand. It turned out that he had studied at Eastern Kentucky University and he'd been at the Kentucky Derby in 1973 when Secretariat won. I fussed over him for that. I also took the opportunity to affirm his government's stance on expanding access to anti-AIDS drugs. Since he had been in office, dozens of hospitals in Thailand had stepped up distribution of the potent antiretroviral cocktail that was keeping patients alive. And the government was defying the pharmaceutical companies by using cheaper generic drugs to keep the costs down.

Because PSI was new to his country, this was our big chance to introduce him to our programs and gain his support. The PM listened with great interest as we described what we do, emphasizing prevention and government partnerships. We were all thrilled when he offered PSI the full support of his government. I felt like high-fiving everyone but worried about how I stank from all the adrenaline that was running through me.

Then, at last, having made it through the day, I went back to the hotel and took a bath. I watched TV for the first time since I'd left America, a Discovery Channel program about chimps. Perfect. It helped me realize how deeply I had gone into the trouble of our world, how much I had almost lost myself in it. I determined to keep my equanimity, to find a way to stay in the work and not burn out. I then proceeded to sleep twelve and a half hours—by no means a personal best, but still impressive. When I woke I was still shaky, but I was not throwing up, I was not crying, and I was ready to fight.

~ ~ ~

Most of my week in Thailand was taken up with events surrounding the huge international AIDS conference, organized by the Geneva-based International AIDS Society and the Thai Ministry of Health, being held in a vast conference center on the outskirts of Bangkok. There were seventeen thousand participants from 160 countries. These unwieldy meetings are held every two years to keep the flow of information fresh and promote the exchange of new ideas to fight this mutating monster. The theme of this conference was "Access for All," referring to the disparity in AIDS treatment and prevention between rich and poor countries in the global North and South. But the big news was the increasing impact of the epidemic on women and children caused by gender inequality and harmful gendered cultural practices: There were an estimated thirty-eight million people on the planet living with HIV/AIDS, and for the first time, the number of women with HIV surpassed the number of men. During the previous year alone, there were an estimated five million new cases of HIV infection, including more than six hundred thousand children younger than fifteen. By now I had become a full-blown evangelist for PSI's emphasis on prevention, using private sector techniques to deliver health products and services to the poor and vulnerable, and my confidence increased with every press conference, panel discussion, and cocktail party I attended that week. I tried to be methodical and calm and completely prepared. I saw the great Jim Kim, the Harvard doctor I'd befriended on the "Heart of America" tour. A brilliant and beautiful spirit, cofounder of the community-based NGO Partners in Health, Dr. Kim was now running the World Health Organization's HIV/AIDS program and heading up an initiative called 3-by-5, which lobbied to get three million HIV patients in the developing world on AIDS drugs by the year 2005. The fact that he was having trouble meeting the goal said a lot about our inability to deal with the pandemic.

I quickly learned that these huge international conferences are three-ring circuses: In the first ring, there's the formal meeting of delegates who listen to lectures and speeches (this year by dignitaries such as Nelson Mandela and then UN secretary-general Kofi Annan) and then break into sessions to share the latest AIDS research and data. In the second ring, nongovernmental organizations set up little booths to explain and promote their programs and strategies. This is always the livelier gathering, part carnival, part trade show. One afternoon, Kate and I decided to take a tour of the exhibits and stop in at the PSI booth. But on the way we had to pass through the third ring of the circus, a section of the conference center set aside for displays by the corporate sponsors. When I had a look at the GlaxoSmithKline installation, I stopped dead in my tracks: The global pharmaceutical giant was celebrating and promoting itself in a two-story "booth" within the cavernous hall, which included a chic café/bar, a posh lounge area (ample enough for sleeping, which some people were), and no fewer than *four* two-story waterfalls. GSK were giving away free stuff and were mobbed by a long queue. They had massive full-color displays and sharp-looking executives who'd buzzed in to see what all the fuss was about.

I whirled and huffed at Kate, "How much do you think this cost?!"

"I'd say about five million," she said. (Kate loves to wind me up.)

I stormed into the minimall of a booth and collared the man who seemed to be in charge. I guess I could be methodical and calm for only so long. "Why are you spending such an obnoxious amount of money on this exhibit?" I demanded. "Don't you see how wrong this is?"

The guy glanced around the room for help while Kate and Papa Jack sidled closer to me.

"Think of how many sick mothers you could help for the cost of those waterfalls!" I said. Now Kate was tugging my arm. "Or better yet, you could have given that money to PSI to *prevent* a bunch of at-risk kids from becoming infected in the first place."

I had more points to make, but some GSK security guards came over and basically threw us out. Kate had to struggle to keep a straight face.

"Ashley, what was the point of that?"

"I don't know, but I feel better now!"

When I phoned my mother and told her of my antics, she told me she was very proud of me and my actions would no doubt resonate.

Later on I went to the plenary hall to open a session on "cross-generational sex" (a now common term coined by a PSI researcher), a practice that is deadly and alarmingly common in sub-Saharan Africa. Basically, younger, vulnerable women—often children—are taken in by older men, used for sex, and frequently infected with HIV. Girls have to be educated about the dangers and empowered to say no to the sugar daddies. The speakers were so impressive, and my mind kept drifting to thoughts of Africa. It was the continent most affected by HIV/AIDS: Twenty-five million people were already living with the virus, and 95 percent of the world's twelve million AIDS orphans lived there. I had heard so much about it from Bono, its ravages and its dreams, its elegance and its despair. I had not yet finished this journey in Asia, but I already knew where I had to go next.

Chapter 9

EURYDICE IN AFRICA

In an odious brothel, holding the sweet and sad Shola.

Our recovery can be measured by the ease of our comings and goings.

—VIRGINIA SATIR

The sights, smells, and customs of Thailand and Cambodia lingered with me for weeks after my return. With each person I greeted, I naturally put my hands to my heart in *namaste*. If I saw a Buddha, I placed my hands in prayer at my third eye. I could feel the presence of my farm friend in the fabric of the grubby linen pants that I wore in Bangkok, which I folded and stored away without washing as a precious physical reminder of the trip. I could be transported back to the pagodas at the sound of a wind chime on the porch. Kate had warned me that I might have some trouble with reentry, and she was right. It was lovely to be home again at our farm in Tennessee, but I felt uneasy. I was shocked by the opulence in America, overwhelmed by the colossal shiny trucks on the highway, the towering stacks of produce at the supermarket, the fifty choices of breakfast cereal, the trash bins overflowing with casually wasted objects that would have been treasured by my friends the *wat* grannies or the orphans of Phnom Penh who have so little.

Day after day I sat at my desk, attempting to write letters to potential donors, trying to reduce the story of my journey to a few attention-grabbing anecdotes that would compel them to send checks to organizations like PSI and grassroots programs that save lives.

How could I tell them that Ouk Srey Leak was real, that she needed us? That the exploited women in Pattaya were not strangers, but our sisters? The only way I could express my thoughts was in a diary, just like the one I wrote in hotel rooms in Southeast Asia:

August 2004

> *And now, once again, I am home, and at a loss.*
> *I am surrounded by beauty, and I have my routines—whether it's drinking tea in bed or baking fresh peach pies or laboring over a dinner table to bring it to its ultimate high summer perfection. Some days I*

go through my roses, plant by plant, and devise the demise of hundreds of Japanese beetles, then gather baskets full of botanical glory and fritter away hours making them look just right in little vases all over the house. I read scripts lying in the sun and in the steam room. We go to Sister's for supper. I occasionally help looking after our family's young'uns, I win and lose at badminton. I go to my husband's races and sleep twelve hours a night on the bus, even with those noisy race cars on the track. And sometimes, like tonight, in spite of all my life's beauty, abundance, comfort, and grace, I lie awake sleepless and disturbed.

I wonder what sort of day Ouk Srey Leak has had. I picture her on her nylon mat in the corner, blanketless and pillowless and I worry about a young man I met in his tiny, clean hut, so ill he could not lift his head, his one-armed father peddling herbs to raise capital to buy medicine for his child. I wonder if the other son, the mentally ill one, will ever have any kind of proper mental health care, if he is abused as he wanders around the slums every day. I wonder about all the desperately ill people I met in hospices in both Cambodia and Thailand, and whether they are dead or alive, and if they have passed, did they go gently? I hope so. I hope so.

Oh, this little old house, this humble farmhouse that has held Meacham dreams and sorrows and prayers for so many generations, decade upon decade of supplications for healthy crops and safe children, can you hold my dreams? Can you hold my tears cried again and again for the unsafe children and the sad women I met, and for the millions upon millions I did not?

Much has already come from my trip. We've raised almost half our goal monies, *Glamour* magazine is incorporating fabulously helpful YouthAIDS stuff in my October cover story. Sister is involved, corralling talent for a World AIDS Day concert, and Kate and I are a knockout on the phone together pinning down donors to write those checks.

But for some reason . . . that's silly, I know what the reason is . . . but tonight, as I do many nights, I am suffering. I miss my husband, who is away preparing for a race. I am still carrying a deep cough in my lungs, a holdover from the Myanmar hill tribe kids at the homeless youth shelter. Our cats are deeply in love with me, but rather than enjoying it, it merely highlights how casually they can treat us when we're away a lot. (Much to *my chagrin, Dario does not seem to be relenting on the "No cats on the bus for race weekends" rule.) I am hardly writhing in bed as I did in Bangkok, but the malaise is real.*

And so the only thing to do, as ever, is to pray. I'll listen to the depth of the countryside on this fresh August night, unroll a yoga mat, and take it to the Lord in prayer.

~ ~ ~

Upon my return, PSI invited me to join its board of directors, an honor I was overjoyed to accept. I would now have a seat at the table among highly qualified public health and technical experts such as Professor Malcolm Potts, a world-renowned reproductive health specialist. I would learn about problems and solutions in greater detail, provide my board cohort with detailed information about our programs on the ground based on ever-increasing personal experience, and help shape the organization's future. My first order of business was to earnestly advocate diversifying the board in terms of gender, age, race, and geography. Perhaps my proudest moment thus far has been helping to secure an enormous, anonymous donation to provide long-lasting, reversible contraceptives to women in fourteen countries in sub-Saharan Africa. (The program became an unqualified success by 2010, helping to avert three million unintended pregnancies among poor women every year.)

We began planning my trip to Africa as soon as I returned from the Bangkok AIDS conference. We decided to focus on PSI partners in Kenya, Madagascar, and South Africa and the distinct challenges each faced in the fight against HIV/AIDS and other preventable diseases. Because I would be on camera so often on this trip filming a VH1 AIDS documentary and I would also be doing a cover shoot for *Condé Nast Traveler* in South Africa (another way to promote grassroots work), I decided to invite my longtime friend, gifted painter and makeup artist Moyra Mulholland, to come along. Moyra grew up on a farm in South Africa during apartheid and studied fine arts at the University of Cape Town before moving to the States, so she was already familiar with some of the grimmer realities of life in Africa. Over the years we've grown very close, and I couldn't think of a better companion for what I knew would be another emotionally grueling journey.

But before we embarked, Moyra and I had one piece of business to finish: the 2005 Golden Globe Awards, which were held the night before I was scheduled to depart for Kenya. The Golden Globes are the season's first display of Hollywood opulence and glamour, and they have always been special to me because of my best actress nomination for *Ruby in Paradise,* which auspiciously launched my career in films. This time I was up for best actress in a musical or comedy for my role as Cole Porter's wife, Linda, in *De-Lovely.* My costar and screen husband, Kevin Kline, was nominated for best actor, so it was going to be a fun night.

On the day of the show, our suite was bustling with activity. The best part of events like the Golden Globes is the chance for me to visit with some of our far-flung friends and people in the film business who share that part of my life but whom I don't often get to see. Salma Hayek popped by with her dog, Blue, whom she'd been inspired to adopt because of Buttermilk and Shug, and we compared stories about our passion for roses. Salma and I are like sisters and have been even before I played Tina Modotti in *Frida,* which this amazing woman both starred in and produced. I had been telling her all about my work with PSI, and I had already convinced her to come with me on one of my trips.

By midafternoon it was time to pile into the limo and head to the Beverly Hilton. Dario looked so handsome in his tuxedo. He is always a good sport about dressing up for these events and facing the banks of cameras with me, and we always take our own pictures before we leave the hotel—the Mamaw and Papaw, I call it, because my grandparents took great snaps on occasions when they dressed up. Awards shows are merely a part of what I do—they certainly don't represent who I am—but I really enjoy making movies, and red carpet events are now inseparable from the creative part of acting that I love.

De-Lovely had been released by MGM, which also had a hand in distributing *Hotel Rwanda* that year, and we were all seated together at the Globes: I was able to spend more time with the terrific Irish director Terry George and with Don Cheadle, who played the hotel manager who sheltered and saved hundreds of Tutsis from the genocide-sweeping Rwanda in 1994. Terry and Don had invited the real manager, Paul Rusesabagina, who was seated at our table, and we visited all evening, mostly about his trip to the States and what an amazing movie had been made from such a painful story. I couldn't fathom what he had been through during the slaughter, although I could clearly see the weight of it in his eyes and in his posture. He told me that he now lived with his family in Belgium. I wanted to learn more about his life but felt it wasn't an appropriate setting to ask, so I simply offered him my friendship and told him I hoped I could visit Rwanda someday.

Wherever I am, I hope to focus completely on the task at hand, banishing any thoughts of the past or the future, engaging fully in the moment. But I was very aware that night that I had a foot in two worlds. Not many of my colleagues knew the first thing about my international work (most still do not!), and it wasn't something I could casually share with people in that setting: "Hey, tomorrow I'm going to Africa to visit some slums and brothels. Would you please pass the champagne?" I was caught up in the paradox of my life, feeling neither here nor there—which is generally a tricky place for me to be.

~ ~ ~

The next morning I kissed Dario goodbye and started packing for the trip. Not unexpectedly, some of my old coping behaviors started welling up in the stress and excitement of leaving. I wandered around the large suite in a daze all day, knots of anxiety and jubilation warring in my stomach. I'd cross the room, then retrace my steps because I had "destinesia" (heading somewhere, then forgetting why I'd set out in the first place), or hid some necessary thing from myself, or packed away something I still needed.

I decided to do myself a favor and attend Seane Corn's late afternoon yoga class on my way to the airport. I floated through my practice, hearing nothing. I occasionally noticed I was out of sync with the class but kept on following my own breath and trying to open as much as I could, especially my heart. In my back bends, I prayed. Seane likes to walk around the room, softly speaking encouragement or instructions to her students. When I started my finishing poses, Seane sat next to me, and we whispered a little. I told her about my chaotic, weepy day and about how preparing for this trip was different from the time I'd prepared to travel to

Cambodia and Thailand. Then I was *willing*, incredibly willing, but now I was willing *and prepared*, which brought a prescience of grief.

In my closing prayer, I asked to remember that I already possessed in great abundance all that I needed to make it through a trip like this and to be able to tap into the Source that would sustain me and enable me to be of service.

Bobby Shriver was in class that day, and we sat down to talk afterward. It was he who had introduced me to Seane's yoga class back in the mid-1990s, when we first became friends.

Bobby's life is anchored in spiritual practice. His words that day, as always, touched my soul. He reminded me that there was so much love and sweetness in life that you could hardly bear it. And when you remembered that we all die, it didn't seem like any of it was possible: the loving, the ultimate leaving. That was where my mind was—in the dichotomy. The incredible love I had for my husband, and leaving, traveling to Africa for adventure and pain. Kate had warned me that the brothels of Africa were even a little worse than those of Southeast Asia, where at least there was liquor and music and makeup and dressing up, a veneer over the ugliness. But they say everything is more vivid in Africa: sunsets, foliage, landscapes, vistas, the human dilemma.

Certainly the HIV/AIDS pandemic was more florid and brutal than anywhere else on the planet. And in Kenya, my first stop, the virus was already entrenched in the adult population, with 1.4 million infected. The challenge was to keep it from spreading into the next generation.

~ ~ ~

It was early morning when the jet touched down at Jomo Kenyatta International Airport on the outskirts of Nairobi. The approach took us low over plains dotted with flat-topped acacia trees, their feathery green limbs casting long shadows on the bright orange soil. The sight moved me enormously. I had always harbored the most romantic notions of Africa: the wild golden landscapes Isak Dinesen and Beryl Markham described and, even more enthralling, the idea of "Afrika"—a cauldron of liberation struggles that forged great political and moral leaders like Nkrumah, Mandela, and Tutu. But as is often the case, my idealistic visions quickly dissolved in the face of reality.

Once again, Papa Jack was waiting at the gate to whisk me through the airport. We were hitting the ground running. After a quick stop at our local PSI office in a modern, disheveled office park, we headed straight to the Huruma estate, a crowded slum of one hundred thousand souls squeezed improbably into two square miles. A blazing sun glinted off the tin roofs of shanties that flowed into the arid plains, literally as far as the eye could see. It took my breath away. The enormity of the poverty was blowing my mind while the glare was killing my eyes. I took advantage of a slowdown in traffic at a congested roundabout to buy a pair of knockoff Ray-Bans from a street vendor just before we left the pavement behind.

Our wheels kicked up clouds of hot dust as we rolled through a maze of makeshift shacks and crumbling apartment buildings. Kenya has the largest economy in Africa, but about half of the people live in poverty. The government owns the land in Huruma, but the squatter landlords charge exorbitant rents to the migrants who settle here from the countryside in search of a better life. I heard of one housing complex where fifteen hundred people shared a single toilet. Open sewers ran along the rutted roads past pockets of rubble and trash. The air stank of human waste mixed with the sickly sweet smell of vegetables and meat left out in the heat. I tried to imagine all this in the rainy season and shuddered.

We pulled up in front of a wooden church to meet a group of HIV-positive peer educators and youth outreach workers. After the usual howdy-dos, we followed on foot behind the YouthAIDS team as they set out to show me their stuff in very dramatic fashion. They use ingenious ploys to attract a crowd, pretending someone is being chased or beaten in an act of mob justice, or in this case carrying a colleague on a stretcher, shouting that someone had tried to kill himself. Word spread quickly, and within minutes hundreds of barefoot kids were sprinting toward the action.

Once the crowd was big enough, it was bait and switch. The PSI youth team broke into one of their fabulous, charismatic, powerful skits that has many plots but one message: HIV/AIDS kills, and prevention is fundamental to staying alive and healthy. When the skit was over, the team capitalized on the crowd's thrall and began a question-and-answer session about HIV/AIDS. One young woman in the audience asked whether or not you could get HIV from mosquitoes (FYI, you can't)—a sadly revealing mix-up with another big killer around here: malaria, a disease PSI also had innovative programs to prevent and treat. AIDS had been ravaging Kenya for more than twenty years, but there was still so much to learn.

We poked around the slum, waving, saying hi in bad Swahili, and admiring tiny, colorful shops. Fifty percent of Kenyans make their living through agriculture, mostly subsistence farming, but in cities and slums they survive by scavenging and selling little things in the informal economy: onions, perhaps, or secondhand shoes (or a single shoe), or by sharpening knives. There are small stands and makeshift businesses everywhere, announced on crude but colorful painted signs, and I loved paying effusive compliments to the owners.

I was thrilled to see how many young people in Huruma knew about "Chill," a wildly popular social marketing campaign. It used fun, hip-hop sounds in commercials to create an upbeat and empowering message about delaying the first sexual experience—or reclaiming abstinence if one had already been sexually active. It was aimed at ten-to-fourteen-year-old children—who are just about to make the choices that would affect the rest of their lives and are often being pressured to do so. Wherever we made the "Chill" hand sign to young people—it looks like a "V" for victory or a peace sign—the kids cheered and flashed it back at us. Abstinence has become cool. The kids join Chill clubs in school, where the code word is *Nimechill*—Swahili slang for "I Am Abstaining."

We walked up a flight of crooked, decaying stairs in a cement-block building to visit the flat of Abiud, one of our peer educators. He unlocked a bright green door and ushered us into a six-by-eight-foot room with a spigot and squat hole toilet on his floor. By Huruma standards, Abiud lived like a king; he had the entire place to himself, whereas most such rooms accommodated entire families. He had a bed off the floor, some stereo equipment, knickknacks, soccer posters, and a David Beckham T-shirt for decoration, along with scores of motivational and reflective quotations placed everywhere. His rent was $10 a month, which he paid with his PSI earnings. I sat on his bed with my arm around him, looking at his photo album, telling him how proud I was of him and to keep up the good work.

He was twenty-one, HIV-positive, trained to give his testimonial to others to help educate and protect them. For his work he was given nutritional supplements, some health care, counseling, and support. Like other peer educators I met in Kenya, Abiud told me PSI had saved his life, given him an identity, and made him useful. We might not be able to save everybody, but we could make a difference in the life of this one young man, and he, in turn, was helping to save others.

~ ~ ~

Our next stop was a voluntary counseling and testing center, one of those vibrant storefront gathering places full of motivated, empowered locals who bring the gospel of medically accurate sex education, reproductive health, and the prevention of HIV and other sexually transmitted infections (STIs) to young and at-risk people. There were posters on the walls such as "A Human Being's Sexual Bill of Rights," including the right to know about your body, the right to have sex only with whom you choose and when you choose, and the right to be protected from disease. The centers also provide a forum to dispel dangerous rumors and misinformation about the virus. For example, many believe that it's simply not possible for people who go to church to be infected with HIV. This myth fills coffins faster than small businesses responding to the demand can construct them.

Misinformation, however, is only fuel on the fire of the AIDS crisis in Kenya. The root cause of the HIV problem here is gender inequality and violence against girls and women. The sexual objectification of women leads to ongoing inequities in education, economic, property, and legal disempowerment, which in turn, of course, keep women and their children stuck in the violence of poverty. For me, the most fundamental expression of this poverty is a woman's inability to negotiate, much less have control over, her own sexuality and fertility.

In Kenya, this inequity can been seen in cultural practices such as wife inheritance (a woman being required, upon her husband's death—often from AIDS-related causes—to become her brother-in-law's wife) or in the lack of economic opportunity for women, which leads to transactional sex—which is also often cross-generational sex, a ubiquitous phenomenon here. Sometimes it's so simple as to cut like a knife: In the Lake Victoria region, the men fish, and the women sell the fish, and the men insist on sex in exchange for giving them the fish to sell. Cross-generational sex occurs when an older man uses his relative status and power to coerce a girl into sexual acts, sometimes in exchange for subsistence items she needs for her family or herself, such as a liter of fuel, or for aspirational consumer goods, such as minutes for a mobile phone card. Infuriatingly, there are documented cases of teachers demanding cross-generational sex from girls to permit them to remain in the classroom or to record accurate grades on their schoolwork. In such asymmetrical power relations, girls and women cannot negotiate condom use—much less abstain—and are totally vulnerable to the virus, pregnancy, and related negative cascade of poor life outcomes.

As grim as it can be here, there are some faint rays of hope. Some of the Protestant churches—a growing force in Kenya—have been backing away from their unrealistic stance on condom use. The night I arrived in Nairobi, the All Africa Conference of Churches was wrapping up a three-day-long HIV/AIDS conference. This ecumenical fellowship, representing more than 140 million Christians in thirty-nine African countries, had been slow to awaken to the reality of AIDS and had even contributed to the stigmatization of sufferers. But all that was changing. I felt very comfortable speaking at the conference. I am always most at home with people of faith and am heartened by talking about the HIV emergency in such a setting, because only when we all believe and accept the intrinsic worth of each and every person on this earth will we have the full motivation needed to stop the disaster of HIV/AIDS. And churches are accepting that they have to preach from the pulpit the truth about how HIV is transmitted and that they have to address within their faith the many social ills that contribute so mightily to HIV's rampant devastation of Africa. I believe an effective wave of the future is faith-based organizations working with public health NGOs. Together we have the ability to reach, empower, and save tens of millions of lives, unleashing human capital that can then focus on lifting their societies out of poverty.

There were some great spirituals sung at the conference, too, such as "We Shall Overcome," which moved me to tears, reminding me that Monday was Martin Luther King Jr.'s birthday. And have no doubt about it: This is the civil rights movement of our time.

As if our day hadn't already been full, later that evening we visited three brothels. In between, I had collapsed from fatigue born of incredible heat, noxious pollution, traffic, noise, and the intense throbbing of 2.7 million difficult lives. My nap had the dual purpose of essential rest and psychological relief, knocking me out so my unconscious could have some time to reset and fortify itself for the assault on dignity and humanity that is a brothel. I woke up calm and ready.

First we parked on a crowded, heaving street lined with electronics shops, across from a run-down, five-story tenement in a broken-up, tough part of town. Every now and then my view of the tenement was interrupted by tricked-out buses ripping by, lit up with what I am sure were meant to be festive lights and decorations that only seemed sad and tawdry to me; the back of the buses had crudely hand-painted Hollywood cartoon figures plastered on them.

Entering the brothel, I felt like Eurydice being led into Hades. The halls were completely dark, apparently because the electric bill was rarely paid, and women worked with one candle per room, adding to the frightening, macabre nature of the scene. As soon as we entered, the women started screeching and throwing plastic bottles at us. They thought we were reporters, like the ones from the national TV news station who had recently done a story on this brothel. Many of the women's secret lives as prostitutes had been exposed to their families, and they were still shamed and furious about it. Papa Jack and our escort finally calmed everybody down and assured them we did not have cameras with us, that we were there simply to talk with them about their reproductive health.

We were allowed to go deeper into the brothel, but the atmosphere was tense and explosive for the duration of our visit. The place was revolting. Even in the darkness we could see green slime on the walls of the corridors that led to thirty small dorm-style rooms. Dozens of women came every day to pay 150 shillings (less than $2 U.S.) for the use of a filthy mattress on a lopsided spring frame, separated from the other two or three beds in the room by threadbare sheets strung from ropes. They sat on chairs in the hallways, waiting for clients, of which, based on what I saw firsthand, there was no shortage. This was different from my experience in Asia, where the pimps and madams kept business away during my visits—or was that Papa Jack at the door, turning clients away as I bonded with the women? Here, business was going on as usual the entire time, with the sound and sights of crude sexual couplings all around us illuminated by flickering candlelight.

Kate and I finally gathered up about eight women to sit down with us in one room, while Papa Jack stood guard at the door. Outside we could hear scuffling and yelling. Papa Jack later told me that the desperate women would actually assault customers as they came in, competing with one another, trying to force the men onto their beds, extracting money out of them if they were successful in unzipping their pants. Sometimes the men would simply pay the aggressor 100 shillings to get rid of her.

The women we interviewed were a fierce, proud lot. Their dreams were humble and realistic by our standards yet remained distantly out of reach for them: to be a cook, own a small hotel, receive computer training, become a hairdresser. But the bus fare from home to town was more than a day's wages doing hair. Even if they could access training for these dream jobs, they could not afford to live. They were admittedly illiterate, but they were no fools, I will say that, and their exploitation was by their own desperate decision making in the absence of other choices, unlike many of the women I met in Cambodia and Thailand who had been coerced and kidnapped. They all had children, had been abandoned in the rearing of them by boyfriends or husbands, and were starving to death. The uniformity of their stories was numbing. All became prostitutes on the advice of someone already in the business, as a last-resort means of feeding themselves and their children and paying their kids' school fees. (Education is the Kenyan ideal: Skits and plays with happy endings invariably include a graduation. For far too many, it never happens.)

We shared information, and they spoke intimately, but without the trust and confidence I have cherished from so many others. They were hard women, and they had every reason to be.

In a narrow stairwell, I had an encounter with a customer that I have never been able to shake. Our eyes met, and neither of us relented as we held each other's stares. There was violence in both of us: challenge, aggression, frank judgment, and contempt. I had the power of my principles, but he held power over every woman from whom he had ever coerced sex.

When we left, the women up and down the corridors covered their faces, but ironically, none of the men did. My bitter thought was: *Why do women carry the shame? Why?*

We could have walked to the next establishment, but the streets weren't considered safe. It was a scuzzy fleabag hotel right out of a movie. Sammy, the owner, inherited the place from his dad in 1967 and kept up the family business. He rented rooms in fifteen-minute intervals to prostituted women who scored clients on the street below. For the cost of the room, one had to pay an extra 10 shillings for a condom, and we were stopping by to thank him for that. It was, to say the very least, an encounter about which I had very mixed feelings. I looked at Sammy's room, painted a painful electric blue, containing his few possessions, a fridge and hot plate, and tried to picture his entire life unfolding in it, trying to summon compassion for a pimp. Not much luck. I was ready to get the hell out of there when I was told a woman on the street wanted to talk to me. I ran down the stairs to make her welcome, and the beautiful Shola came into our lives.

She looked different from the hardened women across the street. Shola was still a teenager, at least six feet tall, rail thin, and heartbreakingly gorgeous, with small, elegant features. Her skin was like velvet, and she had liquid eyes. We settled into Sammy's sofa as I tried not to think too hard about what exactly I was sitting on (thanks, Papa Jack, for the wink-wink, watch-out-for-the-bugs look, that was real helpful). And the dear girl, in a quiet voice, told us this story:

She was from the Meru tribe and one of seven children. Her mother died in an accident when she was twelve, and when she was fifteen her father died of tuberculosis. Her father's relatives took their land, and three of her siblings vanished. She had no idea where they were. Shola said she'd had six years of school, with a little sex education in the fifth year, but she'd had to drop out to look after her siblings once her mother died. She got pregnant at fifteen and again at eighteen, at which time her boyfriend left her. Two months pregnant, hungry, and unable to feed her toddler the increasing amounts he required, she began taking the bus to that street to sell herself between five and nine o'clock every night while a kind neighbor watched her child. She worked until her eighth month of pregnancy and was back at it a month after delivering. She said the baby had an infection in his umbilical cord and ran up a 16,000-shilling bill—the equivalent of $216 U.S.—only a part of which she could pay, and she was now even more desperate.

Kate, Papa Jack, our PSI team—all were mesmerized, horrified, as Shola spoke. She seemed so innocent and fragile and ashamed of what she was doing. She said the work was difficult at first; she was very shy and would only hitch up her skirt. She would not perform oral sex, saying it was dirty. She was obviously still lactating.

"I don't let the men touch my breasts, because that's the food for my baby," she said. She could not stand to go home to breast-feed with the grime of strange men on her as she held her son.

"What would you do if you weren't doing this?" I asked. She said she would want a small business, selling secondhand clothes.

Kate looked at me and I looked at Kate, and suddenly all her warnings from Thailand went out the window. We had to help this teenager right away; no NGO programming, however expertly designed and administered, was an immediate enough intervention for Shola. We knew the nature of PSI's work was not to rescue women out of prostitution, and gestures like these rarely worked without an established support mechanism. For Shola, we made an exception. She was too compellingly tragic. We dug into our pockets and came up with about $250 U.S. It was enough to pay Schola's rent for two years. We explained how much it was, admonished her to tell *no one* she had the money, and gave her the number of the local PSI office with the plea to call us to check in, explaining that they could help her convert the dollars to shillings and keep it safe for her. She rolled it up in a tissue and put it in her bra. Our local staffer told her the name of a modeling agency and how to look it up, something that irritated me and I disagreed with but had to admit that in the short term, while she still had no skills, might help her generate income apart from outright sexual exploitation. We gave her a lot of love and encouragement, then drove her to the bus stop.

When I think of Shola and that foul blue room jumps to mind, I blot it out with the memory of her pressed into me, my arms wrapped around her, in the backseat of the car, that ephemeral moment when she was safe, surrounded by people who had rallied to her defense. But it was a brief moment indeed; I never heard whether she followed up with our office, and there was no way to track her down in the transitory vortex of Nairobi's slums.

In countries like Kenya, where HIV/AIDS, malaria, diarrheal diseases, poverty, and all manner of social problems plague the population, life can be very, very cheap. But the value of a woman in such societies is cheapest of all. That afternoon I had paid 800 shillings for flimsy sunglasses on a Nairobi street; all the women I had met earned 100 shillings for a trick turned on their backs, 200 shillings for one on their hands and knees. Now, that's cheap.

~ ~ ~

Back at the hotel, a perky tourist from Texas recognized me in the business center and asked me if I was on safari. I let her blithe obliviousness and her expensive khakis irk me, and I blurted out bitterly, "No. In fact, I am on a HIV/AIDS prevention trip and have just been to three brothels." I hoped I had ruined her evening.

~ ~ ~

In the morning, we drove several hours on ridiculously bad roads through the countryside to see a malaria program at a rural clinic. On the way, I received full immersion education about malaria, at that time the world's biggest killer of children under five.

Because malaria is carried by female mosquitoes that feed on human blood at night, NGOs battle the disease by making it possible for hundreds of millions of people to sleep under nets treated with insect repellent. This works best because entire families often sleep under a single net together, and if it isn't treated, those whose arms and legs are touching the net will still be bitten unless the repellent is present. The repellent has the added benefit of chasing the mosquitoes out of the room, thereby offering protection to those not under the net almost as well. In this way, multiple huts with long-lasting treated nets in a village can have the wonderful benefit of providing some protection to those who do not yet have nets.

The challenge has been educating folks about the cause of malaria and the need for every household to have and sleep under a net, the distribution of the nets, making antimalarial artemisinin-based combination therapy drugs available, and teaching those infected to seek treatment. These are the kinds of obstacles NGOs specialize in overcoming and on which good progress has been made.

It costs $6 to manufacture nets, which are sold for the heavily subsidized price of 150 shillings, or less than $2 in the villages. In 2008, this price was reduced to a mere 50 shillings. We deliver the nets to Kenyan health facilities at which we implement community behavior change communication, while selling the nets at these reduced prices, which can increase a sense of prideful ownership and use of nets. (By 2011, a happy confluence of political will and funding would allow PSI and other NGOs to undertake massive campaigns to distribute nets for free.)

Most rural Kenyans know about their clinics and women aim to go to them for ante- and postnatal care, even though it is sometimes a two-day walk to the clinic. Knowing the arduous journey will also yield malaria protection, they are more motivated to make the trip. A pregnant woman is highly susceptible to malaria; it makes her extremely sick and can cause a world of ills to her fetus, such as early termination or low birth weight if she is able to deliver. They constitute the highest risk and most vulnerable group and are a core focus of malaria campaigns.

From what I had observed, it made little sense to confront each condition—AIDS, malaria, unsafe drinking water, malnutrition—as a separate threat to the health and well-being of women and children. This old, siloed approach to health care and development aid was already on its way out. Now PSI Kenya integrates reproductive health, maternal and child health, and HIV prevention communication and services on every level.

One of the behavior change communication challenges in Kenya is teaching women and caregivers the value of mosquito nets and how to use them correctly. And this was what I was going to help demonstrate at a rural clinic.

A large crowd of nearly two hundred was gathered for our outreach event. Women sat on the grass, either pregnant or holding babies, and everyone was very curious and attentive in spite of the equatorial sun at midday. There was the usual pomp and circumstance in the form of repetitive welcomes and some fabulous singing to compensate for the stultifying protocol, then I demonstrated how to use and treat a net. I was given a typical plastic basin and showed how to use the gloves and dissolve the repellent tablet in water and saturate the entire net. Wonderfully, even though the event was fun, new technology means such steps are now obsolete, as pretreated nets are standard. And this was only five years ago!

Afterward, I interacted with my audience and felt confident of our day's success: None, when they arrived, used nets. Now all would go home with both a net and information about malaria, how it was transmitted, how not to become sick, and treatment seeking behaviors if they were infected. They also said, when asked, that they would reach out to other families with their new empowerment, and last but not least, they said they would stand up to their husbands, who often insisted on sleeping under the family's sole net alone, even with the knowledge that the mothers and children needed them the most.

To wrap up the demonstration, some wild, boisterous women sang for me again, becoming quite carried away when I joined them and basically creating a mosh pit where they knocked me from hip to hip like a little bouncy toy until I escaped, laughing, into the calm of the van.

~ ~ ~

I had one more appointment before I departed Nairobi. Before I left home, I had asked Gloria Steinem, a mentor and friend, "Who is the one person I simply must meet on this journey?"—something that has become a tradition on my trips. She has thrilled me every time with her introductions. Her referrals have connected me with heroes who have become friends and with organizations I now support that powerfully supplement my engagement with PSI.

Thus I arranged to meet the two women who ran Equality Now's Nairobi office, but because of my crazy schedule, the only time to see them was in my hotel room, the night before I was to leave for Madagascar. When I opened my door in my bathrobe and saw two gorgeous Kenyans, Agnes Pareyio and Faiza Jama Mohamed, one in full formal cultural dress, I ushered them in and hurried to pull my act together so I would give them the same honor they had obviously afforded me. I put on my favorite nightgown that passed as a day dress, ordered them coffee, and prepared to be schooled. I was not disappointed.

Equality Now is a global NGO dedicated to ending discrimination and violence against women; its emphasis in Africa is on property ownership and female genital mutilation (FGM). In their animated, musical voices, the two women described the campaign against FGM, the brutal tribal custom of cutting a young girl's genitals. Sometimes euphemistically called "female circumcision," the practice is so widespread that an estimated six thousand African girls are threatened with it every day. In some tribes it is a ceremonial nick, but usually the clitoris and labia are sliced off by a traditional circumciser, usually without anesthesia or any regard to hygiene. A tremendous amount of blood is spilled when a girl is cut (many girls hemorrhage to death), and circumcisers often use the same filthy tools on more than one girl in succession, spreading disease. The resulting damage to the genitals makes girls more susceptible to STIs and HIV. It happens at various ages, but invariably, it happens. The desired result is a girl with reduced sexual function, who will remain a virgin until marriage and a faithful wife thereafter. It is an exceedingly grotesque example of pathological attempts to control female sexuality. FGM is so difficult to stop because it is an entrenched and pervasive practice, and women are conditioned to believe that they can never marry without being cut. Because every woman in the group has been mutilated, the peer pressure to conform is enormous. In many places, a mythology has evolved around female genitalia to reinforce the practice. In some tribes, it is believed the clitoris will hurt a baby upon delivery, and that it will kill a man. (Well, of course it does, but it's a delicious death men love and from which they recover! *La petite mort*, as the French would say.) FGM is so important that should a woman in Tanzania die uncircumcised, she will be cut postmortem, or it is believed she will not go with her ancestors.

In Kenya, Equality Now representatives travel from village to village, explaining that the clitoris is an organ with an essential function, just like an eye or a hand, using anatomical models of healthy genitals and ones that have been circumcised. They explain that the early onset of vaginal dryness makes sex unbearably painful. The extraordinary pain and difficulties women have with childbirth are related to the lack of elasticity in all the scar tissue where the genitals have been mutilated, including the removed labia. When they do this education face-to-face with both men and women, the practice changes, but Africa is a big place and it's slow going. They also appeal directly to the older women who perform the mutilations, essentially trying to persuade them to hang up their rusty knives and razors by reeducating them into a small business of some sort or taking the religious route (you'll go to hell for hurting all these girls so unmercifully!). They are doing fabulous work, and while it is hard, there is progress. Equality Now has partnered with a grassroots group in Maasailand to implement "alternate rites of passage" for schoolgirls. They have engaged in training police officers in ways to enforce anti-FGM laws and have a presence in the courts to hold judges accountable for upholding the rule of law.

Americans might be shocked to learn that FGM practices have spread to this country along with the African diaspora. A federal law passed in 1996 specifically outlawed female genital mutilation in the United States. Equality Now is at the forefront of the campaign to expand the reach of the law to prevent girls from being shipped across the borders on "vacations" to be mutilated. Sadly, the bipartisan Girls Protection Act did not make it through the House of Representatives in 2010; there are plans to reintroduce the bill in the next session.

By the time Agnes and Faiza said their goodbyes, I was so fired up that it was hard to sleep. I could feel my horizons expanding as I contemplated the network of organizations like Equality Now that I could support. Each was like an instrument in an orchestra that, when played together, made a glorious symphony of hope.

Chapter 10

THE RICE TENTS

Prostituted women testing HIV-negative in Madagascar.

There is a crack in everything. That is how the light gets in.

—*LEONARD COHEN*

$\mathcal{A}$fter a week in the sunstruck urban wastelands of Kenya, the lush rain forest of Madagascar was a balm for my eyes and my soul. Kate had arranged a brief respite for us at a lodge on the edge of the Andasibe-Mantadia National Park, deep in the eastern mountains of this exotic island nation in the Indian Ocean. My plain wooden bed was under a mosquito net, and my windows and doors opened out into a place rich and lush in life and noise, a jungle filled with colorful birds calling in the trees, eight-foot-tall hibiscus plants rustling in the breeze.

I desperately needed this communion with life, as Nairobi had taken it out of me. I am not an urban person in the best of circumstances, and I'd never been to such a place before, so hard and dirty and tough and desperate. I'd thought everything in the developing world was either like Phnom Penh, basically a large rural town, or Bangkok, modern and muscular with freeways and skyscrapers. I hadn't known there was such a drastic place with millions of people trapped in slums, barely getting by every day. I had been fully disabused of my romantic notions of Kenya, born of films, books, and tented safari brochures. The Maasai I saw were herding thin cattle on the sides of cratered highways chugging with cars on the verge of collapse. My naïveté made me feel foolish.

All the domestic animals I'd seen in Africa were very thin, and I said a compassion mantra each time I saw some: *Om mane peme hung*. It was how I could feel somewhat useful in my total uselessness to them, and how I could keep from crying. Our young guide from the lodge had an amber-colored dog named Ginger that he called over to meet me so I could love on her. She was awfully friendly and sweet, and I vowed to provide her some food. Papa Jack told me no matter how much money I gave our guide, the dog would see none of it, so I retrieved my lunch scraps from the bin to feed Ginger and her friends. I got some especially good sugar from a lovely brown male, and it was confirmed yet again: There is nothing like the love of a fine dog.

In the morning, we visited an incredible little animal habitat that had chameleons, lizards, snakes, geckos, and the like. It was fascinating that so many unique species had developed in isolation, 240 miles off the southeast coast of Africa. I ended up wondering: How have these creatures so ingeniously and brilliantly evolved to where even their eyeballs make them blend in safely, and we humans have evolved into an eighteen-year-old girl, eight months pregnant, being bought and sold for sex so she can feed herself?

That afternoon, I clumsily tried to evade Papa Jack for a solo hike and was caught red-handed fetching a map at reception. He was kind enough to go against his own instincts and respect my fanatical need for aloneness, and I gratefully trekked up the rich mountains by myself, where I immediately began to weep. I walked and cried, and nature, as always, was overwhelming enough to absorb my grief and allow me to heal some. After Nairobi, I was starting to feel I could no longer be shocked. I could be touched, I could be moved, I could be distraught, but I couldn't be shocked—at least not by bad stuff. The worst sights and stories were all different versions of the same tragic tale of poverty, lack of education, gender inequality, disease, exploitation, inhumanity. The variety was in nature and in love, where wonders never cease: the colors of the chameleon, memories of Papaw Judd scrambling my eggs for breakfast, Dario's humble contrition when he's wrong and his gentle way of helping me learn when I am, twenty women meeting as strangers at a yoga retreat becoming sisters by the end of the week, a thunderstorm in Big Sur, a flock of thousands of birds gamboling and landing on a loch in the Highlands—I could go on and on. The beauty of the world could break my heart, but its ills could no longer break my spirit. At least not today.

By now Moyra had joined me on this painful, glorious adventure. I was deeply grateful for her company, and I'm amazed at how we love so many of the same things. As we drove through the countryside, both of us gaped out the window at the cheer the Malagasy put into their tiny clay huts, at the beauty of wild roses, St. John's lilies, rushing rivers, waterfalls, graceful, inventive orchids, and ridges of green as far as the eye could see.

But after this brief, restorative visit, it was on to the teeming capital, Antananarivo, and the challenges of a once isolated people now being slammed headlong into the twenty-first century. I quickly began to see beyond the physical grandeur of Madagascar and into its extraordinary poverty. Even though the land seems abundant, 88 percent of rural Malagasy do not have safe drinking water, and they suffer the consequences of that with the usual tragedies, all of which are preventable, including unacceptably high maternal and child mortality. The land produces fruit, but it earns them little money, as 60 percent of it rots before it can be exported; farmers cannot afford to pay to transport it. The once magnificent forests are being razed for timber and firewood and by slash-and-burn agricultural practices. And while it seems lovely that there is no litter on the ground, it is because there are no goods to throw away. Only half the children are vaccinated, and half the children are malnourished and stunted. The rural infrastructure is extremely minimal, and our mission of delivering lifesaving messages and goods, such as clean water treatment (which costs only 1 franc per liter), insecticide-treated mosquito nets, maternal and child health education and products, and, of course, HIV/AIDS prevention, has been confronted with a whole new galaxy of challenging puzzles. Fortunately, we do have some good funding here from both USAID and the Global Fund, money I was seeing in action in terms of both ideas and programs and the motivated, dynamic local personnel who implement them.

Although AIDS had been slow in coming to Madagascar, in 2005 it was waiting like a ticking time bomb to explode into the general population. Madagascar's remoteness, coupled with an isolationist, Socialist government, helped protect its people from the AIDS pandemic that swept the mainland during the 1980s and 1990s. But in recent years, a new leadership had thrown open the doors to private investment, travel, and tourism—and with it, HIV.

At the time of our visit, between only 1 and 2 percent of the population of nineteen million was HIV-positive. That was the good news. The frightening news was that what little the Malagasy people knew about HIV was mostly rumor and misinformation. It reminded me of the United States in the early 1980s, when there was so much fear and such a terrible stigma attached to the virus that HIV carriers were afraid to be tested. But with the Malagasy government's support, PSI was unleashing a massive social marketing campaign to educate the people about HIV/AIDS and how to prevent it.

Part of my job here was to use my high profile to crack open the social taboos surrounding HIV/AIDS and to find at least one HIV-positive Malagasy to go on television with me to put a human face on the epidemic for the first time. It took Tim Hobgood, PSI's young country director, most of the week to track down a willing subject. The woman who had agreed to meet me wanted to back down, because she was afraid that if her relatives found out about her disease, they would reject her bones upon her death and she wouldn't be buried with her ancestors. In the culture here, that is the same as being sent to hell for eternity. We had to keep trying to overcome the stigma: If people couldn't even talk about the virus, how could they be educated about how to prevent it?

~ ~ ~

While we waited for Tim to work his magic, I had the distinct pleasure of visiting the clinic run by one of the many unsung heroes in the fight against HIV/AIDS, Dr. Rene Randrianga. Dr. Rene is a large man with skin the color of milk chocolate, wide cheekbones, and almond-shaped eyes that reflect the mélange of African and Asian ethnicities that make up the Malagasy people. Toss in the French language inherited from the island's former colonizers, and the mix is complete. For ten years, Dr. Rene has provided health care and counseling to the capital's prostituted women in an effort to keep them from contracting and spreading HIV. Two factors complicate the danger here: Many Malagasy consider it perfectly normal to have multiple sex partners, in or out of marriage. And this country has one of the world's highest rates of sexually transmitted infections such as syphilis, and the open sores from these infections facilitate HIV transmission. The best solution available was education and condoms—and PSI was providing both. Dr. Rene would be our guide into the streets of Antananarivo, where—to make a terrible joke—the rubber literally meets the road.

That night, the skies opened up like spigots as we drove down dark, sloppy clay roads lined with tiny, ramshackle shacks until we arrived at our destination. As far as I could see, sidewalks were lined with pathetic tarps made from plastic rice sacks—they called them "rice tents"—where the poorest and most desperate women would lie down on the pavement with johns for as little as 15 cents a trick. That thing I was saying that I couldn't be shocked anymore? Ha! This scene was unimaginable. I saw a man holding an infant in the rain as he supervised his wife, a prostitute, with a client in a nearby rice tent.

I got out of the car and from beneath a leaky umbrella called out, "Bonsoir!" as cheerfully as I could.

Dr. Rene's smiling round face emerged from the waiting crowd. "Bonsoir!" he said. "And here are the girls!"

We had arranged a dry place to meet and talk. The women were so poor that no individual could afford to rent a room or even the dollar it cost to buy the sheets of plastic to cover the sidewalks where they worked. So two, three, or more went in together. That type of clustering was apparent as they swirled around me in pairs and threes to be introduced. I needed my local translator, Nouci, because none of these prostitutes spoke French, only Malagasy. The lovely Nouci was such a sweet, compassionate sister to have in these situations. She would always show such sensitivity in incredibly raw, delicate circumstances, and her abilities facilitated remarkably vulnerable conversations.

Everyone was smelly. Many of the people I meet on my trips had little opportunity to bathe. Sometimes the stench was overwhelming to the staff that came with me, but for some reason, I rarely had a problem with it. I like close contact with people, to touch and hug, and tangy, sour smells came with the territory. But this group tested even my gag reflexes—it was a different kind of odor, a homeless smell. The worst smelling was Nini, and she was also the most destroyed person I had met so far in my life. She—just barely—lived on the streets with her children. She told me she was about to have her fifth child any day now, and she'd already buried two of them. Her problems were an acute distillation of poverty, lack of education, gender inequality, preventable disease, unplanned pregnancy, and no way out. She never looked up, always holding her eyes in a dead, downward gaze. Even the abducted women of Cambodia and Thailand had something in their reserves that life in this country had drained out of Nini's spirit. I would caress her, and something like the ghost of a smile, the memory of what a smile might have been in another life, would pass over part of her face, but never all of it, never completely.

We gave her some food, but Papa Jack saw an older woman take it from her, and we fretted for days over whether or not she might have gotten it back.

I asked the women if I could peek inside one of the makeshift rice tents, which were loosely attached to a piece of fencing for height, with a rock or piece of garbage holding the edge down to prevent the plastic from blowing away. I squatted and then crawled through the small opening, feeling how close, how stifling, the tiny space was. I knelt on the muddy plastic for a few moments, taking it in, observing, feeling. It was one of the darkest moments of my life. The ground was littered with torn foil packets and damp condoms—which in its own way was good news. The bad news was that I could not make conscious contact with God in that hellhole. I literally felt a rebuff, like a "not here" answer, that startled me badly.

There was a transcendent moment with this group of new friends, however, and that, coupled with the fact that I spent time with them over a number of days, has imprinted them into my soul. They had their babies with them, even though they were working, and one especially young prostitute let me hold her son, Patrick. Oh, boy. He did that thing babies do when they rest on your chest, then lift their heads a bit to consider the world but decide it's not worth it, why bother with all that, when you can simply sigh and burrow into that safe place of shelter within the bosom. I nearly died on the spot. I began to sing to him a French Christmas carol—incongruous for January, but the words just came to me:

"Il est n'e le divin enfant, chantons tous son avènement." He is born, the divine baby, and is that not what all babies are? A spark of the divine is in us all, immutable, incorruptible. My sisters on the street began to sing with me, and when we finished, the air was different, charged, sacred. We were outside of ourselves, outside of these lives, inside something wonderful and good, the love and promise a baby can make you feel.

We stood quietly for a long moment, then Dr. Rene began a lullaby. This great man had continuously declined other jobs, options, administrative work, raises, whatever, so he could stay with the least, the lost, the last. He deserves to be enshrined. Given the geometric movement of the

HIV virus, it is impossible to estimate the number of lives he has saved by teaching high-risk groups and their clients about condoms and risk reduction. Even more immeasurable is the humanity, so delicate in these circumstances, he has kept alive with lullabies such as the one he sang for us that night.

Not far from the rice tents, on a larger, boulevard-style corner, a group of older, more seasoned prostituted women welcomed me. Among them was our peer educator and shining star of the streets, Sahouly. Plump and ebullient, with bright eyes and a toothy smile, Sahouly had trained herself to offer reproductive health and HIV prevention education, and Dr. Rene had worked hard to give her a sense of self-assurance and authority. PSI paid Sahouly a small salary, as we do all peer educators, but it was unfortunately not enough to allow her to reduce the required number of seven clients per night to feed her family and make ends—barely—meet. The price of a trick on the streets here, I was told, was the equivalent of a dollar with a condom, two without. It was Sahouly's job to keep herself safe and to explain to the others why the extra money wasn't worth the risk.

~ ~ ~

The hotel where we were staying in Tana was under construction, with work on the floor below and the roof above my room, which for some odd reason had seventeen chairs in it. I woke up the next morning to a voice message from Dario, who called as he watched a nearly full moon rise that made him think of me. The sound of his voice made me emotional and weepy, as I'd been so lonely for him on this trip. And there were still nearly two weeks to go. I also wept as I remembered the man I had seen holding an infant as he supervised his prostituted wife while she serviced a client in a nearby rice tent. I wondered: *What separates Dario and me, another married couple, from the grave misfortune of Malagasy I see all around me?*

However, I also felt serene, having created a protected, peaceful space in the room, with an altar on which I put my incense for both harmony and love, powerful spiritual iconography such as a cross, some special stones, Nelson Mandela's autobiography, and other resonating items. Moyra, Kate, and I blessed the space (and ourselves) with a deep yoga practice, concluding with a long prayer, which I dedicated to our teachers: the easy stuff, the hard stuff, the eternal stuff. But it was possible I was confusing serenity and low-grade depression.

~ ~ ~

Later that week, Sahouly invited me to her home. I was having a "bad" day, crying uncontrollably during our short lunch break back at the hotel. I had gone full fetal thinking about baby Patrick's likely life, and it was only the sweetness of Sahouly's offer that motivated me to peel myself by the pony-tail off the mattress. I tried to dress, hardly able to see myself in the mir-ror for the tears, and played the outfit game, trying to choose something I thought she'd like. But the bow on my shirt hadn't been ironed right and looked like a shoelace instead of a lovely ribbon, so I finally just put on Mamaw's pearls. They're the equivalent of my heavy artillery, and I bring them out when I am at my lowest and need her strength and guidance the most. It's never failed.

Sahouly and her family lived in two very small rooms, dirty through no fault of her own, as the courtyard she shared with forty others was unpaved red, raw dirt that tracked unrelentingly. Her water source was a spigot not too far away, and she used our Sur'Eau water purification solution, to pre-vent diarrheal disease in her family. She had a suite of wooden furniture with no cushions and we sat directly on the slats, all except Dr. Rene, who rightly assumed the rickety pieces would not hold his weight. Her two girls sang a few songs for us, and we chatted about this and that. They both loved school, particularly math and science. They had no idea what their mother did to provide for them.

Sahouly had told us she'd turned to prostitution ten years ago to pay for the medical bills after one of the girls was gravely ill. Although her hus-band knew she turned tricks, her children thought she was just a coun-selor for PSI. After the visit, she took us into her crowded neighborhood to show us the stop where she caught the bus to the red-light district every night. Sometimes she met her quota of seven clients in time to catch the nine p.m. bus home, but more often she was stranded in town until ser-vice resumed at four a.m. Once home, she slept for a few hours, then did her day job: mother of three, wife of eighteen years.

Moyra and I had an extraordinary opportunity with Sahouly, and we seized it. We rode the bus with her to work, and I chuckled when she pointed out her in-laws' shack, and we had a conversation so typical as to be ubiquitous: How do you get along with your mother-in-law? In town, she showed us her corner and walked us through what her night would be like, but as it was still daylight, after she traced for us what her typical nights were like, we found ourselves idle. Men would not be trolling for sex until after dark, and that was when Moyra and I hatched a plan. We invited Sahouly to our hotel room, where we could offer her a hot meal and a bath.

She'd never taken a bath before, and as we ran the water for her, we explained the concept, feeling so pleased when she stepped into the water, only to be surprised when she popped back out into the living room. We clearly hadn't explained well enough. Relax, we said. Submerge your head underwater and let it all go. Fall asleep if you like. We ran the bath again after I cleaned the tub (her first dip, however brief, testified to her lack of running water at home) and gave her a bottle of beer. We didn't see her for a long time, and while I took the second of my three showers, I thought of her down the hall, doing the same thing, united by this simple act and separated by so much.

Afterward, we ordered off the room service menu, and she left not a trace on her three plates of food, all of which was typical local fare. I had thought she might choose meat or other rarely accessed delicacies, but she went for the usual rice and pap gravy. When I scooted the bread and butter toward her, she ate that, too. Her hair was wet and fell in ringlets past her shoulders, and as she sat there, gorgeous, clean, in her bathrobe, I saw the change in her demeanor, the understanding in her eyes. She was here among her sisters, who honored her for who she was, the shining star Sahouly, a woman of stunning potential.

~ ~ ~

When we returned to the red-light district, Sahouly took us to a peer education session in a small room in a brothel. All the women sat on the floor, chatting animatedly, legs draped over one another's, interrupting, talking over one another, answering one another's questions before Sahouly or Dr. Rene had a chance to chime in. They had already learned a lot in the program but still had lot of questions, including HIV risks to pregnant women. This topic allowed me to delicately introduce an idea I had longed to bring up: being tested. But I knew I had to handle it with exquisite care or I'd blow it.

Veronica, a prostituted woman who was six months pregnant, was my entrée. Moyra, a mother of two, had picked up on how anxious she was about the health of her baby. Dr. Rene and I talked to her about mother-to-child transmission and how critical it is to know your status, and also about syphilis, which causes birth defects. Then I pounced: "Why don't you and I go to the public health clinic tomorrow to be tested?" She said yes. On a roll, I asked others. Five of them said they would. I couldn't believe it. As I sat there trying so hard not to roar with joy, they bickered among themselves about the time and finally settled on three p.m., plenty of time to grab a little sleep after a night's work and tend to the kids. Our group dispersed into the night, and my satisfaction melted into worry about attrition and who, out of fear, would blow it off and not show up.

~ ~ ~

To our delight, not five but seven from Sahouly's group showed up to be tested for HIV, some with their children in tow. While we ate pizza, I asked if the women would prefer to wait to discuss our tests at the center, out of earshot of the café staff, because the taboo was so extreme. Again this remarkable group of strong women surprised me: They didn't mind discussing it one bit. We talked about Nini, the pregnant homeless woman from the rice tents, whom I was hoping to get tested with us. Even though Dr. Rene had scoured the streets to bring her here today, he had not been able to find her. I was afraid she might have vanished forever.

After eating, we gathered in the waiting room of Dr. Rene's clinic to have our blood drawn. It was a little awkward when the time came, so I shot my hand in the air like an eager schoolgirl and volunteered to go first. By this time I'd had so much blood drawn at clinics and voluntary testing centers that I should have had a tap attached to my inner elbow. Moyra, who is afraid of needles, declined the invitation, but she dug deep to sit by Veronica's side and held her hand through the test.

When it was over, I was more than disappointed to learn we could not get the rapid results we expected. There was equipment available that could get results in minutes, but it was not at the clinic that day. The quick test is so important, because 35 percent of all people who are tested do not return to find out the results. But we were forced to wait in suspense for another twenty-four hours. We hugged and kissed and bade farewell again. I wondered if they would all have the courage to come back to face their status.

~ ~ ~

Meanwhile, a woman named Annie who had AIDS and might be willing to talk about her condition on television—as long as her identity was disguised—had been located in town. She was terrified that her neighbors would kill her if they found out she had the disease, so we agreed to meet in a café far away from her home.

To get there we walked a narrow red dusty street lined with little shops selling small goods. The businesses here were tinier than the stands in American parks where you can buy a pop or snow cone, barely big enough for a person to work behind the rough wood counter. We found Annie sitting in a café patio. She was a tiny, lovely-looking woman, terribly frail and missing some teeth but quick to smile and giggle. She ordered a glass of milk and, speaking through Nouci, told me her husband was also infected, and they didn't know who had given it to whom. Their kids were eleven and fourteen and didn't know the family secret. Only Annie's husband and mother knew her condition.

She explained that she had a message for her people: be wise. AIDS is here, and it is not something the Americans made up as a reason to spend money—which was one of the rumors going around. AIDS will infect and kill you if you don't prevent it in yourself and your family, she said. Unfortunately, she had decided she would not repeat this message on television. It was too dangerous for herself, her family, and her place with her ancestors. Annie was afraid she wouldn't live to see the day when people could talk openly about the virus. She was sure she would be dead in a year. I tried to rebuke that fear and reached out and rubbed her neck as she bit back her tears. Then she looked at Nouci and asked, "Isn't she afraid to catch my disease?"

"Oh, no, no, no . . . ," I told her, and pulled my chair closer. I gently twined my arms around her and hugged her close. She was stiff and anxious at first, then melted into me. I think it had been a long time since anyone had held her.

We told Annie where she could access antiretroviral drugs to treat her illness and about the secret support groups for HIV-positive people where she would be welcome. She was very keen to go, although she said she wouldn't tell her husband. She didn't think he would approve. Too much fear.

~ ~ ~

The next day, I sat in the now familiar public health clinic waiting room, tense about what might happen, waiting for our friends. I was relieved as each arrived, calmly and shyly. Dr. Rene, we were told, was stuck on a bus in traffic. We did not want to receive our results without him because he would need to help with the counseling in the very likely event that one or more of the women were positive. I asked the women about how work had been the night before. They said they had fallen asleep on the sidewalk, leaning against a building, while chatting. And how had they spent the day thus far? Typical housekeeping and child-minding chores. One of them told me she did her wash with our water purification product, Sur'Eau. Ever since a huge cyclone in 2000 caused flooding that ruined much of the country's drinking water, PSI/Madagascar had teamed up with CARE and the Centers for Disease Control to produce and distribute the mild bleachlike solution to prevent waterborne disease. Apparently it's also great on stains, and we know it's cheap!

Dr. Rene finally arrived, his glorious smile in place, accompanied by Nini, whom he had worked hard to find. That was why he was late; he'd been out searching the streets again for her. She looked, if possible, in even worse shape than when we'd first met, or maybe it was just daylight revealing more than her stench, which a breeze from the open window swirled around the room. Her feet, bare as many Malagasy's are, were filthy and crusty, and her legs were far too thin for a woman in her ninth month of pregnancy. Her eyes were glazed and her mouth was raw with open blisters, which she had used her red lipstick to cover with pitiful effect. She told us that her two-year-old was sick, and I could not imagine where the baby had been throwing up and pooping and how Nini had been coping with a sick kid while living on the sidewalk. I made a silent vow to help her if I could.

As the clinicians prepared to give us our results, I sat with one of Veronica's children on my lap, a precious eight-year-old girl in a fairly clean dress with only one tear, dotted with a sweet daisy print. She had on red patent-leather shoes that did not match but were obviously worn with pride on her special day of meeting me. I braided her long ponytail to keep the sour smell of her hair more confined. Then, as I stroked her, I rested my other hand on Nini's belly. Finally, the first number was called.

I accompanied the woman who matched the number (all names were kept anonymous) into a small counseling room. She sat in a chair across a desk from a social worker, and I knelt beside her, my arm around her shoulders, eyes fixed on the small stack of papers that I knew were everyone's HIV test results. The social worker went very carefully over the number on the card the prostitute produced, visually and verbally confirming that the number matched the certificate and that she was the age and gender indicated. The social worker then slid the paper forward with the test outcome validated by an official stamp: NEGATIF. The woman went through a transfiguration akin to Jesus's on the mount, from grim, fearful stoicism to an outburst of relief and joy. "*Negatif!*" she kept repeating, shaking the social worker's hand as if she'd been given a diploma, crying some, but really being far too overjoyed to do any one thing for more than a second. I bawled shamelessly, caught up in the miracle but also knowing that the next woman's result could be disastrous. We had six more to go before we were done.

The process repeated itself again and again, the frightened but resolute woman in the chair, me on the floor beside her, numbers and details verified, and results presented. They were unbelievable:

NEGATIF.
NEGATIF.
NEGATIF.
NEGATIF.
NEGATIF.
NEGATIF.

A series of miracles and the most eloquent tribute possible to the power of peer education. Seven veteran prostitutes with more than seventy-five years on the streets and thousands upon thousands of tricks turned among them had tested negative for HIV.

We all reacted in our own way. The social worker immediately began reinforcing risk management behavior and correct, consistent condom use. Our stills photographer, squished in a corner, a veteran of some of the world's grimmest scenes in countries the U.S. State Department might not be able to find on a map, cried openly behind her lens. The VH1 documentary crew openly declared it the heaviest thing any of them had ever been through. Moyra didn't breathe until pregnant Veronica and the toothless granny—the two we had been most sure would be HIV-positive—were also declared negative. Back in the waiting room, when we realized that all of us were free and clear (this time, at least), jubilation broke out. There was clapping, dancing, singing, and a prayer.

Now I could leave my friends without the sense of panic I had felt a day earlier when we had parted. They were free from HIV, and I fully expected all of them to remain that way. Sahouly and I shared a quiet moment when she said she couldn't wait to go home to tell her husband, although we both confirmed the importance of them using a condom together. Relief must be tempered by reality.

As we left, I spoke with Dr. Rene about passing him money to pay for all the medical care everyone's ailments required and in particular what to do about Nini. We agreed that at our farewell gathering that night, we would give him a small fund out of which he would settle prescription costs. It was the least we could do and in fact was very inexpensive. The costs for delivering Nini's baby at a clinic, plus her medications, her two-year-old's meds, and the meds for all the other women's sick babies was less than $100.

~ ~ ~

We wrapped up our visit to Madagascar with an official press conference to thank the government and our donors, followed by a big party for everyone involved in the trip, which officially kicked off our thrilling collaboration with the Top Réseau health clinics. When we arrived at the hotel ballroom,

I chose for the first time all week to speak English instead of French. I have been told by a marquis that I speak a very good seventeenth-century French, which might have been a bit formal for this setting. I thought I could transmit more spirit and attitude for the kids in the room in English. However, when dear Nouci came to translate for me, she totally froze, numb from exhaustion, and told me *I* had to help *her*! I took the mike back and translated myself into French, satisfying the government officials in the room with a little wave and shout-out when I was finished. The event wrapped when our energetic peer educators did a dance that told the story of the ABCs (*a*bstinence, *b*eing faithful, *c*orrect and *c*onsistent *c*ondom use). After celebrating their commitment and spunk, I slunk out of the reception to sit quietly in my hotel room (the one with seventeen chairs), to pray for guidance about Nini. I called Dario and told him that if I were to leave here without helping her, her life and the lives of her children would be on my conscience. He offered to help, and I decided to present my plan to our country director in the morning.

~ ~ ~

At the airport, I was chased into the lounge by some wild Italians shouting my name. Having been on the front page of every paper (there are six) upon our arrival made privacy a joke, even down to being photographed at a swimming pool. One day I was swimming freestyle, and every time I came up for air I heard a young woman pleading, "Mademoiselle, mademoiselle!" But the attention was good for reducing the brutal stigma around HIV, and I endured the hoopla with more than my typical modicum of grace. Sequestered in the lounge with the Italians still carrying on but Papa Jack standing sentry, I told the PSI team I wanted to set Nini up in a house with no obligation for three months, to allow her simply to care for her newborn and to begin to heal. (She'd had no chance to grieve the death of two of her babies; this is something I continue to rue, the time and space so many poor people lack to process life's insults and catastrophes.) After three months, we would explore what her interests were and put her into some kind of training or school. We would wean her off our provisional support when she had a job. We also agreed I would regularly wire Dr. Rene money for the other children's health care needs. Although I wish I could do this for every prostituted woman in the world, I left Antananarivo somewhat satisfied that I had at least helped a few. I slept most of the way to Cape Town, waking up only to write, my lifeline in this work, and glance out the window expectantly at the South African landscape.

Chapter 11

PRAYING WITH MY PRESENCE

MARSHALL STOWELL/PSI

Meeting my hero, Nobel Peace Prize winner Archbishop Desmond Tutu.

Because I remember, I despair. Because
I remember, I have a duty to reject despair.

—*ELIE WIESEL*

*W*e are born alone and we die alone, and the frequent loneliness of this work resonates with the reality of individuated experience. I write to try to comprehend, process, heal, share news of the human community with those who cannot travel as far and wide as I, to raise consciousness, to raise money, to be of service, but I am ultimately alone with my response to my experiences. We all are. That is why mentors are so important, because they have gone ahead to where we have not yet been, perhaps not even in our dreams, and they look back at us with the love born of wisdom, grace, mercy, and compassion to give us hints as to how to have our own experiences with integrity. Such a mentor to me, first in spirit and now in the flesh, is Archbishop Desmond Tutu.

As a university student, I formed my politics and my activism listening to Archbishop Tutu's speeches on LP records that South Africans, anticipating house arrest, brought to America, when they fled the repressive, racist Nationalist government. Kate Roberts knew this and had surprised me while we were sitting in the hotel lobby in Antananarivo with the news that we had been granted an audience with him during our visit to Cape Town. The floodgates opened and I started bawling, causing Kate to well up, which made the others in our group cry, even though they didn't know precisely why we were crying, and we all just sat there unapologetically laughing and crying in the well-lit lobby, in full view of anyone who looked our way. The idea that I would finally meet this hero of nineteen years' standing to whom I could directly attribute the work I am now doing in Africa floored me. Meeting him when I was at an emotional and spiritual ebb was exactly what I needed.

~ ~ ~

The archbishop greeted our delegation warmly at his offices in Cape Town. His office was off a busy four-lane paved road that had elevated crosswalks used by herds of livestock. The archbishop was smaller than I expected, but as lively and elegant as I knew he would be, wearing his signature gold cross and a casual cotton shirt with an earth-colored print. We posed for a few photos in front of a beautiful unity quilt. Then I went with him to his office to sit behind closed doors for a moment. He asked if I had seen myself in the local newspaper. When I told him I hadn't, he laughed.

"Then you are less vain than I," he said, his eyes twinkling with what I would learn is his perpetual good humor. "Because I always scoop up the papers straightaway if I suspect I'll be in them!" I thought, *Are you kidding me? He genuinely is this wonderful?* I was besotted.

While South Africa had changed a great deal since Nelson Mandela was released from prison and his African National Congress had defeated the National Party in the country's first fully open election, Desmond Tutu had not changed a whit. He could easily have gone into politics and held high public office, but he chose to retain his role as a spiritual and moral leader. Archbishop Tutu was as charismatic and appealing as I expected him to be, but I was surprised that he asked *me* a lot of questions. Instead of the usual friendly small talk, he wanted to hear the details of our work at PSI and my impressions of my trip and what I would tell my people when I returned home. He had a wonderful way of making me feel that we were somehow on the same level—he actually thanked me for my undergrad campus activism—even when I was so obviously in awe of everything he had done in his beautiful, difficult, profound life as a freedom fighter and servant.

In his questions, the archbishop revealed his own thoughts, and I wove them into my answers to bring the conversation back to him—so I could selfishly enjoy his musings. He spoke about gender inequality, prejudice, and the purpose of sex between married couples as an instrument of love and expression, a way to become more God-like. He talked about the foolishness of advocating abstinence without a balanced approach that acknowledged we did not live yet in an ideal world in which everybody behaved sensibly all the time. He had made South African history in 1996 by recording public service announcements for PSI that warned that the terrible challenge of HIV/AIDS required a pragmatic approach to stop it.

"We in the church believe that sex should only take place within marriage," he'd said in the PSA. "However, for those of you who do practice sex outside of marriage, I encourage you to take the right precautions and practice safer sex. Please use condoms." The spot caused a sensation, because until then, the conservative state-run television station had never allowed the word *condom* to be uttered on air.

Ten years later, despite the warnings from Archbishop Tutu and other prominent figures, 5.5 million South Africans were infected with HIV—nearly 20 percent of the population. And only 21 percent of those sufferers were being treated with antiviral drugs. An estimated 320,000 were dying from AIDS every year. The work had just begun.

Although I believe that the solutions to the problems of the world lie within each and every one of us, I also learned anew that no one person, not even someone with the stature, experience, faith, and perspective of Desmond Tutu, can do it alone. No individual can provide the silver bullet that will stop the world's problems in their tracks, reverse the many wrongs that persist. His wisdom reaffirmed that we all—governments, NGOs, faith-based organizations, and corporations—must rally around education and prevention to slow the spread of AIDS, to ameliorate conditions worldwide. Our only hope is to work together.

When our conversation was finished, I imposed on the archbishop for counseling, even though I could tell he was ready to move on with his day. He graciously offered to hear what was in my heart. I told him how, on several occasions during my travels in Asia and Africa, I was worried that I could not feel the presence of the Holy Spirit. I told him about the (seemingly) godforsaken rice tents of Antananarivo and the profound grief of a young mother dying of AIDS at a hospice in Cambodia with whom I could not summon that palpable sweetness God has so often given me in difficult, complex situations.

The archbishop said he would not presume to give me spiritual advice but instead told me a story: There was a Jew in a concentration camp in World War II who was being ruthlessly tormented by his Nazi guard. On one particularly harsh morning, the officer ordered the beleaguered man to clean a foul, stinking latrine. The guard taunted the Jew as he worked and said to him, "Tell me, where is your God now?" The Jew looked up at him and responded, "My God is in here with me."

I buried my face in my hands, realizing that just because I couldn't feel God in the rice tents, just because I couldn't conjure a command performance of the Holy Spirit at the hospice, didn't mean that God was not there with me.

We spoke for another half hour, and he nourished me with the fruits of his experience. He talked about spiritual maturation and how sometimes during our growth we have dry periods, or rather spells that feel dry, because we have moved beyond the need for that blissful flood of grace that encouraged and informed us at the beginning of our journey. I instantly apprehended what he was telling me—I had always been so grateful for the grace I could summon and feel growing in my heart when I meditated. But now I saw that those instruments had served to confine and reassure my thoughts until I was mature enough for something more subtle—when I could sit in a rice tent and feel what it was like, and not flee its reality by asking God to blow me away with some on-the-spot transcendence.

Archbishop Desmond Tutu, my mentor in spirit and now in the flesh, helped me realize that I didn't always have to pray with words or thoughts or have that buzz that came with them, because I was praying with my very body, with my presence. I thank him so much for it, and for everything he has given all of us.

On the flight from Cape Town to Johannesburg, I closed my eyes and all the sense of Spirit that I did not have at the rice tents and hospice flooded my chest as if a tuning fork had been sounded. It coursed throughout my body, especially my chest, and this time the sense of Spirit was accompanied by colors, something I had heard others describe but had never experienced myself. I was flooded with rainbows of color that I could *feel*. I pictured the plastic on the sidewalk and rained down on it with white light, with majesty, with protection, with purification. I pictured the weak and ill at the hospice, and they glowed with keen, brilliant lights. It was a busy ninety-minute flight, the prayers flying through the African sky faster, higher, and more accurately than any airplane ever could.

~ ~ ~

The part of this trip that I most looked forward to, outside of our meeting with Archbishop Tutu, was visiting Soweto. I had always elegized Soweto as the seat of the struggle, where angry, righteous Africans fought against persecution by a monstrous minority government. Images from the news, bulletins from Amnesty International, U2 records—I followed it all. To actually go to Soweto was akin to a pilgrimage.

And as with so many other things in life, I was quickly disabused of my romantic fervor. My Soweto was a hotbed of political activism, militant youth, and safe houses for underground freedom fighters—I had entirely overlooked the shantytown dimension and the seemingly intractable poverty, the appalling reality of slum living. Soweto is a city within a city, sprawling beyond the southwestern suburbs of Johannesburg, home to about a million souls. Even after housing segregation officially ended with the fall of the apartheid regime, Soweto's population remained almost all black. Although there are middle-class neighborhoods and even mansions for the newly rich who choose to live in Soweto for its vibrant sense of community, these stand in stark contrast with the overcrowded cinder-block houses and tin shanties that surround them. The economy of South Africa remains woefully lopsided, and the scourge of AIDS has made it even harder for the poor to enjoy the fruits of freedom.

Our local office arranged a day for me in Soweto to look at some programs and to visit a few people. I love meeting folks in their homes, having a sense of their lives beyond the words we exchange. My first stop was the small, three-room shack of an HIV-positive woman who was struggling to live with the virus. From oppressively crowded streets, we entered through a lean-to kitchen filled with good pots and pans and a vintage stove that would suit a stylish period cottage in America. She was a baker by trade. She told me that if she were well enough to work, she'd love to do catering. The living room and bedroom were crammed with furniture; the floor was covered with dirty, loose linoleum. She told me she had buried two children from HIV-related illnesses and had one remaining daughter. As if on cue, the daughter came bouncing in from school, doing things familiar to kids everywhere: dumping her rucksack, kicking off her shoes, looking for a snack (there was none). Then a chatty neighbor came in, also HIV-positive, and she launched into an animated monologue about her illness and how hard it was to keep healthy in such a filthy environment. Soweto's infrastructure, never much to start with, was falling apart. She complained that there was only one water tap in the whole neighborhood and one rancid toilet for ten families to share, and how sick it was making them. At first I resented this woman for interrupting and dominating the conversation, but I quickly realized that this was my Soweto after all: poor but informed, sick but informed, neglected but informed. And angry. I listened to their considerable woes and asked what I could do. Even though this was a PSI visit, they most specifically asked me to complain on their behalf to the city about their toilet, which I did.

I struggled to reconcile the disconnect between such smart, eloquent women and their ongoing victimization, but whether women rail against it or remain mute, the problems of HIV, poverty, gender inequality, lack of education, and lack of opportunity remain entrenched.

The traumas of apartheid have been replaced by a new array of social pathologies, including a surge in violent crime and an epidemic of rape. A disturbing survey conducted by Interpol and the local Medical Health Association found that one out of three males admitted to raping at least once, and more than 40 percent admit to being physically violent with an intimate partner. Some researchers posited that South African men were reacting to the emasculation and humiliation of apartheid by taking out their frustrations on the disempowered—women and children. Others blamed the rigid patriarchy that cut across ethnicities and sanctioned rape as an expression of male entitlement and privilege.

An estimated 500,000 rapes occur in every year in this country of 42 million (although only about 70,000 are reported). Forty percent of those assaults are committed against children under eighteen, an intolerable number that has been increasing at an alarming rate. Part of the upsurge is credited with a superstition, perpetuated by *sangomas,* or witch doctors, that men can cleanse themselves of HIV/AIDS by violating children. The only hopeful news to emerge from this sickening scenario is that grass-roots groups have been organizing to counter the violence. POWA, People Opposing Women Abuse, provides legal and support services for women survivors of violence and victims of rape and domestic abuse, and the One in Nine Campaign (named for the number of rapes that are reported) advocates for the enforcement of laws against rape and gender violence. Also, various UN agencies are sponsoring "One-Stop Centres" across South Africa to offer a wide array of services to women and children who have suffered abuse and violence, including comfort and medical treatment, counseling, legal services, and crisis accommodation. They also support programs aimed at the perpetrators of violence.

~ ~ ~

Our next stop was a small, tired yard where a decrepit, hand-painted double-decker bus was parked to one side. A hand pump for water was in the center, and around it were a few small tin outbuildings. In one of them I was amazed to discover about thirty calm, wide-eyed babies sitting in an orderly row on the floor. All were AIDS orphans; some were HIV-positive, some were not. The children were subdued because many didn't feel well, and it was terribly hot. The program here was an extremely modest foster care scheme run by a local woman. It had little, if any, funding. Neighbors and churches donated food, but some days the kids did without. They spread the kids around to locals who could handle them, and a child might not stay in the same house two nights in a row.

Seconds after walking in, Papa Jack, Kate, and I had babies to look after. It struck us how each child was placid, unperturbed about being approached and held by strangers, and in fact they reached up trustingly, undoubtedly because they were passed around so much. Papa Jack ended up with a big toddler in his arms, who was sound asleep in minutes.

"Hey, I can put anyone out," he said proudly. He held him the entire time.

It was touching to see how nurturing the older children were to the younger. One could only hope that they didn't end up caregivers with total responsibility for them, as so many orphans did. This contributed to the horrible cycle of cross-generational and transactional sex, when the young girls trying to feed themselves and babies had sex with older men for food and supplies and were then of course at major risk for HIV. Insist on a condom? No power to. Abstain? If you abstain, you and the little ones starve.

After their dinner of rice and pap—cornmeal mush—with gravy, the children became a little more active. I stayed for a long while, working my way through the babies until I got to Nonno, whose name meant "Lucky." I decided to talk a walk with Nonno in my arms to a cinder-block building where I heard singing. It apparently served as a church on Wednesdays for a few adults who came to worship and be fed a snack. There was white bread, peanut butter, and juice. I sat on the floor next to a large woman who passed her sandwich to my baby, who serenely ate it on top of his rice and pap. I took off his sweaty shirt, and he cooperated perfectly, holding out one arm and then the other, and it occurred to me that he needed water. I was not supplementing his care that afternoon: I *was* his caregiver. He was, in fact, dehydrated, and I stayed in church with the praise and dancing filling my eyes with tears, sitting on the floor and giving sips of water to my boy until he was rehydrated. After a while, a reluctant Papa Jack came over and said everyone was waiting for me. I panicked. I couldn't set him down. I was beside myself. After we sang "Amazing Grace," I waved another woman over to me. I prayed with her, and that helped me do the impossible: pull myself together so I could come to grips with walking away from my sweet little Nonno and all the other children I would leave behind.

~ ~ ~

On a busy road with rough tables set up to sell sundry goods, one of our audio-video mobile units was doing its thing. The market was flooded with adults making their daily visit to pick up what provisions they might be able to afford for the evening meal. The market was also busy with kids who had been let out of school, perfect timing for some edutainment. "Fats," our peer educator, entertained the shifting crowd with music that carried the message of the ABCs of prevention. I floated around, trying to stop counting the malnourished kids (identifiable by the rust color of their hair), and kept it more upbeat, chatting up shy (or were they defiant?) young men about safe sex. One too-cool young man explained that the goat-skin-and-hair bracelet on his wrist was worn to ensure his ancestors' protection. I handed him an antirape flyer.

As Fats was winding down, his fellow peer educators started dancing in the street. I began to make my way toward them, then decided instead to ask some small girls to dance with me in a cooler spot under some stairs. A party broke out among us, and we added more girls, then boys, all of them grabbing to be the one holding hands with me. I led, then they led, and soon the shy ones couldn't stand being left out and joined in, too, be-coming the most animated dancers. I couldn't count how many times I fell in love, how many times I said, "You are so beautiful," how many times I said, "You are so smart," how many times I said pleadingly to Papa Jack, "Just five more minutes!" But, as all things do, it came to an end, and I left Soweto perhaps the filthiest I've ever been, covered in dirt, snot, rice and gravy, slobber, my own sweat, and the sweet, tangy sweat of scores of chil-dren I hope help make Soweto a better place someday.

~ ~ ~

Back at the hotel, I soothed and calmed myself with normal, stable rou-tines, such as hand-washing my things in the tub. I skipped my stained, caked linen pants, though, and decided I'd retire them dirty with a few other special things I kept in my closet, such as the sandals I wore my first summer in France and the sneakers in which I survived the ashram's hikes. After so many years of following the liberation struggle, my pants were my own little piece of Soweto's soil, sun, and soul.

It was finally time to go home. I'd had twenty days in Africa, and pro-vided I had some sleep, I felt I could easily carry on with the work. But I wanted to be at Dario's race that weekend. His energy beckoned me, and I couldn't wait to connect with it. I was set to arrive at the track just in time to hustle out to the grid for a bad-airplane-breath kiss before the green flag.

~ ~ ~

During the transatlantic flight, I discovered an entire Joni Mitchell CD on the in-flight entertainment. I covered my head with my blanket and sang along with "Carey" as loud as I could without attracting attention. Then I listened to "California," and the earphones made her so present to me, and therefore me so present to myself. I became the person I was when I was eight and "Carey" was my favorite song, or who I was when I was six and I lost my first serious fight, which happened to be with my sister, over the order of verses in "Twisted," discovering in spite of my fierce conviction that I could be dead wrong. Or who I was in college when I played "Cali-fornia" on my radio show, or who I have been every time I felt the rapture of the rhythm of "Help Me" or reminded Sister on the phone of all the lyrics to "You Turn Me On I'm a Radio," or who I was each time I drove to the theater while doing *Cat on a Hot Tin Roof,* swept away by her brilliant orchestral revisitation of her old material. I felt all I had been, and all I am now, and it was so sweet and so *here,* a beautiful, almost unbearably exquisite *here,* my arc and my life, and the women who have entered it, oh, my hand on Nini's belly, Sahouly's incandescent smile turning toward me like a rising half moon, half radiant, half shy. . . .

"Amelia" affected me deeply tonight:

Me, well, I've been to Africa.

Chapter 12

BUMPING INTO MYSELF

My extraordinary big sister, Wynonna Judd. Of the many gifts she has given me,
introducing me to recovery is the greatest.

The spirit is never at rest, but always engaged in progressive motion,
giving itself new form.

—*HEGEL, Phenomenology of Mind*

*I*n the months after my return from Africa, I should have felt on top of the world. The outer form of my life seemed perfect; I had basically done everything I had hoped to do. My film career was still thriving, and I gave performances of which I was proud in a couple of creative, inspired independent projects. The trip to Africa was a huge success, including *Tracking the Monster*, the VH1 documentary shot in Madagascar about PSI's Global Fund–sponsored programs, which was broadcast in eighty-one million homes worldwide, received great reviews, and won an array of awards. In June, I was invited to testify about the AIDS crisis before the Senate Foreign Relations Committee in Washington, D.C. I told the committee members that the fight against the HIV/AIDS pandemic was indistinguishable from the fight for gender equality, that there was nothing more important in the struggle against this virus than to urge all societies to reject violence against women and any social norms and cultural practices that cause girls and women to exchange sex for economic survival. I also spoke about PSI's mission to a roomful of reporters at the National Press Club in Washington, where I looked in awe at the twentieth-century headlines hanging from the venerable club's walls.

I was finally using my voice to speak out on the political level for the voiceless millions whose lives are affected by the policies being shaped in distant world capitals. Through my work with PSI and other organizations, I was earning a seat at the table, not for me, but for Ouk Srey Leak, Shola, Sahouly, and the women of Soweto whose stories had moved and inspired me to change my life.

~ ~ ~

My confidence and the smooth exterior of calm and professionalism I presented to the world, however, only disguised the growing chaos I felt inside me. On trips to see grassroots programs, I was focused and single-minded, the harrowing feelings externalized by being in settings rife with egregious examples of trauma and grief. But at home, there was nowhere out-side of myself to direct and metabolize my own pain. A familiar, gnawing emptiness haunted my days and nights. I could feel the trapdoor under-neath me opening again. I was having trouble modulating my behavior; I'd swing back and forth between being paralyzed and overdoing whatever I undertook. I might be able to confidently lobby archconservative Senate majority leader Mitch McConnell in his chambers, but I couldn't seem to manage the simple task of finding a comfortable chair for my writing desk. That summer I decided to reorganize our library to accommodate Dario's ever-increasing haul of trophies, and once I started, I couldn't stop. I began sorting through all the unsolicited gifts that were piling up around me, writing thank-you notes and deciding what to give away, then alphabet-izing all the books within genres, steaming with resentment that I "had" to waste my time processing stuff people randomly sent me that I hadn't wanted in the first place. I could become irritable and unreasonable with-out knowing it and was unable to place things in their proper perspective.

I was also concerned about some frustrations I'd had during the making of *Come Early Morning* and a few months later on the set of *Bug*. It wasn't anything awful, just work relationships that became muddled because I couldn't seem to make my assistants understand what I was saying. I won-dered if I was expressing myself poorly or if they simply weren't hearing me. I concluded I was the common denominator and that I needed to take a look at my own behavior to tackle these ongoing communication prob-lems.

I had embarked on a program of radical self-investigation through yoga, where teachers like Seane Corn showed me how a practice could heal on the emotional—not just the physical—level. Now I decided to augment it with a series of intensive therapy sessions with a remarkable and gentle counselor and life coach named Ted Klontz, a PhD with wide-ranging ex-perience who was referred by an admired friend. She had said, "I trust Ted with my life." Her endorsement made an indelible impression on me, as I had the sense that my own life might be at stake—and that I might un-cover more than a simple failure to communicate.

The approach Ted began using with me is called "motivational inter-viewing," which would rely upon identifying and mobilizing my own intrinsic values and goals to stimulate my desired changes in my behavior and improvements in my feelings. In our conversations, my motivation to change would be elicited from within me, and not imposed from without. Ted guided me as we discussed relationships and behaviors, past and present, validating my reality, gently pointing out my contradictions, letting me catch my own ambivalence, and make my own discoveries. Ted referred to this as helping me "bump into myself," and it felt more organic and transformative than anything I had ever done before.

I had seen a therapist or two in the past, mainly to try to respond to episodes of major depression, but I had never before endeavored to look at my childhood and my family's history in the context of my adult perplexities and how the two might be inextricably related. Part of the problem was that large swaths of my childhood memories were voids, so I naturally disregarded them. It had never occurred to me there was stuff buried there that I needed to uncover, discover, and discard. With Ted I began to revisit my childhood and to address my "life scripts," the basic messages I had been given by my family while I was growing up, that have shaped—or, more accurately, warped—my self-perception ever since. However unintentionally—I don't believe anyone did so thinking, *Hey, let's make Ashley feel abandoned and worthless*—my family members' dysfunctional behaviors led me to conclude that I was a burden, that my needs and wants were too much and were inappropriate—and consequently that I was unlovable. Their messages distorted my thinking, causing me to internalize the fiction that I was too hurt and damaged to heal. Ted began to help me see that while I was powerless over others, their addictions, and the way they affected me, I wasn't helpless. As an adult I was now responsible for my own life, which included the legacy of my childhood pain. I was finally acquiring the tools that would allow me to decide what to keep in my life and what to discard—something I had always wanted, but that had eluded me.

Soon after Ted and I started working together, consistent with my characteristic "why not?" attitude in life, I offered that I was happy for us to meet with Dad if Ted thought it was a good idea. Dad and I were in a relationship again, although it was at times uneasy. For me, when something uncomfortable came up in our present dealings, it inevitably dragged along with it, like a fishing hook that dredges up tins cans and other unintentionally found junk, the unresolved, unaddressed past. It held my attention that Dario loved him, as did his friends, who uniformly enjoyed his company. I accepted that I must be part of the uneasiness between us, so in the safe space of my home, with Ted to guide us, Dad and I arranged to have our first professional therapy talk. On the appointed day, my bravado wavered. There was so much unacknowledged pain around that relationship, so much loss and grief. The idea of being vulnerable with him, showing him (and myself!) the real trauma from the terrible losses overwhelmed me.

The three of us sat on velvet sofas in my sleeping porch, where I feel held and comforted by the hillside visible through floor-to-ceiling windows. But shortly into our appointment—I don't even recall exactly what had been said, but obviously we were approaching something big from our past, previously never discussed—my throat started closing up and I felt as if I were going to pass out.

In a burst of formal manners I assume I used to try to cover my feelings, I said, "May I go to my husband?" and then I fled. I ran to Dario's office, knowing the distress on my face was shouting, "Help me!" and then I ran to our nearest guest room and threw myself on the bed. I felt as though I were suffocating, I was crying so hard. Dario looked at me, wide-eyed, witnessing this eruption of years and years of feelings, and wordlessly held me until my crying began to subside. Eventually I pulled myself together and went back into the sleeping porch to resume the session.

In spite of the inexplicable terror I felt, and the considerable shame around not only having such big feelings, but feeling them in front of adult men (truly horrifying!), I did trust Ted and believed I was safe with him. Supported by him and yearning for growth in my life, I leaned into the fear and made another appointment with Dad. There was long-haul work to be done on this fragile relationship. I credit my dad enormously for his willingness to keep showing up for me, for his open-mindedness about participating in modern clinical therapy and practicing the tools Ted began teaching us.

I was able, for the first time, to tell my dad what growing up had been like for me and how often I was left alone—much of which shocked him.

And I was allowed to tell him how his behavior while we were together (and apart) had made me feel. Ted remarked that my father was one of the best listeners he had ever encountered. Dad took it all in, occasionally offering observations, giving me more information (even about his own shortcomings), and asking questions, but never interrupting and never making excuses for himself, with weasel words like "Yeah, but . . ." or "What I really meant was . . ." He was thus able to validate the reality of my childhood perceptions, even though some of his had been very different from my own. My father gave me gift after gift, acknowledging with each recounted memory that his actions and inactions had devastated me many times.

I often discuss with friends from similar backgrounds what happens inside of us when our experiences growing up are minimized and denied by adults, both then and now. In response to the minimizing, we imbue our painful memories with even greater intensity, with anger that becomes rage, shame that becomes humiliation, and loneliness that becomes a hole in the soul. In short, the memories became indictments, of self and of others.

Ted had a huge assist from Dad. Aided by his utter lack of defensiveness, the nature, quality, and tone of what I did recall from childhood began to morph. My memories progressed from being an indictment to simply being a description. I was being taught ways to let go of my reactions to those who had wounded and neglected me and the carried emotions that had become toxic to me, and kept me isolated, especially from my dad. Even during our periodic truces, I had maintained a cautious mistrust, and kept him at arm's length. Although the process we began with Ted would take time, I eventually began to realize he was back in my life for good this time. I began to trust him. I became my father's daughter once more.

~ ~ ~

What I had understood about previous generations of our family had come from snippets of conversations with my grandparents and other family members, naturally filtered through my own subjectivity. Most of what I knew about my parents and my childhood was heavily dominated by my mother's version of the story, which often differed sharply from how everyone else in my family remembered things. Their perceptions and memories were only whispers compared with Mom's full-throated aria. My mother is a highly imaginative person who has always enjoyed a yarn. But I believe it was her darkly urgent need to protect the story of my sister's paternity, which she had invented and perpetuated, and early childhood traumas of her own, that allowed very little room for my own or anyone else's understanding of who we were and how we had arrived there. My own perceptions were molded, naturally, by the amount of time I spent with her, compared with my extremely limited exposure to my dad for years at a time.

When parents divorce, it's not unusual that their kids become pawns in a sad game of resentment, accusations, and revenge. It is also not unusual for each parent to create a personalized narrative of what happened, who was at fault, how, and why. In spite of the tendency in each of my parents to paint the other as the "bad guy," I have learned that in all relationships, both sides share pretty much equal responsibility, even when one's actions are more visible and seem more egregious.

Mom certainly wanted to make everything Dad's fault. Her role was to discredit him, create distance, make us distrust and maybe even hate him all the while hopefully building herself up. I believe that she needed to, given that he knew that he was not my sister's father, and she feared that at any time, he might unload the truth, which for some reason she genuinely believed would be catastrophic for her and for my sister. Thus the obloquy she had begun back on Larrabee Street continued unabated throughout my childhood, and long into my adulthood, accusations that he never loved us, he never paid child support, he lied, he cheated. Mom's campaign against Dad was often very successful. I absolutely internalized some of those attitudes toward my dad and, contaminated by her invective scripts, developed my own wariness toward him.

I was in my thirties before I was able to calmly evaluate for myself Mom's version of events and come to my own peaceful conclusions. For instance, my mom had always told me that Dad didn't want another baby when I was conceived, that he had even pressured her to have an abortion. However, that was not the way Dad remembered it. He had told me I was planned and wanted. I could not reconcile their completely different versions of the story of my place in this world until my wedding to Dario in 2001, when my parents were uneasily but amicably placed in the same room for the first time since I was in first grade and living at Camp Wig.

The celebrations took place at Skibo Castle in Scotland. I had been very assertive with Mom: Dad was invited, and there was nothing she could do about it. Even her default position of needing to "protect" my sister from him would not work. She did not have a vote in his attendance. I was just beginning to suspect that my mistrust of him was something I had inherited from others and not wholly organic. So I had a stern word with my key family members in advance, indicating that no bad behavior would be tolerated, and I felt reasonably comfortable that everyone on my side could "act right" for the occasion. Plus, I felt well defended when Dario threatened to physically throw anyone off the property who was out of line. Dario and I offered different moments during which toasts could be presented. Dad chose the parents dinner, a time when Dario, his folks, Mom and Pop, and Dad would be sharing a special, private meal. (*Man,* I think now, *was I brave!*) As the evening unfolded, I realized Dad's toast was the story of how I was planned, and loved, when brought into this world. It was a stunning revelation for me, and to my astonishment, my mom, to her great credit and my benefit, did not contradict him.

"Diana and I talked about having another child," Dad said in his toast. "I said, 'We're going to California, what do you think?' She said, 'Well, I'll let you know.' And the next night I came home and there was a candlelit dinner and a bottle of wine. Di, was it beef Stroganoff?"

"Lasagna," my mother confessed.

I was gobsmacked. And I began to wonder what other things I had been taught to believe about myself and my father might be fabrications.

~ ~ ~

I continued to be surprised. Dad recalled our early years, of which I still have very little memory, as a "storybook father-and-daughter relationship." Perhaps I had to wipe those recollections out of my consciousness in order to endure the long separations when I didn't know whether or not he loved me. I continued to struggle to generate any connection with the times we had been close when I was little. In our sessions with Ted, I did begin to remember more of the abandonment, which, however painful, was a necessary step toward healing.

There was a lot of ground to cover. We talked about those early years in Sylmar, California, which my mother had always said were so miserable for her. Dad was at ease remembering he was still in love with Mom during this time, although he thought they would have been better off choosing a different community in which to settle initially, one where Mom would have been less isolated. In pictures, my family looks normal, my mom in a pixie hairdo and short skirts, Dad in bell-bottoms with some gnarly sideburns, standing in front of goats at a petting zoo and at other family tourist attractions. I love the photos of my sister dressed up in her cowgirl outfit, strumming a tiny guitar with a harmonica in her mouth. My favorite video is of her appearing with flair from behind a curtain, performing a magical show, singing into a xylophone's drumstick, giving a confident shimmy of her wee shoulders. The photos of me show a smiling, dark-eyed baby who seems well fed and well loved.

We talked about my earliest memories in Hollywood, and Dad filled in some of the gaps for me. After he left the house on Larrabee Street, moving to Manhattan Beach, Mom had told us that he was a good-for-nothing bum, or words to that effect, but in fact he was going to grad school at UCLA, earning a 3.89 average toward an MBA. (If his being in school came up, she cut that conversation short with a dramatic, "He cheated.") But he never finished his master's.

Mom and Dad's divorce was final in 1974, and Dad requested, and was granted, a promotion and a move back to Chicago at the home office. He recalled that she asked him to come by before he left for Illinois, and over breakfast in a McDonald's she said, "I want to tell you that you're not Christina's father." He responded blithely, "Yeah, I know." They had simply never discussed it before. Despite his suspicions, he had always unequivocally accepted my sister as his own daughter. For that one morning, there were no accusations, there was no acrimony. They finished breakfast, and he started up the new MGB he had bought for the trip to Illinois. "I drove off into the east into the sunrise, to a new job and hoping for a new life," he said.

He came back fairly often to see us. Always one for an adventure, he took me on a long road trip up the Pacific Coast Highway, all the way to rural Oregon, just him and me in his MGB, making stops along the way to see friends. I was still in kindergarten, and Dad was engaged and caring, working on spelling lessons with me and patiently helping me learn to eat new foods, like yogurt, that I wouldn't try at home. It was an interesting odyssey into the alternative lifestyles of the Pacific Northwest, circa 1974. My list of new experiences included sleeping in a yurt; stopping in on a friend, who happened to be in her hot tub, and thus seeing a grown woman who was not my mother topless; playing hide-and-seek after dark in a national park in which friends were squatting; watching a ten-year-old handily roll a joint; and various other oddities of the era. The trip became a mainstay classic of my show-and-tell performances.

~ ~ ~

My memories turn spottier and darker the next year, when, after the usual blissful summer with our grandparents, Mom moved us back to Kentucky and we lived on and off with Dad at Camp Wig, south of Lexington. Even at that tender age, I understood that my parents were not reviving their marriage, we were just grouping up for a while, trying to make the best of things. My feelings from that time are mostly of low-grade, chronic loneliness and fear, with hazy suggestions of a few good memories.

Along with the blackberry bushes and swimming holes at Camp Wig, I loved the cats we kept there. They were definitely pretty wild and free, so when they materialized, it was exciting. I remember them having ear mites and the like and my arms welting up from flea bites. But they were entertaining, and I could spend hours tracking them. My dad is a great cat lover, enjoying them with deep attachment, sensitivity, appreciation, respect, and humor. It's something we have been able to share, and I enjoyed learning all about the cats he kept during the years we were not close, as they were such an important part of his life.

There were other, more disturbing memories from that time, though. The road from Lexington to Camp Wig was narrow, winding, with elevation changes, and had only a puny guardrail. Dad gave me rides on a borrowed motorcycle a few times, and I remember being very scared. The motorcycle did not have a backrest, and it felt as if the only thing preventing me from falling into the hollow, as we tipped from side to side, taking the curves, was the strength of my seven-year-old arms. To this day, I have an unreasonable fear of tipping. Nothing else, only tipping, and I know it is from being on that road. I am perfectly at ease in a car with my husband driving 170 miles an hour. I'll sit cross-legged, giggling, popping Malteezes, a Scottish malted milk ball. I can go upside down on any roller coaster in the world (after multiple corn dogs, even). But I cannot ride a golf cart up a modestly sloping putting green or anything else that creates in me the sensation of tipping.

~ ~ ~

What happened after that year at Camp Wig was mainly lost to me. While I know facts, I don't recall basic experiences. As I've said, my mother, sister, and I moved, without Dad, to Berea, an idyllic and creative town forty miles south of Lexington. But how did I land there? One day when we were visiting our grandparents, Mom came by and swooped us up. At our new home, Dad never came to visit, and no explanation was offered for his absence. He had vanished once more, establishing patterns of deeply traumatic, abrupt changes that scarred me. But once we began therapy, Dad informed me that Mom never told him we were moving. In a way, she had stolen us. He shared with me how he drove around central Kentucky feeling equal parts rage and despondency, looking for us until he found out weeks later where we lived. But he realized there was no point in confronting her about visiting us; she would just disappear with us again.

I had a strange physical experience as he described what had happened, a nonthinking, nonverbal sense of memory sluiced within my body. I felt my feet tingle on the floor on which they were placed, and a feeling of hyperreality buzzed through me, culminating in dizzy light-headedness. The more we talked, body memories such as this began to occur frequently, as my body confirmed that what my head was hearing made sense.

~ ~ ~

After our one year in Berea, in the lovely home on the hill, Mom's next cross-country move was triggered by her mother asking her to testify against her dad in their divorce proceedings. Unable to figure out how to respond, how to set boundaries, she chose to flee.

My sister was furious at being uprooted from a place she had come to love, and she started acting out her anger on me during the drive to California. Mom and Uncle Mark had rented a U-Haul truck and laid a mattress in the back for our travel space for the 2,434–mile trip, propping open the rear door a foot to give us some air. During one long day of driving, in an inexplicable rage, my sister started climbing onto the high piles of furniture and boxes and jumping on me, then holding me down and licking my face until I was hysterical. Desperate for it to stop, I took off my small shirt and waved out the back of the trailer, trying to flag down some help. I was more afraid of my sister than of falling onto the interstate. Sister remembers that a state trooper pulled us over, and she received a humiliating spanking from our mild, kind uncle for being so cruel to me. I don't remember most of it. I know it's something she regrets deeply, and I have done what I can to help relieve her of her guilt. I regard her behavior, like that of every child, as a perfect reflection of the environment in which she was being raised. And just as I was in many ways not having my needs met, neither was she.

During our two years in Marin County, I don't remember hearing from my father once. The few times I saw Dad at Mamaw and Papaw's while living with them during summertime, I felt so awkward and shy around him. He acted as if we knew each other, but I wasn't so sure. I don't remember asking him why he had disappeared, and he doesn't remember trying to explain. I recently asked Mom if I asked her about him, and she admitted she was so immersed in her own world that she doesn't remember, either.

One of those summers, he showed up at Mamaw and Papaw's in the MGB to take me on a road trip to see our wonderful cousins in Pennsylvania, and I felt very weird that I was going to be with him after not having seen him for at least a full year, which to a young child can seem like a lifetime. As we set out, he put something from a small gray film canister in his mouth, and when I asked what it was, he told me plainly it was speed. That was my dad's way, being transparent, and plainspoken, thinking such honesty was the enlightened way to parent. Even though I was only nine or ten, I had been around enough drugs in my short life to know what amphetamines were. I was scared to death, and the speed seemed to fit the portrait of my dad painted by my mother, as well as my grandparents' concern about his "lifestyle," as they called it. When the MGB broke down in Catletsburg, only a few miles from Ashland, I was enormously relieved our trip had come to naught, feeling I had narrowly escaped something terrifying and would be safely returned to Morningside Drive.

~ ~ ~

Breaking into the entertainment business had become Mom's obsession while we were living in California. One night she and Sister went to a Merle Haggard concert and managed to meet him in the parking lot. My mother is nothing if not beguiling and they ended up traveling with the great star on his tour bus for the next few days. I was left home alone during their escapade

I have pieced together that this sort of thing happened a lot. I tend only to recognize the absences when a story is being told about my family and one of the listeners will look at me and ask, "Where were you?" My mother and sister's adventures, positive and negative, had so dominated my own life that I often had no idea where, in fact, I was while they were living theirs. I have put things together by asking family members and friends and doing childhood work with professional clinicians. So often when I start such work, guided back in time, giving that little girl who still lives in me a chance to express herself, the first thing out of my mouth, or the first thing I write, is, "Where is everybody?"

~ ~ ~

I spent another joyful, mostly carefree summer after fourth grade with my grandparents, but this time my sister stayed in California while she and Mom worked on their act. I missed her, but I flourished under the attentive care of both sets of grandparents. I guess my mother and sister had a promising summer, because I would later learn Mom decided Sister, who was only in eighth grade, would not be entering high school in the fall, so that the two of them could pursue Mom's burgeoning quest to make something special out of her life. I would hear snippets from family and in some cases friends, such as my old pal from Hollywood, Gabrielle, who wrote that my mom and sister had crashed with her mom and her for a while in L.A., and often fought terribly in their small apartment. I later learned they also spent time working on their act and hanging out with musicians in Las Vegas and Austin. As for me, one evening toward the end of August, the phone rang, and Mamaw answered it in the kitchen. After a few moments, she told me to go play outside. I was climbing our wonderful big friendly tree in the front yard when she came out and said, "Ashley, you're not going back to California to live with your mother and sister. You're going back to the river to live with your dad." She was clearly upset. I went and sat on the side stoop, stumped. I hadn't spent any time with, much less lived with my dad in years.

Mamaw told me she and Papaw wanted to keep me there and wondered how I would feel about that. I was surprised they wanted me—that anyone wanted me—and I naturally loved the idea. I had often fantasized about it. They really wanted to keep me, and it was the first of several conversations we would have about me living there with them. But Dad wanted me, too. He and Mom had been having a drag-out fight in court, where she was suing him for back child support. He told me that although he keenly wanted both of us girls to come live with him, Mom was wholly uncooperative. Sensing a possible compromise, he offered to make her a deal: "I'll give you $2,000 if you give me Ashley." Mom took the money.

I had deeply ambivalent feelings about being with Dad again. He was still living the bachelor-hippie leather worker life at Camp Wig. It was clear Mamaw and Papaw did not fully approve of his choices, and I was very aware of their unspoken attitude and concern. They were classic American dreamers, having arrived in the upper middle class through hard work, self-employment, and flawless respectability. Dad was a creative free spirit, and his way of life seemed a bit scandalous to them.

The morning I was leaving Morningside Drive, I stuffed as much of Mamaw's costume jewelry as I could into the many pockets of my blue jeans—I have no idea why, except that perhaps I wanted to take a piece of her with me or to control something, anything, pushing back against my obvious powerlessness in the family. Or maybe I wanted to squirrel something away that I could look forward to later, anticipating I would be lonely, imagining bringing each item out, one by one, remembering the fun times I'd had with Mamaw. Our two-hour ride was quiet, each mile deepening the silence as we drew closer to parting. Papaw was so mad about leaving me in a situation he feared was not appropriate for me, about not getting to keep me I recall he wouldn't pull the car into the long driveway or set foot in the yard at Camp Wig. Mamaw walked me to the house, and when it was time to say goodbye, she turned to me and searched my face, giving me a chance to come clean. Eventually she said, "Ashley, I would give you anything I have. You don't have to take it from me." I reached into my pockets and handed my grandmother her things. I was devastated that I had hurt and betrayed her and was very ashamed of myself. I have always thought the way she handled this moment exemplified her dignity and grace.

My first months back at Camp Wig were indeed very lonely. I remember playing alone every day after school, sitting in my austere room, trying to pretend it was comfortable, that I liked it and that it was my "own." I had a stiff plastic horse that I played with on the windowsill, and I tried futilely for a short while to read music out of a collection of Peter, Paul and Mary songs. At the same time, Dad treated me well and was committed to parenting me as best he knew how. For a while, I had a father again. He fed me hearty bowls of oatmeal with raisins and honey in beautiful hand-thrown pottery every morning. It was delicious, but I had a hard time telling him that the breakfast didn't stick to my bones long enough and that I needed him to pack me a lunch and a snack because I became hungry again every day well before lunch, which made me struggle in school.

Whenever I went into of my "spells" of depression, the ones I'd been having since I was eight, I would become mute, limp, and lethargic. I would be frozen in some intractable silence that I could not break out of. Dad would ask me what was on my mind, trying to draw me out to find out what was wrong. He would attempt to reason things out with me, to encourage me to speak, to describe my feelings. This line of questioning was so perlexing to me, so foreign, I would stall and often went to one default word: "Mom." I also could not understand how he, a grown-up who should have known how things worked, could possibly have expected me to be verbal in that condition. Didn't he know I was down a deep, dark well, where no talking could take place? Also, he tells me that sometimes I was so angry, I would just stand there in front of him and shake or bite my arm—my sister has told me this, too—and I could never articulate what I was angry about. (Dad and I now both know that depression is anger turned in upon oneself, but at the time, neither of us had a clue what was going on.)

But at least he was *there*. He sat on the edge of my bed when my first little boyfriend broke up with me, saying, "Poor baby, poor baby." (Of course, I recognize now that the level of grief I experienced had little to do with the boy and everything to do with retriggering major feelings of abandonment.) Dad was also great with me when I returned the five-dollar bill I had pinched from his wallet. He recognized the risk I had taken by being honest with him and rewarded me with his joy, kneeling in front of me and even crying a bit over my truthfulness, which was a revelation. With Mom, the punishment rarely fit the crime, and even telling the truth earned a spanking, additional grounding, or worse, the dreaded "silent violence" of more neglect.

We had some good times living like river rats along the Kentucky that fall. Dad had made a lot of improvements to Camp Wig. He was growing weary of eating peanut butter and living the life of a starving artist, so he cut his hair and started selling advertising for *Blood Horse* magazine in Lexington, which bills itself "the Horse Capital of the World." I enjoyed our drives to and from Lexington, now in a proper car, Mamaw and Papaw's salmon pink Imperial, loaned to us while they wintered in Florida. I played with the myriad fancy buttons just as I did on the long road trip vacations on which they took me every summer. Dad and I listened to National Public Radio, and there was a sense of routine, even though the loneliness never left me. I didn't reconnect with the little girls I had known on the river back in first grade, and the kids at the private school I now attended were culturally and physically far removed from Camp Wig. I never had a friend over, or stayed with one, for that matter. So once school let out every afternoon, it was just Dad and me. Sometimes he couldn't pick me up on time, and he arranged with the school for me to hang out in a classroom until he could fetch me. There was one other boy, a bit older, who was in the same predicament, but we never spoke to each other. I just remember his preppy shoes and figured he was "better" than I.

I was also uncomfortable with Dad's occasional girlfriends, who sometimes came to the river and spent the night. Once, when he had a date to spend the night with a girlfriend in Lexington, he took me along. I recall feeling insanely weird sleeping in the strange home, knowing we were there so my dad could be romantic and sexual with his date. When I thought it was about time to wake up for school, I went looking for my dad and walked in on them having sex. On the way to school, Dad said, "Well, now you know why we spent the night in town." The "ick" factor for me was stratospheric in this department, as it would be for most fifth-grade girls. Dad says he was motivated to be honest and open about the human body and sexuality because he had zero sex education as a child. But, as with many of my parents' choices, he realizes now his open attitude about nudity and sexual information was an overcorrection. While he absolutely meant well, it did not have the desired effect; it repelled me.

Eventually, strip coal mining up in the hills caused so much erosion and flash flooding that the camp flooded for good. With the river rising in our house, we had to escape in the middle of the night to a Red Cross shelter. Camp Wig was a total loss, so we moved in with one of my friends from my school, Fielding, and her mother, Willie. Fielding and I shared a room as if we were sisters and slept in matching twin beds, which I thought were grand. I helped her little brother Austin pick out his Garanimals in the morning, and I felt responsible and needed. The house was a beautiful old Victorian, with gorgeous porches and fish scale tiles in deep colors. To me it felt almost like being a family, something "normal," which I craved: a mother figure, a dad, and some kids who could play and hang out together. Fielding and I sat in a living room nook playing backgammon. I did not understand the nature of my dad's relationship with Willie, which had initially been romantic and then was not. He confided in me that he wearied of her leaning on him, but I didn't really care and didn't want more insider scoop on the adult dramas. He picked me up from school on Wednesdays and took me to the ice-cream parlor near Rupp Arena and let me eat a hot-fudge sundae while I told him about my day. Those were the sorts of things that mattered to me.

Meanwhile, Mom and Sister were busy hanging out with the musicians they met as they rambled around the country, practicing their singing, trying to find their entry and niche in show business. Soon, I received a letter from my mother in which she told me that she and Sister had changed their names. Mom picked "Naomi," a name she admired from the Bible. In court, she had retaken Judd as her last name. Furthermore, Christina Claire Ciminella was no longer; her new name was Wynonna Judd. I lay on the floor practicing how to spell it and say it. Why. No. Nah. Now that they were the Judds, things were changing with them, and it seemed I no longer had a place in their world—or any other world, for that matter. I had just turned eleven.

Chapter 13

DELIVERANCE

NAOMI JUDD

Ashley Judd

Ht. 5'5
Wt. 105
Hair Sandy
Eyes Hazel

Homemade modeling shots Mom took of me, age 13.

You lie, a small knuckle on my white bed;
lie, fisted like a snail, so small and strong
at my breast. Your lips are animals; you are fed
with love. At first, hunger is not wrong.

—*ANNE SEXTON*, "Unknown Girl in
a Maternity Ward"

In 1979, when I was finishing fifth grade, Mom decided to stop wandering around the country with Sister and settle in Nashville, Tennessee, where most of the country music labels were based. After four months in motels and house-sitting for friends, she rented a small, hundred-year-old farmhouse on Del Rio Pike in the town of Franklin, a forty-five-minute drive south of Nashville, and arranged with Dad to take me back. He was becoming more involved in the world of thoroughbred racing and would soon be moving to Florida to work for a promotion. They had apparently agreed to share custody again, letting each other take me during alternate years. I had no knowledge of their conversations or their plans for me.

And so, at the end of my typically nurturing and sustaining summer with my grandparents, with days spent at the pool, trips to the Ohio State Fair, hot afternoons spent helping Papaw Judd at his filling station, Papaw Judd and Cynthia, whom he married after his divorce became final, informed me that instead of returning me to Dad in Lexington, they would be taking me to Tennessee to live with Mom.

I don't remember that reunion, only the drive, lying in the backseat of Papaw's Buick feeling scared and intensely sad. They dropped me off at an I-65 exchange in Brentwood, Tennessee, where Mom met them.

The transition was very hard on me. The farmhouse on Del Rio wasn't ready for us yet, so Mom was still house-sitting while she worked during the day as a receptionist at a firm on Music Row. I spent my first night with Mom, whom I hadn't seen since Christmas and before that, the previous May, in a strange house. When I woke up, I was alone. I fell into my deepest depressive spell to date and commenced sleeping around the clock, waking up only to watch a few shows on TV, such as *The Price Is Right*. I would search this stranger's house, and when I found products mentioned on the show, I would clean the living room, interacting with the happy people on TV or pretending to be in a commercial. Once the soap operas came on, which I did not understand, I would go back to sleep. I remember waking up and not knowing if it was dawn, day, dusk, or night or how many days had passed. I remember Mom coming in to check on me a few times, partially waking up while she sat there for a minute. I do not recall us interacting much during those moments. I do not know how long this lasted; I do not recall moving into Del Rio. I don't remember my sister being at this house. Maybe she was; maybe I was so depressed that I can't remember. (Or maybe Papaw and Cynthia took her to Kentucky for her own visit with grandparents.) My memories of her begin only at the next house at which we house-sat. I can't recall if I was happy to see her or how we greeted each other. I just recall that she sat on the back porch learning to play Rickie Lee Jones's "Chuck E.'s in Love." Then there is another hole in my memory, and it resumes when I am lying in bed in my new room on Del Rio, and I can hear Mom hanging the few pictures we owned, arranging our familiar things, including a few family pieces such as Grandmommy Burton's sideboard, in such a way as to make a home.

~ ~ ~

I entered the sixth grade at Grassland Elementary School, while Wynonna, after her hiatus, was finally starting high school at Franklin High. Early on, we used to do the laundry together at a laundromat I still pass often, and once when Sister and I were folding towels, she cracked, "If you are going to live with us, you have to fold the towels our way." I guess I had picked up a different technique over the years, spending time in so many different households. How did Mamaw fold? Nana? Cynthia? Dad? Willie Wood? So hypervigilant and unsure of where I belonged, I took my sister's remark very seriously, believing that one wrongly folded towel and I'd be turned out to live somewhere else.

I continued to fantasize about moving to Ashland to live with my grandparents, but neither of my parents would abide the idea. Over the years, both sets of grandparents had been concerned enough about my living arrangements, yet they never managed to form a full alliance to actually rescue me from my chaotic, nomadic life. Once, even my aunt Margaret hired a lawyer to discuss the possibility of obtaining custody of me, which he explained a judge would never grant. Both my parents were living, and he said she wouldn't stand a chance. She still looks at me with soft regret, offering her apologies that she couldn't help when I needed it, and only when I was in good recovery did I stop wondering about how different—how much better—my life could have been if my grandparents had succeeded in adopting me.

Cynthia and Papaw Judd started talking about adopting me as soon as they learned Mom wanted me back again. I would have loved nothing better. They lived right down the street from a school, and I used to walk to it after dark, and in the very picture of a forlorn lost child, wrap my slim fingers in the fence, staring longingly at the playground and buildings, imagining that it was my school, that I had just walked there from my home with my grandparents, after a hot breakfast they had cooked for me (Papaw Judd made a mean country breakfast), and sat at the kitchen table eating with me while we talked about my upcoming day. Cynthia knew Mom needed money and told Papaw Judd the way to make this happen was to pay Mom $10,000 for me. Before they could make arrangements, Papaw's kidneys failed, related to his alcoholism, and he had a transplant. The medical process was not near what it is now, and he was a sick man off and on for his remaining years, making incessant trips to Lexington for his complex care. He admitted to Cynthia that he was too sick to keep me. I am still so grateful to Cynthia for how very well she took care of my grandfather. She was a faithful caregiver until he died, and it does help knowing they had wanted me.

~ ~ ~

My feelings about where I actually belonged in the world fluctuated even within my peer group. I had friends from a grade above me, and in my frantic attempt to be accepted, I tried to gain their approval by "acting big" and carrying on the way they did, which at times included smoking cigarettes and behaving like a cool teenager. I was devastated when friends my own age rejected me as being "too fast." But by now I had no idea what it meant to be "normal."

Mom took nursing jobs to pay the rent, eventually settling into a three p.m. to eleven p.m. shift at Williamson County Hospital. I nagged her to switch to the seven a.m. to three p.m. shift so I could see her sometimes. She explained those were popular shifts and gave other reasons why she would stay on the three p.m. to eleven p.m. I rarely saw her except on weekends, when she would often fry chicken in an old family skillet, which I loved taking cold in my lunch on Monday mornings. My sister and I occasionally bonded in our shared neglect. She could take good care of me, being protective and fun, letting me do her civics homework for her or be around her friends (both of which I loved), but she could also turn domineering and crabby, hollering at me from her bed to bring her a glass of something to drink so she could take her asthma medicine. I would take her water, but she didn't want water. I'd take her milk, but she didn't want milk, either. She wanted juice, and when I brought it, I would be released from my butler duties to resume whatever I had been doing that she had felt entitled to interrupt.

By now my mother and sister had intensified their pathological attachment to each other. They needed, despised, and loved each other desperately, and were often at each other's throats. Sister constantly obsessed about Mom, how to make and keep peace and earn her approval, which even I could tell Mom would extend and withdraw on a whim in order to dominate and control her older daughter. After one typical period of them not getting along, which could include fistfights that I heard and watched from my bedroom, and after which my mother would show me her bruises, saying, "Look what your sister did to me," my sister placed little pieces of paper all over the house, taped to doorjambs, creatively hidden inside cabinets, even in the washing machine. They all said, "Let's get along." Mom, coming in from I didn't know where, saw them and imperiously decided to allow herself to be provisionally charmed. She progressed through the house, finding the notes, a smile on her face, until she came across some household chore Sister had left undone. The smile dropped off her face, she withdrew her approval, and they were fighting again within seconds.

There was a fragile peace when they practiced their music. When they were singing, I could hear them behind Mom's closed bedroom door, collaborating, respecting each other. Without the music, I realized as an adult, there might not have been any good times at all.

Gradually, I went from being somewhat content in my isolation, able to self-soothe and put a happy face on things, to figuring out that my job was to stay out of the way or out of the house.

I often spent school nights with my best friend, Beth Inman, whose own mother, when she gave Beth and her brother their good-night and off-to-school hugs, wrapped her arms around me in a way that both pleased me and made me feel ashamed, because I needed the affection so badly.

Initially while on Del Rio, I tried to stay in touch with my dad. During my first autumn there, I recall we spoke on the phone once, and he said he'd like me to spend Thanksgiving with him. Although I was only eleven, I proceeded to research Greyhound bus schedules, finding the gas station in Franklin at which a bus made a stop, and how long the trip would be, and how much it would cost, for me to ride to Lexington. I presented my plan to Mom with confidence. I remember I was sitting on a cabinet, chatting away about my wish to see Dad, swinging my legs. My high spirits were met with a curt and imperious, "You do not spend Thanksgiving with your dad. You are coming to North Carolina with me and Larry, to meet his family." My legs stopped swinging midair.

Larry Strickland was a handsome gospel singer for whom Mom had fallen hard as soon as she arrived in Tennessee. Larry soon moved in with us on Del Rio Pike, and Sister and I began calling him "Pop."

The trip to North Carolina was an unmitigated disaster. I was depressed, for one. Mom and Pop were wildly sexually inappropriate in front of my sister and me while we were in the backseat during the long drive. Once there, Mom, intent on making a good impression on Pop's folks, had me on a very short leash. Pulling me aside, she explained how she wanted me to behave, and that she would wink at me when I needed to perk up. I was unable to conform to her vision and she looked like she had something in her eye all weekend. By the end of Thanksgiving, I was grounded until my birthday, which is mid-April. Worse, I do not remember seeing or talking to my dad again for nearly two years.

In the summer of 1981, just before I began eighth grade, I did successfully book myself a Greyhound ticket to see him. One evening, my sister dropped me off at a depot in Nashville, and I rode alone for eleven hours overnight on a route that required multiple stops and bus changes to Ocala, Florida, where Dad had moved.

By then Dad was manager of sales and marketing at *Florida Horse* magazine and had also married a Lexington belle from a horsey family named Eleanor Van Meter. They were living in a cottage on a horse farm outside of Ocala. The arrangement was such an improvement that as my scheduled departure for Tennessee approached, I was relieved and pleased to hear that Dad, Eleanor, and I were harboring the same idea: I would live with them for my eighth-grade school year. Mom did not object, and Dad enrolled me in a private school, which I picked because they had cheerleader tryouts in the fall and I could maybe make the squad, and for a few months everything seemed great. Dad and Eleanor, however, were not as happy as they had seemed to me. Dad later shared that he had been too rigid to adjust to some of the changes and compromises a coupleship requires, and the brief marriage soon collapsed. One day before school, they were sitting at the kitchen table, looking quite somber. Strangely, Eleanor gave me a card that simply said, "Cheerio." When I came home from school, she was gone and I never saw her again.

The split caused Dad to go through his own deep depression. When I approached him in the grocery store aisle, where he stood not moving, arms limp by his sides, and I asked if I could have a crap sugar cereal, and he said yes, I knew I was in trouble. That was completely against his fatherly values, and I knew something was wrong and he would not be able to care for me anytime soon. When I rode the bus back to see Mom for Thanksgiving, I was already devising my plan, writing letters to friends in Tennessee about how I couldn't return to Florida after the holiday but how I couldn't tell Dad in advance, because he'd be so mad at me. I thus wordlessly ditched my dad, and unintentionally gave my mother a smug victory over him, more fuel for her anti-Dad campaign.

Once I was back in my mother's house, the savage scripts about him resumed at full throttle, and she was bound and determined to make sure we hated him as much as she did. I can recall only two visits he made to see us during the remaining years we lived on Del Rio Pike. But Dad told me that there were times when he drove to Tennessee to pick us up for a visit and Mom would make us hide in the house on Del Rio, turning out all the lights, until he finally gave up and left. I think I remember one of these stunts, hunkering in a dark house below window level, while Dad circled the house, hollering, but I can't be sure.

The atmosphere in our shabby farmhouse careened between utter quiet—the kind of quiet that can only be caused by abandonment and neglect—and raw drama. Although they eventually married in 1989 and mostly settled down, during the Del Rio Pike years, Mom and Pop were locked in a toxic cycle of jealousy and betrayal, breaking up and getting back together. Periods of Pop's extended absences were punctuated by his returns to Del Rio Pike, when we would play family. We'd have more meat with supper, and Mom would tell us girls to cheer up and act right when he was around. A horrific reality for me was that when Pop was around I would have to listen to a lot of loud sex in a house with thin walls. The tall wooden headboard of their bed would bump against a door between our rooms, which was excruciating to hear night after night. (As a result of treatment, I now know this situation is called covert sexual abuse.)

While Pop was away, Mother would steam open his mail and secretly follow his tour bus out of town, sometimes catching him with other women. She'd throw him out and then send my sister to talk him into coming back, or she'd compose lengthy letters for Sister to read to him on the phone, while she sat silently by and semaphored, coaching Sister's performance. Their fights were epic. Sometimes Mom would go for her revolver, and several times Sister called the cops to break it up. I heard and watched all of this, every bit of it, and I never understood why the police didn't take me with them when they left. How I remember standing barefoot on the back porch in my nightgown, watching the officers' backs as they returned to their squad car, and the quiet of their leaving.

One of my behaviors during this period was to plan my time at home in meticulous detail. While the school day was winding down, I would write out the flow of my afternoon and evening in quarter-hour segments, deciding in advance how to spend each successive fifteen minutes, desperate to fill the long, empty hours or keep myself busy and out of the way while the dysfunction played out. Once, when I just couldn't stand it anymore, I ran over a mile to our closest neighbor's house, people I had never met, intending to shout at them, "Help me! There are crazy people living in my house!" I rang the bell, chest heaving, out of breath, and their giant, terrifying dog bounded out, snapping its jaws at me, eye-level. It was the most frightened I have ever been in my life. My knees buckled and I nearly fainted on the spot. By the time someone answered the door, I was completely broken; the wind was out of my sails. The neighbor drove me home without me saying a word.

It was about this time that I took to playing with Mom's gun, trying to decide if it would be worth it to shoot myself. I don't remember the first time I did it, but soon there were many days after school when I was sitting cross-legged on the floor on my mother's side of the bed, facing a long, narrow window that looked out into the side yard. I would expertly check the chamber, load bullets, give it a spin, and with a jerk of my wrist click the chamber into place, cock the trigger, and then hold the gun to my right temple. To me, the way my family lived was already killing me. This sort of death often seemed preferable, the only escape I had available to me. I tried to tell people what it was like to be me, what being here felt like. My reality was that no one listened, no believed me, and even if they did pity me, no one acted. Episodes of suicidal ideation to cope with searing emotional pain continued into my adulthood, and to this day I have no clue how I survived, other than by the grace of God, especially in the form of angels intermittently put in my path who showed some interest in me. They kept me going.

I returned to the dream that maybe Papaw Judd and Cynthia would try to rescue me, if they only knew what living on Del Rio was like. So I wrote a long letter casually describing the details of my everyday life, the craziness of the relationship with Pop, the days and days I spent alone, the way I never had a ride to or from school or my activities, thinking they would take the hint. But the letter never reached them. I found it on my mother's dresser. I looked askance at my mother, who had obviously opened and read it. "Don't you ever talk bad about me to my daddy again," she said. From then on, I kept my various plans of escape to myself.

~ ~ ~

The irony is that if you'd met me at the time, you would have thought I was an all-American kid, and in some ways I was. I was a cheerleader my freshman year in high school, was voted vice president of the student body as a sophomore, went to the prom with a well-liked football player, and had lots of friends. In a way I was living a double life, keeping my loneliness and my deepening depression to myself. If I mentioned it to anyone at home, I would be given a speech as to how difficult Mom's life was, in which she would dominate the narrative with her own hardship. I eventually learned how to act "normal" in an abnormal world, developing scrappy coping strategies and survival skills that helped develop both my resilience and my dysfunction. Everybody thought I was a well-adjusted, adaptable kid, an overachiever who earned good grades and was going places. I was not so sure. When people liked me, I didn't know why. When their parents approved of me, I felt empty, because I knew I was lying to them. If they'd really known what was going on with me, the sorts of things that happened in my household, they would not have allowed me to darken the doors of their homes.

~ ~ ~

In a random stroke of fate, one day a man from New York City knocked on the door of our secluded rural home. He was a print ad producer, in the area scouting locations to shoot a cigarette billboard. He was interested in the fields around our house for the ad and was looking for the property owner. Instead, he found a fourteen-year-old girl, home alone, to whom he blurted out, "Have you ever modeled?" I thought nothing of inviting him inside, sitting on the floor with him on my mother's bedroom floor, and showing him our homemade modeling head shots. He encouraged me to enter a modeling competition in New York City, sponsored by one of the top agencies. It was something I wanted badly, but I didn't have the money to make the trip. I shared the exciting information with my godmother, and she stepped in to help me.

Piper McDonald Evans is one of the powerful people who were miraculously put in my life at crucial times, times I otherwise might have endured a worse fate or perhaps not even have survived. Apart from my grandparents, she was the first and most influential of these guardian spirits and someone who still holds a treasured space in my life. She was born Linda Ann McDonald, and grew up across the street from my mother in Ashland. In fact, she had introduced Mom and Dad on their first blind date. Her brother played with my uncles; our families were "yard kin," as I like to put it. Piper had gone to the university, pledged a top sorority, and graduated with impeccable grades. She moved to San Francisco before I was born and became a woman of the world, versed in art, literature, history, and fashion, always displaying considerable intellectual gifts as well as a fantastic sense of humor.

When Dad and I made our road trip to Oregon years earlier, we stopped for a while to visit her in San Francisco. I was in awe of her and spent much of our time in the car with my windshield visor down, looking in the mirror, trying to arrange my hair to look like hers. She has often popped up in our lives at the most auspicious times. When Mom decided to move to Marin County, Piper was there to meet her at the airport (wearing a mink coat, of course) and helped her out while she looked for an apartment. Piper had an inkling of how chaotic our lives were, but there was little she could do except be there for us when she was needed.

Over the years we grew closer, and she became a safe haven for me in my adolescence, much as Mamaw and Papaw Ciminella had been in my early childhood. I don't remember if she called me or I called her, but one day after school when I was about fourteen, and I was sitting there beside Mom's bed holding that gun, I ended up talking on the phone to her. While I didn't mention that I was actually playing with a gun, I did share that I was extremely miserable. Because she knew my mother, she both believed me and did not judge anyone involved. Instead, she expressed her confidence in me and thus gave me something else to focus on: the novel idea that someday I could live differently.

She later gave me a book entitled *Tiffany's Table Manners for Teenagers,* and in her inscription she wrote, "If you have the kind of life I think you are, you're going to need this!" One of the many things she taught me was how to be at ease with all kinds of people, because she was inclusive, celebrated diversity, and honored everyone, even though, paradoxically, she could be an unapologetic and incorrigible snob when it came to society stuff. She later took me to France and Italy, where for several years in a row we blissfully spent the month of May. She opened up the world to me.

When Piper learned I had a chance to compete in the competition, she offered to pay for the trip and accompany me to New York. It was a magical experience for me. We stayed at the Waldorf Towers, and visited the Metropolitan Museum of Art and the Algonquin Hotel, where the famous Round Table originated, and the fountain at the Plaza where F. Scott and Zelda Fitzgerald took their drunken midnight dip. She took me to dinner at La Grenouille and Odeon. She met the man who had knocked on my door in Tennessee, telling him, as well as her New York friends, about my bright future, a future that, until those conversations, I had been unaware I even possessed. I had read *Cosmopolitan* and *Vogue* magazines and thought myself very sophisticated for a fourteen-year-old. I had almost grown to my full height of five feet seven, and I suppose I had just the right look for the agency's talent scouts, because I won in all the categories. The prize was a paid two-month contract to model in Japan.

Two weeks after my fifteenth birthday, I walked off the plane at Tokyo's Narita Airport. Having no chaperone assigned, I looked around the gate area for someone from the agency to meet me, but there was no one. I had no idea what to do or where to go. The signs were all in Japanese; it was the week of the emperor's birthday and thus a big national holiday. I saw an American couple on the airport bus that I had randomly decided to take (hoping to wind up at a hotel) and tentatively explained my predicament. But my story must have sounded fishy—a kid babbling about a modeling contract and no place to stay—and they muttered something and turned away. They did not help me, and they made me feel that my predicament was my fault.

After giving up on trying to read a Japanese phone book and discovering their equivalent of 411, I finally figured out how to make a call and placed one to Piper. Always thinking, she had put some yen in my wallet before I boarded the plane in San Francisco. She told me to phone her back in a minute, and in the meantime, she booked me a room with her credit card at the only hotel she knew in Tokyo: the five-star Imperial Palace. I arrived at the posh hotel, a bewildered unaccompanied minor out of the United States for the first time, and ordered room service for two days—weird-tasting hamburgers—and wandered the Imperial Gardens while she straightened things out. The problem was my name. My passport and plane ticket were in my legal name, Ciminella. But the agency was expecting to pick up Ashley Judd, and when they didn't see that name on the manifest, they didn't think I was coming. It was a confusion I'd lived with for many years. Depending on which parent I was living with, I was either Ashley Judd or Ashley Ciminella. My last name was another piece of the battleground where Mom and Dad waged their wars. My school records zigzagged between the two names. As a late teen, Ken Stilts, Mom and Sister's manager, told me I needed to legally change my name to Judd for contractual reasons, as a Judds TV special was being negotiated in which I would take part. I believed him, but I remember how when I went before the judge, he grilled me paternalistically and clearly did not like my story—and neither did I. I was allowing myself to be pushed into something rather than making a choice I felt comfortable with. I loved both my last names and the branches of my family they represented. It never felt good when one parent tried to leverage their name at the expense of the other.

An agency rep finally picked me up at the hotel, and I was popped into a single bed-sitter apartment in a little two-story building filled with other young models, male and female. I would hang around the agency, waiting for my booker to hand me a slip of paper with the details of a look-see or job on which I was being sent. I would ride the subway and take taxis, often on my own, all over Tokyo, doing print (magazines, catalogs) and TV work. Once I was even flown to Kyoto for a job. The atmosphere was very loose, even as work was being done.

I didn't realize it was anything out of the ordinary when one of the agency bosses singled me out for particular attention. He would seat me beside him at parties and would lie down with me and molest me without ever removing my clothes, on the sofa at his house, while someone on his staff remained present. I guess he was making sure that if it was ever his word against mine, he had someone to corroborate his story that there was no nudity to speak of. I really didn't mind his attention, although I knew he was being patronizing and condescending, often scorning my best pal and me for our crude teenage manners and southern Americanisms in front of the others at the dinner parties he insisted we attend.

When the boss wasn't demanding my presence, I was hanging out with the other models at bars that loved having us, as we drew large crowds. I spent many summer nights dancing to David Bowie, drinking sloe gin fizzes. There was a creepy Frenchman who hung out at that bar who offered me a ride home. He was much older and suggested we stop at his apartment first. I vaguely remember that he lived in a Japanese-style apartment he shared with others. I was so young and confused that I had no idea that what followed was rape, because of both my objections and my age, or that there was anything wrong with it, even when it happened again. Later, other models told me he was a scumbag and rumored to have something to do with gangs in Marseilles. Gee, thanks for letting me know. An adult male model who lived above me in my apartment building attempted to force me to perform oral sex on him, and I was able to persuade him to stop and leave me alone.

I think I told the other models about these incidents, and I suspect they passed on the information to the agency, because very soon after, I was abruptly moved out of that building and into a safer one, with an older girl from New Jersey as a roommate. My summer improved after that. She was very protective of me and good fun, and we did things like cook supper together (well, if spaghetti with cottage cheese qualifies as cooking) and dance around to music we liked . . . but in safety and in private, the way teenagers should. When I started to become homesick and shared that I yearned for the routine of classes, crisp autumn air, and Franklin High School football games, she yelped with joy. She had been fearful of what was going to become of me, and she was relieved when it seemed I would go home to Tennessee and resume school.

Those two months in Japan made me decide that modeling was not for me—at least not as a full-time occupation, although I didn't have much of an idea of other ways to escape Del Rio and earn money to enable the independence I reckoned I would need. Piper met me at the plane in San Francisco, where I collapsed into the kind of hug I had been dying for all summer. I handed her my purse containing $10,000 cash. I didn't share the sordid details of my summer, both because at the time I didn't grasp that there was all that much wrong with what happened and because I was afraid I would be the one to be in trouble. I wasn't far off. In the spring of the following school year, my mother searched my room, as I think she often did, and found my diary, which I had wrapped up in a sleeping bag deep under my bed. She read it, and unfortunately, her reaction was to sneer at me: "I read all about you and your boyfriend. . . ." As was so often the case, I was shut down, my own experience and reality invalidated and denied. I was punished once more for having been a vulnerable kid, when what I desperately needed was adult intervention, help, and support. My mom took the money I had earned and spent it on some self-improvements she had been wanting.

Mom and Sister had released their first album in the spring of 1983, and they were already recording their follow-up. By the end of my sophomore year, they had their first gold record and a number one single on the country charts. They were able to lease their own bus and started touring constantly. Recently, I was visiting with Don Potter, the gifted guitarist who helped create the Judds' signature sound and was on the road with them that first year. He described how when they left Del Rio Pike, I sat on his lap, even though I was fifteen years old, and sobbed, begging them not to go. I have no memory of that.

Tenth grade was a long, lonely, dangerous year for me. I was more alone than I had ever been (which was saying something) because now my sister was gone, too. I mean, she had run away before, but now she was seriously *gone*. I'd been indoctrinated to believe that I was self-sufficient and it was normal to be alone, but at times I naturally was making some perilous choices. Sick of never having a ride, I began to drive without a license. Sister had been a great one for having fun parties in previous years, when Mom was out chasing Larry around and we were left alone, and the tradition continued, sometimes even when I didn't want it to. Kids just knew my home was often an empty one, and sometimes they would show up with a case of beer and I couldn't seem to make them leave. One such night, a boy I had asked to the Sadie Hawkins dance called and asked, "You there alone?" Not knowing any better, I told the truth. He said, "We're on our way!" and hung up before I could protest. It was a school night, for crying out loud! He brought a friend, and they hung around drinking beer. I had some. Mamaw happened to call while we were drinking. I was mortified, feeling so much shame, as if my precious grandmother could tell through the phone line that I was alone drinking with boys. When Mom came home during one of her rare visits to Del Rio Pike, they were still there. She chased them around the house with a long kitchen knife. Believe it or not, we're able to look back and laugh about that one.

I was grounded—which was nothing new. I was grounded for breathing, it seemed. Although sometimes I deserved it. When I was only fourteen, I was goofing off in the yard alone one Saturday afternoon when some of Sister's friends stopped by to see her. She wasn't home, but Sister's pal Lance was very friendly and asked me if I wanted to go to Nashville with them to take in the scene while Vanderbilt played a home football game. Mom was on her usual three p.m. to eleven p.m. shift, so I thought, *Sure. Why not?* But by the time we arrived in Nashville I was already frightened, in over my head, with older, strange high school boys. Plus, I didn't have any money and couldn't buy anything to eat. Their plans kept escalating, and I was absorbed into the whirlwind. They party hopped around campus and the stadium, and soon everyone was very drunk, dragging me with them. I was panicked, nagging them to take me home, but no one was in any mood to make a forty-five-minute run each way to the country for some fourteen-year-old. The party landed at the house of one of Lance's friends. I was stashed in the bedroom of his little sister, who was away at boarding school. I lay down on this strange girl's bed, sensing I was in great peril, frozen, unable to figure any way out of this awful pickle. I didn't even know where I was. I knew my poor mother, at work at St. Thomas Hospital in Nashville, would be out of her mind when she arrived home to an empty house. I had no idea how to call her at the hospital, and I was far too scared of her to pick up the phone and call home after midnight.

I somehow made it home the next day, and I was grounded forever. My mother even made my sister put all my cheerleader uniforms in a garbage bag and return them to the school principal, saying I was in big trouble at home.

My friend Lisa Cicatelli, on whom I often relied, admitted my mother had asked her parents if I could live with them full-time when I was in tenth grade. They had said no. Realizing there was really no plan in place for me, I decided that, just like when I was seven years old, and I had hung on the back of Dad's borrowed motorcycle by the strength of my own small arms, it was entirely up to me to save myself. I packed all my things, called Sister's boyfriend, and asked him to drive me to Lexington. I announced that I was moving in with Dad again to begin the eleventh grade, even though I had not lived with him and had no memories of seeing him since that brief time I spent with him in Florida when I was in eighth grade. I don't remember telling anyone before I made the decision. I just did it. I had had enough.

~ ~ ~

At first, Dad seemed happy to have me back in his life. He had begun producing a syndicated cable TV show about horse racing called *Starting Gate* and was now splitting his time between an apartment in Lexington and the house in Ocala. I had no idea that in the meantime his recreational drug use had progressed into serious addiction, something over which he no longer had any control.

So my move to his apartment in Lexington was the equivalent of jumping from the frying pan directly into the fire. I enrolled in the Sayre School, the private academy where I had also attended fifth grade, in downtown Lexington, which was several miles from Dad's apartment. He stuck around for the first couple of days, driving me to and from school in his Porsche 911 and nursing a strong cup of coffee as we listened to *Morning Edition* on National Public Radio. He seemed hung over and distant in the mornings and restless, irritable, and discontented in the afternoons. Soon he made the first of many business trips to Florida, and I barely saw him most of the time. He would put a few dollars in an envelope and leave for weeks at a time. I didn't tell anyone in my family that I was basically living alone. And I didn't complain to my father. I simply adjusted to the new installment of "normal."

My school was populated, or so it seemed, by wealthy, happy kids from safe, nurturing families who lived on horse farms and had two parents at home. My home life, on the other hand, was steeped in shame. The school did not offer transportation, so once again, I never had a ride. It was too far to walk. I dreaded the daily humiliation of calling around to friends who had licenses, trying to be cool while actually begging for someone, anyone, to take me to school.

When one of my friends finally expressed her exasperation at my persistent requests for rides, I was so ashamed that my spirit broke. She had said no, I didn't have a ride, and I was unable to think of another way to get to school. I stayed home. The next morning I woke up, dressed, and ate, but then the crucial moment came, and I could not bring myself to call someone for a ride after yesterday's abasement. The moment passed. I watched the clock. Classes would be starting now. Defeated, I took off my clothes and lay on the sofa, watching TV. All that week, day after day at home, my shame mounted. When I finally pulled myself together and went back to school an entire week later, the headmaster passed me in the hall. I coughed, a weak attempt to suggest I had been ill. Mr. Grunwald said to me derisively, "Nice try, Ashley."

I have a lot of blackouts in my memory of that year, too. I still don't know how I ever paid for food, much less went to and from the grocery store. I sat in my room alone, day after day, drawing houses so large that I had to tape pieces of paper together to accommodate my sketches, homes that I pretended were mine. I went through a period of obsessively calling posh boarding schools in the Northeast, acting out a long fantasy of pretending I could apply to, be accepted at, and pay for such a school. I remember several occasions when the person on the other end of the line believed I was my own parent. How right they were! Once I admitted that I was actually the student, and the admissions officer was alarmed. But that is as far as I or anyone else ever went to address my sad situation—with one notable and lifesaving exception.

Colleen was one of my next-door neighbors in the apartment complex that year. One day when I was out of clean clothes and trying to figure out how to do laundry without a machine, without a ride to a Laundromat, I gathered my courage to knock on her door and ask if I could do wash. The way Colleen tells the story, she was five years sober in Alcoholics Anonymous. She was recently divorced and felt she was a failure at the "relationships sweepstakes" in life. Brought to her knees by her inability to forge a lasting relationship outside her family of origin, she simply asked, based on her sponsor's suggestion, her Higher Power to "teach her how to love." That day, I knocked on her door. She still tells me I am a gift from God in her life, an answer to her prayers. I cry every time she says it.

Colleen let me do my wash in her apartment. She also roasted me a chicken almost every weekend. She took me to Baskin-Robbins for ice cream from time to time, and she gave me the Big Book of AA to read. She said she suspected there was addiction in my family. Addiction was a word I had never heard, and the idea my family might have it was a wholly original observation. I remember feeling a spark of elation, the sense that maybe there was a name for what plagued my family so severely and caused so much dysfunction, and that if it had a name, and someone like Colleen could talk about it so readily and had in fact herself somehow moved past it, then maybe, God willing, there might be hope for a different kind of life for us. When I asked her why she didn't do something about my dad if she knew what was wrong, she told me there was nothing anyone could do until he hit bottom and asked for help. She taught me that one can carry the message of recovery, but one cannot carry the person. As helpful as this relationship was, I still find it incredibly odd that no one else noticed or intervened on my behalf—to say the least.

Colleen's friendship made a profoundly lonely and ignominy-filled year endurable. But it was not enough to keep me safe. Although he never used in front of me, it was obvious that my dad's disease worsened with each passing month. He has since been candid with me about the extent of his addiction while he was home and how obsessed he was with me going to sleep so he could get down to business. While away, he would call me in the middle of the night and rage incoherently; when he was in town, he was by turns paranoid and angry. His thinking grew increasingly distorted, and he began telling me it was in my power to remedy some of our family's interpersonal ills. He would demand I do something about Mom, complaining about the way she treated him, how she prevented him from seeing Sister, and the Judds, on the road. He was in this mode when he decided that I needed to know the "big family secret." In the living room of the apartment, he told me that he was not my sister's biological father. I'd had no idea until that moment.

I took this information stoically. Although it was shocking, it also made sense. I already felt our family was a screwed-up, crazy, irredeemable mess, a family full of hatred, fighting, accusations, manipulation, abandonment, and emotional and physical violence. Disapproval, contempt, manipulation, and demonizing others—this was the major currency of each relationship. This information fit perfectly into the helpless, hopeless container of my broken heart. It made such screwed-up sense that Dad knew this thing that Mom hated him for knowing, this thing that she manically feared he would use against her. I realized it was as if he had a loaded, cocked gun and he just . . . walked around with it all the time, and she was desperately, creatively scrounging for ways to restrain, control, or trump him. And both of them used us kids in their power struggle. The lie took on ever-greater meaning, proportion, and without being spoken about out loud, it actually dominated our lives mercilessly.

It didn't occur to me to tell my sister. I had no voice and no power in this family, so why would it? Instead, along with the many other secrets I was well practiced in keeping, this became one more that weighed me down with a crushing sadness that was nearly killing me.

And if that weren't making me crazy enough, the midnight phone calls grew worse and more frequent. I was so unskilled—I was a child, and it never occurred to me not to answer the phone. I would be lying in bed, alone in my dad's apartment, the phone would ring, and I would pick it up and brace myself. He would start cursing about Nana and work his way through the family from there. Once, when I was so utterly shattered that I hung up on him, he called back and threatened to kill me.

After many of these nights in a row, for some reason I received a phone call from Ken Stilts, Mom and Sister's manager. It is possible I called him; I don't recall. He could hear in my voice that something was wrong. I broke down, and a staccato description of how I had been living poured out.

My mother, sister, and Nana happened to be together that day in Washington, D.C. Ken told them what I'd shared, and within minutes it was decided that I should go live with Nana. She had gotten remarried to a man named Wib Rideout, and she and my mom had finally repaired their relationship. Nana would be happy to take me. But of all my grandparents, I had spent the least amount of time with her over the years. It had simply never occurred to me that she would want or accept me.

I leaped out of bed, packed up the Honda Accord that by that time my sister had given me for my sixteenth birthday (which arrived too late to be of much help during the actual school year), and drove back and forth to eastern Kentucky twice, moving myself to my ancestral and spiritual home. Avalon, at last!

Dad, to say the least, did not take it well. When I told him over the phone, he started screaming at me for being ungrateful, for leaving him after all he had done for me. He tracked me down at Nana's and flew into another rage. I don't remember the details of what happened next, but this is what Dad tells me transpired: It was about ten o'clock at night when I met him in front of the hotel where he was staying on Winchester Avenue, right down the street from Papaw Judd's filling station. He demanded to know why "I was doing this" to him.

"I did the best I could for you," he bellowed. "But if it's not enough, if you don't accept it, fuck you! I'm out of here."

I don't remember if I said anything back to him, if I ran away or stood there and took it. I was obviously not going back with him. He had, to use his own words, publicly "divorced" me. He was saying he was out of my life for good.

~ ~ ~

Finally moving in with Nana was my redemption. She proceeded to give me what I had had for only brief stints in my entire life: three hot meals a day cooked by a grown-up rather than by me; someone to wash my gym clothes on Fridays; a safe, consistent, and abuse-free home. She listened to me. She supported me. She bought me pearls when I made straight A's. When I asked her why, shocked at the gift, she said she felt that others did not give me the recognition I deserved. I didn't really know what she meant.

In addition to having Nana, my beloved Mamaw and Papaw were of course nearby, prior to and after they came home from their usual winter in Florida. I could go there for breakfast. I could stop by every day after school. This, for me, was nothing short of heaven. It was what I had been trying to organize, manipulate, connive, and make happen my entire life; I had begged, in many ways, many times, to be allowed to live in eastern Kentucky. I finally was, and I know beyond a shadow of a doubt that it saved my life.

I had one year of being a normal teenager. I confess that I had a *Miami Vice* poster taped to my bedroom wall. I fell in love with the movie *Out of Africa*, listened to Billie Holiday records and U2's first album, and dated a smart, kind, delightful boy. And once again I loved going to class. I went from nearly failing geometry at Sayre to finishing eighth in my class at Paul G. Blazer High School—the same school my mother had attended twenty-two years ago.

I had known I wanted a higher education since I first learned to spell the word "college." But when the time had come to apply to schools during my senior year in high school, I was flummoxed by the process. I remember sitting at my Nana Judd's kitchen table in Ashland, struggling over the forms. My godmother, Piper, had stepped into the breach, providing an effective adult presence in my life in the area of higher education. When no one else was paying attention, it was she who adamantly insisted that not going to college was not an option. She supervised everything, right down to making sure I had asked people for letters of recommendation. Nana was supportive, too, as I struggled to find a suitable topic for my essays. But even with Piper's firm guidance, I bungled much of the process, in part because of the heavy burden of shame that undermined my every step. There was a severe internal critic that told me I was not good enough to go to the schools that teachers had suggested and which Piper expected of me. I sabotaged myself to the extent that I didn't mail in most of my applications on time. I had my heart set on the University of Virginia, which was the only application I actually mailed, but I didn't make the cut. So I hastily applied to the University of Kentucky and was accepted into the class of 1990. As it turned out, it was the best choice of all.

This period of reaclamation was deep. But it was not perfect. It was embedded in the broader family context of ongoing, untreated addiction and dysfunction. I rarely saw my mother and sister, who had progressed in their increasingly unhealthy relationship, which was exacerbated by their professional success and their cojoined lifestyle on the road. My grandparents still were unfriendly with each other. But they all declared a truce and attended my party at Nana's house to celebrate my high school graduation. The only one missing was Dad.

~ ~ ~

My father and I remained estranged for years. In college, I would occasionally run into him at my favorite Mexican restaurant, High on Rose, and because he was my dad, I would reflexively go to him, expecting to speak to him. He would be terribly chilly to me, and I couldn't understand why. When a sorority sister with whom I did most of my running around commented that she did not like the way my dad treated me, I realized that hey, maybe it wasn't so good. I had accepted unacceptable behavior for so long, from so many, I didn't know that I had the right not to tolerate it. He shared that we ran into each other once on an airplane and another time at the Breeders' Cup, and that both times we passed each other without a word. Sister made an effort in fits and starts to keep up with Dad—occasionally inviting him to concerts (which caused massive drama between Mom and her) and taking him along to meet the Rolling Stones, a band he'd always loved. When he was around, I had no idea what to say, think, feel, or do.

After making an indelible debut when I was in high school, the Judds rocketed to superstardom during my college years in a story that is by now a familiar staple of country music lore. Suffice it to say that I was content to stay out of their spotlight, celebrating and enjoying their successes mostly from a distance. Sometimes I would join them on the road for a date or two, and everyone made me feel welcomed. In spite of the considerable hardship offstage and what their music cost me emotionally, I was always tremendously proud of the Judds. The band welcomed me warmly, and I enjoyed hanging out at the crew meal after watching soundcheck, which I made a point of attending. I loved listening to my sister, relaxed and carefree in this setting, experiment vocally and musically, reprising the Joni Mitchell and Bonnie Raitt sounds I had grown up listening to her sing in her bedroom. In these informal performances, I glimpsed the vocal virtuosity and commanding stage presence that would eventually characterize her solo career, and lead reviewers to declare her "Elvis-like" and the "greatest voice since Patsy Cline."

Come evening I loved attending shows, slipping out into a sold-out arena just as the lights went down, feeling the crowd's excitement, and watching, with deep pleasure, the joy my mother and sister brought to tens of thousands people each concert. I had my own favorite songs and waited to hear how my sister would hit certain notes, appreciating creative treatments she would give signature Judd licks, especially savoring the bluesy numbers that really showed off her remarkable voice. I beamed when folks recognized their favorite songs, watching women cut loose to "Girls' Night Out," loving it when couples wrapped their arms around each other's waists on "Love Is Alive," and laughing at the bit in "Mama He's Crazy" when some poor fool of a man near the front would be put on the spot to sing into my mother's microphone. After shows, I would sleep with my sister on her pull-out sofa bed, and some of my fondest memories are of those calm nights after electrifying shows, reading Ellen Gilchrist and Flannery O'Connor to her, with her little dog, Loretta Lynn, curled up with us, Mom up front in the jump seat looking at "life's highway," as she called it, eating her nightly bowl of popcorn with Banjo by her side as the miles rolled by.

Mom slowed down a bit after she discovered in 1990, while I was a senior in college, that she had contracted hepatitis C, a chronic, potentially fatal liver disease. The Judds embarked on an emotional farewell tour, after which Wynonna had to launch a solo career. My sister was bereft, while also stunningly successful. I continued to participate from the distant sidelines, as usual. I found that tour to be an especially histrionic one, and in general I didn't enjoy the drama. I had already had too much of it.

Mom's semiretirement from recording and touring gave her some time on her hands, and she used it to write her memoirs. In 1993, the whole life story that she had invented for herself and told to others for years was suddenly put out there in black and white. *Love Can Build a Bridge* was Naomi Judd's self-portrait as a quirky but lovable single mom who became a star after overcoming great hardships while raising her two daughters by herself, after being abandoned by her no-good husband. The problem was some of it was simply false, and often what was not patently false was at least hotly disputed by family members, who remembered things very differently.

For instance, in the book she described the heartbreaking time when her beloved brother Brian was diagnosed with lymphoma when he was fifteen and she was seventeen. She named the doctor who saw Brian and the type of cancer: reticulum cell sarcoma. She said that her parents made the trip to Ohio with Brian and left her home alone so that she could attend the first day of her senior year. She described the clothes she laid out the night before and the sharpened pencils and notebooks lined up on the dresser. But she did not name the boy who came over that night and, she wrote, "took advantage" of her emotional vulnerability and also took her virginity. By omission, she implied yet again that her occasional boyfriend Michael Ciminella caused her pregnancy.

Unfortunately for everyone concerned, not only did Dad know the truth, but by now so did almost everybody else in our family—and in Ashland, Kentucky. It was an open secret. I remember one family friend, thinking it was normal chitchat, pulling an Ashland High School yearbook off the shelf to show me Charlie Jordan's class picture, commenting on how much my sister favored him. But astoundingly, unbelievably, none of us had ever told Sister. She was almost thirty years old and she still didn't know that her biological father was Mom's old boyfriend Charlie.

When Dad was interviewed by Mom's collaborator for her memoir, he was put back on his heels to learn the extent of the unflattering things she had been saying about him. He realized that his relationships with his daughters had been poisoned since we were little girls, and he wanted to set the record straight. And he was particularly disturbed that Wynonna still didn't know the truth about her paternity. Dad had always thought that Sister should be told, but he'd decided it was her mother's place to tell her.

Finally, with Mom's book coming out, he decided that the lie had gone too far and that he had to tell Sister himself.

I, too, was tired of all the lying and secret keeping. I occasionally went to family therapy with my mother and sister—something, I have to say, from which I gained minimal benefit, in spite of my fondness for "Joanie," the practitioner. (I still puzzle over why she didn't diagnose the addictions or suggest treatment.) But during one such appointment, my mother and sister started arguing about whether Dad should be invited to a concert—the kind of classic power struggle of wounded wills that had destroyed so much of our home life. I watched, really seeing for the first time. For some reason, I didn't feel so overwhelmed with my own debilitating frustration, helplessness, and pain, and thus I suddenly saw in stark relief the neon pink elephant with a frilly tutu dancing wildly in the room: the Lie. With detachment, I saw the extraordinary energy, the wile, the brilliance, really, that Mom had employed in maintaining the Lie. I knew that for my part, it had to stop. I would soon be done keeping toxic secrets.

The decision to tell Sister was gaining critical mass. Dad attempted to speak to her after she and Mom sang at the 1994 Super Bowl halftime show, but Mom caught wind of his plan and made sure Sister was never alone with him. Mother continued to be tortured by a powerful belief that she would be destroyed if Sister found out, bolstered by her conviction that if she should be told the truth, my sister would need to be "institutionalized." Dad called Joanie to set up a meeting with my sister so that he could divulge this momentous news in a safe setting.

The night before their appointment, I had a spiritual experience. I remembered the scripture "The truth shall set you free." I realized it was faith-in-action time. God is everything, or God is nothing. I shared my certainty with Mom.

"Tell her," I said plainly, flatly, directly, "or I will." I felt hopeful and sensed freedom was nigh. I had faith beyond the fear.

When Dad arrived at Joanie's, he was surprised to find Mom's car parked next to Sister's. He had been trumped. Mother had booked the appointment prior to his, and I came along to enforce the disclosure. On that day, I made the best decision I knew and decided that my sister was more important than my parents' court-style intrigue and machinations. What mattered to me was being there for my sister, whichever parent told her.

We sat in Joanie's office in silence, except for the sound of our mother sobbing. Sister was wondering if she had been summoned to hear more bad news about Mom's hepatitis. I was in my detached, hyper-rational watching mode again. I was given the gift of some patience, and I waited a while. It eventually seemed clear that it was up to me, because Mom could not go through with telling her. In a strange way, I was happy to have this sober responsibility. I knew . . . I *knew* . . . it was right.

"Dad is not your biological father," I said. "Your father is named Charlie Jordan."

Mom sobbed and crawled on her knees across the office, burying her head in my sister's lap.

Sister blurted out something about how this made perfect sense to her and explained some important things she had never been able to figure out. Mother sobbed harder. I watched as my sister's wheels began to turn, as she began rapidly to process, to finally arrange this information in a way that fit together the puzzle pieces that had been maddeningly scattered her entire life.

In her memoir, Sister wrote, "I wasn't angry. I wasn't sad. I wasn't anything. And I belonged to no one. I felt like I was in a space between earth and hell. I looked at Ashley and saw the pain on her face. . . . This kind of sorrow never truly goes away. It was devastating for all three of us."

Although I am not sure it was devastating for me, I was immensely sorry for the years of unnecessary anguish she had endured, all that the lying and evading had cost her. I was sorry, as well, for how much maintaining the Lie had consumed our mother and what it had caused her to do to our dad, her compulsive need to demonize him. Although I imagined her knowing would be an uneven journey, with aftershocks and powerfully mixed emotions, and I couldn't know how long it would take for there to be acceptance and peace, I knew discarding the lie was a major improvement and held great promise.

Dad says that when he arrived for his appointment, the receptionist told him to wait a bit. Then he, Joanie, and Sister had some time together.

"I've just been with Mom and Ashley," she told him. "Ashley told me."

"Well, now maybe we can develop a relationship based on truth," he said.

As you can imagine, there was a great deal of healing to do in our family after that day. Sister and Dad began to build a relationship, having a lot of fun with each other along the way, until they stopped speaking to each other in 1997 after a falling-out over an unrelated matter. Sadly, that's the way it has always been with our family: one step forward and two steps back.

Chapter 14

SHADES OF HOPE

My grandmother of choice, Tennie "Mennie" McCarty, and me
at my Harvard graduation.

One cannot begin to learn that which one thinks one already knows.

—*EPICTETUS*

*T*hrough my sessions with Ted, I was beginning to understand the roots of the depression and behavior disorders that had caused me grief for most of my life. At the same time, my sister was moving toward healing in her own way. As she has said in many public forums, her own painful childhood has fueled an array of problems in her adult life, including a life-threatening eating disorder. Finally, she decided to do something no one in our family had ever done before: seek help for her addictions. It was an enormously brave step, one that would help all of us begin to push back individually and collectively against the inherited, multigenerational dysfunction that often dominated our lives.

In January 2006, my sister checked herself into rehab at a residential treatment center called Shades of Hope, in the tiny town of Buffalo Gap, Texas. Until then, I had no idea what went on in treatment. Actually, I did not know what rehab was. I had no idea that alcoholism and other addictions were diseases. I didn't even know my sister suffered from something called compulsive overeating: I just thought she liked to snack, and I certainly didn't know it threatened her life. I knew a tiny bit about AA from Colleen, the woman who had befriended me in eleventh grade, when I lived mostly on my own in my dad's apartment. But I had never heard of Al-Anon, which helps friends and families of alcoholics, or Overeaters Anonymous. I mean, for being thirty-seven years old in modern America and someone who's generally interested in my own well-being, I was completely ignorant about addiction and recovery.

The inpatient program at Shades of Hope lasts forty-two days. During the fifth week of treatment, the family of the patient is strongly encouraged to visit the facility to partake in "family week"—five days of supporting their loved one, which includes evaluating one's own responses and role in the family system and learning about solutions and tools. When I was invited to attend Sister's family week, I took a look at the schedule they emailed to me and picked out one day that looked kind of interesting. I called Cam, the administrator, and said, "Okay, great. I'll be there Wednesday."

"No," she said, "it's really important you be here for the whole five days."

"Wait a minute, do you have any idea . . ." I sighed, then explained my work and travel commitments and my husband's schedule and how it was impossible to cough up five days on short notice.

It was suggested that I call the owner, and I was given her home number. I let that rub me the wrong way. I was already thinking, *Oh, is my family being treated as special and different? Call the owner at home? What's up with that?* I generally do not appreciate my family being singled out for special attention. Much of our lives have been lived in public since I was a teenager. Stories about the scrappy, struggling single mom, her musical, rebellious daughter, and the constant bickering and fighting between them became integral to the act, the dysfunction became part of the family "brand," and it's often been exploited—internally and externally—to my detriment. Additionally, anything we did in public—a movie, a meal after church—became the Judds making an appearance, and I resented the way my mother and sister could not set and maintain boundaries with fans but just welcomed them into what should have been a moment of family time. I have at times also grown terribly weary of the copious amounts of misinformation that have become part of the Judd canon. I once attempted to correct a gross inaccuracy printed in an interview I gave to a British publication. The editor in chief of the magazine responded, "This information is on *The Times* microfiche. We will not change it." The family myths were increasingly entrenched and apparently incorrigible.

So I was fixing for an argument when I called the home, and a gentleman named R.L. answered the phone. I love country people and rural accents, and he had one of the best I'd ever heard in my life. But it didn't make me feel any more confident about Shades of Hope. *These people are trained professionals? What is this place?* I was thinking, quite unfairly, while R.L. went to fetch his wife. Then another voice came on the phone, as soft and dry as a West Texas breeze. "Hi, I'm Tennie. And I want you to know how much it means for you to be here. . . ." Before I knew what had happened to me, I had been charmed. I was arriving on Sunday and leaving on Friday. What's more, I was excited about it.

I hung up the phone and said to Dario, "You have to come do this thing! It sounds amazing!" But he was not having any of it. He had something to do that week and could not be persuaded to be anything more than mildly interested in Shades, even though he loved my sister and was glad she was somewhere she could be helped.

On Sunday evening, I arrived alone at a charming village in the farm country south of Abilene. The tiny, bewitchingly decorated bed-and-breakfast where I was staying was a short walk from the cozy-looking treatment center. Actually, everything in Buffalo Gap is a short walk from everything else. After I settled in, I took a stroll around the quiet streets lined with picket fences twining with roses, rows of ancient-sized live oaks, and winter plants such as lamb's ear, which I loved as a child. I noticed that in lieu of garbage cans, each block of modest homes shared a Dumpster set right out on the curb. To spruce them up, people had painted them with fanciful sunsets and forests, or bucolic pastoral scenes with horses, which I found annoying. They seemed tacky and interfered with the otherwise picture-perfect loveliness of the village.

The destination of my evening ramble was a cluster of yellow clapboard buildings set among leaf-blown lawns and little rock-lined flower beds. There was no fence separating the Shades of Hope center from the rest of the town, and nothing seemed institutional about the facilities. The main building looked like an old, overgrown farmhouse, a bit frayed at the edges, with rocking chairs and porch swings set to enjoy the views. I stood in the dark street, trying to peer inside from a safe distance, and sure enough, I saw my sister through a large beveled window. She was standing at the water cooler, having a conversation with someone just out of view. She obviously belonged. It was a wistful moment for me; I was the outsider looking in, a deep, unarticulated idea already forming that I wanted some of the benefit of this experience for myself, but with no clue how, or why, or that in a week's time I would be the one standing by that water cooler.

I woke up early Monday morning and met joyfully with Sister in the center, where we were permitted to visit for thirty minutes before the serious business of family week began. I was impressed with the client art on the walls, replete with healing and promise, the upbeat and loving atmosphere, the obvious support directed toward my sister by her peers as she greeted our family. Once our thirty minutes ended, we transitioned into something called "no talk," meaning interactions with my sister were strictly confined to the context of group meetings expertly guided by clinicians who would lead our suspicious, tense bunch from a scary start to a wildly improbable, healing end on Friday.

Out of respect for their privacy, and to maintain the necessary confidentiality of what occurs in treatment, I am deliberately vague about the identities of most of the various family members who gathered in Buffalo Gap. But I can say that, as always, I had no idea what to expect when everyone assembled. Family gatherings can be volatile affairs, and adding Dad skyrocketed the tension. My dad and my sister had not spoken in nearly ten years. It was nothing less than extraordinary that he was there and that their greeting was not charged with hostility. His readiness to show up, especially with others present who utterly reviled him, was flat-out astounding. When Ted had called Dad to inquire about his willingness to attend, he said, "Anything for my girls." And, of course, the willingness of the others to stay in the room, however tentatively, is enormously to their credit, too.

All family weeks take place in a lovely group room at Shades, with hand-painted vines climbing the walls and a quote that repeatedly caught my eye: "Our spiritual purpose is to fit ourselves to be of maximum service to God and our fellows." I was handed a family-week booklet that I began to devour. I was intrigued that it contained questionnaires for me and very little information about how to fix my loved one, the "client," or her mother, who in my eyes was clearly the problem! We met a well-dressed, confident, and gregarious woman, a marriage and family counselor who would be in charge of our family week. Rather than presenting her academic credentials and rattling off the many impressive letters that trailed her name, the therapist, whom I'll call Erica, introduced herself to the group by running through her own list of "claims," addictions from which she was now in recovery. She seemed so human sharing her own litany of things likes debting-spending, codependency, and survivorship of different kinds of abuse. It was all so interesting! She had such a clear bond with my sister and her peers.

The counselor then explained how the week would progress and was up front that at times things would get very rough, emotionally volatile, and polarized within our group. She described how each of us was there to throw personal ingredients into a stew and that during certain exercises, the fire would be darn hot and things would bubble over. She also vowed that by Friday we would—each and every one of us—break bread together and partake in peace and friendship of that same stew, sitting at a family table. I didn't know if I wanted to scoff more at the corny stew metaphor or at the delusion that my family would "break bread" together.

I went with, "Yeah, right, lady. That might happen with other families, but you ain't got a chance with mine."

"Trust the process," she said. "Don't quit before your miracle happens."

Didn't you hear me? I thought, but decided not to say anything further aloud. She would see for herself: As much as I hated it, we would absolutely be the exception. There was no such miracle available for my family. Individuals? Well, I would hope so. I think so. As a family? *There is no way on God's green earth.*

During this orientation, I met Tennie McCarthy, who turned out to be a striking woman with short black hair and pale skin, wearing bright red lipstick and nail polish that matched her beautiful kimono-style jacket. She seemed elegant and loving and formidable all in one package. She was quiet, yet clearly a great authority. I also met her professional partner, a no-nonsense, grandmotherly woman named Phyllis, whom I came to know as "Granny P."

The basic orientation was followed by the key message the treatment team would underscore all week: Addiction is a *family* illness. It involves far more just than the "identified patient." *Everyone* in the family system is affected, particularly if there has been untreated addiction over generations. We were told that our own illnesses and reactions to childhood abuse might look very different from those of our loved one, but we came out of the same wounded family system, we shared a common source of pain, and some of our behaviors were adaptations to cope with that pain. Those behaviors, such as denial, minimizing, medicating feelings with people, places, and things, had probably served us well initially but eventually became obstacles to our own spiritual growth and well being. I also learned that there was help available for all of us, and the treatment repeatedly stressed, surprisingly, that the absolute best thing I could possibly do for my sister . . . for my entire family . . . was to get my *own* help and give recovery a try. We were told things like "Don't walk, *run*, to open meetings of AA, to Al-Anon, to Co-Dependents Anonymous," whatever that was.

I still could not imagine what all this had to do with me. I wasn't an addict, and although I had to change my answers around a few times to do so, I answered "yes" to fewer than three questions on the alcohol abuse questionnaire. But my butt was in the chair, and I was listening.

As the clients who were in treatment joined us, we shifted our chairs from our small circle into many rows. I was asked not to sit by my sister or other family members, so as to maintain enough physical space to allow me to have my own distinct experiences, feeling my feelings autonomously, without the risk of filtering them through another's, or adjusting my feelings to match someone else's, or distracting myself with rescuing or caretaking someone who seemed uncomfortable. So I sat, rather like a big girl, with total strangers and listened with my own ears and my own heart. Next to me was a beautiful young woman with enormous doe eyes, eyes I realized later looked so big precisely because everything else about her was small from self-starvation. All around me, in fact, were otherwise warm and welcoming, empathetic, seemingly "normal," typical-looking people. But as Granny P began to explain the "umbrella of addiction" concept, and she interacted with the clients (she knew all their stories, and although some were shy, they were startlingly honest with her and the entire group), it became clear that this was indeed life-and-death business.

The concept underlying the umbrella of addictions is that at the core of every addict of any type is loneliness. As Bill Wilson, cofounder of AA, wrote, "Alcoholics are tortured by loneliness." The all-addiction model shows we can use anything, and I do mean anything—alcohol, drugs (street or prescription), shopping, sex, relationships, work, debting, spending, nicotine, and so on—outside of ourselves to try to soothe our core pain and loneliness, fill the hole in the soul, to try to change the way we feel.

The most generally known type of addiction is chemical dependence, including alcoholism and narcotics addiction (nicotine and caffeine are in this category, too; they are mind- and mood-altering substances that enter the bloodstream and affect brain chemistry). There are also behavioral addictions such as compulsive overeating, compulsive purging via vomiting, excessive exercise, laxative abuse, and anorexia (restricting food), among many others. Sex, shopping, and gambling addictions fall into the category of process addiction, because the gratification often comes not only from the behavior, but from the anticipation of that behavior. The idea of executing the act begins to build, living rent-free in one's head. It becomes an idea that overcomes all other ideas (an obsession) and culminates in the act itself. Coming down from the act sets into motion a cycle of "pitiful and incomprehensible demoralization," intense shame, and self-loathing . . . which sets up the desperate need for relief once more. These process addictions, Granny P was explaining, are actually the hardest from which to get sober and abstinent. Like alcoholism, they are progressive, meaning the more you do it, the more you need it—with ever-diminishing returns—and they can be fatal if left untreated. Such behaviors can initially be quite brilliant, in that they do make us feel better; we do something only because it *works*, even if the behavior seems ultraweird, like cutting. But after a time it quits working, and our delusion is that *this* time it will be different, it will work again. The persistence of this delusion is astonishing.

After revealing all the different types of chemical and process addictions folks may use to medicate, Granny P talked more explicitly about exactly what it is we try to medicate. I am not sure I had heard of codependency before, and I certainly didn't know what it was. Codependency is a relatively new term in psychology that describes an array of behaviors and choices that are formed as strategies to survive dysfunctional family systems and are a direct result of trauma and abuse. The first cases were identified among spouses and family members of substance abusers who had become enmeshed with the addicts they were caring for and were driving themselves crazy trying to control the addicts' behavior—make them change, clean up, go to bed, get up, go to work, sign the Christmas cards, whatever. The definition has expanded to include anyone who tries to control the behavior of others (or themselves) as a coping mechanism to medicate loneliness, that hole in the soul left behind in the aftermath of abuse—which does not have to be radical, dramatic, big-time abuse. Codependence can be a hard concept to grasp because it's so broad, so by looking at its core symptoms is useful. According to Pia Mellody, a nurse and recovering codependent who has written extensively on the subject, codependents have difficulty

1. experiencing appropriate levels of self-esteem
2. setting functional boundaries
3. owning and expressing their own reality
4. taking care of their adult needs and wants
5. experiencing their reality *moderately*

This first, fleeting encounter with the term was sending little shock waves through my system. It was as if I had been living alone in a sound-proof room with no way to express myself with my family, and now I was acquiring language for the first time. I would glance at the patients around me, whom I strangely already considered *my* peers, and they would offer a squeeze of my hand or empathetic glances that seemed to understand far more than our brief knowing of one another would merit.

After a much-needed lunch break, we returned to the group room for Granny P to deliver a classic introductory lecture on the Twelve Steps as a way to restore sanity to our lives. A succinct summary I will never forget is this: In steps one, two, and three, we make peace with the God of our own understanding. In steps four, five, six, and seven, we make peace with ourselves. In steps eight and nine, we make peace with others. In steps ten, eleven, and twelve, we grow in peace.

Yowza. That sounded to me like a pretty good deal.

Granny P told us she was a longtime member of Alcoholics Anonymous. One of the most remarkable things to me about Shades was that every counselor at the center, including Tennie and her daughter, Kim, are recovering addicts themselves who rely on the Twelve Steps fellowships, while also availing themselves of appropriate professional help during the course of their recovery journeys.

And Granny P's story was stupendous: She took her first drink—a long pull from a hot bottle of Four Roses whiskey found under the seat in her granddad's truck—at age seven; had four husbands; and engaged in all manner of kooky, painful adventures. Having recently celebrated forty years of continuous sobriety, a journey that early on also included inpatient treatment for codependency and anorexia, she sure seemed to know what she was talking about.

~ ~ ~

By the end of the day, I was swirling. I continued to study the family week booklet they gave us and tried to fill in the addiction questionnaires that would help identify our own problems. I was drawn to a series of pages in particular that illustrated the roles people play in a dysfunctional family, along with their internal and external traits, and to what special assets, in good recovery, those traits could be converted. There is the Victim, the chemically dependent person who is hostile, aggressive, and self-pitying on the outside but filled with shame, guilt, pain, and fear on the inside. There is the Chief Enabler, who is emotionally closest to the Victim and who martyrs him- or herself to the Victim's care; the Mascot, or the family clown, who covers his or her insecurity with childish antics and humor; and the Scapegoat, the family rebel who is always in trouble, hiding rejection, hurt, jealousy, and anger inside. None of these seemed to fit me, even though I could pin onto others the right assessment. Then I looked at the Family Hero, a responsible, high-achieving "good kid" who follows the rules and is super-responsible, while inside he or she feels guilt, hurt, and inadequacy. I suspected an outsider might think that one fit me, except for the part about following rules (I liked having my own way, thank you very much). But I didn't feel like the hero child of my family; in fact, it felt more like a convenient label placed on me so as not to have to deal with me.

Finally, there is the Lost Child, who feels rejected, hurt, and anxious on the inside but to the outside world seems quiet and shy. He or she is solitary, lives in a fantasy world, seems mediocre, attaches more to things than people. Shy? Mmm. Mediocre? Not on your life. I pondered if my wonderful fairies, having Catherine the Great as an imaginary friend at age seventeen, fit the "fantasy life" criteria. I certainly went through a hypermaterialistic phase in high school, when all I cared about was the right type of clothes—anything with an alligator on it would do—so that I could fit in with my preppy friends. And I drew those elaborate houses in grade eleven, thinking I would be happy if I just lived in one like that. It passed, thank God, but I could identify. Then I arrived at the bottom of the list for Lost Child and found a characteristic on which I could absolutely hang my hat: "Pets are very important." When I saw that one thing, I began to have trust in the treatment team. It was only one sentence out of all those pages, but it nailed me. *I am a Lost Child.*

~ ~ ~

That night I had a conference call scheduled, and all the bed-and-breakfast had was one old rotary phone, and my mobile didn't have service. The call was important enough to me that it pushed me out the door, willing to approach and knock on a stranger's door to borrow their phone, using a calling card. The first door I knocked on turned out to be Tennie and R.L.'s house. That was my first interaction with her outside of the group room, and I tried not to look too obvious, surveying her beautiful screened-in porch with a full-size bed as a swing, laden with inviting pillows. When my call was finished, we stood in a plush sitting room full of folk art and oozing family feel. We had a little chat. She asked me straight out if I was anorexic. (Knowing now that bulimia is about anger, I realize that if I had an eating disorder, I'd likely be bulimic.) I knew I wasn't anorexic, but I told her, "I don't know," because I had already figured out that at Shades, a vigorous denial was the same as an admission! She said something about listening to the similarities over the course of the week, not the differences, or something comforting like that, nonjudgmental and inviting. I don't really know. I just knew I wanted her to keep talking, even as I didn't want to admit I wanted her to keep talking.

It was a brief exchange, but long enough for Tennie to make the strangest suggestion out of the blue: write my mother a letter with my nondominant hand. She said it would be awkward, illegible, slow, and that was fine, just to do it.

I woke up early the next day, well before I was adequately rested, with the usual brew of anxiety and pain. I thought, *Well, I lie here every morning, trying to figure out how to get through these feelings, why don't I follow the suggestion given to me by that woman? Why don't I, for once, try something different?* I sat down at the table, stiffly held my pen in my left hand, touched it to the paper, and to my amazement I began writing like my seven-year-old self. All this . . . *stuff* poured out that I clearly recognized as coming from the time we lived in Berea, when I had my first episode of depression. It was fascinating, painful, full of a child's indignation and resilience. Now I was really starting to wonder if there wasn't something to this place.

~ ~ ~

The therapies used at Shades of Hope call for a tremendous amount of written work to make an honest appraisal of one's difficulties and strengths, including an "auto"—a long, unfiltered autobiography and histories of all one's addictions. Tuesday of family week is set aside for the client to read his or her written work aloud to the family. My job was simply to witness Sister's process, to hear what it was like to be her, how being in our family affected her, to hear her courageous admissions of powerlessness over her addictions and the heartbreaking descriptions of the unmanageability of her life, including how she hit bottom and her plan for going forward. We weren't allowed to write or take notes and were asked sit still and be perfectly present. Nobody could minimize or say, "No, that's not the way it happened," or, "You've been such a jerk!" Hearing my sister's story in that setting was one of the greatest experiences of my life. I thought it was rock and roll. It was something I had wanted for her and something I'd been looking for my whole life. It was what I tried to do for other people in my advocacy work—to allow them to be truly witnessed in their context, in their process, in their reality. By the end of the day I was exhausted but exhilarated, and I had loved repeating back to her, even the wildly painful parts, exactly what she had said. It was empowering. Others in the family weren't as tickled, and that corny stew was starting to bubble.

Wednesday is devoted to a form of experiential therapy called "the sculpt"—a three-dimensional representation of a family's dynamics. It is directed and managed with great creativity and skill by the therapists, but it's scary as hell for the family at first. Sister asked a few of her friends in treatment to represent various people in our family. Then she placed each member of the family in a symbolic position. One member, for instance, was asked to stand on a chair, because they had ruled the family, functioning as ultimate authority. Being up high like that illustrated how they were up on a pedestal, in a position above and separate from others, wielding inappropriate power. And then divorce was represented, addiction, enmeshment, all the different manifestations of the disease. Questions were asked and answered, dynamics explored, memories unpacked, the effect of things on her revealed. When it was time for me to be born and join the family, I was asked to play myself. I sat on the floor, representing the time in my life when I was the baby.

Tennie asked gently, "What are you doing down there?"

"Oh, I'm praying," I said. "I'm constantly looking for some sort of spiritual solution."

"But what are you thinking?"

"Um, well, right now, how ridiculous this is, how [So-and-so] always gets away with this bullshit." I had been watching all the family stuff I had already been witnessing helplessly for thirty-seven years, and it was crescendoing inside of me.

Tennie asked me to stand up. "How do you feel?" she persisted.

"I feel absolute and total rage in the seat of my soul," I said.

"Who are you so angry at?"

I looked around the room, my arm flew up, and I pointed at someone. And Tennie said, "Tell them."

The first thing I said was, "How do I know you are lying? Your lips are moving."

As for the rest, well, the things that are said in treatment are confidential for good reason, and individuals typically discharge hysterical, historical emotions *without* the family present. This moment was unorthodox. Afterward, the treatment team told me my anger preceded me into a room, that on a scale of one to ten, I was a fifteen. It was something I had heard before, but most people either couldn't tell me in a way that did not constitute abuse or simply wouldn't tell me I seemed angry. Either they raged at me about my rage, which prevented me from being able to consider that what they observed might have some basis in truth, or they said things like "You are so intimidating, you seem invincible." *Imperious* was another word I heard from time to time. Both approaches, of course, made me angrier, the former entrenching me in how justified I felt in being angry and the latter baffling me when I felt exceedingly vulnerable inside and yearned for that part of me to be acknowledged. Since first thing Monday morning, the staff had been saying, "If you hear something about yourself three times, you may want to take a look at it. There just might be some truth in it." Well, I heard all the time from certain people that I was angry, and in this setting, it was becoming harder to duck the feedback.

It was extremely unconventional, to say the least, but the treatment team began as a group to lead me in anger work, a process that moves old, stuck energy out of the body. In a room full of strangers and my family, in front of whom I had not felt safe to express my real feelings for decades, with the staff's encouragement, a primal roar came out of me. It was shocking for me, and the anger work took on a life of its own. Later, I was told that I seemed to be "doing" my whole family's anger, which was considered an unacceptable emotion in many ways. That I took on not only my own but other people's, people who were so enmeshed with others that they could not risk ever expressing anger toward them (because they might alienate the person on whom they were reliant). It was a brand-new idea, and it made perfect sense.

Eventually, my head of steam—which dated back to . . . oh, what? Age seven? Eight?—began to dissipate. When I sat next to clients, they quietly celebrated me, congratulated me, held my hand, gave me those empathetic knowing glances again. (By contrast, of course, my family was stupefied and horrified.) At the beginning of sculpt, as everyone was settling in, offering their feelings check, and being given an explanation of what lay ahead, I had been nearly passing out for some inexplicable reason, nearly levitating out of my chair with feelings I did not understand. After the anger work, I could feel something was happening, and it seemed good, as though I had burst out of a too-tight husk, as though I could breathe.

~ ~ ~

There were more lessons to be learned that week, effective ways to improve communication and approach one another directly about hurt feelings or disagreements without causing harm. But after that sculpt, everything seemed anticlimactic. I found myself increasingly identifying with the other clients at Shades during our group interactions, and I picked out a couple I particularly liked to sit next to at meetings. Meanwhile, physical symptoms resumed and became more alarming, waves of dizziness and sensations that made me feel as if an electric wire were being touched to my body. Episodes of near hyperventilation and almost passing out increased, apparently in reaction to the painful childhood memories being dredged up and daylighted in group sessions and exacerbated by seeing my parents in the same room, at the same time, and by the idea of my sister finally having her long deserved moment of being heard and validated. All this triggered the first layers of years and years of my own pent-up feelings. They were roiling right under the surface of my skin, quivering in my lungs, coming out any way they could. It was becoming clear to me that all the stuff I had been trying to manage with the same ole same ole coping behaviors could no longer be contained. I was like a papier-mâché sculpture, trying desperately to patch my peeling layers, while something about being in this place spoke to a part of me that was so ready to stop the patching. My emotions were beckoning me to relax in the nascent knowledge that it was okay to come unpeeled, something my conscious brain was not quite ready to believe.

On Thursday night, Shades invites the whole community to an open all-addictions Twelve Step meeting for friends and family of the clients as well as any former clients. Apparently, folks drive for hours every Thursday to reconnect with what has become hallowed ground, the place where they found their recovery. I had no idea what it was all about, but I was curious, open-minded, and hopeful it would have something valuable for me. As I was dressing in my room, my mind started to drift back to what the next week at home held in store for me. I heard a voice from deep inside of me say, *I don't want to leave.* It was so clear and so startling that I froze. It wasn't an idea or a thought—it was a voice coming not from my head, but from deep inside my chest. I sat on the edge of my bed and thought, *Would there ever be a place for me in a place like this?* All the questionnaires I had filled out on Monday didn't seem to apply. I didn't have an eating disorder. I wasn't a drug addict. I didn't have a gambling problem, a shopping problem . . . When I introduced myself at the beginning of each group, I said I was codependent; now "rager" had been added to my claims. But was that enough to earn a bed in a joint like this?

I walked over to the friends and family meeting in the dining hall and sat in a folding chair next to a client I had befriended. There were about forty people, all seated in a large oval so we could face one another. When it came time for people to volunteer to share their experiences, strength, and hope, someone from my family began talking about me, describing me, sharing stories and facts and traits in a way that felt very wrong, very painful, as if they were taking ownership and credit for the survival skills they thought were so charming, such as my highly inventive fairy world and passion for reading, strategies I had developed to endure and survive their addictions. The tsunami in my body started, and I almost hyperventilated again. Then suddenly I found myself speaking out in front of the whole group, saying, "Please stop! Those are my personal things and it's inappropriate for you to be talking about me in this way. And by the way, the time frame you are talking about, bragging on me? By the time I was in sixth grade on Del Rio, I was coming home from school and putting a gun to my head on a regular basis, thinking about killing myself." It was pretty amazing. I had spoken up, shared my reality, debunking powerful single-strand narratives that had dominated the family mythology for decades, and finding the voice—without having to isolate or rage—that I had lost when I was seven years old. Another family member, one who used their voice even less than I and was notable especially for never standing up to anyone, actually spoke up and also asked the person to stop talking about me that way. It seemed a few of us were ready to begin making some big changes.

~ ~ ~

On Friday, the last day of family week, we met once again in the group room. We each sat with our loved one and said five things we liked and loved about her. We made collages based on suggestions by the treatment team, topics to do with our relationships with one another. It was such a great, loving experience. The staff gave us suggestions about how to support Sister after she got back home, explaining the basics of ED (eating disorder) recovery: no comments about her body. Stay out of her plate when she eats; it's none of your business. If she is in recovery, you will know from her behavior.

Then they started going around the room and making suggestions for each family member, in some cases recommending Twelve Step programs they should seriously consider attending, books they should read, professional help they might consider. I went last, and the woman who was the head of the treatment team looked at me and said, "We'd like to invite you to stay."

I was startled. I told them I'd love to come back sometime for the six-day intensive course they offered, but—

"No, Ashley, we'd like to invite you to stay for forty-two days of inpatient treatment. The Band-Aid was pulled off this week. We'd like to help you heal the wound."

Now I was absolutely staggered. Of course, the thought had already occurred to me, but it was a difficult thing to hear in front of my family, some of whom began clucking about how badly I needed help (oh, the pot calling the kettle black!). I was getting more and more infuriated, feeling that overwhelmed, helpless, voiceless torture again. I felt picked on, when others, with obvious multiple addictions, could also use inpatient treatment. (The staff would tell me later that the invitation was also based on how much hope they felt for me—but I had no way of knowing that yet.)

My head was spinning, and I quietly inventoried my life. I had rock-solid commitments, including a ten-day trip to Central America for PSI. But I knew that trying to tell this bunch, "Oh, but I have this three-country tour with appointments with heads of state, and the military is providing security," was not an adequate reason, in their eyes, for me to defer going into inpatient treatment. I had already seen the staff convince mothers who were breast-feeding newborns that the best thing they could do for their child was to get clean and sober.

So I knew not to argue or bargain. I sat quietly in the midst of the chaos of my family and looked to my left, and there was Tennie. She looked at me, not saying anything. I kept looking at her, because somehow, in spite of how she seemed to know things about me that I didn't yet know about myself, things that seemed shameful to admit, she had become my safe person in that room. As I kept looking, something was being communicated to me through her gaze. She had something I wanted. I had no idea what it was, but she had it. It radiated out of her, easily, effortlessly, a sense of recovery, emotional sobriety, and most of all serenity. I kept looking at her, feeling something wordless pass between us. I nodded my head slightly. That was my surrender. I agreed to stay on the spot because of the way she looked at me. Just as I knew I was a Lost Child because "Pets are very important." That little, but that much.

I returned my attention to the head of the treatment team, who had witnessed my nod. And then Tennie said the most remarkable thing: "Nobody ever thinks to do an intervention on the Lost Child."

I wanted to bawl as I had never bawled in all my born days, but after showing my family the pain of my anger, I'd be damned before I would show them how much a remark like that cracked me open, especially when I had suddenly, unexpectedly, become the new "identified patient" in the room. As I choked back my enormous swell of emotion, though, I knew in that moment that these people understood something about me that even I didn't understand. And with very little information, but emerging trust, I made my decision. And as it turns out, there would be plenty of time for deep crying—and the gifts that come with constructive catharsis—ahead.

Chapter 15

THE LOST CHILD FOUND

When I received my honorary doctor of humane letters degree, another miracle,
conceived in my family week, was born: Both my mother and father attended.
I have waited a long, long time for moments like this one.

We think each family which has been relieved owes something to those
who have not, and when occasion requires, each member of it should be
only too willing to bring former mistakes, no matter how grievous, out of
their hiding places. Showing others who suffer how we were given help
is the very thing which makes life seem so worthwhile to us now. Cling to
the thought that, in God's hands, the dark past is the greatest possession
you have, the key to life and happiness.

—*The Big Book of* Alcoholics Anonymous

They do not mess around at Shades of Hope. My nod was received as a firm "yes," and I was dispatched from the group room immediately to retrieve my things at the B&B and check into treatment at the front office.

I admit to walking rather slowly to that B&B, breathing in what I misconstrued as my last taste of "freedom" as long as I could. I noticed the painted scenes on the curbside Dumpsters again, the ones that had irritated me earlier in the week. Why they bothered me so much dawned on me: They could be a metaphor for my life. Painted up on the outside, looking good from a distance, and full of heaping piles of rotting stuff on the inside.

Once in the B&B, I wrestled again with the old rotary phone and how to place a long-distance call with a calling card without buttons to push, to share such strange news with my husband. It was both simple and difficult to explain. "I am staying for inpatient treatment." There was not much else to say, because I didn't know anything else. His questions were smart and concerned: "What does this look like? For how long? Do I see you? Talk to you?" I had no answers. Wait. I did have an answer.

Trust the process. Don't quit before your miracle.

I think he was in shock, understandably. Dario being Dario, in spite of how it affected him, was supportive of me. Not only is that his nature, he had a powerful incentive. He would soon become the first and biggest beneficiary of my wonderful new way of life. In the meantime, he was on the first plane home to Scotland, literally that night, where he spent my time in treatment with his family, reading my letters and writing me back. (I did not have visitors on Sundays and Wednesdays like my friends, but I did receive a lot of mail.)

When we hung up, I felt deep fear and a chilling uncertainty. Not seeing my husband for that long suddenly seemed too dramatic, too drastic, and the bargaining bloomed in my head: *I can go home, this is all overstated.*

Ted is one of the greatest clinicians in the country. I can create a plan with him to tackle the things that have been revealed this week. I'll sustain my good start and take it seriously. This inpatient business is over the top.

I rang Ted, pretty much to tell him this. I did not get past "The treatment team just did, what do you call it? An intervention? On me, for adult child of dysfunctional family issues. They've invited me to stay for six weeks. I initially agreed but I have changed my mind and am coming home, and boy, Ted, we have work to do!"

Ted, the great communicator, the gentlest of souls, floored me with his response: "Ashley, I have wanted this for you since the first time I met you."

I stood stock-still, speechless, and my bargaining, so convincing mere moments ago, vaporized.

He said a few other things, I imagine, but "I have wanted this for you since the first time I met you" reverberated in my ears, drowning out everything else. I must have been moving very slowly. We had said our goodbyes, but I was still standing, holding the receiver, mouth probably hanging open. And I heard Ted, as he was hanging up, crying with great joy in his voice to his wife, "Margie! Margie! You'll never guess what happened!"

I was stunned once more. Overhearing that remark, not intended for me, but about me, and said with such glee, was like having read, "Pets are very important." I did not understand why Ted believed this was fortuitous. I sure as heck did not understand why it was such a damn happy occasion. But it was clear others believed that it was, others who expressed nothing but great compassion and concern, who somehow, in spite of my scrambled confusion, were emerging as very safe and trustworthy. Comments like that, so brief and small, assimilated into my insides, and gave me a hook, the beginning of something to hang on to, a way to grasp that they believed, and to begin to suspect that if I did what they had done, I, too, could have what they had.

I zipped my case and wheeled my small bag down the tree-lined street, the center drawing closer, looming larger. I crossed the threshold and sat in Cam's office, answering questions and doing paperwork. I remember being so grateful I had good insurance and the ability to pay for this treatment. I remember Cam saying she'd put me in a room with my sister. Cindy Henson, then head of the treatment team, was sprawled comfortably in a chair beside me. I had no idea that she was already deep into her assessment of me, formulating the basis for my first assignments she would direct my case manager to proctor.

The tech (treatment team assistants who are always present to support clients) on duty went through my things with me, taking from me items not allowed during treatment: cell phones, any type of music-playing device, books, anything with which one could harm oneself. I looked up phone numbers before turning in my phone and stood in the tech's office letting certain folks know I would be out of commission for at least forty-two days. Kate Roberts was one such person. Without divulging much detail, I apologized deeply for the massive inconvenience. I stressed I was not canceling our complex trip to Central America, only delaying it. She received the news graciously and wished me great good luck. I shared my news with a few other souls, and all responded similarly. I found that strange, even as I was grateful for it. Soon I was holding the receiver in midair, trying to think of another person to call, one more chore to do, to delay what I had set into motion.

The tech, seeing this, said, "Ashley, I need you to finish up."

Fear closed in my chest like a fist. I replaced the receiver, stepped out of the office, and became a patient.

My case manager, Kristen, a kind and very young-seeming clinician, was introduced to me, and I was provided a Shades of Hope tote bag with the tools I would need to commence the work she gave me. A large three-ring binder, a fat ream of paper, pens and pencils, and most important, my own copy of the Big Book of Alcoholics Anonymous. I had seen other clients with their binders, written work spilling out of it, inspirational notes slid under the clear plastic cover, family photos taped in collages. I wondered what I would do with mine.

She gave me "first step prep" to write on codependence, instructed me how to write my own autobiography (before we can straighten out our present, we need to have straightened out the stories of our past as best we can), and asked me to write a history of depression, self-harm, and suicidal ideation. I felt baffled, as I had *no idea* where she had come up with that very personal information, why she took it so seriously, why me hitting myself from time to time was anything anyone would want to talk about. I remembered Cindy in Cam's office, so relaxed in that chair, and I realized that in this place, what you say in front of anyone is shared with everyone. I was bummed. I would have really preferred to keep that tidbit to myself.

I don't much recall a lot of what I did next, but boy, oh boy, do I remember supper and snack, filling out my "feeling sheet," and going to bed. During the meals, I was sitting precisely where all week I had rather longed to be: at the round tables filled with clients. I had heard something about affirmations and different assignments clients had with respect to meals. And now, I knew. My meal plan was written on a board, and I went through the buffet trying to measure and plate my food as described. (This would begin one of my many attempts to control my experience; not having an eating disorder, I wondered why I had to eat the way eating disorder clients did, and depending on my opinion of the menu, I would want to under- or overserve my portions. And the lemon ration with water? Well, it was a full five weeks before I quit conniving how to obtain more than allowed.) I watched fascinated as an anorexic put a kerchief on her eyes and was fed by a bulimic. The assignment was to help the anorexic give up control of what and how she ate and for the bulimic to learn how not to despise food put into the body for nourishment and sustenance. After the meal, everyone stood up in turns and said five affirmations about her- or himself, with the peers reflecting back to that person the positive statements. ("I love my stomach." "I am loved, loving, and lovable." "Just for today, I will do the next good, right, honest thing.") I am not sure what I said, but I know I was scared to death, trying mightily to pretend I was not while I choked back tears and sputtered through it. I would later lie awake in bed trying to think of good things to say about myself that would convince the others I really felt that way.

On the screened-in back porch, I met Jake, a wonderfully furry gray-and-black tomcat who would become my dearest friend and closest companion. I stood at a painted wooden box, looking into the dark back garden that sloped toward a creek, and paused, unsure what to write about what I felt.

My sister walked me to my room. To my forlorn dismay, I had not been put in a room with her (it turned out Cam was the campus softie). And because of the number of clients at the moment, I ended up in a four-person room, totally alone. We stood in the large, plain room, adorned only with two sets of bunk beds and a few chests of drawers, and my big sister gave me "the hug": the wonderful, nurturing, motherly, all-embracing hug she gives so very, very well. I was cracking, I was coming undone. She said as she held me, "Let it all go." I didn't know what "it" was, but I had come far enough in one week to know that I had a lot of "it." She put me in bed, tucked me in, and walked out the door.

~ ~ ~

I had chosen the top bunk, and my eyes looked around wildly as I struggled to find purchase, a way to reason things out, to make sense of the cauldron of emotion and the baffling new setting. I saw the only decoration in the room, a paper plate hanging on the wall with a cross made out of glitter stuck to glue.

Lord have mercy, I was in the loony bin.

I stared at it. I wondered about the woman who had made it, if she, like me, had been in pain, and if in this strange place she had found peace. I wondered if someday I might look back on it in my mind's eye, recalling it with fondness. In retrospect, I identify those thoughts as part of my strong will to survive, my earnest yearning to heal, and my nascent *hope*, despite how bad I felt.

Thus began the loneliest walk of my life. The first nights in treatment are excruciating, and clients often declare they've had miraculous spiritual experiences and spontaneous healing transformations that send them right out the door and back into their lives before completing a full week. This, I understand. Boy, do I understand. In spite of being unconditionally loved and accepted, and supported by a talented treatment team who often worked around the clock, I was in the most acute emotional pain of my life, at a baseline of deeply grieved loneliness with surges of near panic and wretched anxiety.

I didn't sleep much. The techs would check on us at intervals throughout the night, for a variety of reasons. My sleep was so tortured that every time one entered the room, it sent adrenaline rippling through my system. A tech rises early at Shades: Blood pressure is taken, on certain days of the week clients are weighed, meds are dispensed. (In the beginning, they detox clients off all but the most essential meds, to see, often for the first time in a client's life, what they are really dealing with, what their actual baseline mood is. So many folks are misdiagnosed, meds misprescribed, meds dosed improperly. Many of the medical conditions codependents deal with are induced by emotional stress, and substance abusers often withhold so much information from health care providers that one can't always blame them for putting patients on stuff that they either don't need or is actually dangerous for them.) I found the routine exhausting and was relieved that I was initially on "no exercise," which is standard for a client's first ten days.

My first full day in the center was a Saturday, and my free fall into aching loneliness accelerated. With reduced staff and less structure, I felt the quiet around the facility as nothing less than a vacancy in my own soul. The clients went on an outing, which both my sister and I did not attend, as the center took extra measures to protect and preserve our confidentiality and anonymity. Being left behind meant there were just three people having lunch in the large lunchroom (the third was a client too ill to go out). I sat facing the door, looking at the crossroads on which the campus is situated. I could a see long ways down the country road, its slight undulations from the giant live oak trees' roots that wove and bulged underneath. In my mind's eye, I imagined standing up, walking to the door, placing my hand on the knob, and walking out. Just walking out. That simple. I had no car, no phone, no money, but I could walk, and I imagined doing so. I have walked many miles on country roads in my life, and I could just . . . walk out of there and see where the road would take me. I had the vague sense that doing so would be none too smart, that the pain I was in would accompany me wherever I went. Those thoughts were vague, and I am not sure what prevented me from leaving. After lunch, when I crossed the street back to the center, I did look down the road once. A dim, fuzzy thought formed that I could indeed walk out of here someday, and maybe—just maybe—I would do so as a changed woman.

The weekend activities included a lot of quiet time for written work, Big Book study, Twelve Step meetings, an occasional movie with recovery themes, and process groups in which clients could share in depth about something going on with them, facilitated by a member of the treatment team. I felt ashamed as I struggled to learn the language of recovery: what to say in my "feelings check," when to give peers feedback, and when such feedback was considered "cross-talk," offering comments about another person's sharing that is not appropriate in Twelve Step meetings. I began to use the dreaded "confrontation" format, as required, at the beginning of each group. People who wind up in treatment generally have trouble expressing their feelings and their needs moderately; often they've not been taught how to, having never seen healthy communication modeled. Using a standardized script with fill-in-the-blank sentences, I practiced owning my reality with simple statements devoid of under- or overdescribing and ultimately taking responsibility for how I was going to respond to another person's behavior and take care of myself. (Mind the final statement: "To_____. When you rage at the staff after lunch, I think you are doing the anger you have toward your dad. I feel fear and pain. I need and would like you to do anger work with Tennie and Kim. And, I intend to remember 'if I spot it, I got it,' do my own work, focus on my own recovery.") People with healthy internal and external boundaries can listen with detachment and know the exchange is not just about *them* (even though it seems directed at them), but is a reflection of what is happening inside the person who is sharing. It took me a while to arrive at that place of loving detachment. When one of our peers gave my sister and me a confrontation for perhaps not considering how our closeness might be painful to watch for clients who missed their families terribly, I took it personally and totally shut down. I felt that no matter what I did, I was doing it all wrong.

That Sunday, I was up most of the night, wild with irrational fears and anxiety that felt like worms in my chest. I felt I needed to tell the tech what I was experiencing, yet as I lay in bed, I imagined I was locked in my room, which increased my anxiety. When it finally drove me out of bed, I was so surprised and relieved when the knob turned smoothly in my hand. It never occurred to me that a) this was not a lockdown unit; and b) locking clients in was an illegal fire hazard. I stumbled across the garden, found the tech, and in gulps of air punctuated with heaving sobs managed to say something about how no one has ever believed me before when I said I was in trouble emotionally, that I had been in bed really coming unglued. The tech soothed and consoled me, validated me, reminded me she was not trained to do much more than that, and offered to call in other staff. I was blind with emotion, but calling staff was too much of a brouhaha, I thought. God knew what assignment they'd give me if they heard about my meltdown. I went back to bed and rode out the spell.

By morning, I was utterly worn out. I decided this was unsustainable. I could not live without adequate sleep. I marched to the foyer and, seeing Erica there, said, "Hi, look, yeah, I am just gonna go to a nearby hotel, grab some sleep. I am sure a few hours will make a big difference. I don't need my whole suitcase, I'll just take a day bag, and I'll be back later. Thanks."

She stared me down.

"A.J., it does not work that way. If you walk out that door, you are taking your stuff with you, and you aren't coming back."

Silence.

"Come in here," Erica said.

I was led into the treatment team's staff room, where their long morning meeting was well under way. The entire gang, or what felt like a coven, was assembled around a paper-strewn table, with client cases opened, charts on the wall. It was like walking into a genius's laboratory, where obvious creativity and skill kinetically charged the air.

Erica may have said something to explain why she'd brought me to nerve center. I think I feebly built my case for sleep. But what happened next was what really mattered and was another of those life-changing moments.

"Ashley, what are you so afraid of?"

I was amazed to hear the confession, the incredibly vulnerable truth, come out of my mouth.

"I am afraid I am going to lose my mind."

There. I said it.

The energy in the room changed. The very air became gentle. There was a palpable softness.

An array of eyes looked knowingly at me. People who had been where I was, who were now somewhere much further down the recovering road, nodded their understanding.

"We will never let your mind go somewhere we cannot bring you back from," Erica said.

Although my chest clamped and I had no idea what they were saying would look like, I accepted their promise. I walked out the door, rejoined my peers, and proceeded to work very, very hard on my treatment plan for forty days and forty nights, sleep or no sleep.

~ ~ ~

I took ownership of a middle chair on the glassed-in porch, facing the garden and the creek. I spread out my paper, pens, and other tools. I wrote during every free minute, answering the questions of my now numerous first step preps (if step one is to admit I am powerless over something and my life is unmanageable, a "first step prep" is informally known as step zero: "This shit has to stop"), my auto, and all the subsequent assignments I would receive. I attended, and actually enjoyed, every group: process, Twelve Step, cognitive, behavioral, spirituality, experiential, and art, among others. I found the work fascinating, in spite of being painful, and found that when I was deeply engaged, either by listening to my increasingly loved and valued peers or by doing my own work, I didn't feel tired. I gave my all to the work.

One night in art group, we were asked to draw the body part that gives us the most hassle and then process out loud why we dislike or feel shame about that part of ourselves. Clearly an exercise designed for disordered eaters, I nonetheless had no trouble identifying the body part that grieved me most: my brain. I drew one, and in a creative, messy-but-still-somehow-makes-sense series of designs and statements, I shared that I knew my brain was my greatest asset (especially when used in conjunction with my good and tender heart) and that among other things it was a smart one that allowed me to experience great beauty, joy, and pathos. But too often at this stage of my life, my brain was racked with difficulties, consumed nonstop with trying to manage anxiety and emotional pain, sorting out multiple channels of static like a radio knob being spun back and forth across the dial, never tuning in one strong, clear channel. I knew there was plenty of hope for my brain, but this wonderfully strange thing I drew visually reflected the chaos and darkness too often in it. I also related my brain to my body, the low-grade, chronic lower back pain, the deep wound I felt in my actual, literal heart during my worst depressions, a pain so harsh and unbearable that I could think only of killing myself to make it stop.

I also began to benefit as much from my friends' work as from my own. In experiential group, held in a cozy, small, womblike room, a recovering drug addict who in her previous inpatient treatment practiced her eating disorder the entire time (a sadly common occurrence, it was soon clear to me) began to do deep work on the core pain that set up her addictions in the first place, triggered by abandonment and neglect of an alcoholic mother she loved "like a drug." She read aloud a letter she wrote to her now deceased mother, and by the time she was on line three, I was the one in a heap crying. Our stories were quite different, but that did not matter. I *identified*. A grief I could not contain swelled up in me, and by now I was willing to let it do so. As I had been encouraged to do on my first night, I began to let it all go.

My friend, unsurprisingly, vomited after she read her letter. Purging was how she had been handling her feelings for years; by now it was an automatic response. While she was being attended to, the treatment team focused on me. "Lord almighty, what was going on with you?" they asked in their inimitable West Texas accents. It was wonderful to say I didn't know, to just be, to feel, to cry, to be paid attention to in this way while I grieved, to be accepted and validated without being minimized or told I had the story wrong and facts mixed up, and to begin to see for the first time that with enough of the right kind of work, "this, too, shall pass." My deepest fear had always been that I could not heal. In spite of how agonizing the work was, it seemed I was not terminally unique, as it says in the Big Book of Co-Dependents Anonymous, and that it would finally be "possible for me to mend."

I haltingly read my first big chunk of written work one evening in a reading group. In such groups, held a few times a week, those ready with written assignments would read them to peers and staff, who would reflect back what they had heard, as well as offer observations on the text and how to go further with the work. I tried to read in a clear, confident voice, hoping my presentation would make sense of the insensible, this baffling, cunning, and powerful disease of codependency and the behaviors it spawned. I had difficulty with the questions, from section headings such as "noetic disorders" and "otheration," and I took a tentative stab at providing responses. There was one paragraph I wrote that came to me in a burst of hyperlucidity. For the first time, I intuitively captured and described how whenever I called a certain person in my life, my voice mails followed a pattern: friendly, warm greeting (make you like me, make you glad to hear from me, make you want to listen more). Description of my day (make it upbeat, interesting; engage them: seem attractive, independent, someone to admire). Emotional content (glimpses of how I really felt, truth coming out, hint at that hole in my soul). Download my thoughts about them and how much I love them, what they should be doing (present in a "good way," but goal is to make them do what I need and want them to do; address my deeply hurt feelings. The "If only you would . . . I would feel better" section). Summarize all of the above, condense into a nice little paragraph nugget that would be very clear (Goal: make them think this all makes perfect sense, do not think I am crazy). Inquire about their day (be interested in them, altruism, back to upbeat woman at top of message. Goal: Hook them into calling me back). Repeat, day after day.

My peers that first week included a sixty-three-pound anorexic who couldn't be in a top bunk lest she break a brittle leg descending from it, a crystal meth addict who had been forced into prostitution, and others with serious chemical and process addictions. Yet when I finished this work, as well as the uncertain beginnings of my exploration of childhood depression, they were dead silent. They looked at me a long time before anyone spoke up. Finally, someone spoke.

"I am so glad you are here" was her feedback.

I was stunned and agitated. They were addicts, alcoholics, and the like, but what was wrong with me? I was nuts, by their reactions.

Well, I *was* nuts, I have learned to say, but with a huge grin on my face, because today, I am glad of it. Because of Tennie and the others who intervened on my behalf, I was beginning to receive the best treatment in the world, but for codependency and depression, perhaps our society's most underdiagnosed and untreated emotional problems. Without their keen observance of my emotional pain, who knows how many more voice mail messages like that—and worse—I would have left in my lifetime.

But it would be a while before I could shuck off my disease and laugh at my former insanity. That night, my new friends, taken into my confidence, helped me begin to see and reconcile how abusive my childhood was. In particular, I began to learn about the effects of neglect and abandonment on a child, how different a day in the life of a child is from a day in the life of an adult. How although it may not have been a caregiver's intentions, the effects of their actions registered deeply as abuse and trauma. I was taught that the modern definition of abuse is "anything less than nurturing," and I began to grieve for the small, precious girl I was, needy and vulnerable, exactly how God intends children to be, and the many, many less than nurturing experiences I had. I was told that slapping a child in the face is a uniquely humiliating experience for her. The Karpman drama triangle was explained to me, a pattern of individuals triangulating, jumping from prosecutor, victim/martyr, and rescuer roles, and boy, could I easily see it at work in many of my family's relationships. It was an extraordinary relief, finally, to have something to call the tortured dynamics with which I had been raised: abuse. I began to recognize the behaviors I had developed in my adult life as attempts to restore within me the many losses of my childhood. Having been taught from an early age that who I was was not okay, I had used people, places, and things as a basic source of my identity.

I was taught about the shame core that develops in abused kids when their abusers, for whatever reason, are *shameless* and thus teach the child to be *ashamed*. They began to teach me about the insidious effects of witnessing others being abused. And they explained I had a long road ahead, because sadly, in a way, healing from these types of trauma can be harder. There is a lack there, a nothingness, a void with which to work. Clinicians even say that sometimes severe physical abuse is at least an interaction between perpetrator and victim, an indication of some kind of interest in the child. But with neglect and abandonment, the message can be that the child isn't even worth the bother of beating. It can be hard to find a way into the damage done, to begin to undo it. With abuse to one's actual body, there are powerful modalities that trigger those memories, stored in the very cells of the body, and move out the abuse, memory, and emotional energy. But when it didn't happen to one's body all that often, but was played out before one's eyes . . . well, one of the consequences is you draw your brain in art group when asked, "What part of your body troubles you?"

After that first night in group when I read for the first time, I was disturbed by the feedback I received. It was a watershed moment in treatment when the dam really burst and the floodgates opened. I did not sleep a wink and had one of the worst nights of my life. The real work was beginning, both identifying what had been eating me alive and applying a simple plan of action to address it.

Shades of Hope teaches it is abusive to point out a problem without highlighting a solution. Wow, was that a radical idea! In my family, relationships and communication seemed to be all about the problem, particularly as it was observed in one another. I have piles of scathing letters and faxes written to me from my relatives inventorying everything they thought was wrong with me, detailing my failures and shortcomings as a daughter, sister, and woman; vitriolic essays (and voice mails left overnight) about my not doing the right things on holidays; sweepingly negative statements about my personality and soul. If I had a beautiful party, I was a snob. If I burped, I was crude and rude. In their eyes, I couldn't get life right, at least not for any sustained period of time. Often, other people are dragged into the letters, outsiders used to bolster the damning case built against me. And to be clear, my own disease did complicate and burden my relationships. In doing my work, I began to identify and take responsibility for my symptoms, such as denial, poor boundaries, low self-esteem, toleration of abuse, compliance, and dominance, and the way they affected others. I was learning how typical these antics are in alcoholic and dysfunctional family systems, where the rules are constantly changing and no one can ever be, or do, good enough. In these situations, there are no solutions. That Shades would teach me solutions that led to serenity, solutions I could apply to all these situations, was revolutionary.

So that night, after reading my work for the first time, I began to apply the solutions suggested. Lying in bed with the old, familiar crushing pain and loneliness, I realized that the principles I had heard in Granny P's lectures could be applied to my feelings. I reached for the strange new words. Wheels turning, I thought, *I am very powerless right now. I am powerless over this old pain, what others have done and left undone. I am powerless over the fact that the only way out of this old grief is through, and that only I can take this journey. No one can do it for me. And yes, right now, my life is indeed unmanageable by me!* And I remembered what I had heard emphasized: Being powerless is an act of surrender, but it does not mean helplessness. I had choices. So I chose to move on, to open my mind to the idea of a Power greater than myself, who could do for me what I clearly could not do for myself: restore me to wholeness, sound thinking, sanity. For had I not been strangely insane? I contemplated my God concept: loving, nurturing, gracious, and accepting, a whole, perfect, infallible, eternal parent. Next, I found myself at the turning point. What was it going to be? Keep doing what I had been doing, keep getting what I had gotten? Or try something different? Was I finally in enough pain that the risk of changing, using these strange new tools, hurt less than the pain of staying the same?

And then I made the decision. I decided to abandon myself to the care and protection of this Power, as I understood it that nanosecond. I turned my will (my thoughts) and my life (my actions) over to the care of my Higher Power.

To my astonishment and eternal gratitude, relief was instantaneous. The anxiety vanished. The pain lifted. I could breathe, but I almost held it in this strange new space of calm and placidity. I felt like looking around in the dark, to see what had changed. But the peace seemed secure. It lasted a minute, then another, and another after that. I became comfortable in bed. I relaxed. And blessedly, I dozed.

About twenty minutes later, the big feelings began to creep back in, the emotional disturbance returned. I remembered that honesty, open-mindedness, and willingness was all that was asked of me, so I repeated the three steps I had taken earlier. Amazingly, it worked again. And it kept working: that night, and every day since.

~ ~ ~

I continued to work on my autobiography and inventories, and as I wrote out each year of my life, I relived the emptiness of my past. I thought once more about leaving treatment when that periodic pain in my physical heart recurred while writing about that pivotal seventh year when the childhood depression began. But by the grace of God, I stuck with it. It wasn't easy, though. Even the pastor with whom I did one-on-one spiritual counseling once a week asked if I needed to be on meds (I did treatment medication-free). That hurt. Everything hurt.

Being put on "no talk" hurt, too. On Thursdays after lunch, we clients queued nervously as we were admitted, one by one, into the treatment team staff room, where they had collaborated on our new round of assignments. One week, mine was "no talk." I have never been more ashamed in my life. I was sure I was being told not to speak because, just as the kindergarten teacher had said, I "talked too much." I was sure they needed me to shut up because my needs and wants were just too much, because I was a burden . . . all the things I had felt growing up. Although I was told the assignment was to help a person go deep within, feel all the feelings—sometimes for the first time—in this safe place where one could do that, I didn't hear that. I heard the old messages from long, long ago. But I persevered, and I did good work. I was miserable, but I took the action, and I found myself benefiting from it. I had to let go on a very, very deep level, and I began to see how much conversation is unnecessary, how much it can be used to chat feelings away, sidestep uncomfortable emotions, attempt to control, avoid focusing on oneself, and so on.

After "no talk" ended, I was partnered with a three-hundred-plus-pound compulsive overeater, and she was designated as the leader of our duo. I walked out of the staff room impressed by their insight. I grasped they were giving me a vital chance to truly break my denial (which stands for "don't even know I am lying"), to accept eating disorders as a lethal disease when untreated, and to make some major facts about my family and the legacy of addiction crystal-clear. Oh yeah, and I also got, loud and clear, that they were still working with me on my tendency to lead and asking me to experience what it felt like to step back, not be in charge, not use the old will to survive and hang on for dear life.

I became known for giving excellent feedback during those portions of our groups. I listened keenly and watched transfixed by all that happened. I reached to see connections, patterns that I could apply both to others and myself. I liked waiting until the end, hearing everyone else's remarks first, then working on assimilating, synthesizing.

Although I worked hard and participated fully, I was hardly a model patient. I tried, as all patients do at different times and in different ways, to control my experience and defy the rules I didn't like. I came to despise Irma, now one of my favorite people at Shades, whom I greet so joyfully each time I return to visit (which I do at least twice a year). She was the tech who mostly did the night room inspections, and I blamed her mightily for my chronic sleep disruption. I resented the excessively early mornings and approached them with a hard-done-by attitude. I wrote Irma up repeatedly for talking too loudly, hollering from one room to the next, which I found rude and disruptive. While allegedly working on a resentment-forgiveness meditation practice, I more than once snuck in forbidden naps. There was also the high-stakes "Affair of the Teabag." Each meal, clients are provided one hot beverage, either decaf coffee or herbal tea. I had selected coffee, but when Trey, that hard-nosed tech at Shades and unfortunately (I thought) the spouse of my case manager, happened to look away just as I passed the teabags, my hand reached out, grabbed one, and stuffed it in my pocket. I sat down with a smirk on my face, ate my meal, drank my decaf coffee, and returned my dishes to the kitchen. I walked away, a lift in my step. I didn't have a mug. I didn't have access to hot water. *But by God, I had a teabag.*

I continued to think about my precious contraband. And before I knew it, during a long quiet spell during a Twelve Step meeting I attended but did not qualify for, and thus at which I did not share, I said I had something on my mind and asked if I might share. The group conscience voted yes, and I proceeded to tell my teabag story.

The most wonderful, remarkable thing happened. Hearing it out loud, I was struck by the absurdity of my actions and rationalizing, and I began to laugh. Others laughed, too—with me, not at me—and before I knew it, I was crying, I was laughing so hard. It was the first time I had laughed in treatment, the first time I'd had fun. Something inside me was beginning to change. My peers told me they could see it!

I had another breakthrough: After photocopying my work for my case manager, I snuck in a fax to my housekeeper, asking her to send me more Varsity fountain pens, for I was almost out and mailing a note would take too long, because, dang it, I want what I want, when I want it. I finished my fax with a postscript: "Do not fax me back. I am not supposed to be using this machine." I did not know the fax was set to provide a miniature copy as confirmation of a successful transmission until Kristen, my case manager, simply handed me the paper trail.

It was a turning point in my time at Shades, for I began to see what they were doing and how they worked. I was so afraid I was going to be in superscary trouble, maybe secret double probation, when Kristen showed it to me, but all she did was lay it on the table where I worked on the porch and walk away. I began to realize she was simply reflecting my actions back to me. I realized she had been so simple, so direct; she had not shamed me. Thus began a rapid evaluation with a new perspective: No one had ever shamed me at Shades. When I had felt shame, it was the core shame that had been inside of me when I walked in the door. I began to accept that I had been so ashamed of my shame, I could never name "shame" as what I felt during a feelings check. I also saw that the treatment team was both encouraging and leaving me to a process, a journey, that only I could undertake, in a place where it was finally safe to do so. It made perfect sense to me when Tennie later said, "Ashley, you know what we are really treating at Shades, don't you? The big 'C.' " I was about to guess, "Codependency?" when she said, "Control." Shades of Hope took everything out of my control: what time I went to sleep, when I woke up, what I ate and how much (including slices of lemon and the temperature of my water), my access to the phone, and when, who, and how many calls I made. There was no computer, no music, and no TV, and my self-soothing routines and practices, both nurturing and harmful, were taken away. I sat there, literally, for forty-two days, everything out of my control, so I could feel the emotions I had worked so very, very hard all my life to avoid and, if that wasn't possible, control. It was the greatest gift anyone ever gave me, and in spite of the considerable agony I was in for much of it, I would do it again in a heartbeat. The rewards are worth it. I used to say that the way I now sleep like a baby every night of my life, made it worth the price of admission. But the gifts and promises of recovery are so rich in my life, the abundance and joy so great, that wonderful sleep is but a minor chord in a great symphony of healing and joy.

In the months before I ended up at Shades of Hope, my thinking about my service work was alarming. Each morning as I woke up, a single anguished thought would rush into my awareness: 28,000 children will starve to death today. I forced myself to trace the trajectory of their deaths, from hunger to malnutrition to stunted growth to the body cannibalizing itself to wasting of flesh and organs to expiring, knowing it is a long, slow, painful deterioration. I would think about a mother, if she were still alive, witnessing the decay of her child, helpless to stop it. Times 28,000. I would think about the Pulitzer Prize–winning photograph, "The Vulture," of a hunkered child, teetering mere breaths before she will topple over and die, a vulture patiently waiting for her carcass. I would think about how the photographer, haunted, would later commit suicide. I would panic. I would think: I have to sell the farm. I have to move to a refugee camp. I have to give up my whole life as I have known it to be useful to any degree, to take responsibility for the lives of those 28,000 children. They died yesterday. More will die tomorrow. This was all before my feet had hit the floor. Ultimately, I mobilized myself with excoriating thoughts about my own pointless ineffectuality. I would rage at myself to create some kick-start in my brain chemistry that would allow me to get out of bed and drag myself through another morning. I was hitting bottom, and I had no idea. I just thought I cared a lot about the world.

At Shades, we were able to talk about the incredible all-or-nothing, black-or-white nature of my distorted thinking, the abject lack of moderation. The counselors and my peers helped me believe I actually can care—deeply, passionately—and that there is only so much I can do, and even that, in spite of good intentions and energetic motivation, I will do it imperfectly. They constantly admonished me to seek God's will for my life, not my own, even if my own will is that today, 28,00 children will not die of starvation. They asked me to see myself as a small cog in a great whole, or, less poetically but no less helpfully, as in a Hula-Hoop. I can only control what is inside my Hula-Hoop, and having obsessive thoughts about great forces and processes outside my Hula-Hoop actually render me useless within the only domain in which I do have the chance to be effective. They also challenged me about my alleged belief that when I change myself, I change the world, that when I take responsibility for myself and my healing, I am effecting ineffable change on a spiritual level that I may not be able to see, but is no less real.

A woman came in for treatment while I was there who had been, among other things, an injecting drug user, and in her circle of addicts, it was common for both men and women to trade sex for drugs. Now clean and sober, as well as abstinent from her eating disorder, her thoughts turned to how her high-risk behavior had possibly exposed her to HIV. During group, I was asked about my international service work, and I was momentarily lost. I had not, apart from the conversations about my all-or-nothing thinking, which had been very inwardly focused examinations of the innermost workings of my psyche, thought about the work itself. I was cautious, as I did not want to inadvertently abandon my treatment process, and mentally "go away," or let my focus stray back to the outside world, which I would be rejoining soon enough. I had come to believe that in many ways, Shades of Hope represented the real world: A place where the truth is told, the Self is sacred, and I wanted to absorb as much of this great reality as I could, ensconce myself in it so that I could have it firmly embedded in my consciousness before I went back to the distractions, the hyper marketplace, the love song codependency, damaging belief systems that can make up daily life in America. So I haltingly began talking a little about some of my work, especially, obviously, HIV prevention. Perhaps it was the first moment that I was able to bring my recovery and new personal skills to the domain of service work. I shared my experience, insights, and hope around HIV testing, how to handle results (positive or negative), healthy behavior change, and carrying the message to other vulnerable people. The woman listened gratefully, fearfully, and cried when she asked me to go with her while she was tested. I did. She cried again when she was given her results, which she had asked to hear in group. She was negative.

~ ~ ~

Eventually, I began to sleep again. It wasn't nearly enough, but I did sleep for six and seven hours at a time. Once, oh, blessedly once, I was actually fully rested! I was moved into a smaller room, and I began to feel less like a misfit lost child. I remember taking one day off from my work the entire time I was there. When I was going to bed, I felt really good about myself and the choice I had made to give myself a break for one day. I didn't need anyone's approval, permission, or forgiveness. I felt zero need to explain, justify, or convince anyone. I was starting to develop some healthy, autonomous boundaries and self-esteem. Dario says that around this time, he, too, could tell I was improving; something about my letters told him so. It always makes me cry, I feel that beautiful joy-filled pain when he describes that moment. Thank you, God!

We had been writing lots of letters, and I phoned him twice a week once I was off that "no talk" assignment. Once, I noticed I was unobserved and told him I could talk longer, but he would not break the rules with me. He's a good man, my husband, and he assumed the rules were there for a reason and would contribute to our welfare somehow. He was right.

I began to look forward to seeing him and the others who would be attending my very own family week. I had completed the bulk of my written work, which was now bulging in two large three-ring binders. I was saying affirmations after meals with confidence and ease. I came forward to do my work in group, sometimes fearfully, but trusting there were gifts for me on the other side. When challenged about things I hadn't looked at or worked on yet, I remained open-minded, even though that shame would crop back up. Most important, I trusted the staff and knew that in their expert hands, guided by a Higher Power that loves me, interesting and great things could happen.

The Monday of my family week, on my way to six thirty a.m. yoga, I approached the same crossroads I had studied during that lonely lunch on my first Saturday at Shades of Hope. That day, I had contemplated walking out of treatment, seeing how far my two feet could carry me from this bewildering place and these crushing emotions. This day, as I stood in the intersection, I found myself turning in a circle, arms flung open, head thrown back in joy, then dropping to my knees in wonder, awe, in gratitude. It was April 13, 2006, and the full moon, known as the pink moon (and it was!), was on the horizon directly to my right, at one end of the country road, and the sun was rising directly to my left, at the other end. I was held between them, my grandmother the moon, my grandfather the sun, an awesome moment of balance, majesty, and power. Each crawled imperceptibly in its path, and time stood still. I knew I was loved, and I knew I was going to be okay. I knew all was well. I ran into yoga, but no one else had seen this remarkable sight. It seemed to be a gift just for me. When I would later research the April full moon, I was unsurprised to read it would be the brightest moon of the entire year.

~ ~ ~

After breakfast, I sat in a rocking chair on the front porch and watched my husband's rental car pull into the group room parking lot across the street—something I would do every single time he drove onto the campus during my family week. It was so strange and exhilarating to see him in this setting! When he crossed the threshold of Shades of Hope, we grabbed each other in what is still the best, most memorable hug of my entire life. We wrapped our arms around each other, buried our faces in each other's necks, and did not let go for a very long time. I could feel the fullness of his emotion quivering in his chest. Eventually, I kissed his beautiful face, held his precious hands, and after introducing him to my friends who had been such faithful companions to me on this incredible journey, we ran to the swing under an especially fine oak tree, where I had often read his letters after lunch, and wrapped ourselves around each other. Apparently, such intense physical warmth was outside the rules, but members of the treatment team, able to see us from the windows of their staff room, were deeply moved and let us be. They still talk about it, in fact, and tears still come to my eyes when I remember it.

At nine thirty sharp, we disentangled and looked at each other (we'd be on "no talk" the rest of the week, until my outing on Friday), and then Dario walked to the group room. I returned to the center, picked up my now well-worn tote bag, took a deep breath, gathered up my courage, and crossed the street to face my family with truth and hope.

The morning was identical to every Monday in a family week. I enjoyed the welcomes, outlay of facts, ground rules, and explanation of the program being done on *my* behalf. I felt important in my family for perhaps the first time in my life. This week, these lessons, this work, was about *me*.

Oh, I had been the center of attention before, but not like this, not when it was about my reality growing up, how I had been affected and impacted, without someone either hijacking the story, because they'd had it worse, or trying to minimize or deny it or tell me I really needed to just get over it. I knew I could neither predict nor control how it would go, how folks would react, but I would give myself the dignity of my process, and I knew there were miracles waiting for me, in spite of and no matter what others would do with these five days.

Ironically, my dad—the one who had bravely crowed, "Anything for my girls," when he attended Sister's family week—and I had a near miss on that Monday. Because he had attended before, he had felt he did not need to be there for the Monday morning group. The treatment team had been firm and clear: You come for the entire thing. This is Ashley's. It is similar . . . and different. He walked in rather late, and a scandal erupted. The treatment team was not amused. They read him the riot act and told me their suggestion was that he leave and not be permitted to participate given his apparent unwillingness to respect the center's policies. I plummeted into my helpless Lost Child place, registering how quickly I could still free-fall through that trapdoor. I thought about my choices, and while I knew and was scared of that part of my dad that was "terminally unique" and did not follow rules (the "hip, slick, and cool" syndrome), I also knew this week could be phenomenally powerful in helping us turn around our relationship. I spoke up and said I wanted him to stay. I was proud of myself for taking charge of what my week would look like, and we settled down to business.

Reading my written work was a pivotal component of my family week. To be given the space, with advocates present who would help protect me and others, to share my childhood truth was simultaneously terrifying and liberating. Giving voice to my reality, such a powerful theme in feminism, was the empowering part. The scary part was that I had to accept, and yet take the risk anyway, that some people who were listening might never be safe or healthy and therefore might never be able to regard my story for what it was: my story, something to which we each inherently had a God given right. I knew that particular parts of the pain I was in growing up, and the thoughts and behavior born of that pain, would be ridiculed, rejected, pathologized, and held against me, maybe until the day I died. Unfortunately, I was right: Certain things I said were isolated and thrown back at me in the years since that day. But I do not regret standing up and saying, "*This is what it was like for me.*" I owed that to the small child I had been, for whom I am now responsible, whose advocate I am and must continue to be. A lot of people weren't there for me while I was growing up, but by God, I am here for myself now. Not at the expense of others, mind you: Reading such work is but one stage of family of origin work. It's not about staying stuck in it. It's about having my story straight, so I can genuinely, finally arrive at the place where I can say, "That was then, this is now. So what? Now what?" But believe me, there are no shortcuts to arriving at this place. I had tried them all. They do not work. They can seem an easier, softer way, but in fact they are not.

My sculpt was another intense and revealing experience. The family was re-created, with obvious similarities to how it appeared to my sister, but it was actually also very different. Siblings often have vastly incongruent experiences growing up, as if they are being raised in different families. I asked my family members to place themselves in positions that reflected aspects of their relationships as I perceived them. I asked people to say the words, express the attitudes, beliefs, and emotions with which I was raised—including those horrible incessant streams of verbal abuse. When the picture that I experienced growing up was arranged, I was asked to place my small self in the scene. Where would I be? What would I be doing? What would I be feeling?

I did something I had never seen anyone else do in the now numerous family weeks I had witnessed, and I did it instinctively and quickly. It required not one iota of thought. I turned away, walked very fast, and I exited the circle of the sculpt, the staff, and all my peers and almost went out the door. There were about forty of us altogether, and I went as far away from everyone as I could while remaining in the room. I lay down on the floor, curled in a ball, put my left thumb in my mouth, and began to sob.

Yes. That is *exactly* what it felt like for me, growing up in my family.

Tennie, with her fierce and gentle brilliance, with her gifted expertise born of decades of this kind of therapy, began to work with me while in this state of regression. I couldn't believe it when someone put a black cape over me to represent the depression that had both smothered and strangely kept me safe growing up. I had seen this done with other clients, but I was paralyzed when the cape was placed over me to represent my very own disease. Tennie continued to work with me, and together we told the story of my childhood visually, viscerally. Soon, we reached the crucial turning point, the "That was then, this is now. So what. Now what?" I began to use my empowered adult voice and claim my recovery, my future, free from depression and codependency. I robustly detailed what my solution is today, itemizing the kit of spiritual tools that Shades of Hope had placed at my feet and how I was going to use them. But one oddity remained: I was still on the floor. Tennie was pushing me very hard, challenging me. I was racking my brain, going through every single thing I had learned in my six weeks in treatment: my relationship with my Higher Power, taking the steps, writing with my nondominant hand—I cycled through all my hard word. But I was still missing something, and that woman would not let up.

Finally, Tennie said, "People, Ashley! People! We need other people to recover! God lives in and speaks to us through our healthy interdependence with others. We experience God through *relationships*."

Oh. People. I whimpered and could feel the lonely Lost Child place open up in me again. "I'd really prefer to recover without people, if you don't mind," I said.

"We cannot recover alone, Ashley."

Okay, I get it, you old bat! I thought, and I picked myself up off the floor, shucked off that wretched black cape, and smiled at this great woman who pushed me so hard and gave me so much.

My eyes now wide open, I saw the looks on my family's faces. They were absolutely devastated. Some had physically cowered, covering their heads, they were so disturbed to see the distress I had been in for the whole of my growing up. Perhaps the main new thing that emerged that day is that it was exceedingly, sadly clear that to a very large extent, they had had absolutely *no* idea what family life had been like for me growing up, so absorbed had they been in their own pain, dramas, addictions, and obsessions.

Tennie instructed me to pick out some people with whom I felt safe and to ask them to join me. First I asked my peers, but soon I was saying family names while firmly instructing them to treat one another with kindness, respect, and dignity in my presence and letting them know I would no longer tolerate unacceptable or abusive behavior. Best, I knew now that I meant it, how to detach with love, take care of myself, and maintain this healthy boundary! I placed those next to me with whom I felt most comfortable and cautiously expanded the circle to include everyone. In this way, we were sitting on the floor when something miraculous indeed happened—something I had thought impossible.

My dad took my mother's hand. (Okay, that in and of itself is like from outer space.) Next, he opened his mouth. Then he began to offer his heartfelt amends. He took full responsibility for himself, spanning the decades they had known each other, and with humility, tenderness, and unmistakable culpability, cleaned up the wreckage of his past.

From that harrowing afternoon in the apartment in Lexington exactly twenty years ago, when he told me he was not my sister's biological father, when I knew beyond a shadow of doubt that my family was condemned to irredeemable hopelessness . . . to this. It was only Wednesday of my family week, and the miracles were rolling.

Dad and I still talk about that moment. He says that in it, everything was lifted from him: every resentment, every grief, every urge to get even. But the mercy was not confined to the moment; it has deepened and expanded. He shares about being given great gifts of compassion and empathy for my mother, a new ability to consider life from her point of view and to contemplate how events, such as her own upbringing and the events of 1963 and 1964, affected her.

This recovery thing works, if you work at it.

Not everyone, however, was able to participate on such a deeply positive level, and one family member did not return. The staff requests that all participants not drink alcohol or take drugs—including prescription drugs unless absolutely necessary—during family week. And in spite of the constant reminders from staff to "trust the process, don't quit before your miracle" and steady encouragement to see my work as something that I had a right to, a necessary stage of my own catharsis and healing, they couldn't hang. Sadly, I'm told they are one of only two family members ever to bail on the family week process in Shades of Hope's twenty-five-year history. Maybe my family is just a bit terminal after all. But as Tennie says, as long as they are sucking air, there is always hope. I truly believed what I was being taught: that no situation was hopeless (although at times I might feel hopeless), that there was no difficulty too great to be lessened, and that it was possible for me to find contentment and even happiness no matter how my various loved ones were behaving. And so I took my focus off the disappointment of this loved one's behavior, dealt with my feelings in a healthy way, and proceeded with my own recovery. Imagine, then, how delighted I was recently when this person called and told me they have a year's sobriety in Alcoholics Anonymous.

Thursday involved more deep work and processing, including a potent chance to offer direct statements about things that needed to improve in different relationships and forgiveness processes. The work was not uniformly smooth. Naturally, the many family dynamics were pinging wildly off the walls. Once, I sank into despair as a couple bickered nastily about an incident they'd had buying materials to make the collages they had been assigned. After twenty minutes, Erica looked at me and asked, "How much more of your family week are you going to let them hijack?" I used my voice and asked them to settle their beef later, reminded them and me that this group was about my recovery, our time was limited, and we needed to move on. But there were also sublime moments of incredible vulnerability and tenderness, such as when my dad cried so hard that he doubled over, once he had offered and I had accepted his amends for having "divorced" me on Winchester Avenue all those years before.

On Friday, I sat knee to knee with loved ones while they each told me five things each one "liked and loved" about me. My God, after having each pitched in seemingly inedible and rotten ingredients, we were actually partaking of that corny stew that had simmered and boiled all week, sharing in a rich meal love, laughter, and fellowship.

I kept the papers on which, in easily recognizable handwriting, were itemized some things each one liked and loved about me. What a far cry this "inventory" is from the old letters, faxes, and interminable voice mails they used to send me! They are gems that consecrate special moments, memories, and connections I share with my loved ones, positive aspects upon which to build with those who also choose to recover. What they describe about me runs the gamut from the way I dance as though no one is watching, to my smile, to the way I make a mess when I cook, to my casual indifference about my appearance, to how beautifully I keep my home and entertain, and my zeal for Kentucky basketball, and the way I smell like violets just as Mamaw did. But one poignant theme repeats and is mentioned by everyone who was present: "Your strong sense of right and wrong; the way you help people; your service work; your ability to still love; your empowerment of others; your commitment to fairness; your unbreakable spirit; your integrity; your respect for your fellow men and women on this journey; the strength of your convictions; your fearlessness in advocating on behalf of others; the way you embrace those who are sick; the way you fight for those who have nothing; the way you hold orphans."

Yeah. I like and love that about me, too.

~ ~ ~

For my outing, we had lunch at a beautiful local café. It was my first time off the Shades of Hope property in more than a month. As Dario and I took a nap later, I listened, as I was falling asleep, to the everyday sounds of this beautiful and heartbreaking world: the sound of my husband breathing; a family checking into an adjoining room, the distant sound of traffic, a dog barking. Nothing in the world was different, but I sure was.

I spent my last week at Shades debriefing from my family week, completing follow-up assignments. This included dealing with a newly revealed round of childhood incest. There wasn't time to unpack it completely, and take advantage of the resources Shades offers for survivors, but we made a good start.

I had considerable codependency with a family member who attended family week; an important, valuable relationship, but one I had idealized, yet others could see was troubled and strained. During one summer of my early adolescence, when I had stayed with her, her husband had molested me. In finally having the courage to share the details with someone, I learned the chillingly accurate term, "grooming," as well as the typical stages and when I heard it, the visceral feelings of repugnance and shame confirmed that was indeed what this trusted adult man had done:

groomed me, to set up the pattern of sexual abuse in such a way that I would be compliant and even flattered. First, he began by hanging out with me when I watched late-night TV after everyone else went to bed (the isolating phase). During that time, he sat a little too close to me on the sofa, telling little jokes that created our own insider relationship, talking just a little bad about others but building me up to gain my trust and confidence, initiating the secrecy phase. During the day, just before others entered a room, or after they left, he would give me a wink, a lingering touch on the arm, doing things to "invest" in our "special" relationship—the desensitizing to inappropriateness phase. He exploited my vulnerabilities and neediness for attention and validation. He would quickly volunteer to drive me wherever I needed to go. He took me to special places, involving me in his life, saying his wife wasn't interested, and how much he appreciated me (the "our relationship is unique and special" phase). Soon, he made the relationship sexual. When we were alone in the house he came into my guest room at every opportunity. I was so slow in realizing this had been a classic, highly abusive pattern of incest committed by a scheming and clever sexual predator because in his very success as a perpetrator, he convinced me we were having an affair. He insidiously made me believe that I wanted the relationship, even though it revolted and scared the hell out of me. In what could have been a disastrous turning point in my life, my family member and he, aware of my dubious living conditions at home, briefly discussed taking custody of me, having me live with them for a school year. Oh, my god, I shudder to think how much further the molestation would have gone, how much worse it could have been. Even though my next school year was a typically difficult one, I think, *But for the grace of God go I.*

Even after I left that house, the man continued to write me, and begged me to write him letters in return, giving me his friend's address to which I could send them without my family member knowing. Completely freaked out, I told one of my parents about it, and their response was, "Well, is he your boyfriend?" I managed to avoid him and his attempts to contact me, and then I proceeded never to talk about it. This was one of the many reasons why my after-care plan included a commitment to ongoing trauma, adult child, and abuse survivor work.

I moved on to the other end of the treatment exercises, which, for me, included making a collage of what life had looked like as the depressed Lost Child in my family, and in recovery, what my role in the family might look like. I created my after-care plan and processed it with staff and peers. My minimum commitment to myself was to spend time every day with other recovering people, to read recovery literature every morning with my prayer and meditation practice, to apply the principles and slogans of recovery in all my affairs, to reach out to others on this journey by phone, and to give away what had been given to me so freely. "We cannot keep what we have, unless we give it away," Shades stresses. I also committed to do an intensive six-day family-of-origin, and survivor-abuse and trauma workshop every calendar year, to continue the deeply healing process of "uncovering, discovering, and discarding." I made a promise that were I ever to relapse, I would return to inpatient treatment. Simply put, I committed to continue to go to any lengths for my recovery, to clean house, trust God, and help others.

Perhaps most saliently, I wrote a goodbye letter to depression. I had witnessed other clients reading powerful goodbye letters to diseases they had come into treatment not even knowing they had, or denying had been killing them. The work had been exhilarating merely to witness, and so it was perhaps this assignment more than any other that let me know I was completing something, dying to an old way of being, being born into a new life of freedom. I was moved and surprised by the words that effortlessly flowed from my pen. It was an ode, a farewell, a thank you letter, and most important, a triumphant statement of "good riddance." It said, in part:

Dear Depression,

You have, indeed, been dear to me. You were my way of life, and such a natural part of my existence, I hadn't even known you were smothering me, so completely and thoroughly were you my companion.

I remember night after night of lying in bed, and you coming to me in the form of those dark, negative thoughts, and how I'd collect them, each one a precious chink in my armor. I'd draw those thoughts to me, turning them carefully into the poisonous refrain, and when they settled deeply enough in my brain, and the much-needed chemical relief came, I'd let it evaporate. Another one would instantly materialize, much like the subsequent waves in the ocean—the tide draws the form back into the sea, where another has been simultaneously prepared. And so these thoughts would collect relentlessly until I got what I needed—proof I was wrong, proof I was unloved, proof everyone chose the words and actions they did to disregard me, their desire to let my needs go unacknowledged and unmet an indictment of my very existence being wrong. I could review the day with your devious help and reframe it to my most severe disadvantage.

The effects of this were numerous. I could make sense of moments earlier I had not understood. I could pull into the cocoon of my bed and avoid the dangerous man whom you lied about to me, telling me he had all the power to hurt and save me. I could connect the thoughts within my body and freeze, go idle, go mute—oh, the pall you cast on my solar plexus! You could trap with your vicious cycles of thoughts, the endless, rampant loops that somehow never became tedious, in spite of the same hurt being replayed ad infinitum. I could watch the reruns; speak the words in my head, and get the same hit of worthlessness and despair, over and over and over.

Living with you has been torture. My resiliency has tried with poignant courage to kick your ass out of my body, and such wholesome tactics, craving a cup of tea to set the tone for my day, another person's love to refute your antic in my soul.

It was said here at Shades you were my first love. What a peculiar thought. You did isolate me, like a greedy lover, you distracted, soothed, and absorbed me totally. How very odd.

But all that is over now. I have a husband, a Dad, and a Pop. They aren't perfect, but they're mine, and I've learned I can be mad at people and still love them—that was perhaps the sharpest double-edged sword of all your lies. I needed to protect myself, but I also needed to trust. You kept me from doing that. You had me convinced that anger excluded love, both in me and in others.

Which has been worse? Assuming what I'd received was tainted and fraudulent, or not giving at all, especially to my mother?

But now I have a plan, and I have other thoughts with which to replace you. Where you once took up residence, affirmations now live. Where you fed my tissue and cells and immune system with toxic messages of self-hatred, self-acceptance now ripples and shines. Where you dropped heavy stones in my heart or put the elephant on my chest, I now have the gentle presence of God as I surrender.

Where you told me I was worthless and unlovable and that all was hopeless, I have recovery and Steps and fellowship. Where you told me there was hatred and dysfunction, there are miracles and reconciliation.

Where I once had only you, my beloved friend, I now have Hope.
And so to you, loyal depression, I bid farewell. Rest in peace.

I do not give you permission to move on. I do not send you to another being. I bid you transform, composted by Mother Earth, dispersed by the universe, energy neither created nor destroyed, but transformed from negative to positive, shadow into light. I harness the energy, the lesson, the benefits of the journey, to the betterment of all and the harm of none.

I am free.

~ ~ ~

In the Dallas airport, I bought a large hot cup of jasmine tea and savored every sip. I held my cell phone and giggled while sending texts, laughing equally at how very little I had missed while secluded from the world. I accepted without bargaining my business class seat, and felt my Higher Power reward me for accepting life on life's terms when I was upgraded to first class without having asked. On Dario's bus, I sprawled legs out and arms akimbo on the bed, an enormous smile on my face, feeling free, joyful, empowered.

"What's that yoga pose called?" he asked, amused by me.

"Goddess," I said without missing a beat.

I taped a Shades of Hope pass to the wall on my side of the bed, on which I wrote out permission to myself to sleep late for the first time in forty-eight days. Near the racetrack where Dario was competing that weekend, I found a dilapidated but wonderfully cheerful old clubhouse where recovering folks gathered, and I visited with them every day, enjoying my new cohorts enormously. I practiced making "reach out" phone calls and bringing into my daily life (and especially my relationships) the solution, the practical plan of action, and the spiritual principles I had been taught.

Back at home, I was grateful to see the redbud trees were still in bloom, I hadn't missed the dogwoods, and plenty of my daffodils were still showing their happy yellow trumpets. I happily reunited with our animals, whom I had not even missed, so focused on and committed to the task at hand had I been, and I settled into my beautiful new way of life. Soon, I was ready to reengage with the wider world and what gave my life such purpose and meaning: service work. I was eager to see how what I had learned about myself, and the new tools with which I was empowered, would show up in this part of my life. Having finally become an advocate for the beautiful little girl who lived inside of me and who needed a healthy adult on her side, I predicted I would now feel even better equipped to advocate on behalf of others with more usefulness, compassion, and integrity.

Chapter 16

PROJECT LIFE

Kate, Salma, and me at one of our many press conferences.

Not enjoyment, and not sorrow,
Is our destined end or way;
But to act, that each tomorrow
Find us farther than today.

—*H. W. LONGFELLOW*, "A Psalm of Life"

*A*fter a very late arrival in Guatemala City, I woke up early to dash out of bed straight to a waiting helicopter. It was a Eurocopter, the same kind that Dario flies, and I was pleased with how familiar and comfortable it felt to jump in, use the five-point restraint, and grab my headset. Our destination was Coatepeque, a small city in southwestern Guatemala, near the Mexican border, where we would be meeting a military escort to accompany us to a clinic. I've always been grateful for governmental cooperation and protection, which supplements Papa Jack's service, and I knew that the need here was non-negotiable. In the aftermath of decades of civil war, where two hundred thousand civilians died, mainly at the hands of U.S.–backed military dictators and their death squads, Guatemala is now a democracy, but it is also one of the poorest countries in the hemisphere, with 75 percent of the population living below the poverty line and a dangerous, heavily armed postconflict zone. We had been instructed not to travel long distances by road, even in broad daylight. I was grateful that a wealthy supporter had donated the use of his helicopter, while I internally saluted and admired the humanitarian and aid workers who regularly make perilous overland journeys without protection, risking their lives to be of service. It isn't fair I have such assistance, and they do not. I would be meeting two such intrepid and unsung heroes at the end of this flight.

As we flew over sharp volcanic peaks and hillsides checkered with bright green coffee plantations and pastures, I pulled my eyes away from the stunning scenery to write for a while with my nondominant hand. I'd been up a good bit of the night with anxiety, and I needed to process a lot of emotion. Ever since I left Shades of Hope five weeks earlier, I had faithfully followed the after-care plan that included fellowshipping with other recovering folks, morning meditation, recovery and inspirational readings, and other exercises—even when I had to do them in the backseats of cars or on an aircraft. I realized now that I was freeing a lot of fear about the feelings that would inevitably come up on this trip, as I ventured into areas of our global reality that can be agonizing to acknowledge and witness. On previous trips I had felt such pain; I wondered if I would now feel even more.

It would have been wonderful if six weeks in treatment could have magically erased all my difficulties, but it doesn't work that way. Recovery is a process, lived one day at a time as a reprieve, not a "cure." It does not promise me perpetual, emotional equanimity (what sort of life would that be, anyhow?). It does guarantee me a design for living that works under all conditions, a process I can count on always, and healthy ways to feel all my feelings safely. The lived effects of abuse and trauma do not vanish overnight, and neither do the coping behaviors developed over decades in an attempt to manage such deep wounding. I had already noticed that a few of my old stress-induced cleaning habits had reemerged during my flight south. At least now I could do a spot check of my behavior and self-correct.

I was intrigued, curious, and open to observing the changes in me, witnessing my new self in the context of my work. My three previous activism journeys were fixed points, frames of reference against which I could compare how I now functioned and responded. I didn't expect to be invulnerable; I most certainly wouldn't even want to be impervious. I did want my turn at this powerful work in such a way, as Mother Teresa said, that still allows me to have a smile on my face. I was already feeling more joy in my work than ever before. Interestingly, the quote in one of my devotionals today was from Ralph Waldo Emerson: "People only see what they are prepared to see." In spite of my fear, I chose to be prepared.

I knew I would need all my tools on this trip, which promised to be every bit as challenging as the previous ones. As always, I would be visiting the at-risk, vulnerable populations, situated mostly in slums, brothels, and hospices. In the spring of 2006, there were an estimated four hundred thousand HIV/AIDS infections in Central America. Our goal was to prevent an explosion of new cases, understanding that migration patterns put large numbers across borders at risk of contracting HIV. In Guatemala, a key aspect of the challenge was cracking a taboo against condom use by men who thought it was somehow unmanly to use protection. This dangerous belief was reinforced by the Roman Catholic Church, to which 60 percent of Guatemalans belong, which officially condemns all "artificial" and modern forms of family planning, including condoms. Here and throughout Central America, the Catholic hierarchy is entwined with a macho culture that enforces gender inequality and severely constrains a woman's reproductive autonomy. But, as I was about to witness, there are outposts of the Church, far removed from the decision makers in Rome, on the front lines of the battle against AIDS and the impoverished conditions that facilitate its spread.

~ ~ ~

Our military escort was waiting as our helicopter landed in a cow pasture on the edge of the town of Coatepeque. So were two Maryknoll nuns, Sisters Dee and Marlene, who were waving wildly and looking so sweet and gentle standing there next to soldiers in camo fatigues with automatic rifles slung over their shoulders. But it turns out they are indeed warriors as fierce as any soldiers in a munitions army. Their weapons are love, compassion, service, devotion, hope, and faith, and I believe they are mightier. I have to. My own hope and sanity depend on it.

Coatepeque is a border town on Highway 1, which runs along the Pacific Coast of Central America, a major trade and smuggling route. Along with the traffic comes HIV, which is prevalent here in much higher percentages than in other parts of Guatemala. Sisters Dee and Marlene run Proyecto Vida (Project Life), a comprehensive care, testing, and prevention program in a region with very scarce services for people with HIV/AIDS.

Sister Dee, born Delia Marie Smith in Lancaster, England, is a stout, energetic woman with close-cropped red hair and a gentle, high-pitched voice. No wimples and habits for this nun; she wore stud earrings and was dressed in a T-shirt and slacks as she showed us around the facilities. It was a bare-bones operation in a run-down building in a town where the electricity goes off at least once a week. The narrow hallways were dark for a while this morning, but the staff was sunny and upbeat—all HIV-positive women who came to the sisters for care and stayed on to help. Sister Marlene, wearing a plain cotton skirt, was more reserved and stayed in the background during the tour, but she joined us when I yet again exploited the opportunity to ask beautiful, devout people to pray with me (one of my selfish trademarks!). Sister Dee started us off with a simple, gorgeous meditation about the nature of our work, reminding me that prayer doesn't have to be verbally acrobatic. It's just chatting with the God of our understanding. She said, simply, we are women gathered here to help people living with HIV, and indeed, that is what Proyecto Vida is all about.

She and Sister Marlene had more than seventy years between them with the Maryknolls, an order for which I have the utmost admiration. The Maryknolls' mission takes them to some of the most precarious and forgotten locations, where they minister to the poorest and most rejected people on earth, regardless of their faith. The saintly Father Michael, whom I met in the Buddhist AIDS hospice in Thailand, is a Maryknoll. And, as I remembered from my days as a college campus activist, two Maryknoll nuns were among four Catholic missionaries who were raped and murdered by a death squad in El Salvador in 1980 as a warning to those who would advocate for the poor. During the civil wars in El Salvador, Guatemala, and Nicaragua, Catholic priests and nuns were often persecuted for siding with the people in the struggle for human rights and economic justice. Another exceedingly blatant attack occurred when the archbishop of San Salvador, Óscar Romero, was gunned down by an assassin while serving mass in his chapel.

Sadly, the prelate who later stepped into Romero's position represented a far more conservative faction in the Church. I had met with Archbishop Fernando Sáenz Lacalle during a quick trip I had made to a regional AIDS conference in El Salvador in November 2005 to try to open a dialogue about the Church's stance on prevention. He was cordial, but it was clear that his ears were firmly closed to any discussion about reproductive health. He even said during the meeting that he thought women used abortion as birth control. He also held to the hard line that Rome had adopted against condom use, even to prevent HIV infection. I was unsurprised, given the Vatican official who in 2003 had said something equally ridiculous: that HIV can pass through condoms. Thank goodness that in 2010, Pope Benedict XVI said condoms are justifiable in limited cases, in order to prevent AIDS. A modest statement based on the public health reality, but quite revolutionary from the Vatican's previous hard-line stance.

I couldn't help but contrast the rigidity of the Salvadoran archbishop with the loving pragmatism of these luminous Maryknoll nuns. Sisters

Dee and Marlene told me that they believed that in each person, dignity inheres, and that dignity entitles them to bodily, sexual, and reproductive autonomy. Proyecto Vida provides condom education with PSI's help. Whether or not they want people to use them, the nuns believe that people have the right to know how to protect themselves and they, and they alone, without interference from a patriarchal superstructure, must be empowered to make that choice.

The mission of the Maryknoll sisters is simply "to make God's love visible." I saw their work in action in the women who worked for Proyecto Vida, such as Luz Imelda Lucas. Luz had lost an infant to AIDS, as well as her husband, who had infected them. She was brought back from the brink of death with antiretroviral medication made available by Doctors Without Borders. Now, she worked as a nutritionist. She told me her service to other vulnerable women filled the void these losses had created. I was also introduced to a married couple, both of them HIV-positive, whose bittersweet story was heartrending. Melchor and Catalina had come to the clinic to deliver their second child by cesarean section in order to protect it from contracting HIV in childbirth. Their first baby, delivered naturally, had died of AIDS. As with many couples, it took the death of a child to alert them to the fact that they were HIV-positive.

Melchor, a compactly built man with sun-leathered skin, told me he became infected when he lived in Guatemala City and ran with a fast crowd. Even though many of his friends were becoming sick, he had never been taught how one contracted HIV and had no idea how to recognize its symptoms. When his own health started to fail, he thought his fevers were caused by colds. And so, unknowingly, he brought the virus back home to his young wife. She was sitting quietly next to him as he spoke, great with child and wiping her face with a handkerchief, in palpable fear of the impending procedure. I leaned gently toward her and said, "Don't worry. I was delivered by C-section and I turned out okay." That brought a small smile to her lips. She was also reassured that her baby would be much safer. A study in Guatemala has shown that while nearly half of babies born to HIV-positive mothers are infected with the virus, with interventions such as antiretroviral drug treatment and C-sections, the risk of transmission is reduced to less than 8 percent.

Melchor told me that his own mother had died when he was nine days old, and he treasured his wife, that he'd protect her with his life and would never leave her, in sickness, health, good times, hard times, you name it. . . . He was obviously a kind man, and he was going to be a wonderful father. He testified to the toll AIDS has taken on men as well as women in poor countries. Men see themselves as protectors, but they are helpless to keep their families safe from AIDS if they don't have the knowledge to do so. Men as well as women need to be empowered with the tools to fight the pandemic.

I told my new friend that I had an appointment to meet the president of Guatemala tomorrow to discuss HIV/AIDS. When I asked what message he'd have me give the president, Melchor spoke with vigor about the urgent need for sex education at home and in schools. His spiel was as articulate as any printed NGO material I'd ever seen. I told him he was an activist and encouraged him to continue to use his voice.

However good an advocate I was becoming, I lamented that it was I, and not he, who had an appointment with his president. The world will be more just, more right, when it is Melchor and his wife, and not an American movie star, who has such access, who can tell their stories to the elected officials who represent them.

The next morning, I was told, a beautiful sweet-faced baby daughter named Milche Guadalupe was delivered without complication. Because she couldn't be tested for HIV for eighteen months, I will never know her status. As with so many others whose lives have touched mine, I can only pray and turn Milche and her parents over to the care of a loving God.

As I prepared to say my goodbyes to the Maryknoll sisters, I started to feel a lot of pain well up in me. The suffering I had witnessed was all so unnecessary, so preventable. When I asked Dee and Marlene how they managed to keep up their hope, they both spoke of the need to stay grounded in one's faith, one's personal connection to God. I understood that, of course, but on this day I felt the need to grieve, too, for all that had been destroyed, for all that had been suffered, for all who died so unnecessarily, so traumatically, in poverty, often without dignity.

Yes, I knew all about the need for education, that ignorance is the enemy, that the empowerment of any single individual sparks a miniature revolution. But the injustice of it all made me want to rage and scream and cry. I usually didn't start to feel this way until a few days into a trip, and I wondered why it had happened so quickly this time. The fear I had felt that morning had already traveled into anger. I had to ride it out and hope I could process the anger and come out on the good side of its gifts: energy, strength, and motivation. It was either that or I'd be up again all night with that awful anxiety in my chest.

Luckily, an important ally and dear friend was arriving later that evening to help me on the journey.

~ ~ ~

I was already in bed and reading through the daunting itinerary for the rest of the week when I heard Salma Hayek's voice in the hallway. I could not restrain myself from jumping up to greet her, so I pulled on a robe and ran down the hotel hallway to her room, ending up on her bed and talking half the night. It's like that when we see each other: With both of us as busy as we are (and as much as I had isolated myself in recent years), we always have much catching up to do. I wish I had a nickel for each time I said, "Oh, this is the last thing I'll say, then I'll go to bed!" It was a lesson to reach out more, not to let it all pile up.

The next morning, Salma and I had a discussion about what to wear during the week. I refrain from trying to pass myself off as a business-person or someone in the UN or whatever on these trips. Unless it's a formal meeting, I just dress like myself, wearing what I always wear, my usual gear from Anthropologie, dresses and occasionally linen pants and T-shirts, and Salma decided to do the same.

We started off with an excellent press conference announcing Salma's arrival and her participation in our AIDS awareness campaign in conjunc-tion with ALDO, the Canadian shoe and accessory company (which Salma handled seamlessly, like the pro she is). Then we visited a free AIDS clinic and hospice in one of Guatemala City's toughest neighborhoods, La Ter-minal. The facility was run by Fundación Marco Antonio, one of PSI's partners. I was delighted to find it spotlessly clean, the sheets matching, and the dozen patients living with HIV wearing new sleeveless flannel gowns. I crawled onto one bed, Salma sat on another, and we each listened to the stories of women who were dying of AIDS. Salma was a natural at the work, because she loves being with people and they know it. Being a native Spanish speaker and gifted translator further enriched the experience for all of us.

My new friend, a frail woman with a gaunt face, had two children living in Atlanta whom she hadn't seen in ten years. Her grief surged up each time she mentioned them. They didn't know she was HIV-positive, and she was afraid to tell them. Her family here in Guatemala had shunned her; her father-in-law threw away a cup after she drank from it. She spoke of the clinic as the only bright spot in her painful life, a place where she was accepted and loved. She talked about trying to be the best lead "cow"— an idiomatic expression—meaning she could influence other HIV-positive patients by keeping up a positive attitude of her own. But, she said, she was struggling. She had attempted suicide twice. In the few minutes we had together, I shared with her what I'd learned during my own hard times about the need to love myself and offered that there was much to love about herself.

As Salma and I were working our way through all the patients, we heard a commotion on the street below that signaled the arrival of another of my guests: Juanes, the Colombian rock superstar and one of the biggest celebrities in Latin America. Outside the clinic, Papa Jack's security team had their hands full as word spread of Juanes's arrival and thousands of Guatemalans filled the streets for a glimpse of him. He was a slender man with a boyish shock of brown hair and eyebrows that Frida Kahlo might envy. Juanes bounded up the stairs to greet everyone, then took out a guitar and gave an impromptu concert for the patients. Then, just as Salma and I had done, he sat down to talk with AIDS patients, hugging them in front of the cameras to transmit the powerful message that while the virus should be feared, the people who suffer from it should not. Later, he recorded a public service announcement for us that would reach millions of his fans with the message that real men use condoms to protect themselves and their loved ones.

Meanwhile, Salma and I raced back to the hotel to change clothes for our "private" audience with Oscar Berger, the president of Guatemala. We arrived at the palace to discover that he had pulled a big switcheroo on us.

Instead of a substantial, behind-closed-doors talk with him about policy and programs, he staged a raucous press conference, apparently in order to preempt our own events and attract the lion's share of attention for himself. Salma, Juanes, and I had to plaster polite smiles on our faces as President Berger herded us through a mob of reporters and camera crews toward a waiting dais.

Berger's press conference coup had been elaborately planned—right down to the nameplates and water glasses and a conference room that was filled with government officials and invited guests. We all took our seats and had to roll with the circus as it unfolded, the price we apparently had to pay to bend the ear of the head of state. I was called on to make a speech, which I did; thank God I was already warmed up and had a little experience at being ambushed. The president then produced a guitar, which he presented to Juanes on the dais in an attempt to force him to perform. Juanes was a good sport and sang a bit of his colossal hit song "La Camisa Negra," and then Berger clowned around with him, joining in a Guatemalan folk song. In his own remarks, Berger made a patronizing aside to his minister of health about the country needing to double the funding of its efforts to fight AIDS. We took that as a serious statement of intent and were glad that the media were there to record it.

During the photo ops after the news conference, the president kept up his antics. He squeezed me and Salma close to him and made some extremely inappropriate, gendered comments about our bodies. Salma told me she thought she smelled alcohol on him as he talked about "the honey of power." Did he mean that we were the bees? Or maybe he was calling us "the honeys of power"—I never quite figured out his intention beyond the obviously sexist nature of the remark.

When it was all over, we climbed back in the car and finally let loose with howls of outraged laughter. Again, I was so glad Salma was there. I might have spent the rest of the day fuming over the president's publicity stunt, but she could find the humor in anything. In addition to being a world-class actor, she's a natural comedian; my mom calls her the Latina Lucille Ball. All the way back to the hotel she kept up a commentary on the afternoon's events that had us in stitches. She was wearing a beautiful low-cut dress with a tight bodice that barely contained her voluptuous

bosom, to which the president had apparently directed many of his remarks.

"It's just physics—*fee-seeks*," said Salma. "I can't help it! There's too
much mass to fit in most clothes."

Salma is so beautiful, she just kills people. You mention her name to
men and they emit a little noise. Part sigh or part squeak. I call it the
Salma sound. But she manages to deflect attention with self-deprecating
humor—a classic thing that women do, but very few can pull it off. "Ashley
came to my room this morning," she said, "and she's complaining, oh, she
has a pimple, she doesn't feel pretty. I say, 'Look at you, you're like this ga-
zelle, with your long neck, so elegant in your carriage, so poised and regal.
So simple and classic.' And then there's me. I've got a big ass, and big tits,
on a short frame, and Ashley, I'm vulgar! You know, even when I'm just
talking, I'm just vulgar! Look at me!"

Salma is a serious person who simply doesn't take herself too seriously.

~ ~ ~

That night, I hosted a cocktail reception with business leaders and dip-
lomats and yet another press opportunity at the hotel. But the part I was
looking forward to most was meeting Rigoberta Menchú, who won the
Nobel Peace Prize in 1992 for her work advocating with the oppressed
peasants of Guatemala during the civil war and championing the rights
of indigenous people. Menchú is a member of the Quiché Maya ethnic
group and was draped, as always, in colorful handwoven cloth. She was a
quiet and dignified person with nut brown skin and a face as round as a
harvest moon. We spoke in Spanish; I can understand a great deal but still
need some help with translation, which Salma provided. I was blown away
when Rigoberta invited me to return to Guatemala to take part in a Mayan
ceremony. It was one of those moments when I fully realized the phenomenal options with which I've been blessed. I could stay at home in a beautiful, nurturing environment in Tennessee, or I could just climb on a plane
and join Rigoberta Menchú for a traditional ceremony. My life could be as
big as I wanted to make it.

~ ~ ~

I have learned that the tragedy of AIDS cuts across the lines of wealth and class and wreaks devastation on the rich and powerful as well as the poor and oppressed. Although poverty and ignorance are the petri dish of the pandemic, no one is immune, not a basketball star or businesswoman, a top model or the son of a president. The disease affects us all. We wanted to illustrate this fact by bringing a film crew from the Discovery Channel, which was making a documentary about our Central America trip, to tape an interview with members of a prominent Guatemalan family who had lost a son to AIDS.

Even though Blanca and Luis Garcia had become outspoken advocates for AIDS awareness since the death of their son, Luis Angel, they were reluctant to appear in the film. It was still such a sensitive subject. Fortunately, there was a new member of our PSI team who possessed a gentle power of persuasion and had a surprising personal connection to the Garcias' story.

Marshall Stowell, who is now PSI's director of communications, had joined the organization in 2005 to work with Kate on the YouthAIDS campaign. I instantly fell in love with Marshall for his elegant, soft-spoken manner and his calm hazel eyes, which radiate kindness and mirth. Like most gay men in America during the 1990s, Marshall was well aware of the AIDS epidemic. Many of his friends in Atlanta, Georgia, where he had been working in marketing, were HIV-positive. But the full impact of the disease hadn't truly hit home for him until Tim, a very close friend, came down with full-blown AIDS. He didn't know how to respond to his terrible decline and felt he had somehow let his friend down. After he died, Marshall decided to devote himself to advocacy work as a way to honor Tim. When our representative in Guatemala called to tell Marshall about the Garcia family and how they were hesitant to tell their son's story on camera, he felt a quiver of recognition.

"Where did their son live?" he asked.

When he was told it was Atlanta, a chill ran down his spine, followed by a huge wave of emotion. He had been friends with a striking, witty Guatemalan designer named Luis Garcia who had died of AIDS during that time. Marshall was able to assure the family that he had known their son well and that we would be very respectful in the filming. They agreed to appear on camera.

~ ~ ~

The Garcias' house was in one of Guatemala City's wealthiest neighborhoods, where stately homes are hidden behind high stone walls covered with fragrant, blooming vines and metal security gates. Luis's grown brothers and sisters were there to greet us, along with his parents, a handsome middle-aged couple with traces of pain still etched in their faces. Blanca Garcia sat snuggled with Salma and me on the couch in the cool, spacious living room as she paged through a thick album of photographs commemorating her son's short life. We all teared up when Blanca told us she had brought the album to Atlanta to reminisce with Luis as he lay dying and to reassure him that he would always be remembered.

Because the stigma against homosexuality and AIDS is so great in Guatemala, stories like Luis's are usually covered up. But the Garcias chose to honor their son by acknowledging the reality of his life at his funeral, wearing the red ribbon symbol of AIDS. This shocked their social circle, some of whom shunned them for a time. They then boldly went further, opening two clinics to care for AIDS patients and offer counseling services for the families.

As Marshall watched the taping from a quiet corner of the room, he felt a moment of completion, of healing. By helping tell the Garcias' story, he was offering hope to those who suffer in silence and was spreading the message of prevention that could save more young people from early death. For Marshall, it was something close to grace.

~ ~ ~

Salma had listened to me talking about my visits to brothels for years; now she would see one for herself. The barrio was called La Linea, a sad neighborhood of garishly painted one-story concrete buildings lining a defunct rail bed strewn with debris. As we walked down the tracks, women peered at us from doorways that led to small cinder-block rooms with narrow beds and sometimes turned to wag their rear ends at us, a form of hello they use to solicit customers. Although prostitution is carried out openly in Guatemala City, many were still afraid to be seen with us. One of the few who would speak to us was Brenda, a teen with long shiny black hair and bright red lips, dressed for business in a tight pink chiffon bodysuit and platform heels. Again, Salma was a natural in this setting. She plunked herself right down next to Brenda on the bed, a thin mattress on creaky springs with one sheet where she had cheap, paid sex, putting her at ease with her warmth and directness.

"Are you afraid of catching HIV?" she asked in Spanish. Yes, said Brenda, but she knew to use condoms, she could insist on it. She also knew how to inspect a customer's genitals for external indications of STIs. Salma picked up a handful of unopened condom strips that were scattered on the bedspread and asked, "How much do you pay for these?" They were given out free at the health clinic, said Brenda. I was more interested in why Brenda had become a prostitute. The answer was all too familiar: She needed the money to feed her son. There was no other work. She had no education or vocational skills. To provide for him, she sold herself ten or a dozen times a day for the equivalent of $2 a client. (This seemed to be a worldwide price point for exploitive sex.) We made our way down the street, knocking on doors and talking to the women. It was a depressing scene, as always, but with my friend by my side it was not so heavy. In fact, Salma was glowing as we drove out of the barrio, leaning through the open window, waving to the women, and shouting, *"Adios, hermanas!* Goodbye, my sisters!"

Marshall was intrigued and asked her how it went.

"Oh, it was fantastic," she said. "These women are incredible, so strong."

"And what did you talk about?"

"Well, I asked one of them, 'Do your children know what you do?' " said Salma. "And she says to me, 'No, I tell them that I sell underwear.' I say, 'Why would you tell them that?' She says 'You know, it's kind of close to the truth . . . because the panties are close to the cootchie.' " Peals of laughter. I could see Papa Jack's ears turning red as he sat in the front seat, trying to keep his eyes on the crowd and the police escort leading us back to La Terminal.

~ ~ ~

Passing defunct cars riddled with bullet holes, we pulled up in front of a stark building and entered a large warehouse space where dozens of prostitutes were playing games with U.S. taxpayers' money. At least that's the way Republican senator Tom Coburn from Oklahoma tried to characterize one of PSI's most successful education programs in a letter to President Bush in 2005. "The project which has been funding these prostitute parties is up for renewal," Coburn wrote. "There is something seriously askew at USAID when the agency's response to a dehumanizing and abusive practice that exploits women and young girls is parties and games." I wholeheartedly agree that prostitution is dehumanizing and abusive. It is gender violence. That is where our agreement ends and the senator's grave shortsightedness begins. PSI's initiatives, which are often funded by USAID, do not always represent the social ideal, which is that someday all girls and women will have sufficient education, empowerment, and opportunity to support themselves with dignity, free from violence. In the meantime, while we work toward that dream, the health needs of exploited populations should be addressed. Otherwise we are complicit in their abuse and misery.

What Coburn—who is a doctor, no less!—specifically objected to is a bingolike game called La Lotería, in which prostituted women are given cards with a grid of symbols that represent concepts about their bodies, HIV prevention, and pictures of venereal infections. Peer educators hold up the pictures one by one, explaining how to recognize the symptoms of AIDS and other infections and how to prevent them. The players check to see if they have a match. The first to cover all nine squares with tokens wins a small prize, such as a T-shirt or a strip of condoms. La Lotería and other approaches like it convey serious, essential information in a lighthearted, understandable, and practical format for the undereducated and illiterate. Life is hard enough, and studies show that instruction in these settings is not effective when it is grim and heavy-handed. Plus, one study showed that those who had participated in the program reported 96 percent condom use versus 78 percent for nonparticipants. USAID cut off funding anyway.

I had made that spur-of-the-moment trip to El Salvador the previous November to lobby for this aspect of our programming at a regional AIDS conference. Our efforts there and in Washington persuaded USAID to renew funding for La Lotería throughout Latin America, including the sessions taking place in this crumbling building.

Salma and I took seats at a table with about twenty prostituted women from the rough red-light district who come together for a few moments of relief and fellowship. In addition to La Lotería, they played a game that involved rolling dice and moving around a ragged game board, asking and answering questions about reproductive health. I'm a fanatic about any kind of board game, and Salma and I dove right in and rather hijacked the play, competing to win. Before long, our new friends were telling us the now familiar stories about how the ubiquitous circumstances of extreme poverty, lack of education, and gender inequality had put them on their backs and knees. When I asked them about their dreams, one immediately said she wanted to be a mechanic. Many wanted to have jobs sewing. So much for Senator Coburn's delusion of carefree "partying prostitutes." But in spite of the grimmest lives imaginable, they had retained their sense of humor, were outspoken, and had managed to find sisterhood and camaraderie in their ranks.

~ ~ ~

After a bloody early flight to Managua, during which Salma let me go through her purse, a quirky thing I find really soothing (I do that to my mother and Moyra, too, and it works great at Kentucky basketball games that become too exciting), we cleaned up superfast at our hotel to turn around for a meeting with the president of Nicaragua. We were met by the head of protocol at the National Palace, who escorted us to President Enrique Bolaños's office, which overlooked a humongous volcanic lake stretching for miles to the hazy horizon.

I was pleased to see that many of Bolaños's ministers were in attendance, which underscored Nicaragua's proactive and bold attack on HIV. Although the country is desperately poor, they have the lowest seroprevalence in Central America—less than .2 percent—and seemed determined to keep it that way. Kate, Salma, and I spoke at length with the president, a courtly, white-haired gentleman, about PSI programs and how they impact citizens exponentially when governments cooperate in serving vulnerable and at-risk populations. The government was just inaugurating a five-year strategic plan to step up its response to AIDS in the health care sector and to coordinate programs such as HIV and tuberculosis prevention as a smarter and more efficient use of scarce resources. After we signed a declaration formally and publicly enshrining the administration's seriousness on the issue, the conversation drifted to more light-hearted topics, such as baseball—a huge sport in this part of the world. I used the opportunity to tell the president about the YouthAIDS mission and how in particular we used local stars from sports, music, film, and television to send out positive, upbeat messages about behavior change and empowered gender dynamics. In fact, our itinerary included a visit to the studios of one of Central America's most popular TV shows, produced in Managua, where we would join the cast to film a public service announcement.

The meeting with President Bolaños was a huge success, as serious as the meeting with Guatemala's president Oscar Berger had been farcical. Next, I was eager to put my feet down on Nicaraguan soil and absorb the history of tragedy and redemption that has marked this country's path into the twenty-first century.

This was a big visit for me, because I came of age politically in the late 1980s, when the end stages of Nicaragua's Sandinista revolution were playing out. And now I had a chance to walk around and breathe the air at the epicenter of the Sandinista revolt.

While they were in power during the 1980s, the Sandinistas began a countrywide literacy campaign, expanded education, and implemented universal health care programs. In spite of its formidable obstacles, the country still displays benefits from those wise social policies—particularly in the area of HIV education and prevention. For example, prostituted women here have the lowest HIV rates and highest condom compliance in the region. And during our visit we were able to see a remarkable program that educates local and national police about reproductive health. Salma and I witnessed a typical peer education session in which police cadets played their own version of La Lotería. There were quite a few women cadets, just as there had been several women involved in our meeting with the president.

It was heartening to see uniformed service members take their first, baby steps toward gender equality. Men in uniform constitute a cohort that is well known for reinforcing unhelpful notions of what it means to be a man. I believe that it is as equally abusive to men as it is to girls and women to constrain and confine them to behavior and roles dictated by social constructions of gender. I was reminded of the old feminist saw, "For every girl who wants to play football there's a boy who wants an Easy-Bake oven." In Nicaragua, women could join the police and win presidential elections, but I wondered if men and boys would ever be able to break out of *their* traditional roles of hypermasculinity in the new Nicaragua.

After years of strife, the country still has a long way to go to realize the open, equal society that seemed so deliciously possible in the early days of the revolution. Human rights abuses have occurred across the political spectrum, there have been reports of corruption, not all of the government's policies have been beneficial to the people it serves, and patriarchal values still dominate norms. Teen pregnancy is shockingly common, and motherhood, even for girls as young as twelve, is considered the feminine ideal. An equally disappointing development in Nicaragua was a draconian law passed by the national assembly just months after my visit that criminalizes all abortions, even to save the life of the mother. Because of this cruel law, there have been widespread reports of doctors refusing to treat pregnant women with life-threatening complications for fear of being prosecuted if the fetus dies. According to Human Rights Watch, politicians pushed through the law to gain political support from the Catholic Church, which maintains a rock-hard line against all abortion and contraception.

But I was able attend a Catholic mass in Managua that showed another side of the Church, one that embraces the social justice gospel of Jesus known as "liberation theology." The congregation met in a broad, airy, simple room, filled with a few dozen kids from PSI/Nicaragua's youth groups, many of whom were HIV-positive. The service reminded me of the Pentecostal churches I so loved at home: charismatic, with joyous singing and clapping and participation from the congregation. Hymns lifted up the little person, the disenfranchised person, who maybe is sleeping on a park bench, or is selling used shoes from a wheelbarrow, or is being beaten by her husband. The songs said that Jesus was coming for that person. I was rapt. When the priest brought me up to speak—a feature of these modern masses—I shared from the pulpit that even though they might regard their church as modest and humble, for me it was awesome (in the true sense of the word). Jesus has always been my favorite radical, and my life is infused with the values they celebrated; in fact, my Christian faith demands I work for social justice and human rights. I still consider that mass one of the highlights of all my work abroad.

~ ~ ~

Way too early one morning, Salma and I visited the set of *Sexto Sentido* (*Sixth Sense*), a hugely popular television social soap opera that creates thirty episodes a year. The studio was a poured-concrete building, very tidy, the interior walls lined with small painted sets built for each character. They had craft services and were especially proud of their modern air-conditioning. The dressing room was equally neat and shared by the entire large cast. It was a cheerful, sweet experience.

Each of *Sexto Sentido*'s intense story lines revolve around social issues. There is a gay male couple, a girl who has been sexually abused, a hero character who becomes HIV-positive, a virgin who is betrayed after marriage, and more. The stories are forthright and dynamic, and they present both real problems and real solutions, along with dispensing medically accurate reproductive health information. We were there to make cameos and film a public service announcement about HIV prevention. They filmed a bit of an episode, and after the director yelled, "Cut!" (a woman director, unusual even in Hollywood) the camera pulled back to reveal Salma and me sitting with her at the monitor. We then addressed the cameras, trading lines in Spanish, saying that it's a lot easier to talk about safe sex on TV than it is to practice it consistently in real life, but it's critically important. The only bad part of the morning was seeing my tired face and that one huge pimple in such close shots on TV and wincing every time I flubbed an especially hard word in Spanish.

I speak Spanish fairly well, and pick up momentum after a few days' practice, but for some reason I kept tripping over the same words on every take. It was embarrassing to hear the director yell, "*Otra vez!* Again!" over and over. There was a time when I might have been flustered, but the new tools of my recovery helped keep me from overreacting. It was a perfectly imperfect performance. I remembered I could make a mistake without being a mistake, and we all had a good laugh when it was over.

~ ~ ~

Back at the hotel, Salma and I sat out by the pool in the tropical evening air and rehashed the journey we had taken together (which, as with all my trips, was far more extensive than the space here allows me to describe). It's so interesting how we each have our own deeply private responses to the beautiful people we meet, the incredible things we see. We compared notes about a stop we made at a drop-in center that offered vocational training to homeless kids as well as those who passed their days on the streets hawking to tourists. I made a small friend who was on my lap or held my hand the entire visit, even when I had my hair braided. He made beautiful, intricate figurines from banana leaves, which he sold at intersections to support himself. He was no more than nine. I was torn up by the pathos of his resiliency. For Salma, the breaking point was witnessing the innocent, creative expression of children in such desperate circumstances. Watching the little ones dancing, twirling with joy, that's when she went to pieces. She continued to teach me about admiring the positive even in abysmal situations.

The next morning I would be off to Honduras, to visit grassroots programs in a community of Garifunas, or Black Caribs, where adult seroprevalence was a shocking 8.4 percent. It would be another movable pageant of tragedy, resilience, and hope, and it was a shame that Salma had to return to Los Angeles and wouldn't be coming along for the ride.

"You're gonna miss me, you know!" said Salma, reading my thoughts. "I'm gonna miss you, too."

Initially, Salma had expressed some trepidation about whether she had the knowledge and skills required on a trip like this one. I told her how impressed I was with her instant grasp of the concepts and her virtuoso performance in the field. All it really requires is humanity, I said, and she had that in spades. "You have, like, a PhD in humanity," I said. "You are totally qualified."

"Did I pass my test?"

Yes, Salma more than passed the test.

Chapter 17

OFF THE MAT, INTO THE WORLD

Receiving a kiss in Daharvi.

What the eye sees better the heart feels more deeply.
We not only increase the likelihood of our being moved;
we also run the risks that being moved entails. Seeing increases
our vulnerability to being recruited to the welfare of another.

—*ROBERT KEGAN, The Evolving Self*

The cabin was dark on my flight from London to Mumbai, so I tapped out a journal entry in the small cone of light by my window seat. While I envy those who can sleep on airplanes, I do enjoy being alone with my thoughts. Tonight, my thoughts were focused on the mission ahead: It was March 2007, and I was about to embark on a three-week journey through India. It was a dream trip straight out of my childhood imaginings. But rather than focusing on Ayurvedic spas and colorful Hindu temples, I would be zeroed in on the largest slum in Asia and the largest brothel district in India. With more than a billion people, nearly one-third of whom live below the poverty line, $1.25 per day, and an estimated 2.5 million infected with HIV/AIDS, India is the mother ship, the big kahuna, of development challenges and an urgent platform for PSI. The pandemic had already infiltrated the subcontinent among the usual high-risk groups: prostituted and trafficked women, intravenous drug users, truckers, and migrant laborers. Now HIV/AIDS was poised to explode through a region that holds one-fifth of the people on earth. The need for measurable, sustainable, immediate intervention was—and still is—critical.

The usual team would be meeting me in India, along with a *National Geographic* crew who would be filming me for an hour-long documentary, *India's Hidden Plague,* about how HIV/AIDS is spreading under the cover of secrecy and ignorance. I would also be meeting up with another special traveling buddy, my beloved yoga instructor, Seane Corn, whom I had invited to join PSI as a fellow YouthAIDS ambassador. Seane's gritty street smarts and boundless compassion made her a perfect companion for an inevitably difficult journey.

I knew I would witness scenes of devastation, and I would listen to the all-too-familiar, always heart-wrenching stories of abused and abandoned girls and women. But a year had gone by since I'd entered into treatment, and I felt better prepared than ever to take on this work. Did I expect to

hurt on this trip? Absolutely. I wouldn't be human if I didn't. But I no longer had to hurt myself. I had *recovery*. I wrote in my journal: "I am often
asked, sometimes quite harshly, why in the world I do this social justice
work in squalid places, and I am, by the grace of God, slowly learning that
piece of my own story. Simply put, I do it because I love it. But why do
I love it? I have always had an absolutely insane sensitivity to sexual exploitation of any kind—overt, covert, institutionalized, spontaneous on the
street, humor in movies that is outrageous yet depicted casually like there
is nothing wrong with it. It hurts me. I know now that I was abused myself, and of course, it makes so much more sense. . . .

"My recovery brings with it healthier boundaries, loving detachment,
and the ability to serve for the sake of serving, letting go of the outcomes,
not because I am unconsciously wrestling my own unresolved grief. The
latter motivation is not a bad thing, not at all. To do this work, it takes what
it takes, but I, for one, am glad to know why the orphans and other vulnerable children affect me in a way that before could make me ill for days.
Now, when I see lost children, I know that I, an empowered adult, am nurturing and loving my own little lost child in me, and that is such a beautiful thing. We are all one, and I am incredibly moved to live this out, time
and again. We are one."

My personal goal on this trip was to feel, just once, compassion, tenderness, and—dare I say it?—love for a perpetrator. To see someone who exploits other human beings and to understand completely that the behavior
is not the soul. To remember that abused people in turn abuse, that behavior is a perfect reflection of the system in which they live. To truly love just
one madam, pimp, or john—even if only for a breath. That is my goal. A
goal that requires a Power greater than myself, for sure. So, I prayed:

*God, I am now ready that You may have all of me, good and bad. Please
remove every single defect of character that stands in the way of my usefulness to You and my fellows. I ask only for knowledge of Your will for me
and the power to carry it out. I trust You completely to teach me how to
take good care of myself, and I know that You do for me what I cannot do
for myself. Thank You for this special adventure.*

And then I could not resist throwing in a small request for myself: "Oh yeah, and I'd really like not to get diarrhea like I did in Thailand, and I'd love to see a pretty temple."

I finally dozed off, to dreams of henna tattoos and homespun cloth, of lotus petals borne on sacred rivers.

~ ~ ~

The tires bumped and the giant jet shuddered to a halt on the runway at Mumbai's Chhatrapati Shivaji International Airport. As we taxied to the terminal, I saw an entire family near the runway, using pails to pull water out of a filthy ditch, in which the children were also playing. Welcome to India.

Marshall Stowell and Papa Jack were waiting, as always, to scoop me up at the gate and sweep me into town. With a population of sixteen million, Mumbai is the third-largest city in the world and the most populous in India, which is saying a lot. The scenery along the route to the hotel hummed with vitality and desperation: the monochromatic shanty roofs of Dharavi, a million-person slum where I would spend much of the next week, in the shadow of business towers and shopping malls under construction. There were families living on sidewalks, beggars, some of whom have maimed their children in a desperate attempt to manipulate money from tourists, hundreds of thousands of matching little taxis, all manner of rickshaws, flowing somewhat miraculously in multiple directions at once, accompanied by a giant symphony of horn honking. They do love to lean on their horns in ole Mumbai.

The Taj Mahal Palace was an oasis amid the chaos, a massive architectural marvel of a grand hotel. My comfortable suite looked out over a motley flotilla of ships bobbing in the Arabian Sea, and I allowed myself to feel for a moment as if I were living out my childhood fantasies of adventure.

~ ~ ~

While I took a day to rest, Papa Jack and Marshall went off to scout our locations in and around Mumbai—no mean feat in such a congested and unpredictable environment. By now Papa Jack had become an invaluable asset for PSI, which used his services to advance important trips even when I was not traveling. In fact, he had seen more of our platforms than I. Jack and Marshall had already been in India for days, making sure all the venues I would visit were as safe as possible and the contacts lined up by our local staff were appropriate and reliable. Jack keeps up with U.S. State Department safety bulletins, he trains the drivers in defensive and getaway driving.

I frankly like the dangerous stuff, the realism and undisguised nature of life as others are living it. I reluctantly accept the security and the help. My husband understandably insists on it, and because I am a kidnapping risk (even though I refuse to see myself that way), PSI and other organizations' insurance also require it. But I dislike the feeling of being set apart, approaching the reality of daily life differently from the citizens I am there to meet, the humanitarian and aid workers who do not have the benefit of such protection and resources. I enjoy journalists, for example, who can blend in and watch life unfold without the distorting presence of SUVs and "fixers." Nonetheless, it's fun traveling with Papa Jack, and reassuring, because of our history, when the going gets weird, which it sometimes does in brothels and seedy neighborhoods. But none of us expected the most dangerous moment of the trip to take place in a movie theater lobby.

The plan was to showcase a dynamic street theater program that sensitizes Indians to the reality of sex trafficking in their communities, to destigmatize and correct myths about women trapped in prostitution, and raise awareness about the public health crisis of HIV among them. In this case, it was the audience at a theater on the edge of Kamathipura, Mumbai's notorious red-light district. Just as in Southeast Asia and Latin America, prostituted women in India have the greatest risk of contracting and spreading HIV. In Mumbai alone there are up to two hundred thousand prostitutes and sex slaves, and anywhere from 18 to 45 percent carry the virus.

I had spent the previous day absorbing the lay of the land in Kamathipura. The brothels were so much like those in Svay Pak, Antananarivo, Nairobi—except they were even more crowded and filthy. Some were no more than rickety rabbit warrens stacked on top of one another, attached by ladders and narrow corridors. Women lived and worked in bunks four or more to a room; their children running around or hiding under beds amid their scant possessions while their mothers serviced customers. It was hell. Each brothel building block had electricity and running water for only two hours a day. The women explained that they had to queue with their small pails at the one spigot in advance of the water's flow, or else they might go without water for days. They said they try to help one another out: If one had a client—and oh, how precious those terrible rupees are—they would try to fill one another's pails, although brothels, like prisons, can have personality conflicts and cliques, and sometimes arguments broke out over scarce resources.

The women we met were aware of the HIV/AIDS crisis but were often too poor and powerless to protect themselves. If a trick would pay extra not to use a condom, and the woman and her children were starving, who could fault her for conceding? It was clearer to me every time I visited prostituted women that the key to stopping the spread of HIV is changing the behavior of the men who exploited them for sex (also known as "demand abolition"), which, logically, would be accompanied by the ultimate goal: a reduction, and eventual eradication of sexual exploitation.

So here we were at the Royal Cinema, where a troupe of interpersonal communicators regularly interrupted the shows—there's always a pause to change reels anyway—with lively skits and demonstrations of the importance of male condom use and other behavior change scenarios. Today's was especially powerful, as women *from* the brothels boldly stood on a public stage, performing vignettes that showed hundreds of people what daily life was like for them. In one, a woman presented her ID card to the ration office for her measure of kerosene, but the bureaucrat, knowing she was a prostitute, discriminated against her, denying her rations. In another, a customer bullied a woman into unprotected sex. In yet another, a pimp took all of a woman's earnings, then beat her to "teach her a lesson." A troublingly common example of generational discrimination was shown, too, in a girl being sent home from school, scorned and denied access because her mother was a prostitute. Without school, the girl's own future as a prostitute is almost a given; a life of penury is indeed certain. And no representation would be complete without depicting police extorting sex for free.

The Mumbai media had been invited to this Saturday afternoon event, which we expected to be followed by a fairly low-key Q&A with me about PSI's mission. Nobody had anticipated the hundreds of reporters, photographers, camera crews, and assorted gawkers who crammed into the theater lobby. While Papa Jack and his security team tried to push back the shouting paparazzi, I huddled in a corner with a beautiful old woman with bad knees and no shoes. She stood creakily, the smells of her unwashed body pronounced, and raised her hands to bless me; I made myself lower than she. She placed her hands in prayer on my head. I reached down to touch her feet. She might have been Jesus Christ himself, but I never had the chance to find out because the mob grew more unruly and were starting to crush us against the wall. Suddenly I felt Papa Jack's strong arm around my shoulders as he and Marshall pushed me through the crowd like a flying wedge of blockers hurtling toward a touchdown. The goal, in this case, was a van that had been backed up to a side door. We were soon inside and pulling away from the silly melee.

I was a little shaky from adrenaline, but I didn't want to waste the rest of the afternoon, so we decided to take a quick side trip to a site I'd long wanted to see: the Gandhi House and Museum. What better way to come down from a narrow escape than to pause to honor the champion of peaceful resistance?

Well, the paparazzi had caught wind of our change in plans, and they were waiting in throngs outside the museum. Marshall bargained with them: Taking a cue from my experience with pesky lookie-loos while filming movie scenes outdoors—a problem I had encountered especially in New York City on *Someone Like You*, when paparazzi actually interfered with our shooting until they were granted snapshots—he told them I would give a quick photo op and say a few words if they would agree to leave me alone to tour the house. To their credit, unlike American paparazzi, they kept their end of the agreement and allowed me to have my sacred moment in Gandhi's home in peace.

The tranquility inside the three-story colonial-era building was palpable and holy. It had been Gandhi's home in the city between the years of 1917 and 1934, when Mumbai was known as Bombay and Gandhi was organizing the *satyagrahas* and acts of peaceful disobedience that would eventually bring down British domination of India. After Gandhi's assassination in

1948, the house was preserved as a museum and turned into a center for Gandhian studies. I read every plaque, studied every picture on the walls. It made such an impression on me: this mighty, humble man, wearing peasant's attire and sandals in the wet and cold, carrying in his arms all he owned at the time, moving nations. I spent some quiet time in front of the plain, thin pallet where he slept, in a room still neatly arranged with his simple possessions, including a spinning wheel. I imagined his hand on his walking staff and was moved by the crude mug from which he drank. It was wonderful.

Of his many, many inspired teachings, perhaps I love best that he said, "I am a Muslim and a Hindu and a Christian and a Jew!" I am a devout follower of his teachings and believe without reservation that nonviolence is the way toward peace. And as I prepared myself for a week in multiple red-light districts and in the vastly sprawling slum of Dharavi, I meditated on Gandhi's unequivocal assertion that poverty is the worst form of violence.

To that end, I was working to help reach the poorest and most exploited for an immediate health intervention at the most basic level. In addition to helping India curb its HIV emergency, preventing unintended pregnancy is a deeply moral issue with profound implications. While we cannot change the living status of these vast numbers of poor overnight, we can help women not have more babies that bind them further to destitution and condemn the infants to needless suffering, to powerlessness, to pimps and madams. We also have programs for malaria prevention, safe drinking water, micronutrient delivery, child survival. But perhaps most exciting for me to see was the Sanghamitra women's collective, a partner that uses Gandhian principles of self-esteem, self-efficacy, and unified action to empower prostituted women, perhaps the most destitute and oppressed population in all of India.

Sanghamitra is the brainchild of Dr. Shilpa Merchant, who at the time was state director of PSI. The prostituted women who founded Sanghamitra named it after a great mythical figure, the wise daughter of Emperor Asoka, who transformed her father from a ruthless tyrant to a peaceful follower of Buddhism. The work of the collective is likewise transformative, turning once isolated, disempowered women into a sisterhood where they can help one another as they learn how to advocate for their own human and social rights. Their motto? "In Unity There Is Strength." Members of the collective and their children are provided a place, called a drop-in center, in the heart of the Kamathipura red-light district to rest and relax away from their swarming brothels. They learn to develop strong women-to-women alliances and to rely on one another in times of need. PSI supplies the women with male and female condoms, and Sanghamitra peers offer instruction in how to use them to avoid HIV, along with lessons in reproductive health and birth spacing. Importantly, the facility offers various recreational and vocational skills such as sewing. Sanghamitra also reaches out to law enforcement to maintain crucial, positive relations with the police. But to me the most exciting outgrowth of Sanghamitra is the Sangini Women's Cooperative Bank, which offers its members (currently about three thousand in all) a chance for economic freedom.

Prostituted women are caught in cunning cycles of vicious debt—to the people who own them, the madams who run the brothels, and then the moneylenders who scam the women with high interest rates when they have emergencies and no other source of credit. The deal is so stacked against them, and they suffer, their children suffer, and the families they are supporting back home suffer. To break that cycle, PSI/India helped set up a lending and borrowing system, following the revolutionary approach of India's Self-Employed Women's Association (founded by Ela Bhatt), that puts what the prostituted woman earns under her own control for the first time. *Sangini* means "friend," and the revolutionary new system is run by the women, for brothel-trapped women.

I sat in rapt attention as a lovely young man gave a PowerPoint presentation about how this particular microfinance and credit and savings program works. To begin, Sangini creates a photo ID for each woman so she can open an account. Lack of proper identification is a huge barrier to banking (and a significant means of discrimination) for women who have been either trafficked, tricked into prostitution, shunned by their families, or born into such poverty that they don't even possess birth certificates. The only requirement for a Sangini bank ID is membership in Sanghamitra. Every day, someone from the bank visits each brothel to pick up deposits, even if it is only 10 rupees (less than 25 cents). While there, the representative counsels the women about the importance of savings and encourages them to set goals: their children's education, for example. The member may withdraw her money at any time, in any amount, without penalty; while deposited, it earns a healthy, fair interest. And she can apply for small loans for emergencies or perhaps to start her own business. It's simply the neatest operation. They have outfoxed the cheaters and owners at every move. In its first year of operation, the bank took in more than 2 million rupees in deposits from seventeen hundred account holders in Kamathipura. Sangini, and initiatives like it, has awesome potential to serve as a model to benefit once hopelessly poor women everywhere. Economic empowerment is an essential piece in the complex puzzle of disentangling women from exploitation. Rock on, Sangini!

~ ~ ~

I was so excited to tell Seane Corn all about Sanghamitra when she arrived in Mumbai with Kate Roberts on Sunday night. While I dragged the *National Geographic* film crew across India (or were they dragging me?), Seane was scheduled to go on an overlapping tour with Kate. It was such a joy to see her lioness mane of golden curls and hear her unmistakable New Jersey accent echoing off the alabaster ceilings of the Taj Mahal Palace. I think of Seane as so sophisticated it touched me to see how giddily thrilled she was to be here, how energized she was by our local missions. We began our time together setting our intention with a seated meditation, at the end of which we looked at each other, heavy-lidded, relaxed, and with a sense that we had been kissed by the divine.

Seane has a remarkable history of resilience and service. She was just seventeen when she moved to New York City by herself and went to work as an illegal underage bartender in a gay sex club. Seane also became involved in drugs. It was the early 1980s, when HIV was quietly surging through the gay community, and one of her closest friends succumbed to AIDS before anyone really knew what it was. Before he died, he passed on a gift: He told her that God was in every person she met, even leather boys in gay bars. "Ignore the story and see the soul," he told her. "And remember to love—you will never regret it." She has said it was her first lesson in the central tenet of yoga—that we are all one. Eventually, she was able to overcome her addictions through a powerful yoga practice and soon became an inspired teacher, verbally brilliant, boldly devoted to Spirit. After she moved to Los Angeles, Seane became an evangelist for yoga as a healing art and spiritual practice. She started a workshop in Van Nuys, teaching yoga to child prostitutes as a way to help overcome their trauma.

Although we come from very different backgrounds, Seane and I have much in common. She's very much a leader; she can hold the space in any circumstance. There's reciprocity in our work. She taught me how to make my physical practice a prayer. I, in turn, have encouraged her social activism. Our relationship deepened after I called her for help when I was so sick in Bangkok, on my first trip for PSI, and she talked me through a night of cramps and mental anguish. I took Seane out to lunch soon after I returned from Asia, to thank her for her kindness. She was full of questions about my activism, and it planted a seed in her soul to use her platform in the yoga community as a launching point for large-scale service work. The conversation eventually led to Seane's becoming the global yoga ambassador for YouthAIDS, bringing the message of AIDS awareness to the twenty million people doing yoga worldwide, and tapping into a billion-dollar industry for fund-raising. She adopted the slogan "Off the Mat—Into the World," cofounded an organization that offers leadership training sessions for yoga practioners who then joined or found community service projects all around the country. It also raises money through service projects that bring yoga students to places like Cambodia, Uganda, South Africa, and Haiti.

On top of that, she's a fun girlfriend who loves to shop. Seane is blessed with the gift of gab, and I couldn't wait to hear her stories after her appointment to teach yoga to the women of Sanghamitra. I would have loved to go with her—but first I had a slum to visit.

~ ~ ~

Everything in Mumbai is extreme: the heat, the traffic, the noise, the crush of human bodies everywhere. And nothing I've done or seen could have prepared me for what passed for a housing compound in the depths of Dharavi, the sprawling area made internationally famous in the film *Slumdog Millionaire*. We were surrounded by dozens of squealing children as soon as we parked the car. I emerged at the opening of a tiny dark tunnel running between two shanties, from which a tiny figure in a bright sari materialized. It was Nasreen, the sixteen-year-old daughter of Kausar, a peer educator, who lived at the other end of this ghastly passageway. It was entirely black, no light source at all, about eighteen inches wide and less than six feet high. The uneven cement was wet from an unseen water source. Was it sewage? I hunched down, let my eyes adjust, and held Nasreen's hand as she escorted me into the reality of this "apartment" complex that accommodates *ten thousand* people. Our route twisted and turned unexpectedly, I never found my bearings. The sounds of people living their lives was all around us, animated conversations, a TV blaring (there is more jury-rigged electricity around here than I've ever seen, it's amazing none of it catches fire), babies crying. The children who had been at the car when I arrived would crazily appear in cracks in the tunnel along our way, popping out of crevices so small that I hadn't thought they were passageways, yet from floor to ceiling, the narrow dark space would impossibly fill with faces. It was like being in a nightmare version of a fun house at the fair, the type where you are constantly jolted by unexpected, unwelcome distortions and surprises . . . but there was very little fun at this fun house.

Eventually, Nasreen and I arrived at a crude wooden ladder, which we climbed up into the two tiny rooms she shared with her HIV-positive mother and her brother. Incredibly, this was a duplex affair, one hovel stacked on top of the other once the horizontal space ran out. I was speechless at the desolation of their living space, which Nasreen had spiffed up by plastering recent newspapers soaked in flour and water over the corrugated tin walls.

When Kausar found out she was HIV-positive in 1999, the doctor told her, "There are drugs, but you cannot afford them, and you'll be dead in five years anyway." Indignant, she ripped her test result paper in half and slapped him across the face. He pressed charges. In court, she spoke out on her own behalf. "Have I raped someone? Killed? Stolen? Kidnapped? What have I done?" The judge saw things her way and demanded the doctor pay her a small fee in damages. Hence, a spitfire of an HIV activist was born. Kausar now worked for PSI, escorting other HIV-positive patients when they went to doctors, mentoring and coaching them through their care.

Kausar has a very charismatic faith and credits God for her strength. When troubled, she prays for thirty minutes, then "goes out and gets the job done." She prayed for me, a long, intent, sincere petition that culminated in a joyous series of alleluias. Like Luz in Guatemala and so many others I had met, she had transformed her life through service to others. It was deeply moving to me.

I was told how, during their hard times when Kausar was so sick from AIDS, Nasreen scrounged for her family to stay alive. She begged. She worked. Eventually, she herself went hungry; a teacher finally reached out to her, learned the story, and personally gave her money for food. A lovely girl, Nasreen wants to be a doctor. I braided her hair, undid it, and braided it again, just to be able to nurture her more. The sweetness of the moment was almost unbearable. Before I left, we had a little talk about our bodies, because Kausar admitted that she hadn't ever discussed sex with her nearly adult daughter. Nasreen leaned into me, holding my hand (she grabbed it back whenever I released hers), listening. I said to her, my own voice surprising me, as it was now thick with emotion and I was flailing inside, trying not to break down. I had suddenly been sucked into a squall of emotion that it took great control to modulate. "Your body is beautiful and sacred. Do you believe me when I say that?" (Yes.) "You are beautiful and sacred. Do you believe that about yourself?" (Yes.)

I came to India for Nasreen.

~ ~ ~

My next meeting was with a very different group of peer educators, ones whom I found especially touching. They were four empowered, recovering, formerly hard-core, hope-to-die, stealing-robbing-thieving-abusing-pimping-homeless street drug addicts who shared with me the miraculous stories of their individual salvation through a Twelve Step program. It was their unyielding devotion to carrying the message to the addict who still suffers that led them to work with their peers. Nearly one in four injecting drug users (IDUs) is HIV-positive; they spread the virus by sharing dirty needles. PSI in Mumbai reaches about four thousand of them through the Green Dot program, which provides clean needles and syringes to keep the addicts from spreading HIV. It also has a drop-in center for them to rest and get cleaned up and where a visiting doctor treats their injection-related wounds.

IDUs constitute one of the most underserved populations in the world. Many aid organizations simply will not work with them, and donors shun them, too. I am proud that PSI is not one such agency, even as we have our own troubles raising "unrestricted" money for their programs, because some governments and foundations stipulate that their funding stream may not help injecting drug users.

My new friends had scars on their faces; one was missing half an arm. They had hellish stories to share; one used to beat his mother for money. Addicts are the scourge of society here, ostracized like the "untouchable" caste. When the police round up suspects for a crime, any crime, they go straight for the addicts, whether or not they were anywhere near the scene. Each of these men managed to clean up and was given a job. However, one in particular was so grateful for his recovery that after putting in a day at PSI, he would leave work and spend hours at the train station reaching out to addicts still in their lowlife using careers. Through his passionate example was born our IDU program. It is now the full-time and paid occupation of all four men, outreach workers who visit the addicts in the streets to exchange needles and syringes and provide counseling.

Sitting on mats in the PSI office with these men, hearing these powerful stories of lives turned around, is absolutely what keeps me going. Gentle, sweet souls, one and all—it was impossible to envision the craven, remorseless shadows they insisted they once were. Like so many of us, they know they cannot keep what they have without giving it away.

~ ~ ~

Except for some lethargy, probably caused by jet lag, I was feeling so very well and balanced on this trip. My first night, I almost skipped the daily inventory of my day, and I am very glad I did not. By keeping it in place, I provide my potentially turbulent days with stable bookends that ground me in familiar spiritual routines. Each morning I study recovery and spiritual readings and then spend thirty minutes in seated meditation (although admittedly some mornings I seem to spend more time checking how much time has gone by, than actually meditating), during which I slowly repeat internally deeply inspirational passages that embody my highest ideals. Sometimes it's the Prayer of St. Francis, sometimes it's the Serenity Prayer or the Imitation of Christ, the Twin Verses from the Damamapada, or the Great Spirit Prayer by Chief Yellow Lark. And each evening I review my conduct, knowing that to spot, admit, and correct mistakes is the essence of character building. I ask myself questions such as, When was I selfish, self-seeking, dishonest? Did I use all my tools today? Did I reach out when I needed to, sit quietly when that was best? Was I on time? Was I kind? Do I owe any amends? Did I allow myself to become hungry, angry, lonely, or tired? Did I repeat the Holy Name, did I surrender, did I have expectations, did I let go of the outcome? How were my boundaries? These routines have brought me *so far.* They have helped me maintain my commitment to honesty and accountability and created changes in both my thinking and my behavior that I am enjoying.

Yesterday, for example, I began hearing a critical voice in my head: *I am not doing enough, I need to do more, I have to do more, I need to work with more NGOs that complement PSI's public health mission, I need to go see the prostitutes around the corner who hollered at me, go back to that one brothel where I held the schoolgirl but couldn't talk because I was getting the "come on, Ashley" wink from Papa Jack, I need to pay for the kids' educations.* It was mental panic. Shortly, though, my recovery rose up to meet this insanity and call it what it was: selfishness and self-centeredness. I was able to hear all the "I, I, I, I, I" that my ego was shouting, and all the other words receded. To the untrained ear, it might have sounded like compassion and goodwill; to me, it was all about what "I" needed to do, which is "edging God out" (ego) in an attempt to stifle my powerful emotional responses to the things I had seen. I was able to remind myself that all that is asked of me is that I increase my conscious contact with the God of my understanding, ask for knowledge of Her will for me and the strength to carry that out. Have I done that as best I can today, understanding that my best fluctuates? Yes. Am I continuing to? Yes. Well then, I can stop abusing myself with perfectionism and trust that, as Father Merton wrote, "I believe that the desire to please you does in fact please you." I am cleaning house, trusting God, doing what is in front of me. That is good, and that is enough. I am enough.

~ ~ ~

I spent time in a secretive brothel in Kamathipura, where cotton cloth covered the entry to each room. These are girls and women who are truly sex slaves, unable to physically leave their rooms, even to go to the health clinic. They do not see the outdoors for years; their only walking is to the toilet at the end of the hall. They are in the *karza* or indentured servitude phase of sex slavery. They have been brought in against their will, tricked by someone they knew in their home village, purchased by a madam for as little as $100 U.S. Each slave has to "earn" back her money, in addition to whatever the madam spends housing and feeding her. They are young, rural, terrified, and unable to speak the local dialect, which intensifies their helpless isolation. If they do dare to flee, heavies are stationed at obvious places such as rail and bus stations to bring them straight back.

The women I met in this human storehouse were actually from Nepal, which has seen tens of thousands of its young stolen for Mumbai's sex trade. Their poverty is so bad, their desperation so intense, that they are often forced to work here with an impossible number of clients per day. They even offer anal sex for a modestly higher fee (about 100 rupees more, about $2 U.S.). It's hard to know the exact HIV rate of trafficked women, as those who are *karza* can't be tested. However, in 2007 the HIV rate of women tested at the Falkland Road Clinic was 37 percent.

This obscene situation was brought to the attention of both the Indian and Nepalese governments by health workers from NGOs who were finding alarming rates of infection in the brothels. The result is that trafficking from Nepal to India has been significantly reduced—an exception being, of course, the women I met today.

It was a relief to leave that stifling room and climb up to the roof of the brothel for some air. I found about ten children there and a woman washing her dishes while rotten food floated in a growing puddle. They were dusty, filthy, but playful and animated by having a foreigner visit. I asked their names, but they wanted to go further, and those who could wrote their names for me on scraps of paper, so I would remember them. The whole life of a child, scrawled in a name. Against the plastic wall of a makeshift room on torn, small pieces of paper, they wrote:

Aadarshini
Yamuna
Nabhendu
Asiya
Aarti

I put the damp, dirty scraps carefully into my tote, and when I returned to the hotel, the instant I hit the door of my room, something exploded in my chest. I was suddenly clawing at my tote, dropping to my knees, nearly vomiting up grief as I crawled to the coffee table, where I laid out each child's piece of paper, looking at their names, seeing the uniqueness of each one's writing, imagining a bit of their essence on the paper from where their hands had touched it.

I thought of their lives—born and raised in brothels, and likely condemned to brothels as adults; the boys were already doing chores to keep things running, and the girls were often sold to men as early as age eight. It was too much for me to reconcile, their free-spirited joy on the roof in spite of the odious reality in the crowded rooms below. Why? How? What was I supposed to do now that I knew this, now that I knew them?

I called Tennie in Texas, described the brothel, and told her of the children I had met on the roof, how they played using that small bit of elevated space to escape their mothers' sex acts and the equal dangers of the streets below.

"How do I pray for these children?" I asked, sobbing. " I don't know how to begin, if I am not supposed to pray for specific outcomes."

In her gentle voice, strong with experience and made gentle with empathy, Tennie began to tell me about her daughter, Kim, and the years Kim lived on the streets, in active addiction and anorexia. Tennie relied on Twelve Step programs as well as professional help to learn how not to enable, how to detach with love from a person's problems and to cope with her own desperate impulses to continually rescue and caretake her daughter. She had to let Kim go, to allow her to find recovery on her own. Tennie even held a symbolic funeral for Kim to assist her as she let go of her daughter. She described to me how, over and over, hundreds of times, as her fears about Kim resurfaced and reanimated her grief process, she would visualize her daughter. In her mind's eye, she gently held her daughter in her arms and carried her to the God of her understanding. Tennie described her God concept as a conventional image of a loving father and said she would lay her daughter in her God's lap, turning Kim over to a Power greater than herself, who could do for Kim what no earthly parent, however loving and dedicated, ever could. Tennie would repeat this prayerful visualization as often as necessary.

I pondered my God concept and to what I might be able to turn over to each child, what I could entrust to them. A river's edge came to me, and I saw a beautiful, mighty, flowing river, which I realized represented God's will. I thought of myself and how I sometimes wade right in, abandoning myself to the care and protection of God's will without hesitation. Sometimes, though, I sit on the riverbank, stuck in my self-will, watching the river flow right by, unwilling to take the steps necessary to put me in the graceful currents. Other times I step in, but only to my ankles, back turned on the river, staring at the bank, thinking about why I can't have it both ways, self-will and God's will. Or I come to God as I did tonight, on my knees, crawling, begging for it.

As this powerful imagery was coming to me, I received it as a gift being washed up on the shores of my conscious mind by something preternatural inside of me. I knew that it would work for me throughout my life. In my mind's eye, I was on the brothel roof. I picked up each child one by one. I cradled them, kissed their foreheads, tenderly said their names, and squeezed them into me, swaying gently as I walked them to the river's edge. There, like Moses's mother, I accepted my limitations and set them in the river of God's love, which could take them someplace I never could.

Aadarshini
Yamuna
Nabhendu
Asiya
Aarti

Utterly drained, but now with some degree of peace, I thanked Tennie and hung up the phone. I carefully placed the small pieces of paper in a small fabric bag, and set them on my bedside table by a flower and a picture of Dario. I lay on my side, staring. I could put the kids in the river, but I couldn't quite let go of the scraps. I trusted I would know when it came time, whether casually or in ceremony, and I knew it would be an enormous act of faith on my part that I wasn't ready for just yet. The scraps were a way of hanging on, just a little longer, to the delusion that I have some control, some influence. Giving them up would mean accepting my limitations all over again, knowing there are things I cannot, and will not ever, know, such as how each child's life turns out, if there would ever be peace. But I can hope, and I can believe. Along with hard work, it's all that is asked of me.

~ ~ ~

That evening, I invited our group to a sharing circle in my room, during which each one could, if she wished, process their Mumbai experiences. Seane regaled us with her thoughts about her time with the women of Sanghamitra. It was ironic for a Westerner to teach yoga in the country where it all began, but the prostituted women of India are so isolated from their society that the benefits of their great traditions are often lost to them. Helping them to bring some healing to their own bodies, an antidote to the abuse heaped on them for years, was her dream. As always, Seane received much more than she gave in this simple act of service. She came back bursting with respect for their activism, heralding their life experience as the expertise the policy-makers and governments actually need.

We tried to process together every night as a way to release the emotions that surfaced during our time in the field. It is important to name our feelings, out them, and release them before they have a chance to become toxic to our bodies and our souls. So many aid workers (and others in helping professions, such as nurses) anesthetize themselves at the end of the day with alcohol, cigarettes, food, or even drugs to numb the effects of what they've witnessed. Too often, gifted, compassionate people burn out. Seane and I encouraged the humanitarian and aid staff to join us to talk honestly about what we had been seeing and feeling, even if those thoughts were not exactly politically correct. In our circle, it is okay to admit, "The stench of that person made me want to gag and run away," or, "I wanted to smash that pimp's head in with a brick." We would listen without judgment in a room filled with candles and friends. We considered how we could overcome the anger, revulsion, guilt, and fear that we weren't doing enough and carry on with greater love.

Our staff members were so used to stuffing down their emotions that this process was alien, even frightening to some of them. Some later confessed they thought it was compulsory, because I was on PSI's board of directors, and I felt bad about that. For myself, I have made it mandatory. Feelings are not facts, and in order to endure in this work, not burn out or give up or just stay home on the farm, I need to express my feelings, even the crazy ones. I need the support of others as I do so, to know I am not alone in my internal struggles. And I certainly need spiritual tools to go the distance and stay present in the work, when it is so tempting and easy to become hopeless, apathetic, cynical. Because if I am one with every being on earth, then I must keep growing in order to arrive at the place of not just intellectualizing, but feeling my shared humanity with both the prostitutes and the pimps, the abused and the abusers, and locate within my own heart compassion for both, equally and unconditionally.

Easier said than done.

I knew that my compassion was going to be tested at the next big event on my schedule: an afternoon with hundreds of truck drivers who exploit men, women, and children to satisfy their alleged sexual "needs" during the long separations from their families. As I said my evening prayers, I wondered how my tools were going to see me through that one.

Chapter 18

ADVENTURES IN BOLLYWOOD

Geeta (who died in the streets shortly after this photo was taken)
and Sushmita Sen.

Leadership is taking responsibility for enabling others to achieve purpose
in the face of uncertainty.

—*MARSHALL GANZ*

They don't call me the Vanna White of condoms for nothing. To teach correct and consistent condom use during these field trips, I travel with a life-size wooden replica of a penis in my shoulder bag. At appropriate times, I whisk it out to demonstrate how to unroll and apply a condom, often to the mortification and amusement of the women, teens at drop-in centers, HIV-positive couples, and others who are not accustomed to openly discussing sexual behavior. I have performed the ritual for thousands of people over the years, but never, until India, all at one time.

This day, I stood on a small wooden platform beneath a colorful tent while five or six thousand Indian truck drivers crowded around for some good ole behavior change communication. They were piling on top of their trucks and hanging off light poles to get a glimpse—not of me, but of my partner in this demonstration, Akshay Kumar, one of Bollywood's biggest action heroes, the Indian equivalent of Will Smith or Bruce Willis, but with a fan base of a billion people. Kate Roberts had done a sensational job of reaching out to India's major film stars to help us in our awareness and prevention campaign. And now I passed my wooden dildo to this gracious and charismatic actor, who held it in one hand while he translated my instructions into Hindi through a megaphone held in the other. The truckers watched, grinning and slack-jawed, while I tore open a condom packet and did my thing: "And make sure you roll it *all* the way to the base of the penis!" It was a lesson in HIV prevention and unintended pregnancy that they would never forget. And with any luck, the message would sink in and save hundreds, maybe thousands, of lives.

This particular event happened in the Nagar trucking "halt point" outside of Jaipur, on the last leg of our trip through India, and it was the culmination of a remarkable and, for me, life-changing journey that had begun in Mumbai's Cotton Green terminal.

On any given day, between two and three million long-distance truckers are crisscrossing the giant subcontinent that is India on its thousands and thousands of miles of national highways. At the end of their runs, they park in huge open-air terminals like the one at Cotton Green, often waiting for days while goods arrive and are loaded for the return trip. The trucks are charming works of art, hand-painted with colorful religious symbols, flowers, and adornments that signify their pride of ownership (I took lots of pictures for Dario). Men live, work, and sleep in their trucks and cook underneath them on tiny kerosene stoves. There is a public bathroom block that charges 5 rupees, or you can pee against the wall, as I saw many doing. Otherwise there are no services. Cotton Green is like a mobile village filled with thousands of idle men, which is a recipe for trouble.

Away from their wives, they often go to Kamathipura for sex—or the prostituted women come to them—which puts them at high risk for contracting STIs and HIV and taking the virus and STIs home to their wives. Rural married women are the highest new infection group in India. About three hundred thousand of these long-distance truckers are already living with HIV, making them one of the most critical groups for interventions.

Our outreach program in Cotton Green has been in place since 1998 and was an absolute joy to see. Interpersonal communicators wearing bright yellow coats were stationed intermittently along lines of trucks that stretched as far as the eye could see. One group was staging a very dramatic and loud play, punctuated by an attention-grabbing drumbeat, the plot of which was safe sex. Another group offered a ball toss game (I missed both my tries). The results lead, win or lose, to dialogues about sex: what is safe sex, what kinds of women might be HIV-positive (Any and all, dude! Looking healthy doesn't mean for sure she's not! Use protection with each partner!), how does one reduce risk (Well, reducing the number of partners would be great, but that's a tough long-term sell with these guys), where products and services are available, and the importance and confidentiality of HIV testing.

I meandered from truck to truck. I chatted with hundreds of men, it seemed, and I was followed by more. I called them my "posse." I sat with them in the dirt under their trucks, where they seek shade from the scorching sun, disregarding the rubbish. We talked about faithfulness, prostitution, and masturbation as an alternative to reduce the number of partners. (Maybe, I was told. But abstaining? No way.) Next we talked about sex with children. I assured them I knew they were good people and that they themselves would not have sex with children, but did they see children in the brothels or know men who did this? Oh, yes and yes, they said.

One new and especially garrulous friend, Yasin, said although he personally would not, he would never tell someone else not to! I challenged that heartily and asked if he, as my friend, would be willing to reconsider. I explained that children were meant to be just that, *children*, and not to be used for sex by adults, and that it was up to us to stand up for children, who alone were vulnerable and defenseless. We spoke at length, and he said he would share his belief that it in fact was not right the next time he saw or heard of a fellow trucker doing so. He told me how children were pimped and made available and described the little signs used to indicate their availability all along the trucking networks. I told him I had heard. And I looked at him and wondered if he was just telling me what I wanted to hear, that perhaps he knew about these heinous acts because he himself was a perpetrator.

And then the most amazing thing happened. I did not judge him.

I suddenly realized that I was in a truck stop cavorting with men who paid for sex, absolutely loving them. I was amazed and grateful for my growth. When I began this work years ago, I was sick and shattered by brothels alone. The idea of facing a man who went to a brothel was impossible; I thought I'd implode because of *his* shameful behavior. Now I had journeyed from wanting to kill (oh, I mean that seriously) the clients with my undiluted rage to standing among *thousands* of them and chatting comfortably, momentarily blessed by knowing the difference between their souls and their behavior, sensing the God seed in each man. I felt the same open-mindedness, acceptance, compassion, love, and concern for them that I did for the women they exploited. It was a total and complete *miracle*. It was not that I had joined the oppressor or that I suffered from a kind of Stockholm syndrome, whereby one is converted to the kidnapper's point of view; it was that I had dealt with my own shame and now I could stand with others in theirs with an open heart. In *no way* did I excuse their behavior, but something about regarding them as the sick and suffering had freed me of the extremity of my own emotions that had previously rendered me useless to them.

~ ~ ~

Truckers in India are themselves exploited at every turn, much like prostituted women. Indians generally believe they are responsible for HIV and ostracize them. One man with whom I spoke longed to marry, but each time a woman's family discovered his occupation, they withdrew her availability to marry him. The police harass them with fraudulent infractions: Your cargo is taxed, give me so many rupees, your truck is overloaded, give me rupees, there is a temporary fee for using this road, give me rupees, your papers are not correct, give me rupees. Of course, the police harass prostitutes, too, so for a few hours I thought, *Aha! I've found the bad guys in this scenario: It's the police!* Then, of course, someone told me how the police were not paid a living wage, either, and their standard of living was also horrible. This person said it so well: "Poverty and corruption go hand in hand." So yet again, compassion extended to another group of people I moments ago had blamed, and once again it was confirmed that poverty is the worst form of violence. Poverty reduction solutions are what each of these groups, without exception, need. My dad taught me a long time ago that shit trickles down; in India it goes sideways.

~ ~ ~

Well, if you really want to jockey for title of most marginalized group in India, men who have sex with men would be hard to beat. I sat with a group of men who cruised the area to service the truckers. Yasin and I had talked about this aspect of paid sex; it's an option for most truckers, who are quite indiscriminate. The attitude is "any port in a storm." I had also heard that some had sex with other male truckers in the sadly misguided belief that HIV couldn't be spread by sex with other men.

About fifteen of us sat in a small yellow room in a shabby building block in Cotton Green, which was a drop-in center for men who have sex with men. It was decorated with tattered curtains and empowerment decals, where the prostituted men gathered to discuss their challenges, their solutions. Some wore eyeliner, one sported a glittery top, all of them were sassy and chatty. I visited with a bewitching, kind, and utterly unique transsexual named Kausur/Mamuia. Kausur was her male persona, which she used in her capacity as a peer educator for truckers who had sex with men, and Mamuia was her female identity, which was where she felt most at home. She was gorgeous, carefully attired, made-up, dainty, delicate, and very sure of herself. As a teen boy, she felt inside she was a girl and began to live her truth regardless of the cost. Her mother had accepted her (and lives with her), her siblings had not. She shared a bisexual husband with a straight woman. She was monogamous and had been since marriage; when she learned about HIV, she immediately began using condoms. Along every step of what was to me a bizarre sexual journey, she had nonetheless exemplified responsible behavior. Of course, we talked about our faith; what else could sustain a person through a story like hers?

She sang two folks songs for me, complete with poised and well-executed dance moves in the classical tradition. In return for the mesmerizing entertainment she provided, I took out my iPod and played Eva Cassidy's version of "People Get Ready."

I was deeply honored by the way people shared their stories with me, with the way they trusted me. Today, that was what floored me, the gratitude and sweetness. And whatever gifts I gave by allowing them to be truly heard returned to me tenfold.

~ ~ ~

Next morning I did my usual routine of meditating, eating quickly according to my meal plan (protein, starch, fruit, and fat for breakfast), making a five-minute attempt at looking sort of maybe kind of cute if you closed one eye and squinted the other, and surrendering the day and the outcome to a Power greater than myself. I knew I'd need to do that more than once, as I was in brothels again, this time with a woman who was a stranger to me but a beloved star to millions of Indians: Sushmita Sen.

As anyone who follows the movies already knows, India has the biggest, most dynamic film industry in the world, and it's based in Mumbai, formerly Bombay—hence the name Bollywood. Indians are absolutely crazy for films, and they follow the Bollywood stars in numbers that make Hollywood agents swoon. That is why it can be so useful to recruit actors to lend their social capital to marginalized and despised populations, to dispel myths and stigma through public conversations and the media about a range of vital issues, from medically accurate sex education and HIV to access to education for girls. But Indian society is so conservative that it's been hard to convince anyone to speak out.

That a person of Sushmita's stature even deigns to talk about this issue, much less hangs out in a brothel, is shocking in Indian society. We approached her to join the campaign because of her willingness to break with convention in her personal and professional life. She was a single mother with an adopted daughter and had played the role of "immoral" (whatever that means) women in films. Typically, the big stars in the global South do not touch roles that are not virtuous, and I was curious to meet her.

At a Catholic school compound (of course I managed to find a priest with whom to talk for a few minutes), I sat in an austere room with nothing but a chair. A tall, regal woman in a lovely pale blue sari came in and immediately captivated me with her womanly brilliance. She reminded me of Salma right away (although let's be clear, S.H. is in a league of her own). Even though she had worked until three a.m. the night before, she was focused, clear-eyed, intent, attentive, dazzling. Her wild, dark hair was unbrushed, she wore no makeup, and her only dressed-up detail were long, lilac fingernails. She oozed star: that "It" factor of confidence, poise, carriage . . . and killer eyebrows!

As we readied for the film crew, she asked me a few questions about my work and shared some of her own story. She is a former Miss Universe who went into modeling and acting. In a maverick move, she chose not to marry and had to fight in the courts to adopt her daughter seven years ago. Her longtime personal assistant had recently died of AIDS. He had been so afraid of the stigma of his disease that he'd told no one, not even her. He might have received treatment and lived a long life, but the shame of AIDS killed him as surely as the disease. It was because of him that Sushmita decided she would campaign to end the stigma and raise awareness that there is help and hope for people living with HIV.

~ ~ ~

Hope, however, had already run out for the first woman we visited together at the Marwari Chawl brothel in Kamathipura. Geeta Sulunke was from Nepal and in her early thirties. Years ago she'd had her name tattooed on her arm; it was misspelled. Her luck went down from there. She was drugged one day at home and woke up in a Mumbai brothel. She waited a month, trapped in *karza* behind a curtain, before she succumbed to her first buyer. It's such an Indian process, that. While rape, and certainly gang rape, is not unheard of in the Indian sex trade, it is not the dominant method of breaking a woman, as it is in Cambodia and Eastern Europe. In India, many girls and women are simply left to sit there in this new, squalid, dark, frightening place until they are hungry and hopeless enough to surrender.

Geeta became HIV-positive quickly. Soon after, she developed tuberculosis. HIV-positive people like Geeta are five to six times more likely to develop tuberculosis, which is already one of the deadliest killers in India. According to the World Health Organization, one person dies from it here every ninety seconds. She never, thank goodness, became pregnant. When we entered the sparse room where she lived, she greeted us with a *namaste* and a lifeless smile, revealing dirty teeth. Her limbs were emaciated, and her skin sallow. She answered our questions in a monotone. She was grim, cynical, illiterate. She looked me dead in the eye and told me neither to fall in love nor to marry. When I told her I had and I am, she turned away from me to focus her attention on Sushmita, and she did not speak to me again. She was one of the few people I met in my travels that I was completely unable to reach in any way. The only thing I overheard Sushmita saying to Geeta was "We are all going to die someday, shouldn't we live while we can?"

Geeta just coughed, covering her mouth with a handful of her sari.

Sadly, she died a few weeks after our meeting. Knowing her end was imminent, and that she could no longer be used for sex, the brothel bosses put Geeta out on the sidewalk—well, actually, in the gutter—to die. A PSI staff member who had been the only person to gain Geeta's confidence found her there and held her as she expired. Then, she washed her remains, collected her corpse, and provided for her cremation.

~ ~ ~

Any trepidation about working with Sushmita evaporated once I saw how wonderfully personable yet gentle she was with shy, vulnerable, traumatized people. It was a horrific time at the brothels, but the highlight of our day together was a ceremony with the members of Sanghamitra at a hall rented by the project. Thirty radiantly excited women of all ages and sizes turned out for us in their best saris. We were greeted with incense, drishti dots, and elaborate garlands. Sweets were fed to us. I loved watching Sush; she's an enormously popular movie star accustomed to this adoration, and I studied how she reciprocated. She kissed heads, took the sweet out of her own mouth, and put it in the giver's. She gave her garland back. That stopped me short. Oh no, all this time, was I supposed to give my garlands back? Dang! I'm pretty selfish when it comes to my flowers. I decided to believe someone would have told me by now if I was supposed to honor the giver by returning my flowers right away. And so, like a child with a favorite toy, I kept my garland!

There were speeches, presentations, affirmations. But the best part was the dancing. A boy child began the festivities with the most extraordinary dance. He was gifted, and the room roared with encouragement and approval. He sweated profusely yet never dimmed in his exertions. I was prodded to join him, so—garland swinging—I twirled around behind him. Eventually everyone joined in, Sushmita dazzling with her graceful Bollywood moves, all of us waving our arms in the air in joyous communion, the ecstasy of sisterhood.

~ ~ ~

"This is big," Kate explained as we drove north toward the giant Bollywood soundstage where Shahrukh Khan was filming a movie—something like his fiftieth starring role.

Kate had met him at a cocktail party the night before. He had arrived at an hour commensurate with his status, meaning one a.m.—which was long after I had left. I have rarely been much of a partier, and I'm constitutionally unable to hang with the late-nighters. I know I miss out on so much fun, particularly when I'm making movies. *Norma Jean and Marilyn,* which filmed in Hollywood, was one of the only movies during which I could partake in the afterhours moveable feast, partly because the feast so often landed at my hotel, the Chateau Marmont. I have amazing memories of being up so late with Mira Sorvino and Sean Penn, both of whom were nominated for Oscars that year, that we were still drinking champagne and swapping crazy actor stories when the daily trade magazines were delivered, with both of them featured on the covers. But last night I had missed my chance to meet Shahrukh because I needed to poke around my hotel room in my nightgown and write in my journal. The irrepressible Kate, though, had been willing to take one for the team and wait for his arrival. He had wanted to meet me, and when he asked her where I had gone, her patented charm had yielded an invitation to visit him on set to discuss his joining the YouthAIDS campaign. She explained what an opportunity this was, quite possibly the biggest box office draw in the world, with hundreds of millions of fans. "He's the Brad and Angelina, the George and Julia, the Bruce and Arnold, all combined," said Kate.

Expectations are usually disastrous, and I assumed that a film set, surely, would be . . . well, a film set. I didn't think I was going to 20th Century Fox or Warner Brothers, but it's such a powerful, influential industry in movie-crazy India, I figured it would be at least a little upscale. Wrong. We turned off the crowded, honking highway onto a dusty secondary road that passed stagnating rivers choked with debris and rubbish. Litter lined the verges. A few tattered picnic tables and snack stands were open to the public. I saw a man, asleep in his rickshaw, looking for all the world as if someone had broken his neck. Ubiquitous stray animals scrounged by the wayside, their ribs as prominent as the flying buttresses of Notre Dame Cathedral.

The studio itself was a plain, large, unadorned building with a tin roof. I wondered immediately what they did for sound during the rainy season. Before we got out of the car, Kate and I invited God into the experience. I realized I was "Bono-ing" this movie star, reaching out to a powerful entertainer to encourage him to use his substantial fame for good, reminding him he could effect great change through the ever-growing pop culture machine.

On the darkened stage were about twenty dancers dressed in a 1970s disco interpretation of traditional Indian classical dance costumes, with dazzling hair and body jewelry. The backdrop was painted an atmospheric gray-blue. Trees, painted silver with jingly bits dangling off branches, added to the Deco-Hollywood-fantasy-musical-gone-Bollywood camp. It was pure moviemaking magic: In person, it was all smoke and mirrors.

We were served tea and our host arrived, wearing an open shirt over his bare-chested pantaloon costume. Pleasantries were exchanged, and then I immediately said, "Please tell me what you'd like to know about what I do." Shahrukh looked at me evenly and gave a most interesting, blunt reply. He said he didn't know why I did it, and he didn't need to know. He believed, based on my commitment, that the work is credible and the situation is urgent. He was happy simply to do whatever I asked him to do, because I was the one asking him. End of conversation. In sixty seconds, we had a commitment and a plan: We would draft public service announcements for him to shoot while on set. He would designate PSI as a charity on *Who Wants to Be a Millionaire,* the wildly popular show that he hosted (and that the world later came to know Indians love via the film *Slumdog Millionaire*). He was willing to talk about "sensitive" stuff, like married men who paid for sex. He offered the premiere of this film as a fund-raiser. He agreed to be the "face" of our new Indian financed hedge fund to benefit grassroots programs.

Kate and I were giddy. This was a *huge* coup in so many ways: This immense cultural figure would be modeling feminist male behavior for hundreds of millions of Indians, directly discussing medically accurate sex education in public, reducing the stigma and myth around HIV, and raising money/awareness for our programs. It was a hallelujah chorus slam dunk.

As we said our goodbyes, members of the costume department brought us gifts, rows of glass bracelets and dangly earrings worn by the film's stars, wrapped in shiny paper. Kate and I oohed and ahhed. I asked them lots of questions. They said they worked nineteen hours a day, slept on set, and had no union. I was shocked. The unfairness and inequity and brutal poverty of India were really beginning to wear me down. Despite the victories of the afternoon, I was finding myself increasingly pissed off at this country. And at my next activity, I was about to become a whole lot angrier.

Chapter 19

A HOLY MESS

Neelam and Komal, the orphans who asked me to adopt them.

Seek refuge in the attitude of detachment and you will amass the wealth of spiritual awareness. The one who is motivated only by desire for the fruits of their action, and anxious about the results, is miserable indeed.

—Bhagavad Gita, *verse 49*

$\mathcal{N}$atasha sat in a large chair in the production office, looking very small, frail, gorgeous, and groomed. Her hair was long and lovely in a Veronica Lake–type wave. Her English was fairly good, and she was soft spoken yet clear. The camera was set up to protect her identity, and in postproduction her voice would be modified, too. One of the documentary film's producers, posing as a sex client, had put feelers out to find a "high-class call girl" I could interview to show how HIV/AIDS is spread to the upper reaches of Indian society by prostituted women who service wealthy clients. That was the story we were looking for; what we found out still gives me nightmares.

When Natasha arrived at the address her "escort service" was given and discovered what we were really after, she told us she was a full-fledged sex slave and her life would be at risk if her owner discovered what she was doing. But she wanted to tell her story, if only to help others in her predicament. And we had to pay her fee—12,000 rupees, about $270 U.S.— so that nothing looked odd and she'd have the right sum of money to give her pimp.

When we settled in, she told me she was about twenty-one or twenty-two years old (many Indians can only approximate their age) and had traveled to Mumbai when she was about eighteen to visit some relatives. Her luggage was lost and there had been a lot of confusion about her arrival. She managed to end up at a girlfriend's apartment to spend the night while she sorted things out. Her friend was going out for the evening and invited her; she was happy to tag along. The friend took Natasha to a hotel. They went up to a guest room, where a man was waiting. The friend smiled and left the room. To her bewilderment, Natasha realized she had been left there to have sex with the man. Fearing physical violence and feeling trapped with no way out, she did. When the man let her go, she went downstairs. Her friend was waiting. She slapped her face. The friend said, "Welcome to the garbage bin."

In a disastrous piece of timing, the relatives she had been looking for had tracked her down through her friend just as she was leaving the hotel. They put together why she was at such a nice hotel and immediately disowned her as a whore. She had nowhere to go but back to her friend's apartment, where her fate, trapped in sex, was sealed. Simultaneously, her relatives were spreading this information back home. She was swiftly, irrevocably ostracized by her family there—even though they took the money she sent them.

Natasha told me she was in a hell she could not escape. Her story is a complex puzzle, a combination of truly being trapped *and the commensurately powerful perception of being trapped*. That makes it hard to describe; it also makes my dismay deeper. Here are some questions I asked and her answers:

Why didn't you then, why don't you now, just go to the police and explain what happened? Why don't you tell them about your life now?

"They would be the first to rape me," she said with a sad smile. "Then they would simply hand me back over, and there would be more trouble when I was returned."

Why don't you secretly, however long it takes, stash away a little bit of money and just sneak away, go somewhere else in India, start over? (Yes, I asked a lot of embarrassingly dumb questions from a Western perspective . . . but I think we all would have.)

"Wherever I go, I will always be *this*." She sighed. "I will see a former client who will reveal my past, and I will never be accepted anywhere as anything but this."

This was so troubling. In a country of nearly 1.2 billion, she had sufficiently internalized her victimization and her boss's fear tactics to believe that wherever she might go on the subcontinent, a former client would identify her and she'd be put back into forced sex. And it might be worse than her current situation. Even though her client's large fees are immediately taken away from her, she holds back a little to send to her home village to support eleven members of her extended family, the same remorseless family that shunned her. Because they "depended" on her, she said she had to continue earning such high fees. She was trapped by her own mind and didn't even know it.

Do your clients use condoms?

"Yes, the boss makes sure they understand they must. I am tested for HIV every alternate month."

Ah, yes, it's not called organized crime for nothing. A healthy prostitute is a better earner.

Has anyone among you tested positive?

"Yes."

What happened? Did she receive treatment?

"I don't know. She disappeared."

Where do you think you will end up? Is it your fear that when you begin earning less you'll be dumped at a brothel in Kamathipura?

"I can't think about that," she said, her face flashing blind panic. The question so terrified her, I instantly regretted asking it.

When I asked her questions about her daily life, her answers were even more chilling. Natasha said she lived in a three-bedroom apartment with ten others, all of whom shared her predicament. She is on call twenty-four hours a day, seven days a week. She never knows when the call will come; she lives knowing at any second she will be sent to have sex with a strange man, and she must do whatever, however grotesque, painful, and degrading, he wants. Her owner is someone she has never seen. In a perverse twist on *Charlie's Angels,* she hears his voice on the phone as he bosses and threatens her. The pimp is the day-to-day manager of her life, checking on her, spying, supervising, and collecting money. Her clients include Indians and foreigners. I asked her if she had been to the Taj, my hotel, and she smiled. "Oh yes, many, many times." I felt sick.

Sensing the destroyed condition of her soul, I flailed for something, anything, positive to talk about. "Your English is so impressive, Natasha. You speak wonderfully. I bet you read very well." She said indeed, she did read some. When I asked what she might envision herself doing as a career, she told me she had long ago dreamed of becoming an Ayurvedic doctor, but insisted that this was now impossible. She did, however, try to surreptitiously teach the others, the little ones, at the apartment to read so that maybe someday they could do something different.

"The little ones?" I asked, a new sickness rising in me.

"I am the oldest," she said. "The youngest is about fourteen."

What? How long has she been there?

"She was eleven when I arrived three years ago. The others are fourteen, fifteen, sixteen, around there."

What does one say to that? How does one react? My time with Natasha was coming to a close. She couldn't be late without arousing suspicion. The next part for me was incredibly emotional. To know she was walking out of that room and back into her life was a pain the likes of which I have felt only a few times in my life, pain like walking away from forty orphans in a well-meaning but underfunded crèche in a South African slum. It was just so wrong, so very, very wrong. I pulled her close to me and held her and tried to burn myself into her eyes.

I said to her, "Will you believe there is hope for you?"

"No."

"Natasha, can you believe, then, that I believe? When you are completely hopeless and despairing, will you remember me, *can you believe that I believe?*"

She broke down. "Yes. I will try, I will try. I will try to believe that you believe."

The time for which we had paid was up. She was crying as she hurried out the door. As a team we raged, sobbed, planned, plotted, and despaired. With Papa Jack guiding us with his New York police and FBI experience, we tried frantically to sort out ways to reach Natasha again, to rescue the children. Every idea was a bust, as each one, given the vulpinic efficiency of organized crime, led to potential danger for Natasha. Their network is so vast, so thorough, so complete—and girls and women are so disposable. It is unlikely we will ever find her. She and the other slaves of her type are a mysterious, inaccessible component of prostituted commercial sex. But we will never forget her. And every day, every minute, every breath, I bless her. I still believe, Natasha, I still believe.

~ ~ ~

The evening with Natasha made my meeting the next day harder. We passed again through rows and rows and rows of houses, many with modest religious icons or now dead flowers over the crumbling portals, crammed full of people going about their daily lives. In one of these houses Neelam, fourteen, and her sister, Komal, twelve, were waiting for me in matching yellow saris. They were AIDS orphans who lived with an aunt in two low-ceilinged, windowless rooms. Both girls were very small and thin, with long dark hair. Komal's was lustrous and smooth, Neelam's was rough, coarse, dry. I wondered if it was from malnutrition. The children each took a hand, brought me in, sat me down. They were eager yet reserved. Indian women sit alongside one another, knees touching, arms draped across each other's legs. I had picked up on this and gratefully snuggled into a comfortable position with these precious girls. They would never sit in my lap, but they did sidle up to lean on me and let me love on them.

Their story was all too familiar. Their daddy became HIV-positive having sex outside the marriage. He died soon after being tested. Their mama also tested positive and died soon after. The girls, plus their then five-year-old brother, were suddenly orphans. An aunt who lived with them was also HIV-positive and suffered from tuberculosis. She slept alone in the back room, as she was highly contagious. They had, thank God, a grandmother, who did much of the cooking. When I asked Komal how she prayed and what she prayed for, she replied she prayed her auntie didn't die, too.

Neelam, at fourteen, exclusively supported this family of five. From eight thirty a.m. until five p.m., six days a week, she worked sewing embroidery to earn 1,200 rupees a month, the equivalent of $27 U.S. (and one-tenth of what Natasha's pimp charged each client). It was not nearly enough to feed them all; Neelam's diet was supplemented through PSI's nutrition program, which provides families in need with rice, wheat, sugar, lentils, cooking oil, and nuts. After work she had a half-hour break, at which time she then went to night school until nine p.m. Neelam was incredibly bright and eager to learn. English was her favorite subject, and she wanted to be a flight attendant. Her brother and sister were able to go to school, but this small child was at home each day only long enough to eat a little bit and to sleep. It dawned on me later that her baby sister's hair was shiny and smooth because Neelam took care of it, as a mother would. But there was no one there to take care of Neelam's hair.

She told me she liked where she worked, she liked sewing. She had no idea that having a job was illegal at her age. She had no sense of our outrage. She had simply adapted, naturally, for the survival of the four who relied on her.

Where Neelam was all gentle responsibility, her baby sister was all attitude. She told me she wanted to be a human rights lawyer when she grew up, to help poor people. I had no doubt she would be qualified, cut out for it, capable to the max. The question was, of course, could she make it out of the slum first? Girls like Neelam and Komal were exactly the kids who were trafficked. Easily, so easily, a man in the neighborhood with financial pressures of his own could invite them for a snack and whisk them to a brothel. Easily, a male relative could show up and say they were his "responsibility," and because he himself was poor beyond poor or he came from a state where child marriage was still common, he could sell them to a pimp, arrange a marriage for the dowry money, dispose of them.

In talking about our dreams, Neelam said all she wanted was to make others happy. Life had taught her, so young, that that was her purpose. But I encouraged her to read, to play, to talk to an imaginary friend, to find something, anything, that could be just hers inside of herself. I explained that unless she built up a sense of her own self, she would have nothing to actually give the others she clearly loved so much. It was not lost on me, even then, that I was in a way talking to my younger self, offering her the lessons it had taken me so many years to learn.

At the end of our visit, the girls looked at each other expectantly and then asked me to bring them home with me to America, saying they wanted to live with me. I realized they had planned this moment. They had coordinated their request, maybe they had even rehearsed it a few times prior to my arrival. I imagined my own sister and me as little girls, collaborating in an effort to have our way about something.

I was having a flurry of fiercely competing thoughts. I wanted to say "yes" although I knew it was not practical. I could not adopt them simply because in this moment I did not want to endure the pain of seeing their faces fall when I denied them their birthright, a childhood free from hunger and want, a guaranteed education—things I obviously could provide. But what about the real complexities of international adoption? Indian bureaucracy? My husband? Did I have the right in this instant to say "yes" simply because they had asked, when I couldn't guarantee it would be allowed, and I would be making a huge unilateral decision within my marriage?

In fact, I believe that I did have the right to say yes. Just as I, as a little girl, had had the right to hear "yes" when I begged a variety of adults to adopt me, to take custody of me, to give me safe harbor away from a life that included terrible abuse. But those adults, even grandparents who cherished me, had said "no." And now, so did I. In that moment, as I quietly turned down two vulnerable girls, I became the kind of adult I had sworn I would never be: a practical person constrained by "reality" who says no to little girls in pain, grief, and need, children who would go hungry and be unprotected when I walked out the door. It gutted me.

Although I could not give them the "yes" they deserved to hear, I gave Neelam and Komal hugs, kisses, strokes, words of positive encouragement and reassurance as I thanked them for the very special day. "I can promise you that I will never forget you," I told them. "I will always pray for you. And I will do my part to be sure that girls like you can be educated, and empowered, and realize your dreams." With one on either side, they escorted me through their labyrinthine neighborhood back to my car. By the time we reached it, Komal, the sassy one, was tired of me. I was tired of me, too, my lame answers, the futility of my speeches to girls like these.

~ ~ ~

That night, I sat alone in my room to contemplate what I could do for the young, vulnerable girls I had met: what was realistic financially, how I could best help, how much/how many of them I could take on. My intention was to increase my conscious contact with the God of my understanding, praying for direction. Would it be letter writing? Simply praying for them? Each had taken hold of my heart in such a special way. It felt powerfully mystical, in a world so crowded with souls, to find my way somehow, through circumstances, coincidences, timing, and fate, to the people I met. I lived halfway around the globe. There were 1.2 billion people in India. How exactly had I ended up in Kausar and Nasreen's slum, climbing their ladder, sitting on their floor, hearing their stories, finding myself in their preciousness and resilience and vulnerability? Or Neelam's? I could not walk away without taking with me some kind of responsibility for the meeting by helping out in some tangible way. I wanted to do more than remember them and tell their stories. Too many children—oh, Ouk Srey Leak—had slipped out beyond my reach.

In New Delhi, on the next leg of our journey through India, I found the answer to my prayers.

~ ~ ~

When we arrived in India's capital city, the first thing we all noticed were the *trees*! And then, along the highway, was a large, hilly verge awash in *flowers*! I squealed. These weren't just accidental flowers making an evolutionary stab at surviving, it was a proper, planted, cultivated flower garden, and it was a sight for sore eyes. We passed a few families and individuals living on the sidewalks of our leafy hotel neighborhood. They had set up little shelters for themselves, stretching a bit of fabric or plastic or cardboard to make a roof. I saw a few small fires built for cooking, but not many. I later learned that Delhi has a draconian antibegging policy, which has effectively criminalized poverty, pushing it back from the streets where visitors might see it.

There were important people for me to meet here and more media events. But the project I most wanted to visit was a community-based antitrafficking NGO called Apne Aap. When Gloria Steinem heard that I was going to India, she told me that Ruchira Gupta, founder of Apne Aap, was the one person I had to meet who would rock my world, and was she right! In the early 1990s, when Ruchira was a journalist, she exposed a criminal organization that kidnapped Nepali girls and sold them into slavery in India. Her experiences with the trafficking survivors inspired her to establish a small group for women to empower themselves through education, vocational training, and advocacy. Since then, Apne Aap has grown into a network of 150 such antitrafficking self-help groups across the subcontinent, and Ruchira has become one of the world's most dynamic and authoritative voices for the abolition of sex slavery.

Apne Aap runs a community outreach center right in the heart of Delhi's red-light district. On the street below, a baby was being bathed by her mother in the street, the water flowing into open drains. Upstairs, the suite of rooms were clean swept and beautiful, with murals painted by members and simple, flat woven mats to sit on. The group has an open-door policy that invites anyone from the 'hood to join for only 10 rupees. Apne Aap uses a holistic approach to empowerment based on "learning, livelihood, and legal protection." The members teach one another self-reliance, self-efficacy, self-respect, self-love. It can be slow and hard going, but achieving sustainability is a process in the individual's mind and soul. It is capacity building at the most essential, elemental level. A trained staff offers vocational classes; I ran my hand over the black sewing machines, blessing the steel that helps a girl learn a trade that can save her life. They have English and computer instruction, classes to build social skills. The small self-help groups within the organization access banking and microcredit programs. And they also have lawyers on hand to train them to negotiate for their rights with the police and government bureaucrats.

I had brought a group from PSI, including Seane, to meet Ruchira Gupta at the center. She's a compact force of nature wrapped in a sari, greeting us with a burst of positive energy that about knocked us over. I could see right away how she could stare down brothel owners and traffickers to rescue sex slaves.

Ruchira is well versed in the reciprocal cycles of poverty and exploitation and how gender inequality sets the stage. The NGO is based on two Gandhian principles: *ahimsa,* or nonviolence, in its methods of confronting the violence of sex trafficking; and *antodaya,* which translates into "rise of the last," which means uplifting the poorest and most desolate girls and women into a world of dignity in which human beings are not bought and sold. Apne Aap also addresses the need to uplift and reeducate the men who exploit prostituted women and sex slaves, acknowledging that the destruction that happens in the soul of an abuser is equal to the victimization of the abused. It's something I talk about often, that misogyny is as harmful to men and boys as it is to women and girls. The prescribed definitions of manhood are as limiting and damaging to them spiritually as the consequences are to women.

Apne Aap groups support more than ten thousand girls and women who have either survived trafficking or are vulnerable to being trafficked. There have been many wonderful success stories, but also heartbreaking setbacks. Ruchira told us a particularly enraging story, involving a woman named Meena who had been trafficked to a brothel as a child. She was able to make a rare escape but tragically had to leave her small children behind. Meena rehabilitated her life, a heroic act in this culture, and tried unsuccessfully to rescue her children, to whom she had given birth in the brothel. When her young son escaped and told her that her daughter, Naina, had reached puberty and had been sold to another brothel, Meena contacted Ruchira Gupta for help. Ruchira pressured the local police to raid the brothel and rescue Naina, whom they found drugged and broken. They returned her to her mother, but Naina's agony wasn't yet over. The pimp from the original brothel sued Meena for custody, claiming Naina was his daughter. The judge deemed the mother of "bad character in her past life" and then declared that the pimp who sold her was the father. The child was sent to a remand home, meaning a juvenile delinquent house. Appalling, impossible? Only if you don't know India.

I instantly offered to stay in India as a public protest until that girl was freed. I was ready for civil disobedience on the curb in front of the remand house, or the judge's house. I was ready to fast, to call friends to travel to India to raise high holy hell with me. But Ruchira told me such a gesture wouldn't help. The Indian bureaucracy could be moved only from within; it took time.

Ruchira Gupta is dedicated to these individual cases, determined to save one life at a time. But her goal is much broader: She wants to fight sex trafficking on an institutional, international, and cultural level by abolishing prostitution everywhere. This position is not widely accepted, but it is gaining momentum as more and more studies show that legalizing and regulating prostitution does not put an end to trafficking, it enables it. A far more effective way forward is to *criminalize demand*. I could write a whole book about this issue, but suffice it to say that my eyes have been opened to the fact that we cannot bargain with the slave traders. We have to put them out of business. It's a practical and a moral imperative. I agree with Apne Aap's policy that prostitution is a systemic form of violence against girls and women, that it is driven by demand for purchased sex, which is driven by a culture of domination, and that exploiting women for sex is not inevitable, it is a choice that men make, and they can be deterred from making it.

Before we left the center, I sat with a group of young women and listened to their stories. One girl shared that her parents had chosen her husband, and she was resolutely denying the marriage. She insisted she would marry in her own time, for love. She was learning there were alternatives; there *should* be alternatives. Her folks were furious. "Apne Aap is spoiling your attitude and mind," they told her. She just kept coming back.

When we talked about abuse, one girl said, "Oh, when they beat us, it's okay if we've done something wrong. That is not abuse." I died a thousand deaths. Cultural change is so slow. I anguish over it sometimes, it is so slow.

I wanted them to know that we were all on a level playing field. When I asked, "Who among us has been abused?" I raised my hand, as did most of the others in the small group traveling with me. I noticed there was a writer from Reuters in the room, and I briefly worried that he would spin a story about how I raised my hand to my own question. Then I thought: *So be it. Most folks know I am in recovery, and I wouldn't be if I didn't have something from which to recover—the logic follows.* At this stage, I am actually beginning to have gratitude for my painful past, in that I may be *qualified* to sit with oppressed people all over the world, to be a part of a grassroots social justice process that speaks volumes about the promise of ending poverty, of an age of justice.

As our time drew to a close, each of us offered something we loved about ourselves. To break the ice, I held my bosom and said, "I love my boobs!" Peals of laughter erupted. Most girls were able to find something . . . teeth, hair, hands, eyes. Oh, but the struggling few who could not put words to one single admirable thing about themselves. Surprisingly, a girl who had been speaking up a great deal was one of these. When I said to her, "Well, I *love* your voice!" she was so pleased. The girl whose parents were attempting to force her to marry was also too ashamed to say anything good about herself; I told her I loved her strength. Funny, isn't it, that the ones who are so visibly special, so clearly gifted, carry so much shame?

~ ~ ~

That night, Seane came to my room and we each shared about our touching yet simultaneously troubling and triggering experience with Ruchira and Apne Aap. We were on our way to yet another cocktail party. Seane looked gorgeous, of course; my hair was wet, and my dress was still wadded up. As we were dashing off, I realized I hadn't said my prayers. I ran to the bedside, fell to my knees, and lo and behold, there she was beside me, also on her knees, hands clasped together earnestly. That's a friend, on her own path, a challenging and empathetic witness of my own. We finally made it out the door for what I hoped was our last late evening event for this trip.

~ ~ ~

The party was hosted by Vinay Rai, a huge philanthropist in India, whose Rai Foundation supports education for girls and women. Mr. Rai is an industrialist, engineer, and philosopher who is spiritually inspired to give back parts of his family's great wealth to help lift up his nation, especially through education. The foundation's motto is "*Manav Sewa Madhav Sewa*"—"Service of Humanity Is Service to God." Right up my alley.

I sat on a small stage while the Rais' well-dressed, beautifully mannered guests took slipcovered seats. Mr. Rai said nice things about Kate and me, described how his family's education fund was endowed with $150 million to send poor girls to college, covering even their clothing, so they would blend well with wealthier students. Then I took the stage.

If do say so myself, I gave was one fired-up, kick-ass, hyperlucid, emotional, effective, come-to-Jesus-meeting of a talk. I had called Bono earlier that night just to thank him so much for having reached out to me five years ago, for getting me into this "holy mess," as I called it. And as I was speaking, one of his great lines came to me: *This is not about charity, this is about justice.* The whole trip and especially the stories of Neelam, the orphan, and Naina, the trafficked girl in the detention home, lit a fire in me. Tonight, I would *not* back down.

I told the stories with all the passion in my soul, then I did something simply not done in Indian society: I asked the guests to give money. I knew most Indians' spiritual practice required them to give anonymously ("the right hand should not see what the left hand gives"). But the point was to break the seal, be mavericks. And it worked. We raised $25,000 on the spot. The money was used for the nutrition camps that provided food for Neelam and others like her.

Mr. Rai retook the stage and seemed not at all perturbed by my impertinence. In fact, he made a surprise announcement: He was going to take care of all the orphans I had met on my trip and pay for their educations! What a remarkable, humbling, and rapturous answer to my searching prayer for these girls. What a priceless, indescribable gift. It seemed it would be radically life-altering for these children. Education is the surest way out, and tonight theirs was guaranteed.

The spectacular nature of the night was not yet over. After Mr. Rai's announcement, I spontaneously decided to retake the podium and make a special plea to the guests. "There is a gross miscarriage of justice to which I would like to draw your attention," I said. "I am a white American. What judge here is going to listen to me? I urge each and every citizen of India here tonight to use your voice to help Naina, a child born in a brothel, rescued by her mother, but now, insensibly, by a judge's order, in a remand home . . ." and I told the story.

Before the evening was over, Mr. Rai told me that two very prominent lawyers had agreed to help Ruchira with the mother and daughter's case. He explained that the lower courts, where this judge made the obscene ruling, are corrupt, inefficient, bothersome, mired. But in India, cases may be taken directly to the highest court in the land—which the lawyers were willing to do to reverse such a travesty of justice. I was ecstatic (and even happier when I learned that Naina was soon released and reunited with her mother).

~ ~ ~

It was ironic that in the days after such good news about the lawyers' intervention on behalf of Naina, and the scholarships for my girls, I finally hit the wall. I was so homesick and allowed myself to go through all sorts of petty angers: I resented that I was going to miss the lilacs and the Bradford pears back home. I looked at India's pollution, the slum visible from my hotel window, and I hated it all. I had been increasingly bothered by what was going on outside of me, unable to withdraw my attention and senses from irritants the way my meditation practice advises. Things clanging, banging, scraping, and slamming in the noisy hotel. It all triggered anger and hopelessness and obsessive worry ("I'll not be able to sleep, it's going to wake me up early, I am going to be tired . . ."), which usually indicated internal anxiety.

I was weary of working so hard at not letting it rankle me, the noise, pollution, sprawl, pouring my soul out in an honest desire to be useful and ending up on the fashion page (and misquoted to boot), watching smiling girls suddenly go blank when asked what they loved about themselves. I was haunted by Neelam's neighborhood, the river of sewage, the family living alongside it, the robotic, exhausted man I saw on the sidewalk ironing still-dirty clothes (who for some reason devastated me especially), the three generations of women sitting in the garbage pile sorting trash, saving useful bits for themselves. I was terrified of my own inadequate vocabulary to describe all this, my own bargaining brain that prevented me from truly grasping it all. By processing, I realized I was in a very negative head and heart space about India. I hated its government, policies, and history and the overpowering magnitude of its problems. Yes, many creative grassroots programs work, lives have been touched, but all of the fixes that any NGOs and government programs offer barely touch the tip of the iceberg.

It was overwhelming. I didn't want to spend any more time sifting through epic despair to find that one shard of hope. I was done. I just wanted to go home.

And then I came down with a case of "Delhi belly," a bout of sickness that nearly rivaled my meltdown in Bangkok. I gave up trying to move or sip even water; everything I did created worsening cramps. Apparently, my body was purging everything I had taken on board. I had to respect its wisdom and accept that for the next little while, I was a passenger.

My sweet friends sat with me for hours to comfort me. Papa Jack read a recovery text to me while I lay still like a wretch. Seane "niced" me, rubbing little circles on my back, so-called because it feels nice, and listened while I sobbed about that man ironing dirty clothes, whose traumatic image kept returning to my mind. I told them about my transformative (though painful at the time) experiences at Shades of Hope, and soon, through fellowship, the downtime became a blessing.

I was reminded once again that I could have serenity in spite of circumstances, in spite of people, places, and things. And I also knew that this despair, too, would pass, despite the impression that everything was hopeless and futile.

~ ~ ~

I recovered quickly enough to fulfill my obligations in New Delhi and to travel to Jaipur, where Akshay Kumar and I reached out to thousands of truckers with the message of prevention. I was holding it together quite well, in fact, until my very last day in India, when I met a group of homeless children.

Anubhav is an NGO that rescues homeless boys from the railway station, where children end up after they have been abandoned or orphaned or have escaped from abusive families. The outreach workers try to save the girls, too, but the gangs/pimps/traffickers are too slick and usually nab them first. In fact, the director sadly told me they have never once been able to rescue a girl. The boys, some of them just toddlers, scavenge for food along the tracks that run through the grubbiest, nastiest, most gruesome slum I've ever seen. The children look like lunatics with their never brushed hair in wild nests around their grimy faces, standing with shoeless feet on garbage heaps and industrial scrap metal piles. The malnutrition was so bad, their hair was two-toned, orange and dull brown. Their homes were rotting sacks stretched on bricks.

The organization, which was started by a group of street children—again, the real experts—runs a drop-in center that provides a safe space where the boys can sleep and spend time during the day. It teaches personal hygiene, feeds them, begins literacy training, and offers spiritual direction. They meditate in the mornings, pray before meals. Some of the boys were AIDS orphans, others ran away from abusive homes. I held a ten-year-old and a four-year-old on my lap, darling little things, and we talked about everything under the sun. Both had escaped abuse, preferring the mean streets to the cruelty at home. The older one had been raped about five times. It was unbelievable that he was so honest with me. (I began to realize some of the gender differences within the sexual exploitation of children. Girls are often kept captive and used chronically; boys are used episodically by occasional predators.) I liked it best when we talked about safe touching. I said one should ask first and remember that everyone has the right to say no, and we should each respect another's "no." The little one had been taken in by the center within two days of arriving at the rail station. The older one had been addicted to huffing paint fumes, something common among urban, traumatized youth. Often it's done initially to ward off hunger, but the high also becomes part of the appeal, a way to numb the pain of reality. Amazingly, I could share some simple concepts with him. After we discussed it, he said he believed he was powerless over huffing, that it made his life unmanageable, and that there was a good and loving God, and he could ask his God for help refraining from huffing, one day at a time. (Of course, I don't think he'll be permanently fixed, but maybe it's a tool that will give him relief from time to time.) I asked them if in honor of the special time we spent together they'd look out for one another after I left. Still on my lap, they beamed at each other, squealed "yes!" and showed me how they were going to hug and hold hands.

I wandered around the neighborhood, going deep into the thicket of provisional dwellings, imagining life here day in and day out. I was sitting in a makeshift shanty, on the bare dirt underneath a scrap of canvas, when I heard a kitten crying plaintively. I panicked. It freaked me out so deeply, I knew I had to flee or I was going to stand up and rip the slum down to *find that cat right now now now now,* or I was going to freeze and sit there and listen to this little mewling sound and completely *lose my mind.* I was afraid I was on the verge of going emotionally somewhere far, far away and not coming back. My brain was flooded. Of course, I was transferring the grief of ten thousand and my own triggered, vicarious trauma onto that one kitty cat, and I had just enough sense left to know it. Somehow I stumbled to my feet and started walking away. And then the children of the shelter brought me back to this world. They surrounded me to say goodbye and sent me off with an echoing chant that sounded like bells in the distance:

Oom shanti shanti shanti . . . oom shanti shanti shanti . . .

In the car, Marshall asked me if the smell of poop had bothered me when the boys were on my lap. "No," I said. I hadn't even noticed.

~ ~ ~

Mother Teresa of Calcutta, when awarded the Nobel Peace Prize, was asked by a journalist what she intended to do with the million-dollar gift.

"Feed the poor people of India," she said.

"You couldn't possibly!" the journalist cried. "Feeding the poor people of India would cost far more than that!"

"Perhaps," she said. "But my God simply asks that I try."

And so I try, too. Mainly I try to have a little peace inside, which in some measure I can take out into the world with me. God knows the world needs it. I have carefully examined what happened on this trip to India, my attitude and my resentments toward the treatment of the poor. This is what I have chosen to remember in future trips: Accepting something doesn't mean I have to like it. It simply allows me to accept reality as it actually is this minute, and then move into the solution, rather than obsessing on the problem. Today, I believe we all need solutions, so I choose the process, again and again, of surrendering, accepting, suiting up, and showing up . . . and letting go of the outcome.

Although sometimes the outcome lifts my heart.

After I returned home, I was shown a tape of Shahrukh Khan recording a powerful public service announcement for PSI/India. My little orphans Neelam and Komal had been invited to the taping, and they were clearly thrilled to be sitting with the most famous star in India. After he finished, Shahrukh called Neelam to stand beside him and announced that it was his great honor to present her with a scholarship from Ashley Judd and the Rai Foundation that would take care of her education all the way through a master's degree. As she accepted the certificate, her serious, beautiful, shy face lit up like the rising sun.

Chapter 20

THE WHITE FLOWER OF RWANDA

ASHLEY JUDD

In the Highlands with my Scottish and Irish heroes,
on my fortieth birthday.

Si tu me connaissais et si tu te connaissais vraiment,
tu ne m'aurais pas tue.
(If you knew me, and if you really knew yourself, you would
not have killed me.)

—*FELICIE NTAGENGWA*

I celebrated my fortieth birthday—April 19, 2008—in the Scottish Highlands with Dario's family and some dear friends, roaring with laughter, running a sack race, and winning the caber toss on the front lawn of Skibo Castle. Five days later, I was in a hotel room in Kigali, Rwanda, gazing out my window at the African sun setting in dazzling shades of orange and red. My last time on this continent, the original home of us all, I was so overwhelmed with emotion that I was nearly distraught. Everything, but everything, provoked a cry: My first African tree! My first African bird! My first African friend! I was returning to my cradle, and everything had the heightened drama of a seeker's first pilgrimage. This time around, I was grateful to be emotionally sober (not somber—sober includes great mirth). Not that I was casual about this journey; far from it. I was simply . . . simpler. My gratitude, awe, respect, and even enthusiasm were more nuanced and subtle.

There was tough work to be done on this trip. Rwanda is the most densely populated African country, with more than ten million people squeezed into an area the size of Maryland. It is also one of the poorest and most traumatized places on earth in the aftermath of a long series of genocides, culminating in the unspeakable genocide in 1994, in which eight hundred thousand people were murdered in the space of one hundred days and millions were driven from their homes. PSI is one of the NGOs that the Rwandan government has invited to help it build a community-based health care system as a foundation to lift its people out of abject poverty. As always, I was here to see our grassroots programs and others' in action—particularly our child survival initiative called Five & Alive—to celebrate what works and the workers who do it, and to help carry the good news back to donors and policy makers that this remarkable country is lifting itself out of the ashes. For example, Rwanda has been outperforming most African countries in meeting its United Nations Millennium Development Goals, which provide a framework and set targets for poverty alleviation, education, child and maternal health, HIV and other disease eradication, and gender equity.

But there is no way to begin to understand the depths of Rwanda's agony, or its soaring promise, without first plunging into the original heart of darkness. The genocide inescapably informs everything in this country and most certainly the public health mission here. It is the background, acknowledged if unspoken; it has set Rwanda's stage.

So once again, as I did in Cambodia, I began this journey with a visit to a genocide memorial.

~ ~ ~

In an angular, sand-colored building surrounded by gardens and graves, the exhibits are divided into three parts: the roots of the genocide, the events of 1994, and the aftermath. The narrative format is so familiar to me: This is what I was. This is what happened. This is what I am now.

The first of three chambers was lined with black-and-white photos from Rwanda's colonial past. First the Germans and then the Belgians claimed authority over this volcanic plateau southwest of Lake Victoria. According to the accompanying text, Rwandans identified themselves among eighteen clans, of which distinctions like Hutu and Tutsi were *occupational* and not tribal/ethnic at all. The colonists made up that all Tutsis were Nilotic pastoralists and Hutus were Bantu peasant farmers. One of the most enraging images was a 1932 photo of a Belgian priest, for God's sake, *a priest*, measuring Rwandans' heads and categorizing them ethnically for registration cards. Once the massacres began in 1994, these registration cards established the delivery system of death for nearly a million people.

Set up by the Belgians and the Catholic Church, the Hutu majority took over Rwanda at independence, and some seven hundred thousand Tutsis fled to other countries to escape an eruption of ethnic cleansing that began in 1959. Still, more than a million Tutsi remained in Rwanda, some intermarried, and most lived in peace with their Hutu neighbors. In 1990, a Tutsi rebel army known as the Rwanda Patriotic Front invaded Rwanda from neighboring Uganda in order to force power sharing with the Hutu government. After years of fighting, the United Nations brokered a peace accord that would allow the Tutsi diaspora to return and establish a multiparty government. This enraged Hutu nationalists, who viewed the Tutsi as "cockroaches." A fanatic Hutu propaganda machine had been whipping up paranoia and hatred of the Tutsi and their sympathizers. On April 6, 1994, a plane carrying Rwanda's president was shot down as it was landing in Kigali. Within an hour of the president's assassination, the army and *Interahamwe* had set up roadblocks in Kigali, and an orgy of orchestrated mass murder began.

There is no part of Rwanda that was spared the rampage of *génocidaires*. Local militias had lists of the names and addresses of Tutsis and moderate Hutus, and they hunted them down and killed them with their bare hands in their homes and in places of sanctuary. It was intensely personal murder. The swing of a 50-cent Chinese machete once wasn't enough; they were hacking and hacking, mutilating, annihilating, burying people alive among the dead, cutting tendons, and coming back later to finish the job.

Half a million women were raped during the genocide, with men who knew they were HIV-positive taking the lead. Many of the women later died of AIDS—a way of extending the killing spree for years. Children were made to murder their parents (and in the case of boys, rape their mothers and sisters), parents to murder their children, before they themselves were killed. As many as ten thousand people who had flocked to a church outside of Kigali for sanctuary were killed by grenades or hacked to death on once hallowed ground. It is unfathomable, yet it must be fathomed.

What is just as unbelievable is that the genocide could have been stopped within days with a modest intervention from outside troops. The general leading the UN peacekeeping forces in Rwanda was begging for assistance, predicting what was coming, and saying how very little he needed to avert the murders. Instead, the UN drew down its forces, and member states refused to intervene in what was insanely branded a "civil war," even as reports of the massacres were appearing in *The New York Times* and other world media. An American transport plane arrived early on to evacuate the U.S. embassy personnel; had it been carrying troops, they might have saved hundreds of thousands of lives. Instead, we—you, me, our government, the world—did nothing.

The killings stopped only when the Tutsi rebel army, led by Paul Kagame, who is now Rwanda's president, resumed its invasion and took over the country. Hundreds of thousands of Hutu refugees and *Interahamwe* escaped across the border into the Democratic Republic of the Congo, where merciless armed militias are still creating havoc in that war-torn region.

~ ~ ~

As I moved slowly through the exhibits, I could feel my legs becoming heavier, almost immobilized. At times I was close to passing out, and I'd have to catch myself up and reconnect with my breath. I would feel pain so deep, the rest of the world ceased to exist and I would be swallowed entirely in it. Prayer did help as I was sucked inexorably further into the memorial. Whenever I started to lose my mind, I would begin to pray for the souls of the dead. *May you rest in peace. May you rest in peace.* One million and more times, *May you rest in peace.*

One of the round rooms of the exhibit had victims' clothing suspended in midair by filament. The arrangement of the clothes uncannily suggested the posture of the body that had occupied them; the empty garments expressed surprise, violence, pitiful and useless self-defense. The clothes were all sizes, and I stood, weeping and haunted, in front of a child's colorful sweater, filthy from where the body had lain in the muck. At that little child's age, that would have been my favorite sweater, it was so cheerful. It reminded me of the rainbow painted on the entrance to the tunnel from Marin County to the Golden Gate Bridge, so optimistic! Next to it was a tattered Superman sheet. God have mercy on us all. Was the person sleeping and hacked to death in her bed? Had a wildly panicked mother grabbed the sheet to tie her youngster to her back so she could run from her rapists?

Another room had horizontal rows of filament to which survivors had pinned photographs of their loved ones. Rows, rows, and rows, images from family parties, official documents, snapshots of reluctant-looking elderly that perhaps an amateur family historian took to have for future generations. The exhibit was almost unbearable. *Murder, murder, murder,* it silently screams.

I paused at the memorial guest book. I couldn't see the page for the tears blearing my sight. What did I say? How did I tell the survivors of such monstrosities anything consoling? How did one apologize to the dead? Feeling useless and incompetent, I wrote, "I am sorry, I am so sorry."

Kofi Annan, head of the UN's peacekeeping forces at the time, and other world leaders, including President Bill Clinton, have offered their apologies for failing to stop the genocide. Clinton says he "did not fully appreciate" the speed and intensity and orchestrated nature of the killings and has called his failure to intervene the greatest regret of his administration. He has been making amends ever since, visiting the country often and committing massive resources from the Clinton Foundation to help bring about Rwanda's recovery.

~ ~ ~

For the rest of my time in Rwanda, as we drove through the now clean and orderly capital, as we drank in the lovely countryside, my mind would occasionally run an automatic slide show, imposing the detritus of genocide on what I was seeing. It really was incomprehensible that such protracted filthy evil transpired ever, anywhere, but especially in a place this pretty and seemingly serene.

This country is close to the very bottom of impoverished nations, ranking 159th out of 177. Yet our hotel was terrific, with a sparkling azure pool surrounded by palms. I had a little suite, and as part of my meditation each morning, I stood at my window drinking tea, watching a woman with a handmade broom sweep the street below. This had to be the cleanest country in Africa, if not the world: All the lavatories in Kigali were clean, and there was toilet paper available in public places everywhere. The streets and fields were free of litter; those ubiquitous plastic bags clogging gutters everywhere on earth were banned in Rwanda. And this was also the safest country in Africa, Papa Jack had assured me.

The government keeps a tight rein on its people to enforce a national identity without ethnic divisions. The downside of this extreme vigilance is an authoritarian streak in the government and a restriction of free expression, particularly among political opponents of the ruling party, that is easy for a Westerner to perceive as over the top. One PSI staffer was jailed for rolling his eyes at a traffic jam caused by the discovery of a genocide victim's remains. As a foreign visitor, I was told to expect that my telephone and emails would be monitored at the hotel. But President Kagame himself told me that when we have lived through their many genocides (1994 was actually but one in a long series), we will have the experience and the right to judge their genocide prevention policies. I really can't come up with an adequate counterargument to that.

Looking at the extreme nature of what transpired, the government reckoned that extreme solutions were necessary, and the positive result is one of the most dynamic governments in the entire world. President Kagame and his cabinet seem to spend every waking hour looking for innovative ways to modernize Rwanda and improve the lives of all its people. They rely heavily on international aid but have a can-do attitude about rebuilding their country themselves. The government partners directly with all NGOs and encourages local participation. For instance, of the 150 people PSI employs here, only 4 are non-Rwandan.

After my wrenching morning at the genocide memorial, I was looking forward to meeting those staff members and absorbing their positive energy. The offices were housed in a two-story brick building set into a small hillside. There was a rondel of cosmos growing by the PSI sign and a small fleet of tidy white trucks parked in front. I met with our country director, Staci Leuschner, and the staff for a briefing about our mission here. The challenges are massive and all too familiar: lack of infrastructure, lack of health care providers, an explosive birth rate and high infant mortality, endemic malaria, lack of safe water (only 2.5 percent of Rwandans have piped water), and the prevalence of STIs, HIV/AIDS, and other preventable diseases and issues that keep the entire population subsisting on less than a dollar a day.

What is quite special about Rwanda is that the Ministry of Health is attacking these problems in a holistic manner, creating a health care system from the grass roots up, with an emphasis on prevention and primary care delivered by community health workers through a network of local clinics and district hospitals. (They even have a basic national insurance plan with 97 percent enrollment!) What NGOs do here, as in poor countries everywhere, is fill critical gaps in services, education, and product delivery where the government and private sectors are lacking. Governments often have little if any infrastructure, yet magically those fizzy soda pop drinks are ubiquitous, as are mobile phones. Hence, PSI focuses on markets—those consumer goods prove they exist—employing private sector techniques to make markets actually work *for* poor people. The same networks that make cigarettes available in every corner of the earth can be leveraged and grown to make healthy products and behavior-change communication accessible to hundreds of millions of people. In this way, positive development contributions are made to local economies, increasing employability by adding to job experience. Plus, the initiatives and campaigns appeal to local folks, because they are generated by locals.

Below the PSI office building is a garage/warehouse for our medical products, many of which bear the proud stamp of USAID, and it is from here we begin to distribute them to clinics and pharmacies and sometimes directly to the poor people who need them. The warehouse staff here, as in most of the sixty-five countries where we have programs, include formerly prostituted women whom we have been able to reach via peer education. As a result, many have been able to exit from prostitution altogether. I visited women who have created a co-op in which they pool their money to buy supplies in bulk, bringing down their individual costs. They make wonderful crafts to sell, and the two sources of income have allowed them to improve their lives substantially, progressing them along the continuum from exploited, informal work to more dignified, formal work with a measure of security and social protections. Plus, they increase their business savvy, allowing them to identify further entrepreneurial opportunities for income generation. There are many reasons to marvel at the "ingenuity of the poor." It is fascinating to see poverty reduction solutions in action and how one good action opens the way for yet another.

~ ~ ~

By late afternoon, I was ready to crash in my hotel room. A familiar crispy, burning fatigue had set in, the kind that feels like grit in my eyes and an aching in my joints, the end product of jet lag and grief. To my surprise, because I am an experienced "rester" but not necessarily a talented "napper," I fell asleep as soon as my head hit the pillow.

I roused a couple of hours later to meet Zainab Salbi, founder and director of Women for Women International (WFWI), who was visiting

Rwanda for a conference on gender-based violence. I had a pot of green tea ready when she arrived at my door, resplendent with chic cropped hair, black silk shirtwaist dress, and fabulous enormous beaded necklace. I've been a longtime supporter, and I was eager to meet the elegant and dynamic Zainab. She is a survivor of Saddam Hussein's Iraq and a human rights activist who founded Women for Women out of the ruins of the rape camps in Bosnia in 1993. Since then, the group has helped some 250,000 women rebuild their lives during and in the aftermath of war. The organization offers immediate food and medical support for women in conflict zones, then lifts them up with counseling, jobs, civic participation and empowerment training, literacy education, and microcredit loans and savings to create leaders out of victims. They work in the toughest places, from Afghanistan to Darfur. The strong women-to-women alliances that emerge during the course of a woman's one-year program participation is one of the greatest assets a woman gains.

Zainab is an intense and rapid talker, and I was content to sip my tea and let her school me in the recent history of the region and hear about the group's work in Rwanda and across the border in the Democratic Republic of the Congo.

"Rape is contagious," she said. "And where it has become an epidemic, it has to be treated like a disease." In the eastern DRC, she said, punctuating her points with jabs of her finger, literally hundreds of thousands of women had been raped since the mid-1990s, and the practice has become ingrained in the culture. The epidemic began during the Rwandan genocide and spilled across the border with the fleeing Hutu fanatics. Before long, the militias regrouped as a rebel army, which began terrorizing the Congolese and using refugee camps to stage raids into Rwanda. In 1996, Paul Kagame's army invaded the eastern Congo to flush out the Hutu militants, while backing a rebel Congolese force to oust that country's dictator, Mobutu Sese Seko. It's a long and complex story, but the invasion touched off what is known as "Africa's world war," with several far-flung nations sending troops to join the fight over control of the DRC. Much of the DRC is fairly peaceful now, but the war rages on in the easternmost provinces between various armed militias and government troops. Along the way, an estimated five million people have died in a conflict that few Westerners were even aware was happening. Zainab explained that this war, like all wars, has become about the economy and land and exploiting natural resources. And rape, as a weapon to terrorize and coerce civilian populations, has become a daily occurrence.

Zainab told me that WFWI, which has an extensive program to help the women of Rwanda, arrived in the DRC in 2004 to launch a multitiered program of direct aid and emotional support, rights awareness and leadership education, vocational skills training and income-generation support. So far it has helped eight thousand women in the conflict zone. But Zainab realized that any gains for women would be short-lived without re-educating men. So WFWI has started up leadership schools to change the behavior of Congolese men, to train them how to respect women's rights, and to educate them in the value of women's work in the development of communities and nations.

"It's *fascinating*, Ashley!" said Zainab in her British-inflected English. "You *must* see our programs there."

I decided on the spot that I had to check this out for myself—how cool would that be, after having been a WFWI sponsor to my sisters in Nigeria for three years? I called Kate and Marshall and told them I would no longer be joining them on a trek to visit the famous mountain gorillas in the Parc National des Volcans. Instead I wanted to slip across the border to the town of Goma to visit Zainab's projects, along with some PSI partner programs. Dario was not amused when I told him, but I assured him that Papa Jack and Marshall would be with me and that Goma was said to be stable these days, with a large UN presence. The gorillas, much as I love them, would have to wait.

Downstairs at what would be healing dinner, rich with new friendships, Zainab introduced me first to the great Rwandan senator Aloisea Inyumba, who hugged me warmly. President Kagame's legislature and ministerial posts are loaded with capable women, the highest female participation anywhere in the world, but Aloisea is a standout. In 1994, after he stopped the genocide, Kagame made her Minister of Family, Gender, and Social Affairs. Her job was to oversee the burial of the dead, resettlement of refugees, and placement in homes for the country's five hundred thousand orphans. Her solution: Everyone must take in a child, and that meant Hutus raising Tutsi children (Gandhi would heartily agree). It was a first step toward reconciliation. Later, she was put in charge of one of the biggest challenges of all: finding a just punishment for the perpetrators of genocide living in Rwanda. Rather than seeking revenge, the Tutsis in charge of the country wanted to find a way for everyone to live together again in peace. When she took the job as head of the Unity and Reconciliation Commission in 2000, the fragile prison system was clogged with low-level *génocidaires* awaiting trial. (The ringleaders are still being tried in an international court in Tanzania.) Inyumba decided to bring back traditional *gacacas*, literally meaning "patch of grass" courts, to try the accused right in their districts. Since then, more than 1.5 million accused have passed through the *gacaca* system. Defendants were offered shorter sentences for confessing and apologizing to the families of their victims and the whole community. It has been a tough, tough process, but a vital step toward healing the trauma and moving ahead as a unified nation.

I spoke for a while with this amazing, special woman (who has since become a close friend and collaborator), and then, when the moment was right, she took me over to meet the First Lady of Rwanda. Jeannette Kagame is a physically imposing presence and somewhat stoic, perhaps even dour. We exchanged a few polite words, but I couldn't really pay attention because I was having an attack of static cling, and my silk dress was naughtily climbing ever upward! I know this because the First Lady's aide-de-camp was on her knees behind me, pulling my dress down and off my backside. Hmmm . . . was it to protect my modesty or the decorum of the entire event? After all, I was smack dab at the front of the room, back turned to the crowd, a movie star chatting with the First Lady. What a lousy time for a bad case of hungry bum!

Better events followed. The most extraordinary drumming and dancing began, performed by the Inganzo Cultural Troupe, and I could feel the pain of earlier in the day being vibrated out of my chest. I was absolutely in awe. This is the Africa I believed in, its traditional culture and arts preserved and shining amid educated, empowered people talking smart about gender equality and development with an eye on seven generations ahead. Even though we were in a hotel's spiffy ballroom, when I closed my eyes I was in the bush, around a fire, the sounds of the wild engulfing me. It was fabulous beyond description. The senator narrated each dance for me: Ah, this is the dance about millet, teaching and celebrating agricultural practices, valuing production to keep everyone fed. Ah, this is the dance for the herd, the grass at the end of their sticks is to dust off the herd. Ahhhh, this is the dance of women, celebrating their beautiful bodies! My gosh, I live for this stuff—it's what I dreamed of in college!

That night when I closed my eyes and visions of broken skulls and bloodstained dresses welled up in my thoughts, I let the drums beat them out of my head. I slept pretty well and woke up curious about another day in this lush land.

~ ~ ~

At first light, we drove out to the airport and boarded a heifer of a government helicopter, a giant military thing with bench seating lining the length of the cabin. Some old Russian Mi-17, Dario later explained, rather confounded that I'd signed a release saying that a) I would fly in it, and b) neither I nor anyone in my family would be mad if it crashed. I was joining Rwanda's minister of health, Dr. Jean Damascène Ntawukuliryayo, crisscrossing the small country to celebrate World Malaria Day with a tour of clinics and programs. The people here need them so badly. One in twelve children born here will die before age one, then an additional one child in seven will die before age five (that's why our child survival program is called Five & Alive). Malaria, preventable and treatable, is cause number one.

To take this on, PSI socially markets Tuzanet, which is pretreated with the appropriate insecticide and lasts for three years. It is available at a very small price or for free in many areas as well. This blended approach of private sector availability combined with recent free distribution of three million bed nets to caregivers of children under age five, pregnant mothers, and the HIV-positive helped achieve a stunning 60 percent reduction in malaria cases in 2007. This is the greatest reduction of malaria rates in the world, something Kagame's government can be very proud of doing for its people. There was a lot to celebrate on World Malaria Day 2008.

From the air, I could see why Rwanda is called the "Land of a Thousand Hills." Its peaks and valleys undulated below me, green and terraced and graced with lakes. While I admired the landscape I began to register what I had heard, that every square inch of the land is tilled in the effort to feed all ten million people living here. They have already run out of space, and there are predictable environmental consequences: massive deforestation, erosion, loss of biodiversity. I was warned that I would never be alone (something I need at least a little of daily), as even in the most remote parts of the country, people would be . . . everywhere. And it's true, they are. No matter how much I hunted for a discreet place to pee, I could never find one. Even unpaved rural roads are lined with folks walking somewhere, perhaps in a blue school uniform or with baskets of goods or a jerrican of water on their heads. There is no way Rwanda and other countries can overcome their problems unless the population growth is reduced.

We landed in a giant field in the Est Province, greeted by hundreds of onlookers who were curious about the helicopter. Cries of *mzungu*— "white person"—erupted as my colleagues and I climbed into our cars. We jolted across rough, red dirt roads to visit a community of health workers in action. Our guide, Pierre, was elected by his fellow villagers to become the village's health worker. Once chosen, he received intensive health services training, which is ongoing. Pierre carries a bag with lifesaving pharmaceuticals, such as antibiotics, family-planning kits, malaria treatment, and first-aid materials. He is available in his home and goes to those who are too unwell to traverse the mountains. If the case is too difficult for him to handle, Pierre refers the patient to the local clinic. He also follows up and makes sure patients take their medications for AIDS and tuberculosis. It's a wonderful program that allows primary care to reach the poorest and most remote areas.

In a small, bare home, we visited a broken woman holding a limp infant. Pierre had diagnosed malaria in the baby and was teaching the mother about her new insecticide-impregnated net and the proper use of Primo, the lifesaving treatment that PSI packages and markets especially for children. When I sat with the woman, she was not easy to engage, she herself was so ill and overwhelmed. I tried to squeeze in a few quiet moments with her, as I am not a breeze in, breeze out, kind of gal. My only real contact with her, however, was that she smelled so rotten I actually had a gag reflex, a first for me in eleven countries of slums, brothels, and hospices.

Water is so scarce here, and it is such hard work to fetch it, that one drinks it mostly, then perhaps uses it for cooking. Washing oneself is a very low priority in this country. I felt very sad. I didn't even learn her name.

In back of the minuscule house, another woman who rented the bedroom proudly showed us her treated net hanging over her bed. She was wearing a matched lavender outfit, and we sat under her net giggling, unable to understand each other with words but giddily connected somehow, excited just to see each other and hug.

The minister, Dr. Ntawukuliryayo, a long, lanky, hyperenergetic man, would not be lingering long at any of our stops. We continued on our tour of rural clinics in a convoy of government, USAID, UN, WHO, and PSI cars. Lurching and heaving over rutted roads, small black faces joyfully yelling, "*Mzungu!*" wherever we went, we arrived at an open-sided building where rows and rows of locals were sitting on wooden benches on a poured-concrete floor under a corrugated tin roof. They were waiting patiently for medical services, and by the look of it, they would need that patience—it was very crowded.

The wards were bare cement rooms with simple aluminum cots lining the walls. The beds were all filled, mostly with mothers nursing their newborns. The minister and I stopped at each bed to talk about how undeveloped children's immune systems are and why sleeping with mosquito nets is essential. I was able to hold a sleeping two-day-old baby, tiny and probably premature. Low birth weight is a very common consequence of both malaria during pregnancy and other maternal health issues, such as lack of adequate spacing between births. Rwandan women average 6.3 babies each. That means if I were a Rwandan, I would have nearly seven kids and I would be almost dead; life expectancy for women here is forty-four years. I contemplated this for a while, but not for long . . . the minister was off to the prenatal ward.

Although we were there to teach the ABCs of malaria prevention and treatment, the minister never missed an opportunity to reinforce other key health messages. At this clinic and everywhere we went, the indefatigable minister also discussed family planning and water purification. He even inspected the outdoor toilets and gave spontaneous talks to observers about sanitation and hygiene.

The sad fact is that 60 percent of rural and 40 percent of urban Rwandans do not have access to safe water. Even the 2.5 percent with piped water cannot know if that water is safe. Unsafe water makes millions sick and kills 2.2 million worldwide every year. The UN clearly states that disinfection of water at the point of use is consistently the most cost-effective way to save lives. To that end, PSI markets our miracle powder, Sur'Eau, in Rwanda to disinfect and purify polluted water. It comes in a small plastic bottle that provides safe water for a family of six for one month for a total cost of 55 cents!

~ ~ ~

After an exhausting day of running around the countryside, our convoy returned to the pasture where the helicopter was waiting. Hundreds, if not thousands, of people had gathered and were lining the field in the most orderly fashion. They were tiered, littlest sitting to tallest standing in the back, staring silently at the big machine. I dove into the crowd and plopped myself down in their midst. I was immediately surrounded by an epic mural of shining black faces, seemingly from grass to sky.

I noticed a boy in a ragged shirt holding a bundle of old plastic bags that he had compacted and tied up with string to make a precious football. I gestured to him and the ball, stood up, and we were off. In one of the most memorable moments of my life, the kids and I began to stream joyously all over acres of green grass, passing the "football," shrieking with glee. I was in a state of grace, and I knew it. It felt as though it lasted forever, the running, lungs heaving, laughing, and seeing their unmitigated joy, the color of their skin so black with my own little white body nestled in the herd. I kicked off my flip-flops and ran barefoot hither and yon. I happened to have on my favorite secondhand dress, an old calico print, and I connected easily with the mountain girl in me. I am sure that was what they connected with, too, and why we fit so well together in spite of all our "differences." When the illusion of differences is rendered obsolete, this, I believe, is heaven.

At last the helicopter people started to shepherd us off the grass, and the minister, who was ready to go, gave me the stink eye. But it was good while it lasted.

~ ~ ~

On the last Saturday of each month, every citizen of Rwanda sets aside three hours to participate in community building. This old cultural practice of helping one another, called *umaganda,* is absolutely glorious—I would love to start the practice in my hometown in Tennessee. Today's *umaganda* project, led by our tireless minister of health, was building homes for genocide widows. (And of course, as there was a throng, he never stopped reinforcing the government's health messages: "A small family is a healthy family! Use soap! Treat your drinking water!") As suggested, we all wore get-dirty clothes, and some of us engaged in tough physical labor. It was an enormous turnout. Laboring together has been influential in healing from the genocide; Rwandans now want to be known as just that, Rwandans, and not Tutsis or Hutus. They help one another without reservation, no questions asked. They manage to live side by side; one may literally live beside a neighbor who tortured or murdered members of one's family and village. It's remarkable.

I was reminded of an image from my visit to the genocide museum on my first morning in Rwanda. Outside the building there are graves where thousands upon thousands of genocide victims were buried en masse. The slabs that cover the graves are fifteen feet wide, twenty feet long, several feet above the ground (the graves are so deep, so deep), and go on for as far as the eye can see. In the poured concrete that is the final resting place for bones hacked by machetes, I saw a white flower, tinier than my pinky fingernail, growing out from within the flat cement of a massive tomb. Rwanda is like this flower, a thing that is blooming out of the detritus and wreckage of the absolute worst humanity has to offer.

The wheel of time turns: Life, death. Life, death.

Life.

Chapter 21

THE REPUBLIC OF RAPE

(right to left) Kavira, Kika, Solange, and Stuka, adolescent survivors of gang rape, at a HEAL Africa clinic.

Quand on disait "plus jamais" apres L'Holocauste, cela concernait-il certaines personnes et pas d'autres?
(When you said, "never again" after the Holocaust, did you mean that for some people, and not others?)

—*APOLLON KABAHIZI*
Alternative translation:
When you said, "never again" after the Holocaust, did you mean that just for yourselves? Or us, too?
Or
. . . . .did you mean that for everyone, or just yourselves?

The border between Rwanda and the Democratic Republic of the Congo resembles nothing more sinister than a gate connecting the pastures on our farm in Tennessee, but what a shocking difference a few feet makes. On the Rwanda side of the crossing, in the city of Gisenyi, the roads are tidy, maintained, lined with tiny, colorful flower gardens. The breezes lapping the shores of Lake Kivu are serene, and the people are friendly and helpful. Passing into the DRC, however . . . Oh, my God. We were leaving a country with virtually no official corruption to go to a place where bribery and coercion are a way of life. It took me, Marshall, Papa Jack, and our driver an hour to navigate through the immigration and customs routine—which involved Papa Jack reaching into his pocket for a steady presentation of $20 bills. We joked that he should be used to it as the parent of a teenage daughter. As soon as we cleared the border post, all color seemed to drain from the earth, and we entered an urban wasteland of some eight hundred thousand people, most of them displaced by war.

As soon as we cleared the gate, we were stopped by a group of uniformed "police" carrying heavy weaponry. No traffic violations, just a simple and typical moment of attempted extortion. James, our driver, spoke Lingala and told them we didn't have anything to give them while I nervously sat on my laptop, suddenly imaging it, and all of my writing, being taken from me.

The lead extortionist shrugged and waved us through. DRC is essentially a failed state, and government, army, and civil service jobs pay nothing. Some are specifically directed, when they begin their jobs, to "live off the land," meaning the people they are supposed to be serving and protecting. Crimes, from the petty to those that qualify as war crimes and crimes against humanity, are committed with impunity.

A few hundred feet later, the road opened up and I saw the notorious city of Goma for the first time: a vast, relentless, dusty slum. There was rubble, garbage, filth, people covered in muck and grime, buildings that were nothing more than lean-to shanties. The earth was gray, drab, choking with dust and ash, courtesy of a volcano just north of town that had been erupting on and off for several years.

Our first stop was a clinic run by one of PSI's partners that specializes in family planning, maternal and child health, and the treatment and prevention of malaria. The clinic's doctor was waiting in his office in a white stuccoed cinder-block building; his hours were painted in a sweet shade of blue paint, and they did not include Sunday mornings, which was when we arrived. I thanked him for making the special effort and asked him about his job.

His main work was in obstetrics, but every week he made home visits in the neighborhood to generate interest in modern family planning, birth spacing, and pre- and postnatal care. He told me that twenty to twenty-five new women showed up each month to access the clinic's services. Although this number sounded small, he said it represented significant cultural change; men here generally want their women to produce as many babies as possible. Seeking to regulate their fertility was big news.

As he spoke, I tried to keep track of the litany of horrors he encountered in his daily work: The babies he delivered were often premature, and infant mortality here was the highest in the world. He treated women who were victims of sexual violence daily. Rape, including gang rape, has become an appallingly common occurrence in militia populated areas around Goma—meaning everywhere, as militias often roam. A frequent consequence of such rapes is fistula, when the wall between the rectum and vagina, or bladder and vagina, is torn open—and more. The doctor told us he had treated children, little girls as young as three and four, for rape-induced injuries. He also saw a lot of obstetric fistulas, caused when such tearing occurs in childbirth. It often happens because the mother herself is a child and her pelvis is not fully formed to accommodate childbirth, or as a result of other complications that in the United States would not have to cost a woman her health or her life. But when you try to give birth unattended, as 66 percent of African women do, fistula is a very real, life-destroying problem.

When I asked where this pervasive practice of rape came from, was it embedded in the culture, he said it was not cultural to begin with. He confirmed what I had heard from Zainab Salbi: Raping began here as a weapon of war, a way to dominate the enemy by terrorizing women, regarded as the backbone of the family, and destroying family structure. Now, gang rape was used by various armed groups, often on behalf of government and army officials and their proxies, in the artisanal mining of Congo's extraordinary mineral wealth. The mass raping allowed groups to access the lucrative elements just under the soil without resistance, clearing out entire villages (hence the massive problem of forcibly displaced persons in eastern DRC). And now there had been violence and instability in this region for so long that war had become a way of life, and rape had become normalized—in the same way that poverty, lack of services, and hardship were the norm. Now, it was all generations knew.

~~~

There's no way to sugarcoat it: Goma is a shithole. The stench is putrid. There is no sanitation. The water is unsafe. The rooms of the next clinic I visited were stuffed with malaria patients of all ages. They looked dazed and miserable, their bodies sagging, their eyelids heavy.

I sat on a few beds, making small talk about how to prevent the disease and, in my own hopeful way, introducing the possibility of each individual making a commitment to sleep under a *mousquetaire*—or mosquito net—at home.

It was a visiting day, so most patients had family in, grandmothers, other children, and siblings. Someone had brought a transistor radio that squawked out a tinny disco tune. My attention was drawn to one man who was feeding his small son. The boy was lethargic and mute, his nose ran, and an IV PICC line was taped awkwardly to his hand, which it dwarfed. The man fed him black beans from a tin plate, around which gnats flew.

This man was a hardened person, and our presence in the clinic that day seemed to irritate him. Unprompted, he started raging at the pregnant women who were given nets free of charge when they came to the clinic. The men still had to pay for theirs, although at highly subsidized prices. And the tough guy with the beans thought this was fundamentally wrong.

"Am I not a man?" he complained. "Should I not be given a net?"

I decided to engage him and try to lighten the mood with some playful questions. I asked him—in French—if nets were available in the private sector.

Yes, he said, but he had no money to buy them.

I scoffed. It is well documented that women in the developing world save and invest every pittance, while men waste money at shocking rates. This man, who was dressed in clean, matching, store-bought clothes, did not seem like a pauper.

"Oh, come on," I said. "I bet you have a little money from time to time for a smoke!"

"No!" he exclaimed.

"Beer, what about a glass of beer?"

Again, "No!"

"Ah, you have so much virtue! Such a clean life!" I said. "But . . . I bet from time to time you have a little money to spend on a woman!"

The room erupted into roars of laughter.

We debated the value of investing in prevention by spending half a franc on a net. "Wouldn't it be wise," I said, trying again, "to spend a little money for a net, so as to save all it costs when you're sick? When the children are sick?" I gestured to the tiny, stifling room loaded with inert bodies. He had no response to that.

I didn't think he had anything against buying products for himself. For example, he had a high-end mobile phone with the latest bells and whistles, to which he turned his attention when our conversation ended.

A lovely little girl sitting near the man's son was eyeing me cautiously. She began to stare at me more openly, and I thought to take her picture and show her the image. Perhaps it would please her. I took my camera out of its bag and aimed it in her direction. The man leapt up in front of my camera, blocking me from photographing not just his boy, but everyone in the room.

I put the camera away but explained what I had meant to do and that it was a means of reaching out to a new friend. The man started mocking me. He took out his phone, scrolled through its zillion features, found the camera, and ran all over the room as if taking my picture with it. I hammed it up, posing from each angle to which he darted—voguing in the DRC. Everyone giggled, and the tension was slightly broken.

Finally it was time to go. I thanked everyone for the visit, wished them a good afternoon, a speedy recovery, and good health. I may have been wrong, but I walked to the car wondering not if but how many women and girls that man had raped.

~ ~ ~

Everywhere the car lurched, children with stunted growth stared. Once eye contact was made and a wave offered, their faces would joyously crinkle into smiles. They wore tattered Western clothes. I saw one little girl in a raggedy pink tutu. The sight of her still haunts me, the distorted Goma version of the precious little American girl who discovers ballet and won't take her tutu off for weeks at a time.

Our next stop was the HEAL Africa hospital in downtown Goma, a 180-bed hospital that specializes in repairing fistulas and reconstructing the damaged genitals of rape survivors. There is so much demand—there are usually 150 women on the waiting list at any given time—that dozens have taken up residence outside and around the facility. I visited with some women who were squatting in the courtyard, washing their clothes or children in ubiquitous plastic tubs that serve many household purposes. Inside, patients were sitting blankly on beds. All looked unbelievably traumatized and dark. Most clutched babies, and a few had been made pregnant by their rapists. One was disfigured from having been burned, her otherwise night black skin raw and pink. A clutch of women in a doorway, mute and scared, stared at me when I wished them a good afternoon and said goodbye and thanked them for letting me visit.

It was like walking out of the gates of hell, and I was ashamed of myself for feeling relief at escaping, to put this place behind me and head for the Women for Women International compound.

In the midst of this ragged and seemingly doomed city is a walled courtyard filled with grass that is actually green, a garden that is actually tended, a building that is clean and proud. Zainab Salbi had notified the women in advance of my visit, and I was greeted with joyous clapping, singing, and ululating, the great African vocalization. I ran to the throng and threw myself at them, dancing and exclaiming my hellos.

We sat together for hours, each woman taking her turn to stand before her sisters and me, sharing her life story. They were each so incredibly beautiful! The eyes, the cheekbones, the lips—but mostly their spirits. They wore traditional, colorful dresses, and I so wanted to learn to wrap a foulard (head scarf) like that! WFWI teaches appressed, victimized, poor women to bathe, to feed themselves and in fact produce and sell food to others, to read, count, and write, and offers them parenting skills, social skills, money skills, a trade. Almost as important, it then gives them a network of sisters to rely on for support. Each woman is in contact with her American sponsor, who donates $27 per month—less than $1 a day—to pay for her counseling and training. All of the women had been in the program for about one year and would soon graduate. Having sponsored in WFWI for three years, I was familiar with the radical improvements self-described in a sister's entry and exit interviews.

This is what their stories that afternoon sounded like to me:

I am an orphan, my husband was killed, my three sons were killed, I could not read, I could not write, I could not count, I lived like an animal, I have thirteen children, I have ten children, I am a widow, I am a refugee, I fled with nothing, not even a cup, I was half-mad, I was crazy, I was a corpse . . . People in the street were afraid of me, I begged, I scavenged in the dump, I treated my children like animals, my husband went to other women, my husband's people pushed me from our home when he died, I was run off the land, I was cheated because I did not know how to sign my name, my children died, I knew nothing, I was filthy, I smelled bad, I came to this area to escape violence, I carried loads with my body to earn money for food, I starved, I had nowhere to go, I was dead, I was in a constant panic, I lived in terror, I abused everyone around me, I was in a rage, I was abandoned . . .

And then, the transfiguration:

I am the happiest woman in the world, I am so blessed, I know my rights, women have rights. I learned to read, I learned to write, I received a small loan to buy fabric, I sew now to earn a decent living, I can calculate my profit so I can manage my finances, I save a bit and I use my capital to expand my business, I learned about nutrition, I know how to eat, look at me I am clean, I use soap, I use lotion, my children eat three meals a day, my husband and I are partners now, I have a voice, I keep my pamphlet that describes my rights in my pocket, it is with me at all times, I was able to save enough to buy a small plot of land, I built my home, my soul opened up, a new woman was born inside of me . . .

Their sacred narratives were mind-blowing, each woman a Congolese Lazarus, nothing short of a miracle. As we listened, members of the group made clucking and groaning noises of recognition and would burst into applause at a particularly heightened expression of empowerment.

When the entire group finished, we talked in more detail about sexual exploitation, rape, HIV, malaria, and unsafe drinking water. Each of these women had had malaria, yet strangely, not a single one had slept under a net last night. Half had babies die from it. A few knew their HIV status, and oddly, only one was using modern birth control.

During this roundtable dialogue, I was able to complement WFWI's extraordinary work by sharing reproductive health, safe water, and malaria lessons with them. We talked about injectable birth control as long-lasting and safe, but how they needed to use a condom each time to protect from HIV. Then I asked if they would be willing to make a commitment to buy long-lasting insecticide-treated mosquito nets.

"Imagine how you would feel," I said, "if you had to write your sponsor that you had missed your WFWI graduation with a case of malaria!" Each woman raised her hand and said she would begin sleeping under a net immediately.

These lessons shouldn't be taken in any way as a criticism of WFWI's life-changing and society-building work. They do so much in such extreme circumstances. But I think it takes all NGOs working in partnership to provide a complete solution to the exceedingly complex and varied series of life-challenging problems that confront the poor.

After our session, we went back on that lush, soft grass for more dancing, clapping, hugging, and smiling. At the very end, I led a passionate salute to Zainab Salbi. Her name rang through the air in a series of mirthful waves, sung by beautiful, clean, fresh-smelling, literate, skilled, empowered standing-tall Congolese women!

~ ~ ~

Passing back into Rwanda was simple. There were no mysterious delays, no attempts at extortion or graft. The breeze off the lake began to blow freshly again, and the leaf cover from beautiful old trees provided shade as we made our way back to our hotel. I spent a whole hour in the bath that night, trying to scrub off grit that seemed to go deeper than my skin.

Then I settled in to process the day's many compelling events. As soon as I began to check voice mail and go online I was deluged with messages: At Dario's race in Talladega, Florida, some other driver, well after the yellow flag had come out, still managed to plow into Dario's car. To dramatically illustrate the crash, an image of the incident immediately popped up on my laptop screen as I signed on. Oh. Sigh. The life of a race car driver's spouse! Dario, his mum, and someone from the team had already left messages to reassure me that he was okay, although his ankle was broken. Dario and I spoke. I can tell everything I need to know by the sound of his voice, and I believed him when he assured me he was all right. Even so, his injury would be putting him out for several races, so our conversation became about that, and what it meant for his ongoing learning curve in stock cars. People cannot stop asking, no matter how many times I answer the question, whether I feel scared about the elements of racing, and the answer is always "no." I decided early on not to be afraid, because that would be a terrible way to live, with fear about things I so obviously cannot predict, influence, or control. My husband said he wanted me to keep my head down and carry on with my remaining time in Africa. I have seen him through far worse than broken ankles, and I appreciated that he did not doubt my concern and supported me to finish my trip.

~ ~ ~

Relations between Rwanda and the Democratic Republic of the Congo were still icy, so there were no direct flights to Kinshasa, our next destination. It took twenty-four hours, including an overnight layover in Addis Ababa, to fly just over one thousand miles, the equivalent distance between Washington, D.C., and Miami, Florida. We skipped the whole VIP line when we finally arrived, as it actually draws negative attention in the form of additional requests for bribes. The ride from the airport was long, and I saw a typical poor African capital out the window, crowded with nearly ten million souls struggling, often creatively and inventively, to make it through each day. Our hotel had red carpet and low ceilings—not a good look—and there were places where they'd patched the wallpaper with matching squares. Overall, the hotel struck me as ragged and depressed, like Kinshasa itself.

Papa Jack's security contact at the U.S. embassy told him, "If anything goes down, just stay put at your hotel. They run out of bullets fast around here."

Indeed, there have been semiregular coup attempts, assassinations, and random eruptions of militia violence in Kinshasa ever since the dictator Mobutu was overthrown in 1997. Robbery, pillaging, and rape are epidemic, and few venture outside after dark. I was immediately on my best conflict zone behavior, putting the chain in the door, looking in the fish-eye with each knock (as if that would really help, but whatever, one does what one can), minding Papa Jack every step. He was physically staying very close to me, very alert. (I get a kick out of seeing him put it into high gear.) It had been fairly stable here for a year now, but nobody was taking anything for granted.

This massive, lumbering, seemingly ungovernable nation, once known as the Belgian Congo and more recently Zaire, has not really known peace and stability since the first bloodsucking European colonists arrived in the nineteenth century. The insane and diabolical King Leopold II of Belgium looted the country for its vast natural resources—timber, copper, ivory gold, and other minerals—murdering ten million Congolese in the process. By the end of the colonial era, the country had been raped and pillaged, ancient cultures and social systems were destroyed, and the people were utterly lost. The Belgians gave nothing back in terms of education or infrastructure. At independence in 1960, there were only seventeen college graduates and less than a thousand miles of paved roads (down to a pitiful three hundred miles today), making transportation impossible in vast areas of this country, equal in acreage to everything east of the Mississippi. Mobutu Sese Seko, as corrupt as he was brutal, picked up where the Belgians left off, plundering the Congo for three decades, propped up by the CIA in exchange for his cooperation in fighting communism. What was left in his aftermath was a chaotic cauldron of warring armies and special business interests. As a result, a population of more than sixty million was left struggling to survive on almost nothing.

~ ~ ~

On our first morning in Kinshasa, Theresa Guber Tapsoba, our country rep, took us to meet Victor and Therese, a couple whose lack of knowledge about family planning ravaged their lives until PSI intervened. Victor is thin and wiry and has a bum eye. Therese has orange-tinged hair, enormous cheekbones, and sweet, soft eyes, especially when her husband is looking at her, which he does often. They have been together since they were children. They live in a little cement house in a run-down neighborhood, with a ten-square-foot main room, and a tiny little room on either side where they and their six children sleep on dirty, ragged pieces of foam on the floor. Altogether, Therese told me she has had nine pregnancies, three of which, out of mad desperation, she aborted with herbs obtained from friends. Each time, this caused protracted agony lasting five days. But it was that or have more babies, whom she and Victor could not offer adequate care, given that they were already barely surviving.

Unregulated fertility is a catastrophe in this country. Congo has the highest maternal mortality in the world, and six hundred thousand babies a year are born for no other reason than to suffer and die. Achieving universal access to family planning, which is Millennium Development Goal 5B, is considered the best way to reduce maternal mortality and is wildly unattainable under current funding levels and conditions in the DRC and throughout the global South, although the subject has recently been given more attention. The demographic household survey in 2008 found that 24 percent of women of reproductive age in Congo have an unmet need for modern family planning. Clearly, PSI and its partners have their work cut out for them in the DRC. Luckily, Therese was one of the few who could be reached and helped.

One day, a community outreach worker knocked on the door, full of information about family planning. The couple was interested enough to visit a local clinic, and since then Therese had been using an injectable contraceptive every three months. At last, the unintended pregnancies stopped. It is very likely Therese would be dead without family planning. But the rest of their lives remained such a struggle. Their one tattered mosquito net, dating to Therese's last pregnancy, was out of date. Their water was not safe, and they experienced recurrent episodes of diarrheal disease. Both did what they could to feed the family, but neither had a job. They ate one meal a day, close to bedtime, and sometimes nothing at all. There was violence in the neighborhood, especially because of moonshine made from a corn processor nearby, and Therese was terrified of the rapes, of which one heard much in the neighborhood. Every day as soon as the sun set she would hide herself and their children indoors.

PSI has a lot to show for its efforts in family planning and maternal health in the DRC. But while our program has improved one aspect of the lives of Victor and Therese, the violence of poverty still threatens to overwhelm them.

~ ~ ~

In a slum called Kingabwa, the roads are steep, raw ribbons that slope down to rice fields that abut the Congo River, which is choked with garbage. On either side are concrete houses with corrugated tin roofs that bake under the African sun. I was fascinated by the market. There was a little corner shack with a spiffy white-and-red paint job that served as a communication booth, and in the middle of the road was a little barbershop, which consisted of three plastic chairs, a small handheld mirror, and a comb. Today was Labor Day and a national holiday, so everyone was home and the kids had no school. It seemed more like National Hair Day, as everyone was being either freshly braided or styled out in the streets. Despite the abject poverty here, life still shines through in the perseverance of the human spirit. What else could possibly explain how the people find the will to live every day?

At the next market, I was able to roll up my sleeves and start doing what PSI does so well: using local markets to allow folk to access health products, services and behavior-change communication. In this case, it was a public demonstration of our point-of-use water purifying powder, with the same ingredients as Sur'Eau but available in this country under the brand name PUR.

I *love* this sort of thing, being on the street, hanging out, trading witticisms, having fun, involving passersby. I stood in front of the kiosk where PUR was sold at a highly subsidized price; about 50 francs (about 10 cents) buys enough to purify ten liters of water. I set myself up with a wooden stool and a big pail of fetid river water, thick with brown muck and filth. Using an enormous wooden spoon, I sprinkled in PUR and began to stir. A great crowd gathered, and we hollered questions and answers back and forth about water: "Where do you fetch your water?" I asked. "Do you have diarrhea? Wait till you see how PUR makes even river water safe! One capful alone cleans twenty liters!" The crowd grew.

After five minutes of stirring, we let the water "deflock." Particles and harmful organisms (visible and not) bonded with the chemicals and settled to the bottom. Using the clean piece of gauze sold with the sachet of PUR, we strained the water into an empty pail. After another twenty minutes had passed—which I filled with more banter—I poured the purified Congo River water into my glass and drank a toast to everyone's health to a big cheer. We began serving glasses of water to the crowd. They drained them greedily, they were so thirsty. I'd bet that part of the reason they drank so robustly was that on an unconscious level they were relaxing, because for once in their lives a vital human need was being met—drinking water—without consequences that would make life even more difficult. Relaxing in a life this hard doesn't come often. I will never forget the great vulnerability of their need for a simple drink of water.

As we made our way back to the car through people begging for food and money, I caught the eye of a young girl who had drunk a glass of PUR. We shared a smile and a thumbs-up. She was beaming.

~ ~ ~

That night I was meditating, and before I knew it, I was sucked into a vision:

I was in dark water. I was pressed deeper into the water, into a chute, and sent downward and under. When I came up for air, I discovered I was in a cave with a very low ceiling. The water was up to my chin. The rock above me pressed onto my head. There were decreasing centimeters in which to breathe. I tried to move forward, backward, sideways, every which way, precariously maintaining my nose just above the water in order to survive, looking for a way out. There was none, the ceiling was too low, the water too high, the margin for error too tiny.

I was suffocating, and I had to snap myself out of it.

It doesn't take Jung to figure out what the vision meant. One is born into it—the water and the cave. The structural factors that conspire against our survival press down on us and box us in. In Congo, the opportunity—the ceiling—is low: corrupt government, failed institutions, an army that harms rather than protects, armed militias wantonly roving, no infrastructure, no public works, low educational and health outcomes, stifling poverty, family and cultural systems destroyed. And the ability to change it is confined to the desperate struggle to actually stay alive, to keep one's head barely above water.

~ ~ ~

There was a reception at the home of the fabulous U.S. ambassador, Bill Garvelink, a former executive at USAID and an expert in complex emergencies and disaster assistance. Bill and his wife, Linda, were wonderfully gracious; they even had a piece of cake and a candle to celebrate Papa Jack's birthday. They made me feel at home, reminding me that their house was supported by my tax dollars, so I believed them. After playing tennis with Bill, I stole a moment in the yard lit by oil torches, walking in the soft, barefoot-worthy grass, with the call of frogs and insects wafting through the lush Congolese air. The great river was mere feet away; I couldn't see it, but I could feel it moving through the night. Africa. Wow. I'll never be over it.

After the introductions and speeches ended, I sat down with the ambassador to hear his take on the condition of the country. In particular, he described the critical importance of the $300 million a year the United States government spends in Congo (a figure that was recently cut by a third). We talked at length about the depth of nothingness here, the utter lack of everything. USAID buys pens and paper for ministerial offices, supplies some books and computers for them and the university. Otherwise, the students and teachers share books, and only from time to time do they have access to a Xerox machine to make copies to spread around. He said all the natural wealth, which is vast, leaves this country, either illegally via permeable borders into the surrounding countries (including Rwanda, which President Kagame and I bicker about—he insists Rwanda has its own minerals, identifiable through their higher quality) or through mining corporations, many of them American, which do not pay one red cent in taxes to the Congolese government. It is utterly grotesque. One of the many consequences of this is that the government's annual budget for DRC is $3 billion, about equal to the endowment of Vanderbilt University.

I saw this paltry budget in action the next day when I met the minister of gender, family, and children, Philomène Omatuku Atshakawo Akatshi. When we arrived at the minister's office, the staff was in a tizzy because the electricity was out. The windows were thrown open, and the street noise billowed up to where we sat. There was only one vintage computer to be seen, but the minister had spruced up her offices with electric blue drapes, a powder blue seating arrangement, and an arrangement of plastic blue flowers as a centerpiece.

Minister Philomène's lovely floor-length Congolese dress was made out of fabric printed with women's empowerment slogans. She is a gorgeous woman, one of those nerdy engineering types (which she is) you just know is trying to tone down her beauty with her professional demeanor. She gave me an exceedingly brilliant and articulate presentation on the status of girls and women in the Democratic Republic of the Congo. However, I can condense the message into one sentence: The budget this year of the minister of gender is exactly $0.0 Zero. Zilch. Nil. That is the state of things here.

In talking about what needs to be done, she was equally clear. Victims of rape and sexual violence need to know how and where to receive help. The help needs to be psychosocial and physical. They need to be destigmatized so they can return to their homes, extended families, communities, schools. They need microfinancing and savings support to start small businesses (she wanted to endow a bank with $5 million in assets for tiny loans to raped women). Women need to make cooperatives, to be together, talk together, work together, heal together. The fighting must end, impunity for rapists must end, along with the brutal environment and mineral exploitation that produces such monstrous behavior against women.

Minister Philomène had a lot to do with writing a set of tough gender violence laws and passing them through Parliament. The laws are comprehensive and inclusive, codifying penalties for all permutation of rape and abuse: elders to youngers, youngers to elders, men to women, women to men, men to men, women to women, body parts, objects, persons of authority, dependents, sex slaves, incitement, pornography—nothing is left out. Of course, the laws must be enforced, and the government, with help from USAID and others, is in the progress of training and sensitizing judges and magistrates. Impunity is a fundamental social and legal laxity that allows wide-scale rape to run rampant. Just as important is changing cultural norms and reaching men with behavior change messages. The torn fabric of this society will take years to mend, but the work, at least, has begun.

~ ~ ~

After nearly two weeks in Central Africa, I was already starting to burn out. Each morning when the alarm went off, I awoke in disbelief and exhaustion, spent the days slogging through the tough times in between clinics, slums, programs; through the joyful discoveries of various successes and ideas, my amazement at the enormity of the problems, the quiet moments of desperation spiked with rage, the rage laced with utter hopelessness, the plaintive seeking of answers from the universe . . .

I needed to hightail it out of Kinshasa and connect with nature and animals to restore my own peace of mind. So for the first time in eleven countries, I gave myself a break and took a Sunday afternoon to visit a very special animal sanctuary I had heard about called Lola ya Bonobo.

Bonobos are a rather forgotten primate, similar to chimpanzees but less fractious and highly endangered because their habitat has been hammered by decades of war and deforestation. They exist in the wild only in Congo and in captivity in a few zoos. Adult bonobos are snared and eaten as "bush meat," a delicacy in this protein-starved region. The babies are captured and sold in markets to witch doctors, idiotic tourists, and unscrupulous animal collectors. In 2002, in the midst of all the chaos and fighting in and around Kinshasa, a Belgian woman named Claudine Andre set up the sanctuary in what had been one of Mobutu's deputy's private estates outside of the capital.

Behind the gate was a sixty-acre oasis of forest and lakes and parkland where more than sixty bonobos of all ages roam about in a protected enclosure. Visitors are separated from them by a chain-link fence, which I walked along until I met the eye of a very fetching male. He solicited, meaning he was trying to entice me to play. I could not believe it. He would run, drop a shoulder to execute a perfect roll, sit up, cross his legs, look at me, and wait. I would imitate him: run, roll, sit. He would then laugh with unmistakable pleasure and joy. We ended up frolicking for an hour, running, playing, jumping, and sitting on either side of the fence, fingers intertwined, kissing. He was mischievous, tender, playful, and in general an angel from God who blessed me with an incredible experience, rare and heart-expanding, that soothed me deeply.

I later learned the name of the handsome bonobo I had loved from the researcher and conservationist, Vanessa Woods, who wrote the fabulous book *Bonobo Handshake*, about her time at the sanctuary. I emailed her photos of him and me running and rolling, laughing and kissing, and she wrote right back, "Oh, that's Keza! And he doesn't like anybody!" Before he was rescued, he had lived for fifteen years in a biomedical lab in Kinshasa, never seeing grass or trees, often so starved that he ate cobwebs to survive. Naturally he was terrified and quite unpredictable when he arrived at Lola ya Bonobo in 2004. The only human he likes is Mama Claudine, so Vanessa felt that Keza's afternoon of play was probably as healing for him as it was for me!

The more I've learned about bonobos, the more enthralled I've become. Like chimpanzees, they share 98.7 percent of our DNA. But unlike chimps, who have a male-dominated social structure and engage in humanlike pathologies such as war, rape, and murder, bonobos are peaceful creatures known for strong female alliances that prevent, contain, and correct male aggression. They might squabble, but they resolve social stress without violence. Researchers like Vanessa believe that the key to their pacifism and remarkable group tolerance and cooperation is a matriarchal society: Whenever a male starts to bully or attack a female, she cries out and other females band together and discipline the males, re-establishing calm and cooperation. Bonobos relieve their tension with lots of sexual behavior, giving new and poignant meaning to the slogan "Make love, not war." They are appealing in many ways, but perhaps what I love best is that a baby can take food out of an adult male's mouth. A baby chimp would never do that, and aggressive male chimps are known to occasionally kill babies. The bonobos' endangered status is salient for humans, as studying bonobos can reveal the key to the one thing we have never been able to figure out: how to live without war.

~ ~ ~

A century ago, Joseph Conrad set his masterpiece novella, *Heart of Darkness,* in the Congo. At its center is the tale of Kurtz, an idealistic adventurer who is sucked into the madness and savagery that he encounters in the cruelest of colonies. There but for the grace of God go you or I. As always, I am in awe of people who maintain their boundaries, who don't succumb to despair. I so admire people like Theresa Guber Tapsoba who persevere daily on in the face of hopelessness, and heroes like Zainab Salbi, like Therese and Victor, like the Women for Women program graduates in Goma and other survivors, and those who dedicate their lives to supporting them. But as I packed my bags in my sad little hotel room to return to my privileged life back home in America, I found myself brooding over my own culpability in the hideous drama of Central Africa.

I thought about Astrid, a tiny starving toddler whose cotton dress hung slack on her frame. I met her outside of a ramshackle health clinic in Kinshasa. Her mother had abandoned her, her grandmother walked to the clinic when she was literally on her last legs, and I watched Astrid clutch a UNICEF-provided refeeding formula with the fury and the rage that only the starving can truly understand.

Yet before I knew it, I would be easing back into my velvety world of abundance and first-class problems. I would be barefoot in my office—the back porch—wearing a white nightgown, looking at fireflies, eating black raspberry chocolate-chip ice cream with Dario, surrounded by our well-fed, inoculated pets, while Astrid and all the friends I made on this trip will still be . . . here.

I couldn't stop thinking about a photograph in the genocide memorial in Kigali, the one of the Belgian priests measuring the heads of Africans and consigning them to their fates through the delusion of ethnic separation. The priests were committing acts of evil, but did they know it? What about the United Nations countries that ignored the genocide spawned by these false divisions? Were those decision makers perpetuating evil by acts of omission? And what about me? I know I am human, I am fallible, I am capable of greatness, and I am capable of atrocity. In these pictures—I could be on either side: the measured or the measurer; the abused or the abuser. My mind's eye kept returning again and again to the image of the white priest, the black women . . . and which side of history I was going to be on.

I am grateful that in countries like Rwanda and Democratic Republic of the Congo, with challenges so great, my work with Population Services International and other organizations helps to put me on the right side of history. And somehow, in spite of it all, my faith, my hope, and my core belief that we can change the world and manifest peace is ever renewed.

Chapter 22

THE CLICK

COURTESY OF THE AUTHOR

Rain or shine, we love to hike. Here we are in the Great Smoky Mountains, accompanied, as always, by Buttermilk and Shug.

O, Great Spirit
Whose voice I hear in the winds
And whose breath gives life to all the world,
Hear me.
I am small and weak.
I need your strength and wisdom.

—*CHIEF YELLOW LARK*, "Let Me Walk in Beauty"

*A*fter twenty-five hours of travel back home from the Congo the plane touched down in Nashville, but my mind was still in Africa. Reentry is always difficult, and the tougher the place, the harder it is to adjust to the affluence and ease of America. I gaped at people in the airport: They were washed, clean, neat, their clothes free of stains. Everything was so bright, too bright.

I asked the driver who picked me up to open the windows and turn off the AC, then I reflexively braced for the potholes of Kinshasa. But the roads in Tennessee are as smooth as ganaches. The hills are packed with densely foliated trees—so strange. I was raised in the South, and yet these familiar sights were overwhelming. I tried to shut down. I closed my eyes and was soon dozing. But my body marked each turn, and once the roads narrowed and I perceived, even in my sleep, the approach to our farm, home called my spirit forth.

Although I had tried to mentally arrive home, imagining walking through the gate, up the garden path, trying to acclimate in advance, the exercise did not eliminate the shock of actually arriving. Disembarking from the car, I stood stock-still in the side garden of our brick farmhouse, shocked by the smothering of green, the lushness, the ethereal beauty of May in Tennessee. It was too beautiful, too cocooned, too soft, too womb-like.

Buttermilk ripped out of the house to see me, soon joined by his sister. I was stunned. I had forgotten we had dogs. Their leaping knocked me back on my heels and I had to kneel, let them wag it out.

I crept through the garden, unable to handle it all at once. I eventually made my way to the backyard, and was again arrested, this time by the explosion of a green undulating valley. I was glad Dario had not heard the car drop me off, did not yet know I was home. I needed some time to acclimate. I said hello to each cat as they one by one discovered their mama was home, and gave myself the space the breathe.

Eventually, I slowly entered the kitchen, taking in with disbelief our calm, ordered home. I opened the fridge. There was a riot of color, so many shapes and sizes.My brain became flooded and my eyes could not individuate any one thing. Finally, I focused on one large block on the top shelf, Dario's leftover lunch. I retrieved the plate. It was enough to feed four people. I removed the plastic film from the feast, and carefully set it aside, having been taught in poor households that such an item is a valuable treasure. But I ceased seeing the food before me, and instead, behind my tears appeared the image of a little boy's legs, shredded, layers of peeling wounds. He had just walked four days to arrive at a hospital, his daddy knowing it was either starve at home, or risk dying on the journey to a place where he might possibly receive food. I waited for the tears to clear, to emotionally come back to our kitchen, then I devoured the vegetables, of which I had recently had none. This food and ease of access to this food brings on a new round of tears.

I headed upstairs and find Dario in the bedroom, doing a Winston Churchill, reading and working from bed, propped up so as to enjoy the spectacular views, and rest his ankle, which he insisted was fine and indeed, he would be racing again soon. When he saw me, there was the moment I love, of recognition and reunion. We hugged, and I took a big bite of his devilishly handsome hair into my mouth. He didn't even say, "quit annoying me," as he usually does, with that secret smile in his voice.

When night fell, with all the windows open and the gentle air cosseting us, I knelt beside the bed, transfixed by the maple trees that nearly touch the windows, benedictions of softness, of generosity. I didn't say much. God understands. In bed, I occasionally blurted things out to Dario, staccato thoughts about my trip. I was physically present, but emotionally, I was in Africa. I was in India. I was in Central America.

The next morning, I sat on our upstairs back porch. I could feel the fecundity of spring on my skin as I regarded the morning glories, how well the hyacinth bean vine had started. The heirloom lilacs, as always, were heartbreaking, wafting fragrance everywhere, and the sweet peas were peaking. Dario brought my tea, having correctly identified the "morning glory teacup," saying he left Buttermilk's poop in the dining room for me to clean up. When he had been let out to do his business last night, Buttermilk made his choice, and running the hills was far more important than pooping outdoors. I smiled. Home.

"Okay," I told God. "I belong here, too. Home, my home, this home, and Africa, both are real, equally real. Thank you for letting me know it's okay for me to be here."

But my energy was very low, and I had to drag myself to my daily meeting. I continually made nests for myself and lay down on the bed, in the backyard, in the woods, with our animals who, with the softness of their eyes, regarded me deeply. I watched documentaries about rape in the Congo, about other African issues, and I tried watching the news. But for the head space I was in, it was too gruesome, and I realized that I needed a break. I didn't feel guilty at all when I relied only on Jon Stewart to keep up with the world, because if I wasn't laughing, I was near tears.

Some days, I did my own Churchill, windows open, skeptically regarding the improbably blue sky, still feeling myself in the liminality between very, very different worlds. Congo is primary colors, vivid, urgent, raw, visceral, a palette of red, orange, brown, black. Tennessee is like walking in the green fluffy grass of an Easter basket, so soft, pale, ethereal, like it's not real, like if I stepped off the bus everything I see would recede from me, like in a dream when I step forward into the dreamscape and it stays just ahead of me, out of my reach, so real in appearance, but untouchable.

I played a song, "Calling All Angels," sung exquisitely by Jane Siberry and k.d. lang, accompanied by cello, an old favorite of my sister's and mine.

Just then, my email inbox gave a ding, and I saw Zainib Salbi had written. She was checking on me after my trip, thanking me effusively for having visited the program, and for what I have written thus far that had been published, describing it as so helpful. I gave myself a few more days to feel rotten but when it didn't lift, I headed to the doctor for my routine, post-trip physical, with the usual parasite test. I studied the awesomely modern, pristine room, and resisted contrasting it with the clinics I have visited around the world. It would be a futile exercise. It is what it is.

My physician was wearing very thick sterile plastic gloves. They looked industrial strength, in fact. When he opened an alcohol swab, I was suddenly confused. I wasn't having blood drawn. I wondered if I was receiving a shot of which I was unaware. He lifted the end of his stethoscope, and wiped it before placing it on the fabric of my dress to listen to my heart. His mouth was moving, but I stopped hearing. I began to cry. He had sterilized the end of his stethoscope. Across the world, surgeons at Panzi Clinic scrub without running water, using bar soap, and sometimes operate without electricity. Many patients leave at night, and sleep in parks nearby, as the clinic cannot accommodate them all.

Although I seemed to be exotic bacteria- and virus-free, I was clearly ill. My doctor then surprised me, this same sweet man who told me years ago if I went to a mental hospital for depression it would go on my "record," diagnosed me with severe reverse culture shock. He said there was nothing he could do but suggest I rest and give myself time to heal from the effects of what I had chosen to expose myself to and take on.

I continued slowly to work at my desk on the advocacy tasks I created for myself during my time in Africa, with each email and call, praying the effort made good on promises made to my new sisters.

Once the Africans had gone offline for their nighttime, I turned my attention westward, to Hollywood. I spoke to my agent who as ever was full of information about scripts and green-lit movies, phone calls and appointments, and all the latest show business news, that nonetheless made my head spin. I started reading a few scripts she had sent me.

Having been offered TV shows for years, I had begun to take the idea of doing a cable series seriously. But I rejected the idea of network, however lucrative, however fantastic the writing in this new golden age of television, however flattering the entreaties. A hit network show would consume nine months of the year for five to seven years of my life—and I would have to make that commitment before knowing whether the show was a hit. I would have to opt out of doing international feminist social justice work, resign from all the boards on which I served. I was unwilling to give up the life I had made for myself, to deny myself the chance to meet another Ouk Srey Leak, to have an old woman with whom I pick rubbish to call me her granddaughter. I remember a labor slave in India whose lair I visited, and the moment when our eyes met in a shard of mirror. I had said to him, "Mohammad, when I see you, I see a beautiful child of God." Holding my gaze, he replied, "I do, too." A deaf mute woman I met in a brothel in Kinshasa, Congo, came to mind. *She was still there.* When the networks call, I say thank you and no thank you, and I have watched beautiful, talented women sweep acting awards for shows I declined. I smile, and bless them, and some I email, cheering them on. I DVR the series I enjoy.

I read scripts for several proposed series on cable. One was about adoption. I perked up. That fit my interests, confronted all sorts of salient social themes, and would allow me to be polemical with a smart character. I would be interested in such a show, but my agent called back later, saying it was a nonstarter. Another script came along, and to my surprise, I loved it. I had been talking with producers who pitch me material about my preference to film in middle Tennessee, and surprisingly, most have been very willing to accommodate. If am going to be on a show for four to six months a year, I would like sleep in my own bed. It would be too much to keep up my current pace of international travel and film something in New York or L.A.

Then, I read a movie script with a lot of buzz, an action thing, written all male, but they sent it to me to read, asking if I'd like this flashy supporting role to be written female. I lied and said yes. Someone associated with the director emailed me to schedule a Skype call with him, and I became more honest with myself. I called my agent and said, "I hated that script."

The tens of millions of dollars I have left on the table rarely crossed my mind. I still pull my weight in the marriage, which is a 50–50 financial partnership, but I long ago stopped participating 50–50 in the posh extras. I chip in what I can for vacations, but for private travel and such, my contribution is nowhere near what it used to be. The days of hopping on a little private plane to attend a UK basketball game are long gone. When I meet with my financial planner, I realize she may assess me as an "under earner," given my potential. She is a counselor, in addition to being one of the top financial advisors in the country, and in her own 12-step recovery. Ted, she, and I talk about the feelings that come up around money as well as the dollars and cents. My feelings are almost uniformly positive, and I live in a sense of abundance. I have no regrets, and that is freedom.

I continued to sleep well, almost twelve hours a night. I enjoyed the weight of my worn daily meditation readers in my hands every morning, and had resumed reading the *End of Sorrow, Bhagavad-Gita for Daily Living* where I left off. Ekneth Easwaran, the great teacher who inspired my meditation practice, would have said I had a golden opportunity to take my practice deeper than I ever dreamed possible, but that it takes consistency to ride the waves of consciousness to arrive at the still, deep ocean floor, where the rubies and diamonds are. But I still felt very sick, and not over the reentry. I decided to see a psychologist I knew in town. After we spoke a while, she offered that what she was observing in me was mostly grief, not trauma, and reminded me of the stages of grief: denial, anger, bargaining, depression, and acceptance. She said "You are still grieving, Ashley, and sometimes you sound like you are in the bargaining, too. And the only way out is through. I imagine you'll kick whatever is making you feel like you are sick, when the emotional part is purged."

Her words were all it took for the dam to break. I began to cry. I could not stop. The force of it propelled my chest forward, which came to rest on the tops of my legs. I sat that way, folded over, limp but for the sobbing, for a while, until the old shame crept up on me, the lie that my feelings are a burden. I began to fear I was wasting her time, excoriating myself for driving forty-five minutes to pay someone so I could cry on her sofa. I glanced up and apologized for being a dork. "You're doing good, Ashley. You are doing so good," she said softly.

I sensed there was double meaning in her offering: the work abroad and taking care of my grieving self within the work. Touched by her encouragement, I let go for good, and cried it out. This was the woman, after all, who after my very first trip with PSI all those years ago, had said, "You know, the little girls are always going to get to you." Though my eyes had filled spontaneously with tears, I had been baffled by what she said.

Soon, indeed, I began to feel better. A sense of something invisible being lifted occurred, and I was no longer dragging around, pushing myself, struggling to stay upright. I flew with Dario to his race in Pocono, and on his bus did some laundry from previous races. I paused, though, and registered in my body how it feels to do two loads, separated by color, with chosen water temps, and custom spin cycles, *on a bus.* I was physically better, but I retained the awareness of, the sensitivities to, the ridiculous abundance of our lives. When it came time, I could not put our clothes in the dryer. I just couldn't. I took them outside and spread them on chairs. I wondered how Dario would feel when he came back from qualifying and all the wash was hanging in plain view of the driver's paddock, a veritable neighborhood filled with racing drivers, their families, team members. He is a natural boy, I suspected he wouldn't mind.

I heard the cars on the track, and I wanted to watch. In spite of trepidation, I decided to experiment, and walk to the pits. If it was too much, if I could not be kind and patient, if I wanted to explain to everyone who asked for an autograph, "No, but have you heard of Rwandan genocide? Are you aware there are more slaves today than at the height of the nineteenth-century slave trade?" I could just return to the bus.

I made it to the pits, and the absurdity, the insane luxury, of putting so much time, attention, and hundreds of millions of dollars into being .001 second faster than the next car—the sums, hundreds of thousands of fans pay each season to sit and watch cars go in a circle could provide school for . . . I couldn't finish the sentence. I put it out of my mind. This was my husband's life. In my sleep that night, I found another way to look at it, to frame it as one of the many extraordinary things humans can do with their potential when we are freed up beyond merely surviving and reacting to violence, hunger, disease, trauma.

On Saturday, we took a rare race-weekend hike after Dario's practice. There was a beautiful state park nearby, and we enjoyed each other's company and the many waterfalls that dampened sharp rocky outcroppings, carefully picking our way along the terracing of creeks. Occasionally, there were deep pools into which the creeks rushed in and out. I cannot resist a good creek, and I paused, looking both ways on the trail. My husband knew what was coming, and made his usual and always futile protestations. I sneaked off my clothes and plunged into a cold mountain pool, exhilarated, needing this, thinking of my Uncle Mark who baptizes in the creek, feeling how water cleans, refreshes, promises, transfigures. I heard, and duly ignored, Dario's insistent pleas of "Babe! BABE! You're a nutter!" because I knew he wouldn't be mad for long. Submerging my head again and again, opening my eyes to see the world under the oxygenated bubbles of moving water, I recognized that something deep inside me had settled, had sorted itself out. It's like an internal click, and it comes when it comes, and it cannot be hurried, the moment when I know I am okay, that deep inside I have always been okay, and when I don't feel okay in the future, I will somehow have a process I can trust, that promises I will be okay again. The click. I stepped naked from the creek, smiled at my husband, began to put clothes on my damp body. I was ready to face the world again.

Chapter 23

CRIMSON DREAMS

My dad and me on my first day of graduate school—
making up for lost time.

may my mind stroll about hungry
and fearless and thirsty and supple
and even if it's sunday may i be wrong
for whenever men are right they are not young

—*E.E. CUMMINGS.* "may my heart always
be open to little . . ."

On June 2, 2008, trembling just a bit with healthy fear, I used my voice to bring the sacred narratives of the vulnerable and mute to the world's most expansive stage: the United Nations General Assembly. As a board member of PSI, I had been invited to speak about the scourge of human trafficking and to promote the solutions that I had seen at work in the field. I used this opportunity to describe the insidious enmeshment between poverty, illness, and gender inequality and how that triad sets up the exquisite pain and degradation that is sex and labor slavery. And, as always, I did it by sharing the stories of the poor and the vulnerable, the disempowered, and the exploited people I had met in my travels, those to whom I had made my one keening vow: I will never forget you, and I will tell your stories. So the representatives of 196 nations were introduced to the transgendered sex slave in Cambodia whose face had been mauled by her rapist's dog; to Natasha, the literate, high-priced "call girl" in Mumbai who could see no way out of the netherworld of sex trafficking; and the children born in a squalid Indian brothel, collateral damage of sex trafficking, who wrote their names for me on dirty scraps of paper: Aadarshini, Yamuna, Nabhendu . . . And I reiterated the basis of my faith: that every human life is of inestimable worth and that when we save one, we save the whole world.

I quoted the effervescent light that is Marianne Williamson, who said, "We are, all of us, not just some of us, children of God, and our playing small does not serve the world."

I was standing before the United Nations because when it comes to human dignity and rights, I refuse to play small. Knowing I was surrogate for the real experts, the survivors whose stories I told, I remembered Elie Wiesel's quote, "Not to transmit an experience is to betray it." And in my head, a plan was already forming that would expand my game beyond anything I had ever thought possible.

~ ~ ~

I had always wanted to go to graduate school, but I never pictured my-self at Harvard. I had briefly considered divinity school and had thought I might go for a master's in public health at Berkeley. I also considered Vanderbilt University, an outstanding school that was less than an hour from my front door. I talked it over with a friend, Dr. Volney Gay, a head of the Religious Studies and Anthropology Departments at Vanderbilt. I ex-plained to him that I wanted to learn, to study, to expand my mind, but a degree should be highly relevant to my interests—not so much a profes-sional credential, but a passion credential. He was prepared for our ap-pointment, offering me names of Vanderbilt colleagues I should look up, suggesting different courses of study. Just as we were about to close, he asked me, "Ashley, why aren't you going to Harvard?"

Thunderstruck, I blurted out, "Why am I not putting a rocket up my ass and flying to the moon?"

I went straight home and called Carol Lee Flinders, one of my men-tors, who cooed, "Oh, the Women and Public Policy Program, founded by Swanee Hunt, is at the Kennedy School. Of course, it's the perfect place for you! " I did some Internet research, cried when I read the WAPPP website (*my people!* I thought), and linked over to the Carr Center for Human Rights Policy site, also at the John F. Kennedy School of Government. I asked a fel-low board member at PSI, one of the first women ever to graduate from Har-vard Law School, what she thought, and the next thing I knew, I was on the phone with the dean of admissions, being recruited to go to Harvard. The Kennedy School offers an intensive, year-long midcareer master's in public administration, aimed at established professionals from all over the world who want to broaden their horizons and increase their efficacy in public ser-vice. Alumni range from Ban Ki-moon, secretary-general of the United Na-tions, to New York police commissioner Raymond W. Kelly. Well, hey! Why not add a Sicilian-hillbilly rabble-rousing actor-activist to the roster?

When it came time to fill out the application forms, I had some wel-come help from an unexpected source: my father.

Dad and I had become increasingly close in the years since we recon-nected during Ted's therapy sessions and our remarkable experiences dur-ing the family weeks at Shades of Hope. He and his wife of ten years, Mollie, are frequent occupants of our smokehouse guest cabin, and they spend summers in our house in Scotland. When Dad sat down with me on our sleeping porch to help organize my essay topics and put together a comprehensive curriculum vitae (not a small task, as I've never kept close track of my zillions of endeavors), I felt as if I were being given a second chance to do over the whole college application process that I had missed out on twenty-three years earlier. I needed him, and he was there for me. It was a joyful time.

In early 2009, to my astonishment and unbelievable gratitude, the dean of admissions personally phoned to tell me I had been accepted into the program. The committee vote was unanimous, he added with a smile in his voice. I threw back my head and hooted and hollered at the top of my lungs, racing from room to room in our big Scottish house, my excitement echoing off the old walls. I kept my new knowledge to myself for a few hours that afternoon, reflecting on this amazing turn of events while hiking up the ben in record time. Now, I reckoned, all I had to do was let my various colleagues know I would be unavailable for anything for a full year. And then move to Cambridge.

~ ~ ~

I still wanted to make movies, but I had purposefully slowed down the pace of my filmmaking career after I went to Shades of Hope to focus on recovery, put it first in my life, and continue digging deeply into my healing process and new way of life. *Crossing Over,* about labor trafficking in Mexico and California, was my first picture in recovery. I played a little supporting role, gently dipping my toe in the water again, and the experience was just what I wanted. Then I took on a much more challenging project, playing the lead in *Helen,* an independent film about a woman who suffers major recurrent suicidal depression. As soon as I read the first pages of the exquisite script by the auteur director Sandra Nettelbeck, I knew I had to be involved with the movie. I was concerned that the material might be too close to the bone, so I had copies of the script sent to Tennie and Ted. My question was, "Can I play the disease without being in the disease?" Both of them read it and quickly called me back with essentially the same reaction: "Ashley, how dare you not?" It was an answer that sent a frisson through me.

Filming *Helen* was a wonderful revelation, and I was reminded of why I love to act. My only bad experience during that snowy winter in Vancouver was not psychological but physical: An attack of acute appendicitis landed me in the hospital for emergency surgery and shut down production for two weeks. I had an otherwise extraordinary experience playing the role, using all my tools while delving deeply indeed into a performance of which I am very proud. I sacrificed a vestigial organ for that movie! I did a delightful and touching children's comedy called *Tooth Fairy* after that and then told my longtime agent, Michelle Bohan, that other projects would have to wait until after my graduation.

Next I found a homey, quiet place to rent in Cambridge, a beautiful brick house with a peaked slate roof, sycamores in the front yard, and lots of evergreen shrubs and trees in a large (for a town!) fenced backyard. We shipped up some furniture and then all the pets. Shug was skunked in the backyard on the first night, and giving her a bath with my magic deskunking potion made it feel instantly like home.

I had shipped up my Mini Cooper, but when I inquired about having a car on the quirky campus streets, the secretary's response was to hold the phone away from her mouth and cackle. So I outfitted myself with a pink Hello Kitty bicycle and began practicing riding back and forth to Harvard. I wheeled up in front of Widener Library, with its crimson flag proclaiming *Veritas* ("Truth"), the Harvard motto, and I had to seriously pinch myself to believe this was all true for me.

Classes started on July 22, 2009. I looked around at my 208 classmates, who represented ninety-eight countries and an encyclopedic array of backgrounds and prior achievements, from humanitarian aid workers to hedge fund founders, cabinet members, and NGO directors. When I inquired what one woman did at the World Food Program, she replied, "I run it." We were all unabashed do-gooders, united by a desire to change the world for the better. I was just about twisted inside out, I was so excited. I was twisted inside out, too, because I was starting to grasp the basics of the academic schedule, which for midcareers included intensive course work in microeconomic and quantitative methods. I had not done math in years, much less math at Harvard. It was easily the most intimidating thing I have ever done in my life. (Sorry, Morgan Freeman, that includes that first day on set with you on *Kiss the Girls*. Even though you are a legend, you're a lot less scary than quant.) There were former ministers of finance in my class, economic policy experts, and other wonks whose math was lightning fast, and I had zero shame about placing in the lowest-level section; I was right where I needed to be.

It was easy to decide to forgo socializing in the quad, and missing the volleyball games to which I had been looking forward. Instead, I set up tutoring in economics and math, the latter with Professor Graeme Bird, a Renaissance man from New Zealand who is equal parts mathematician, Greek scholar, English teacher, and jazz musician. He is so kind, so genuine, and so flawlessly patient that he could actually make me believe he liked sitting in his office with me six hours per week, eraser litter all over my scrambled papers and his desk, doing the work everyone else seemed to have mastered yesterday.

"Graeme," I would choke, "I am making you think I am an idiot, that you cannot believe I was accepted at this school, you are bored sick, and you wish I would leave your office so you did not have to explain this yet again to me, who is clearly remedial in math." He would just smile and talk me down. Then explain it again. (When I graduated, I awarded Graeme a diplomalike certificate students may give select people for whom they have exceptional gratitude for the role they played in helping them achieve their academic dreams.)

We were advised that something was wrong if we were devoting more than ninety minutes per class on homework; in my case, then, something was seriously wrong. But it was what was wrong with the past, not the present. So much old fear kept coming up, I was battling across lifeline time zones. I would have blessed stretches during which I rocked and rolled on homework, ripping through problems, reconnecting especially with anything related to algebra, which I loved in high school and still find very creative. But then I'd hit a wall, and the crap from the past would fill the room like unseen smoke, and I'd be confused, despairing, inept, facing intractable quant calculations. It was definitely consoling to know I was not alone. We midcareers, facing academic rigors in some cases for the first time in decades, would group up in the lunch room and corridors, before class and outside the tutoring hall, comparing notes about our cycles of confidence and doubt, hard work and peace, procrastination and angst. Many of us experienced identical patterns: Satisfied at the end of a long day that we had given it our all, we would lay our heads on our pillows unperturbed (after shoving my school work off the bed; my resolve never to do homework in bed lasted less than a week). But long about dawn, some icy fear would grip us and we'd bolt awake, racked with shame for not having been able to do better or more, and we'd arrive in class exhausted and full of doubt, until some placating professor soothed our spastic emotions and our minds began to work again.

On top of this, I was heartsick because our beloved cat Percy went missing a mere two days after he arrived in Cambridge. I searched frantically for him, my voice bleating his name every moment I was home from school. We put up laminated posters and endlessly called neighbors, businesses. I felt terrible guilt: *If only I hadn't brought him here . . . if the doggie door had been closed. . . .* I would wake up in the middle of the night and stumble around the neighborhood in my nightgown, crying, searching. Then I would go to class, go to tutoring, and do homework. It was hell for me.

Dario was traveling most of the time on the IndyCar circuit, but I think God arranged for us to be together when I finally found Percy's remains in a field. I believe the body is but a jacket, a garment we lay down when it is time for our souls to change rooms. I believe the soul, which contains the essence of all I know and love about a person, is immutable, unchangeable, eternal. Yet I am human, and I have a terrible attachment to the bodies of those I love, the home in which I have known their soul. Finding Percy was a crushing, devastating blow. I wailed and wailed in grief.

I called Tennie in the depths of my pain, and when I was able to calm down a bit, she asked me, "What is the lesson Percy came to teach you?" The answer, clearly, is unconditional love. God is everyone's personal Percy. Totally, beautifully, unflinchingly focused just on that one person. I began to picture every woman, every child, somewhere with Percy, the most beautiful cat in the world, the biggest baby boy, sitting on their chests the way he did mine, paws folded, purring, heavy-lidded, but oh, watching with utter devotion, occasionally reaching up to kiss me. Scraping his cheek along mine is his signature expression of adoration. God as Percy. I loved it. It worked.

~ ~ ~

My final exams in both econ and quant were scheduled for the day after we found Percy. I was reeling and unsure how I could possibly pass these tests. I had been using my recovery tools incessantly, including slogans such as "First things first," "Let go and let God," "Easy does it," and "How important is it?" to help me organize myself, figure out not just how to move forward, but which foot to put in front of the other. I knew, sadly, I would have plenty of time to grieve my Percy and that it was okay to do first things first, which now meant these tests. As I sat for the exams, I felt Percy was with me, and I asked for his help.

A few days later, when my work was handed back to me with A's, I had Percy, along with Graeme, Rachel, my economics tutor, and my classmates to thank for how far I had come. I knew when I held my work that I had *learned* it. I had a newfound, strong confidence in my math ability, I actually found it intensely pleasurable. I had at last exorcised the demons of high school math, so implicated in the debilitating shame I experienced as a kid living on her own, with no one to help me in school.

Soon I was doing original math in further quant classes, for example, bringing together my deep interest in family planning, field experience in Congo, and new confidence in my abilities. In "Population Changes and Consequences" at the School of Public Health, I showed, using the 2008 Demographic Health Survey and modeling software called Spectrum, that by 2050 an astronomical 89,847,607 million babies will be born in Congo to women of reproductive age who have a desire to plan and space births but who do not have access to family planning. I also showed reductions in these unintended births, as well as reductions in maternal mortality, by making family planning available to increasing percentages of women of reproductive age. It was a powerful way to bring home the statistic that though 63 percent of women in the global South use a method family planning, in Congo a scant 6 percent do. I was in wonk heaven!

~ ~ ~

After the grueling intensity of the summer term, I settled into the marathon of my fall semester. In spite of stern warnings, I was carrying more than the recommended number of classes, and even at this fullness, I mourned the courses I could not take and the extra activities I had to skip. On a daily basis my "HKS Today" email invited me to talks, seminars, brown bag lunches, and forums that were enormously appealing. I spent most of my time in study, with every spare moment hanging out with incredible people, students and faculty whom I admired, which was pretty much everyone, but I narrowed it down by field of study, mostly within human rights, social justice, feminism, moral leadership, and spirituality.

Feeling initially like a hopelessly incompetent dork who could never get it—I had been out of college for twenty years, after all—I was amazed at the ease of the uptake and how in no time at all I was a high-functioning graduate school student, reading up to a thousand pages a week and turning in long papers with confidence—by tricked-out course page websites, no less.

Although Dario supported my efforts and recognized that the health of my soul was linked to my service work, he found that living full-time in Cambridge didn't appeal to him: It was too crowded, school and the happenings there weren't interesting to him, and he was taken aback by how class work devoured my time and attention. He likened my summer semester to what his schedule is like when he competes in the Indianapolis 500: totally consuming. And yet I sustained that not for three weeks, but for an entire degree. Not to mention those Yankee roads—those, he really didn't like! We did memorably experience Concord, Massachusetts, and the Sleepy Hollow Cemetery in October and coastal Maine in March, but for much of the time, I found myself going it alone. I also had a series of unfortunate studentlike encounters with sickness: I had a rotten, Centers for Disease Control–verified case of H1N1, complicated by a wicked sinus infection, followed by two post-flu infections, all of which made my life wholly inoperable for a few weeks, even as I maintained the improbable wish that I could keep it all going at such a high level. When my dad came to visit, I took full advantage of his late-blooming, prodigious nurturing abilities.

Dad visited no fewer than five times during the school year, including being there to drive me my very first day of summer semester. He had his own guest room on the second floor of the house, and he would do a lot of the shopping and cooking that would otherwise eat up so much of my time. He enjoyed having something to do, and I loved it. I would wake up in the morning and pass him in the kitchen on my way to do my meditation, saying, "Are you making breakfast for graduate students this morning?" followed by, "What's for lunch." After a reprisal of those hearty bowls of oatmeal from the Camp Wig days, he would send me off with a little lunch basket filled with a sandwich and nuts, teabags, and a thermos of hot water. I would load them into my bicycle's cherry blossom saddle-bags, along with books and notebooks, and pedal across the Charles River to class, saying hello to my friends the geese and the sycamore trees along the way. In the evening, I'd come and lay out all the work I needed to do that evening, organizing reams of paper, coordinating readings with class notes. Dad would have been in the kitchen preparing a beautiful meal, which we would share, and I would talk excitedly about my invariably in-teresting day. When I hosted dinner for classmates, he and Mollie did all the work, making sure the food was wonderful, the table adorned with cherry blossoms. (They, along with me, hung on every word my Palestin-ian and Israeli classmates, who took part in their countries' top-level nego-tiations, were saying.) It was like living out my childhood dream of having full-time parents to take care of me—a need that one doesn't outgrow, whether in kindergarten or in graduate school. It was what I had always hoped family could feel like.

When the weather was bad or I was running late, Dad would drive me to class. I introduced him to all my professors, and he audited a few of my classes. Diane Rosenfeld, who taught a course in gender violence at Harvard Law School, actually sent him home with reading assignments. He told me it was all he could do to keep from raising his hand in class. Although Dad does not share my politics, defining himself as somewhat right of center, we respect each other's opinions and would have interest-ing political discussions. He wanted to read everything I was reading for class, from scholarly articles to entire books. He would look at me when he was ready for more reading material, his eyes tracing back and forth from what I had in my hand to my face, making me smile because it reminded me of what Buttermilk does when I am eating something and he wants a bite of it. It was nourishing having him back in my life.

Within weeks of the fall term, my joy was intense, bordering at times on the ecstatic. In certain classes, such as "Public Narrative: Self, Us and Now," taught by my glorious advisor Marshall Ganz, my biggest challenge was making my papers short enough. More than once, my work would be sent back to me with stern reminders about length. Once, I had a point deducted, which was absolutely the most effective way to induce my respect for page count. (I was obsessed with making straight A's at Harvard and nearly succeeded. Two profs had the "audacity" to give me a B plus!)

My enthusiasm was unbounded. My mind and soul were on fire, which is my favorite mode of being. I sometimes wept in classes, overcome with the connections crackling inside of me, overcome with gratitude and a specific type of happiness I hadn't felt in years. At times, in classes such as "Health and Human Rights" and "Informal Economy: Linkages with Growth, Economic Crisis, and Gender," I stopped taking notes, pushed back from desk, and just *enjoyed the show.*

When Dario won his second IndyCar championship, I fortuitously had a long weekend break from school. Missing class for anything was not an option: Once admitted, we were told to cancel all prior commitments, and I did, including my personal invitation from His Holiness the Dalai Lama to be on a panel with him about the role of girls and women in securing peace. Thus, good ole Columbus Day allowed me to be with Dario at the track when he took the checkered flag. Later, in the hotel room, he basked in the glow of this life-changing moment, answering hundreds of emails and texts while I worked on an evaluation of the Bush administration and Condoleezza Rice's foreign policy toward Cuba for my "Reasoning from History" class.

~ ~ ~

One of the most thrilling aspects of my year at Harvard was reconnecting with some of the remarkable leaders I had met in my travels. Everybody in the world of development and human rights seems to pass through Harvard at one time or another. Mu Sochua, to whom I owe a debt of gratitude for trusting me enough at the very beginning of my international work to take me to the Svay Pak brothels in Cambodia, presented at Harvard for a week, and I was overjoyed to be reunited with her. I was able to invite sex slavery abolitionist Ruchira Gupta, with whom I had such a salient adventure in India, to be a guest lecturer in my "International Childhood: Human Rights and Globalization" class. She captivated students so viscerally and spoke so deftly from every angle of the debate that students followed her to her car and were still engaging her as she had to drive away to catch her flight. I was very proud when PSI president Karl Hofmann presented a seminar on what PSI is and how we work, and the impressed responses from my cohort. "Show-and-tell for the smart set," quipped Dad.

It was meaningful to make the connections between what I had seen in the field and what I was learning in class and develop a new language to evaluate what I'd observed. For example, all over the world I've sat in slums with people selling little things—vegetables or crafts—set out on blankets in a market or in wheelbarrows on a sidewalk, or setting up a "beauty shop" in a field. I know from my studies that these enterprises occur within the informal economy, and I have studied the pioneering theories from the 1970s that first captured and described informality as well as the current prevailing debates. I have been in tiny apartments where I now realize the woman was a home-based industrial outworker, making piece-rate goods for a global value chain. I was now able to evaluate such exploitation from a variety of angles, including from her sometimes not being reimbursed for the materials she used, the lack of enforceable contract that meant sometimes the middleman didn't even pay her for the finished work or when orders were canceled she lost the capital she'd invested, and the lack of occupational safety as she sometimes worked with toxic, hazardous materials in a small, unventilated space. With deeper study, it was easily confirmed that microfinance is valuable, but I learned that it is only one dimension of the financial services and instruments needed by the poor; they also need insurance options, to be able to save, to have more flexibility in the access and timing of their loans. I have learned about informal savings clubs, especially in sub-Saharan Africa, that are fascinating in their sophistication and ingenuity. I have learned more explicitly about legal empowerment issues, ranging from the need to access sidewalks for trade to legal recognition in bureaucracies. It may sound wonky, but these subjects are like homemade peach pie to me—I gobble them up.

It would be impossible to choose a favorite class, but if a measure is how fired up I was, it may have been Diane Rosenfeld's "Gender Violence, Law and Social Justice" course. In my final paper, I was able to metabolize so many of my life experiences to propose a model that encourages women to engage in a feminist analysis of their own lives and, through strong female-to-female alliances, disrupt the virulent problem of gender inequality in their homes and communities. We can do this by the willingness to become aware, then accept, and finally take action to begin to heal from patriarchal wounding, and from increased personal empowerment commit to service work, addressing gender inequality at the grassroots level.

To suggest a solution, mindful of the many times I have witnessed the power of female-to-female alliances both in the global South and in my own life, I built upon Diane's and Professor Richard Wrangham's studies of the bonobos, those wonderful primates I met in the Congo, offering them as a model of how women at the household-to-household level can influence communities into peaceful society. I developed a workshop inspired by the brilliant social architecture of Twelve Step programs, the feminist consciousness-raising groups of the 1970s, and modern sexual abuse and trauma survivor therapy. The workshop would be exportable to any community and open to men as well as women. As Margaret Mead said, every time we liberate a woman, we liberate a man. Also, many men have no idea the effect their addiction to power and degrading women has on us, and them having the opportunity to sit in groups with women who have suffered abuse is an underused strategy. The workshop would incorporate, inter alia, feminist analyses of one's past and present life, include trauma and shame reduction experiential therapy, role playing, inner child work, art therapy, and identification of compulsive behaviors and addictions, and suggestions for after care and advocacy. The crux of the experience would be for each participant to identify core patriarchal wounding in their life, begin to recover from it, and accept responsibility for advocating feminist social justice change in their communities in whatever way is most meaningful to their personal narrative. Once we begin to recover, we can be most useful in precisely the ways we have been most hurt.

I couldn't have guessed that my own story would have everything to do with feminist social justice theory and that the gifts I had been given of clinical inpatient treatment and recovery would bring me back to radical feminism.

The paper won a dean's scholar award. Diane told me when she felt down, she'd read my paper again, and it would put wind in her sails.

~ ~ ~

I graduated from the Harvard Kennedy School on a glorious day in May 2010, surrounded by some of my dearest friends and members of my families of chance and choice. In a reprise of my college graduation, my mother and sister chose not to attend the ceremony, but Dad was right by my side, along with Mollie. And Tennie, my most wonderful surrogate grandmother, brought her quietly radiant, affirming presence to the commencement, marveling with me at the 468-year-old tradition in I which partook. After I had sung "Fair Harvard" in Latin and had run around hugging classmates and thanking faculty, she presented me with a beautiful necklace on which dangled a key, with a framed reading that said, in part, "There is no more 'aloneness,' with the awful ache, so deep in the heart. . . . That ache is gone, and never need return again. Now there is a sense of belonging, of being wanted and needed and loved . . . We have been given the Keys to the Kingdom." The Indianapolis Motor Speedway and Indy Racing League would not excuse Dario from a half day of press obligations related to the 500 (which he would win that weekend for the second time), so he sat in his bus on the track, watching the school's live Internet feed of commencement, while we chatted back and forth via texting as the exercises unfolded.

After the stately procession through Harvard Yard, the various schools dispersed to smaller venues around the campus to hand out the diplomas. The Kennedy School crowd looked like a United Nations General Assembly, with the foreign students wearing their formal native dress: Africans in colorful dashikis and foulards, Asians in jewel-colored silks. Ever the mountain girl, I went barefoot as I bounded across the grass to accept my diploma. As my little cheering section rose to clap and whoop for me, I felt down to my toes that I was just hitting my stride, that truly anything was possible.

I'm not sure where this journey will take me. All I know is that I'll always be traveling on the front lines of hope, expecting miracles to happen.

DARIO FRANCHITTI

Remembering.

On the path to God, light gives way to darkness, and darkness to light, at intervals. A measure of integration takes place, and we enjoy a moment of peace and joy, but the longing sets in again, and we must again exert the terrible effort.

—*CAROL LEE FLINDERS, Enduring Grace*

EPILOGUE

Up on a high ridge in the Great Smoky Mountains National Park, I walk a narrow footpath ribbed with roots. Dense foliage rubs my shoulders. Some trees I know, but there are more than 400 species here. This park, comprised of mixed mesophytic forest, has more biodiversity than the whole of Europe, so, outside my comfort zone of maple, oak, hickory, larch, walnut, paw paw, persimmon, elm, birch, dogwood, redbud, cherry, buckeye, I have at best, a 1-in-400 chance of naming something. Today, I love knowing what I don't know.

It is my first long walk since the July full moon. It's unlike me to not walk, even at night, even if just for a short jaunt to look around, visit the butterflies, watch the turtles in the lake. The woods are spiritually chiropractic. On any given walk, I may not even know I need an adjustment, but once I pass that margin and enter the cathedral of trees and all who live with them, I am changed.

First, I just say, "Hi, God." Second, I declare my proper relationship with my Creator: I am powerless over people, places, and things; there is One who has all power, and that One is a loving God. Third, I recommit myself to the decision I have made to turn my will and my life over to the care of this Power. A hint of Julian of Norwich's prayer floats to mind: "All shall be well, and all shall be well, and all manner of thing shall be well . . ."

Standing on the edge of a creek, my feet yearn, begging me to step in, anticipating the small, smooth stones a thousand shades of sparkling brown, flashing under rushing water. For today, no further thinking is required. My clothes come off. My body shudders a wordless "ah."

There is nothing like being in a creek, resting on my back, the water parting at the crown of my head, running along my body. I am baptized every time I lay myself out on the currents, my world view turned upside down, dappled sunlight moving between thousands of leaves floating against the sky.

As I gaze upward, I ponder a few things of which to be conscious during an upcoming trip to Africa, a return to the Congo:

~ Expectations are premeditated resentments.
~ Live life on life's terms. Be a woman among women, one among many.
~ Do the next, good, right, honest thing. Keep it simple. I am responsible for the stitch, not the whole pattern. Turn the outcome over to God.
~ Ask for help. Write Bishop Tutu, Ted, keep in touch with Tennie. Pray. Cry. Get on the yoga mat. Journal. Read the 104th psalm. Listen to gospel bluegrass.

I feel fear. I have been through this before; I call it a "prescience of grief." It's that daunted, jittery moment before a huge wave crashes, and I, standing in the powerful ocean staring at the advancing crest, beginning to seriously doubt the wild abandon and love of adventure that put me in the ocean in front of a wave that could snap my neck. But the fear does not stop me, because more powerful is the certain knowledge that I am less of a woman when I ignore the plight of women elsewhere. My life is richer when I chose to align myself with their realities, share their truth, witness their lives, and admit their pain into my soul.

~ ~ ~

The August full moon has come and gone and I am home once more from Africa. The dogs and I walk in the woods, the creek that runs through our farm calling me. I pick up a green acorn, and think of the ones the squirrels in the Smokys lent me before my trip, the one I placed against my bosom and carried with me, and gave to a child in a slum. Conditions in eastern Congo were even worse than before. I remember traveling across the lakes and over the cruel, dusty roads, visiting forcibly displaced persons camps, and noble clinics inadequately provisioned, working urgently and under duress where girls and women who have survived gang rape sometimes come for treatment. Kika crawled through the bush for a month to reach help. I fell in love with a group of teenage girls at the HEAL Africa clinic in Goma, particularly a thirteen-year-old named Solange. Like the others, she needed surgery to repair the damage her rapists had caused. I remember thinking of Solange and her friends: When they smile, they are fireflies: luminous, magical, just as fleeting.

I nearly lost hope on this trip. The dark night of the soul hit me faster and with more ferocity than ever before. But that is the way it is with Goma. It's a tough place, perhaps the toughest place I've ever been. It challenges the very notion of a loving God. I might even say, Goma defies God. One night in my hotel room, still reeling from the horrors of the day, I wrote an angry letter to God, rejecting the One I had loved in the creeks and woods:

Dear God, These are your children. What is to become of them? Why have you created a world in which you choose to be 'powerfully powerless?' I think you and your big plan absolutely suck. I think allowing vulnerable, defenseless children to be gang raped and thrown away, illiterate and unable to prevent and treat disease, is beyond a bad idea. The notion you are a God of justice is a savage lie. I think you're a cruel charade and that you're going to be bested by some God who doesn't let crap like this happen.

I thought about Archbishop Tutu. What would he say about all this? I send him an SOS in an email. A few days later, I received his reply:

God is so glad God has someone like you. Available, impotent, wanting, and willing, bearing an unbearable anguish, crying and offering all that you can, a point of transfiguration, offering, being a conduit of grace, of love, of tears, of impotence, and God will thank you for accepting the foolishness of the Cross, the weakness of the Cross. I love you and pray for you to go on being the caring, feeling, crying, weak centre of goodness in a horrible world . . .

My prayer was answered, and I remembered that God lives in the space between people, in relationships, is acted out through our interdependence. God had always been with me.

I remember what I believe: God is love, and when I love, God is with me; and, in order to love, I have to have someone to love. And that someone, well, maybe that someone is you, Ouk Srey Leak. And you, Farm Friend. And you, Solange.

~ ~ ~

As the dogs run ahead, I visit the ironweed, jewelweed, and admire the twining sprawl of passionweed, which looks like a crazy Costa Rican exotic even though it is our state's wildflower. I kneel when "my" red tail hawk takes flight in front of me, keering. At the creek, I put my feet in the cold water and savor the delicious tingle and relief that swells in my entire body. I will rededicate myself to the Good God who made all this.

I wade a spell, the hem of my knee-length nightgown getting wet. However, I will not take off my gown, I will not swim. I want to keep the Congo on me. I do not want to rinse off where I have been.

I want to remember.

ACKNOWLEDGMENTS

Although it is an account of my individual journey, the making of this book in many ways represents a group conscience, the sustained work and suggestions of, in particular, Maryanne Vollers, Trena Keating, and Pamela Cannon. I am deeply indebted to Maryanne's unflinching, steady hard work, which included becoming intimately acquainted with no less than six hundred fifty pages of diaries I have kept on trips to the global south, plus my other writings (published, unpublished, academic, etc.) and speeches, which she cleverly suggested I incorporate into the diaries in order to tell more of my personal story (which I resisted, but that's another story, because in the end, here it is). Maryanne also pushed me hard on the structure and sequence of the chapters, and without her, given I was in graduate school and then on two films, this book would remain but a dream. She is scary smart, which is why I liked her in the first place, and I am grateful she wears her intelligence loosely, and never lorded it and her lengthy experience as a war journalist in sub-Saharan Africa over me! Trena had astonishing confidence in my writing and me, believing my diaries had to be published. She gently guided—without ever directing—me toward the right folks. Those ended up being the good people at Ballantine, including Pamela Cannon, whose reputation as a rigorous and hard-nosed editor suited me fine. I wanted to learn, and all three of these women provided outstanding on-the-job training. Thank you so much for every call, email, word of encouragement, and, I might add, extended deadline.

This book has its inception in the experiences of friends and family who read my diaries sent from around the world, beginning in 2002, and gave their feedback and encouragement. Harold Brown, my attorney, firmly maintained there was a book in these writings when such an idea seemed to me far fetched and grandiose; Penny Gummerson said she waited each day for a diary, and at times folded her arms on her desk, laid her head upon them, and wept; Cary Berman said when daily missives arrived, he would close his office door, and read in them in their entirety right away, then help me find work that would pay my bills while I disappeared again into slums and brothels. Cathy Lewis, Ric and Donna Moore, and others like them, sent checks, large and small, to PSI and its partner programs, motivated by the narratives in the diaries. These people are but a few of the scores of my fellow sojourners who, as I endeavored to honor others by witnessing their life experiences, honored mine. And all I do not mention is not from lack of gratitude but from the tyranny of limited space in which to do so.

I thank Kate Roberts, who invited me to these front lines of hope and has with her perorations encouraged me to keep going; Marshall Stowell, who has given me gentle friendship in the most daunting of settings; and Papa Jack, for expert advance work, safety and protection, intelligence, essential moments of levity, and scouting the least stinky places to pee in ten countries, then tolerating my infernal habit of popping a squat anywhere. And, deepest thanks to my PSI family around the world, past and present, who welcome me to their platforms with generous hospitality in the midst of their heroic work advancing PSI's public health mission among the most poor and vulnerable. You have generously provided an aspirational idealist with an exquisite education in generosity, passion, and tolerance. Thanks especially to those of you who read this manuscript to confirm its technical veracity, as well as our able president, Karl Hoffman, and Frank Loy, chairman of our board, who insist, however improbably, that I am indeed an asset to this phenomenal agency. And last, but certainly not least, thank you to PSI's thousands of local field staff who do brave, brilliant, compassionate service work every day of your lives. This book, in many ways, is for you, and it certainly is for those you seek to serve.

Nicholas Kristof sets the platinum standard of comprehensive knowledge about international development, compassion, and incisive, evocative writing. His willingness to provide the foreword for this book is a testimony to his dedication to a world without poverty and not to the quality of my work. I am very grateful for the notes he generously provided, which were as precise and helpful as his legendary *New York Times* columns.

Equally, I thank the many other extraordinary, innovative, dedicated organizations and their worldwide staffs, who work with urgency and love, doing their part to create peace, safety, equality, and empowerment everywhere. I admire you, and am so grateful you allow me to participate in your work. This is but a partial list, and I regret I cannot include everyone who deserves recognition: The One Campaign to End Poverty, Apne Aap Worldwide, The International Center for Research on Women, Women for Women International, The Enough! Project, Equality Now, Defenders of Wildlife, among others.

I must acknowledge my longtime agent and advocate, Michelle Bohan, who introduced me to Trena Keating, and has graciously abided my retreat from acting, and has unflinchingly supported my various and sundry adventures around the world and in graduate school. Equally, I am so fortunate to have a delightful oxymoron in my life: discreet publicists. Annett Wolf and Cara Trippichio help publicize my work with dignity, and protect my privacy with integrity. Thank you!

Several people who are exceedingly special to me took the time to read portions or all of the manuscript, offering sensitive, nuanced feedback from their deep expertise and souls. Ted Klontz, PhD, Tennie McCarty LCDC, ADC III, CEDC, CAS, Gloria Steinem, Sue Monk Kidd, Carol Lee Flinders, PhD, and Archbishop Desmond Tutu: I l love each of you, and you have changed my life, especially because your audacious authenticity emboldens my own.

Ted and Tennie, in particular, have given me as an adult what I so often needed as a child, "a good listening to." Thank you for taking my calls, night and day, and giving me that safe container in which to process, heal, and grow, and the tools that work under *all* conditions. I hope I can give away to others a modicum of what you have so freely given to me.

My time at the Harvard Kennedy School was enriched by powerful relationships with faculty and students, and supported by a nurturing administration. In particular, I honor and thank Professors Marshall Ganz (my glorious advisor), Bernard Steinberg, Diane Rosenfeld, Martha Chen, and Sofia Gruskin, and Ambassador Swanee Hunt, for not only their devoted scholarship of the highest caliber, but how their work and study is motivated by, and infused with, the unapologetically spiritual belief that every single individual is of infinite worth, and that the base must be empowered. Moral leadership, the role of narrative in building social movements and creating peace, eradicating gender violence, economic empowerment of the poor, health and human rights: I was the luckiest student in the world. In addition to these and many other professors, I am indebted to my classmates: your diversity (my midcareer Masters Public Administration group represented ninety-eight countries), your brilliance, your earnest diligence, your humility in sharing how at times you, too, were overwhelmed by everything going on in that school of copious abundance, and your unabashed belief that we can change the world, all while helping me know that while no one can play my role in the struggle for peace, I never have to fight alone. I especially acknowledge my feminist social justice cohort: You light me up. Whether in the classroom, or in corridors where great moments often spontaneously transpired, during office hours, or off campus for tea or "dinners for seven," Harvard was a constant source of stimulation, inspiration, reflection, and challenge. Thank you, Professor Volnay Gay, for having suggested the School to me; I never would have dreamt of it for myself.

Thank you to friends such as Michelle McGrath, Bobby Shriver, and Seane Corn, who graciously permitted what should be private elements of our friendship to be published. Such are the hazards of friendship with a famous person, and I appreciate your trust in allowing me to share aspects of our conversations and interactions.

I thank my entire family, living and ancestral, American and Scottish, perhaps most especially my dad, Michael Ciminella. He withstood numerous inquiries from both Maryanne and me that necessarily rehashed the darkest and most painful aspects of our family's past. His fortitude in repeatedly sharing, devoid of all defensiveness or attempts to duck his former shortcomings, is remarkable. Both my mother and he have given me the gift I have come to believe every child deserves: having her reality and experiences while growing up validated, understanding that a day in the life of a child is very different from a day in the life of an adult. I am profoundly grateful to sit with you today in a circle of unity, forgiveness, empathy, and humor, knowing not just intellectually, but feeling in my heart, that "that was then, this is now." Or, as Tennie would say, "So what. Now what?" Our "now" is a joy, and I love you both. My joyous affection naturally includes my sister and her beloved children, Elijah and Grace.

As for my husband, Dario Franchitti, simply put: I love and adore you. Always have, always will. As some of our more mischievous friends say, "And there ain't nothing you can do about it!" I cherish our home, our four-legged family, and our quiet time, which has so often been my port in the storm. For a girl who grew up unsure who her emergency person was, I sure am lucky it became you.

Speaking of home, this inventory must include Jamie Mangrum, our exceptional housekeeper, whom we rather seriously call "the mortar between the bricks." In a real sense, Jamie, without home, I do fall down, and thus the logic goes, you hold me up. Thank you.

To recovering folks everywhere: Although it has been said, "We are people who would not normally mix," you are my brothers and sisters. Wherever I go, I know we share the sunlight of the spirit, and I am grateful to trudge this road of happy destiny with you. It is my humble prayer that in some way this book thanks you for carrying the hope of recovery to me, and that it can also carry the message to those who still suffer. If one person who reads this book receives the suggestion that a simple and practical plan of action can lead you to a God of your own understanding, relieve you of the burdens of your past, and help you to live as God intended, precious, empowered, and free, then in my opinion, the book is as successful as Kentucky's 1996 National Championship team.

And, of course, to the God of my understanding: Thank you for doing for me what I cannot do for myself, and especially for my beloved grandparents and all the animals you have put in my life, Buttmemilk, Shug, Percy, Audrey—goodness, the list is long! They have shown me what you mean by unconditional love, which in some measure, I am thus able to pass on. Oh, how I love you. Thy will be done.

NOTES

The following notes are not meant to be a complete list of the sources consulted in the writing of this book, but rather a guide for further inquiry. Most of the facts and figures have been derived from multiple sources, including original research by Population Services International and reports published by United Nations agencies and the World Bank. In some cases, I have cited the sources for unique or hard-to-come-by facts, and in others, I have added extra clarification. For more information on each country, please see www.unicef.org/infobycountry.

Prologue

xv. **The residents are mostly women and children:** According to the Clinton Global Initiative (CGI), there are 43.3 million refugees and other forcibly displaced people in the world, and nearly 80 percent of them are women and children. In 2009, fromer president Bill Clinton appointed me to CGI Lead, a group of twenty-five global leaders under the age of forty-five committed to developing innovative solutions to pressing challenges. In September 2010, my cohorts and I announced a Commitment to Action called "Rethink Refugees" to address the refugee crisis, with special emphasis on the Democratic Republic of the Congo. It includes an awareness campaign and a pilot initiative that will help thousands of displaced people in Congo by focusing on replicable programs in the areas of economic empowerment, education, and energy. For more information, please see www.clintonglobalinitiative.org/lead/refugees/.

xvi. **Famed human rights activist:** I traveled to the eastern Congo with John Prendergast, cofounder of the Enough Project, an initiative to end genocide and crimes against humanity. For more information about Enough and its campaign against conflict minerals in Congo, please see www.enoughproject.org. Our meeting with President Paul Kagame took place in Kigali, Rwanda, on September 1, 2010. Foreign Minister Louise Mushikiwabo was also in attendance.

Chapters 1 and 2

4. **Make sense of my own past:** Many of the details of my family history come from stories my parents and grandparents have told me over the years. Several relatives were extremely helpful in filling in the blanks: my father, Michael Ciminella; my great-aunts Todie Beilie and Ramona Sexton; my aunt Margaret Mandell; my uncle Mark Judd; my cousins Sherry Sager, Celia Volbrecht, Viki Clark, and their children. Gabrielle Balazs, my childhood friend, helped me with her recollections. I also referred to my mother's and sister's memoirs: Naomi Judd with Bud Schaetzle, *Love Can Build a Bridge* (New York: Villard, 1993); and Wynonna Judd with Patsi Bale Cox, *Coming Home to Myself* (New York: Penguin, 2005).

Chapter 3

36. **My husband is a race car driver:**   To follow Dario's racing career and his Indy-Car schedule, please see www.franchitti.com, www.chipganassiracing.com, and www.indycar.com.

Chapter 4

45. **At last, here was an explanation:**   For those interested in more information on recognizing and treating depression, there are several indispensable resources: Andrew Solomon's *The Noonday Demon: An Atlas of Depression* (New York: Scribner, 2001); Kay Redfield Jamison, *Night Falls Fast: Understanding Suicide* (New York: Vintage, 2000); William Styron, *Darkness Visible: A Memoir of Madness* (New York: Vintage, 1990); and the websites www.webmd.com/depression/guide/depression-resources and www.suicidehotlines.com.

50. **The spectacular organization:**   Bobby Shriver supports many essential organizations, but the Special Olympics—founded by his late mother and now directed by his brother Timothy Shriver—is still closest to his heart. For more information, please see www.specialolympics.org.

Chapter 5

59. **Most efficient and effective nongovernmental organizations:**   Since 1987, PSI has saved 98,675,548 healthy years of life for people worldwide, for a cost of approximately $30 per person reached according to the latest 2009 figures. In 2009 alone, PSI helped couples prevent 3.5 million unintended pregnancies. In 2010, PSI delivered its one hundred millionth long-lasting, insecticide-treated antimalaria net. For more information, please see www.psi.org.

67. **Female condoms for exploited prostitutes:**   Female condoms are also for any woman whose partner refuses to wear male condoms; in this way, a married woman especially can discreetly protect herself from her husband's HIV and other STIs, as well as unintended pregnancy, reducing the risk of violence that often occurs if a woman asks her husband to wear a condom.

62. **DATA eventually became the revolutionary:**   The ONE Campaign to fight extreme poverty and preventable disease in the Global South continues, with more than two million members. In 2010, ONE successfully pushed for passage of an additional $450 million in debt relief for earthquake-ravaged Haiti. Please see www.one.org.

65. **A Ugandan nurse:**   Agnes Nyamayarwo continues to help others who are infected with HIV/AIDS in Uganda through the indigenous grassroots group the AIDS Support Organization, or TASO, www.tasouganda.org.

Chapter 6

For a comprehensive look at the role of condoms in preventing HIV in high risk groups and in general population see: "Reassessing HIV Prevention," Malcom Potts, Daniel T. Halperin, et al, *Science Magazine*, May 12, 2008.

72. **PSI found partners:**   Population Services International Cambodia, *Annual Report*, 2004.

72. **They showered the brothels with condoms:**   Although successful in this particular context, and while making condoms available is obviously important for multiple reasons, this showering brothels with condoms would later be revealed as an inadequate strategy for specifically containing HIV among this heterosexual risk group. Some sex slavery abolitionists even express concerns based on their first-person

work that the flooding of condoms into brothels in India actually had the unintended consequence of increasing sex slavery.

73. **As many as twenty thousand prisoners:**   There are many authoritative accounts of the Cambodian genocide. For information on the Tuol Sleng prison, please see www.tuolsleng.com and David Chandler, *Voices from S-21: Terror and History in Pol Pot's Secret Prison*, (Berkeley, CA: University of California Press, 1999).

74. **Cambodia was scarred:**   Dr. Kaethe Weingarten, Harvard Medical School, pioneered vicarious trauma research. For example: "Witnessing the Effects of Political Violence in Families: Mechanisms of Intergenerational Transmission and Clinical Intervention," *Journal of Marital and Family Therapy* 30, no. 1 (2004): 45–59. An unforgettable first-person account can be found in *First They Killed My Father* by Loung Ung (New York: HarperCollins, 2000).

75. **We are making amends:**   Some of our good work, however, is being grossly undone by U.S. immigration policies that forcibly send Cambodian Americans back to a country and culture they never knew, if their parents, when they were given political asylum, did not realize that their children were not automatically made citizens and that some paperwork had to be done. Additionally, that lack of judicial review in our bizarre policy that deports anyone for a felony, even if that felony was committed before the law was passed, is abusively "sentencing home" Cambodian Americans. This outrage is exposed in the documentary *Sentenced Home*, www.pbs.org/independentlens/sentencedhome/film.html.

75. **Our guide into Phnom Penh's netherworld:**   To learn more about the amazing Mu Sochua, please see her website, http://musochua.org/. For an American news story on Svay Pak, see http://www.msnbc.msn.com/id/4038249/ns/dateline_nbc/.

75. **She founded Khemara:**   Please see www.khemaracambodia.org.

76. **Younger and younger prostituted women:**   In recent years, it has been standard to call prostituted people "commercial sex workers." The term, which is used by the UN, WHO, and other agencies, was introduced in an attempt to find nonpejorative language to describe prostitutes. It was also hoped that use of "CSW" might help destigmatize prostitutes. Initially I used this phrase, but after extended exposure to prostituted women, I stopped. The term is inadequate, misleading, a hollow euphemism, and it sanitizes horrific realities while helping some users of the term to feel distanced or even absolved (because, after all, it's just "work" they are talking about). Instead, with the guidance and input of prostituted people worldwide and their advocates, I now use expressions such as "exploitive paid sex," "women trapped in prostitution," and "economically forced prostitution," among others. The reasons are many, the debate about language interesting, and unfortunately, most of it falls outside the scope of this book. Because it is very important, I include a brief overview here and hope readers will pursue this subject in their own hearts and minds.

Three points must be made immediately: One, the preferred terminology in no way diminishes or discounts women trapped in prostitution who seek to find and use their voices, develop agency and self-efficacy, and regard themselves as economic actors. Indeed, such a bold and difficult interpretation of and response to one's context is often the meaningful basis for improvements that make the difference between life and death and can help protest gross human rights violations, such as forced HIV testing (see, for example, http://plri.wordpress.com/2010/12/15/ugandan-sex-workers-petition-parliament-over-hiv-bill/). Two, of course, every individual has the right to self-name and designate his or her work, and I honor and respect the usage of "CSW" when it is a prostituted woman herself who prefers to be called such and not a label applied to her by a supranational agency, however well-intentioned (this includes PSI, which still uses the expression, to my disappointment, although we are seeking terms that "bridge the language of our funders with the dignity of our beneficiaries" [Karl Hofmann, PSI president]). Three, the term *CSW* can be appropriate for the tiny minority of people for whom a full spectrum of economic options, job training, and education is available, who genuinely, of their own empowered free will, with a full understanding of the nature of paid sex, wish to sell their bodies. This group, however, is indeed very small and exists largely in the imagination of the patriarchy. See, for example, Helen Benedict, *Virgin or Vamp: How the Press Covers Sex Crimes*, especially "Rape Myths, Language, and the Portrayal of Women in the Media" (Oxford and New York: Oxford University Press, 1992); and Stephen J. Schulhofer, *Unwanted Sex: The Culture of Intimidation and the Failure of Law* (Cambridge, MA: Harvard University Press, 1998).

My reasoning includes, and is not limited to, the fact that prostitution is inherently violent, sexist, and often classist and racist. For example, it cannot meet the Four Pillars of Decent Work, as identified and articulated by labor experts such as the International Labor Organization (www.ilo.org). (In this context, the word *decent* means "not poor, scant, questionable, or marginal." Synonyms of "decent" include "adequate, sufficient, satisfactory." It does *not* include in this usage a reference to morality or character.)

"Decent work" includes the opportunity to earn a larger salary with accrued experience and expertise, whereas women in sex earn less as they accrue experience, and as they age, they are disposable and pushed out of the marketplace. Additionally, occupational and workplace safety is included in the Pillars of Decent Work and is minimal to nonexistent for most prostitutes. Standard workplace perils include risk of unintended pregnancy, exposure to lethal diseases, extremely high rates of violence, torture, and murder, and a lower rate of pay for attempting to avert such hazards. There is swift punishment from "management" for attempting to self-advocate and squalid living and working conditions devoid of basic services such as safe drinking water and sanitation. Furthermore, the vast majority of prostitutes lack the ability to bargain collectively and to create social dialogue that advances their rights, security, and dignity, all constructs that help define what decent work is and means. Additionally, trauma, racism, and mental illness are known to inhere in prostitution, and therefore once more such "work" cannot fit the international criteria of "decent." Please see http://fap.sagepub.com/content/8/4/405.abstract; http://www.prostitutionresearch.com/faq/000008.html; and "Prostitution and Trafficking in Nine Countries: An Update on Violence and Posttraumatic Stress Disorder" (Melissa Farley, 2003).

(For a discussion of how the Four Pillars of Decent Work relates to public health and achieving the Millennium Development Goals, see http://www.ilo.org/public/english/bureau/pardev/download/mdg/2010/mdg-dw-1-2010.pdf.)

Many advocates have adopted (with regard to women who "choose" prostitution) more accurate terms such as "economically forced prostitution," which underscores the choiceless choice nature of the decision as made by men and women who resort to abdicating their sexual autonomy and physical integrity in order to survive. Another term that is more honest than "commercial sex worker" for millions is "exploitative prostitution," which underscores that the nature of the interaction with a client is intrinsically exploitative, given, inter alia, the asymmetry of the power between the person demanding sex and the person who is unable both to decline and to find an alternative means of generating income for herself (and her children).

Evidence that exploitative sex is not work by all reasonable definitions of work is abundant. Perhaps no research is more compelling, however, than a nine-country survey of prostitutes in which more than 90 percent said they desire to exit prostitution immediately (Farley, 2003). Women and men are in paid sex as a sequel to abuse (http://www.prostitutionresearch.com/factsheet.html; http://gateway.nlm.nih .gov/MeetingAbstracts/ma?f=102206974.html; and http://www.prevent-abuse-now.com/ stats.htmcite), out of desperation to survive, and/or because a person more powerful than they are has forced them. This, simply put, is not work; it is abuse. Therefore, calling a woman who endures abuse to survive a commercial sex worker cunningly disguises that the transaction was in any other setting a crime. To summarize Catharine MacKinnon, when a rapist pays his victim, society no longer regards him as a criminal, he's just another john.

For a discussion of prostitution as gender violence, see Sheila Jeffreys, *The Idea of Prostitution*, especially chapter 9 (North Melbourne, Victoria, AU: Spinifex Press, 1997); Catharine A. MacKinnon, *Sex Equality*, especially chapter 10 (Eagan, MN: Foundation Press, 2001); and https://member.cmpmedica.com/index.php?referrer=http:// member.cmpmedica.com/cga.php?assetID=363&referrer=http://www.psychiatric times.com/sexual-offenses/content/article/10168/48311.

76. **Than enforcing the law:** "Off the Streets: Arbitrary Detention and Other Abuses Against Sex Workers in Cambodia," Human Rights Watch, July 2010, www. hrw.org. The abuse of prostituted women and girls is documented in activist Somaly Mam's wrenching memoir of her life as a sex slave in Cambodia in *The Road of Lost Innocence* (New York: Spiegel & Grau, 2008).

78. **Are still sex slaves:** The modern slave trade is larger than the slave trade was at its peak in the nineteenth century and is the second largest industry in the world. There are many outstanding books and resources that deal with the problem and offer viable solutions. For the outstanding 2010 report that reflects the most recent and best thinking, *Developing a National Plan for Eliminating Sex Trafficking*, and others, please see www.huntalternatives.org. For books, see Siddharth Kara, *Sex Trafficking: Inside the Business of Modern Slavery* (New York: Columbia University Press, 2009), David Batstone, *Not for Sale* (New York: HarperOne, 2010), and Kevin Bales and Ron Soodalter, *The Slave Next Door: Human Trafficking and Slavery in America Today* (Berkeley and Los Angeles: University of California Press, 2009).

83. **Addresses unsafe drinking water:** PSI also distributes at no cost our products and services in many settings, especially emergencies, such as the Haitian earthquake of 2010, and in refugee and internally displaced persons camps.

86. **White-shirted Buddhist nuns:** The "Wat Granny" program is funded in part by USAID (www.usaid.gov/kh/health/activities.htm) in partnership with the Cambodian Ministry of Health, PSI, the grassroots Reproductive Health and Child Alliance (www.racha.org), and others.

Chapter 7

91. **Education and prevention program:** Christine Gorman, "Sex, AIDS and Thailand," July 12, 2004, www.time.com.

92. **Not personally at risk:** United Nations Development Programme, "Opinion Poll on HIV/AIDS Thailand, 2004," www.undp.or.th/download/OpinionPollAIDS.pdf.

99. **An AIDS hospice run by Buddhist monks:** Seth Mydans, "Thai AIDS Survivors Ostracized," October 15, 2006, www.nytimes.com.

Chapter 8

104. **A "God who looks like me":** Some of the thoughts in this passage are inspired by Patricia Lynn Reilly, *A God Who Looks Like Me* (New York: Ballantine, 1995), and Sue Monk Kidd, *The Dance of the Dissident Daughter* (New York: HarperCollins, 1996).

110. **The full support of his government:** Unfortunately, despite Prime Minister Thaksin's promises, the Thai government's commitment to AIDS prevention and education waned under his leadership (www.avert.org/thailand-aids-hiv.htm). He was deposed in a military coup in 2006, regained power in 2008, and then went into exile after being charged with corruption. In 2010, his loyal followers staged violent protests in Bangkok, demanding his return to power.

110. **An estimated thirty-eight million:** Figures in this section are from UNAIDS, *2004 Report on the Global HIV/AIDS Epidemic*, www.unaids.org.

111. **Having trouble meeting the goal:** Sarah Boseley, "Bangkok Blog," *The Guardian*, July 16, 2004, www.guardian.co.uk.

Chapter 9

121. **Half of the people live in poverty:** United Nations Development Programme Human Development Index, http://hdrstats.undp.org/en/countries/profiles/KEN.html.

121. **"I Am Abstaining":** PSI's 2010 monitoring, evaluation, and research on the Chill campaign reveal its ongoing success: 95 percent of the targeted youth continue to abstain.

123. **In thirty-nine African countries:** United Nations High Commission on Refugees NGO Directory, October 1, 2008, www.unhcr.org.

123. **Slow to awaken:** World Council of Churches, "Partnerships Between Churches and People Living with HIV/AIDS Organizations," November 2003, www.scribd.com.

130. **Equality Now:** For more information, please see www.equalitynow.org.

131. **Many girls hemorrhage to death:** Sadly, deaths of girls who have been mutilated have never merited proper inventorying and statistical analysis.

132. **Spread to this country:** To read about asylum cases heard in American courts pertaining to FGM (for example, Abay v. Ashcroft), please see www.openjurist.com. And a case with a happy ending, in a precedent-setting decision in 1996, the U.S. Board of Immigration Appeals granted asylum to Fauziya Kassindja, a Togolese teenager who had fled to the United States to avoid FGM and a forced polygamous marriage. This was the first decision establishing the precedent that women escaping gender-based persecution could be eligible for asylum in the United States. Before Kassindja, they were automatically deported. The case was (erroneously) labeled by the court *Matter of Kasinga*. Please see http://cgrs.uchastings.edu/about/kasinga.php.

Chapter 10

136. **land produces fruit:** Global Horticultural Initiative, "Post-Harvest and Transport Technologies, Reducing Losses and Improving Quality in Fruits and Vegetables in Eastern and Southern Africa Madagascar Position Paper," June 22, 2010, www.globalhort.org.

136. **A new leadership had thrown open the doors:** Four years after my visit to Madagascar, President Marc Ravalomanana, who had ushered in an era of change,

was abruptly removed from power in what the U.S. State Department has categorized as a de facto military coup, creating civic unrest and further isolating the country. The United Nations Security Council and the African Union have called for a return to democracy. Most donors, including the United States and the European Union, have suspended all non–humanitarian assistance programs in Madagascar (U.S. Department of State, Bureau of African Affairs, "Background Note: Madagascar," November 4, 2010, www.state.gov). Meanwhile, PSI continues to work in Madagascar delivering healthy products and services.

148. **Set Nini up in a house:** Sadly, Nini's life took another tragic turn. Although we found her a home of her own, she was unable to overcome her chemical dependency and, one night, rolled over and smothered her newborn.

Chapter 11

152. **A spiritual and moral leader:** Desmond Tutu and Mpho Tutu, *Made for Goodness: And Why This Makes All the Difference* (New York: HarperCollins, 2010), and Desmond Tutu, *God Has a Dream: A Vision of Hope for Our Time* (New York: Doubleday, 2004), among other titles. For more information about Archbishop's Tutu's ongoing work, please see www.tutucenter.org.

156. **A disturbing survey:** Nastasya Kay, "South African Rape Study: More Than 1 in 3 Men Admit to Rape," Associated Press, November 27, 2010.

156. **Rapes occur in every year:** Before one "tsk-tsks" the high rate of gender violence in South Africa, don't forget we have our own gruesome intimate partner violence (including homicide) and rape epidemic in the United States. Please see www.now.org/issues/violence/stats.html, and Bureau of Justice Statistics, Intimate Partner Violence, 1993–2001, bjs.ojp.usdoj.gov. For a sobering and essential reality check about violence against women worldwide, please see the World Health Organization's Multicountry Study on Women's Health and Domestic Violence Against Women, www.who.org.

156. **Some researchers posited:** For studies of the causes of gender violence in South Africa, see Rachel Jewkes et al., "Understanding Men's Health and Use of Violence: Interface of Rape and HIV in South Africa," Medical Research Council, Pretoria, South Africa, June 2009, www.mrc.ac.za; and Lezanne Leoschut and Patrick Burton, "How Rich the Rewards?: Results of the 2005 National Youth Victimisation Study," Centre for Justice and Crime Prevention, Monograph Series, No. 1, Cape Town, South Africa, May 2006, www.cjcp.org.za.

156. For more information about **POWA**, see www.powa.co.za/; also see the One in Nine Campaign, www.oneinnine.org.za/ipoint.

156. **Various UN agencies:** UNFPA News, "South Africa: One-Stop Post-Rape Care," United Nations Population Fund, August 19, 2008, www.unfpa.org

Chapter 12

163. **I could become irritable and unreasonable:** Language inspired by the Suggested Welcome, Al-Anon Family Groups.

163. **Motivational interviewing:** For more information, please see www.motivationalinterview.org.

164. **What to discard:** Inspired by the November 14 entry, *Hope for Today* (Virginia Beach, VA: Al-Anon Family Groups, 2002).

Chapter 13

205. **"I wasn't angry":**   Wynonna Judd, *Coming Home to Myself*, p. 147.

Chapter 14

212. **"Alcoholics are tortured by loneliness":**   *Twelve Steps and Twelve Traditions*, (n.p.: Alcoholics Anonymous World Services, 1981), Step Five, p. 57.

213. **"Pitiful and incomprehensible demoralization":**   *Alcoholics Anonymous: Big Book*, 4th ed. (n.p.: Alcoholics Anonymous World Services, 2001), p. 30.

213. **Delusion is that *this* time:**   Language inspired by the *Big Book* of AA.

213. **Sign the Christmas cards, whatever:**   Language inspired by Mellody, *Facing Codependence*.

214. **Codependents have difficulty:**   Pia Mellody with Andrea Wells Miller and J. Keith Miller, *Facing Codependence: What It Is, Where It Comes from, How It Sabotages Our Lives* (New York: HarperOne, 2003), p. 4.

Chapter 15

233. **Would be none too smart:**   Language inspired by the *Big Book* of AA.

236. **The Karpman drama triangle:**   Please see Steve Karpman, with comments by Patty E. Fleener, MSW, "The Drama Triangle," www.mental-health-today.com.

236. **Losses of my childhood:**   Language inspired by the Welcome of Co-Dependents Anonymous, *Big Book of Co-Dependents Anonymous* (CoRe Publications, 2008).

237. **Compliance, and dominance:**   Symptoms list is from the *Big Book of Co-Dependents Anonymous*, pp. 3–5.

237. **Solutions that led to serenity:**   Language inspired by Al-Anon Family Groups Suggested Welcome.

242. **28,000 children will starve:**   http://www.wfp.org/hunger/stats, and http://www.worldhunger.org/articles/Learn/world%20hunger%20facts%202002.htm.

250. **Find contentment and even happiness:**   Language inspired by Al-Anon Family Groups Suggested Welcome.

Chapter 16

261. **Hard line that Rome had adopted:**   Richard Owen, "Pope Says Condoms Are Not the Solution to AIDS—They Make It Worse," *The Times* (of London), March 17, 2009, www.thetimes.co.uk.

262. **Less than 8 percent:**   Blanca Samayoa et al., "Experience of a Pediatric HIV Clinic in Guatemala City," *Pan American Journal of Public Health* 25, no. 1 (2009): 51.

268. **A documentary:**   *Ashley Judd and YouthAIDS: Confronting the Pandemic*, premiered December 1, 2006, on the Learning Channel.

271. **78 percent for nonparticipants:**   Pan American Social Marketing Organization, "An Effective Behavior Change Module for Mobile Populations in Central America," paper presented at the International Conference on AIDS, Barcelona, Spain, July 7–12, 2002, abstract no. TuPeF5315.

272. **Inaugurating a five-year strategic plan:**   From USAID Nicaragua HIV/AIDS Health Profile, www.usaid.gov.

274. **Because of this cruel law:**   "Nicaragua: Blanket Ban on Abortion Harms Women," Human Rights Watch, August 29, 2007, www.hrw.org.

276. **Adult seroprevalence was a shocking 8.4 percent:**   *Science* 313 (July 28, 2006): 481.

Chapter 17

278. India is the mother ship: Statistics about poverty and AIDS in India derived from the United Nations Development Programme, www.undp.org.

279. Letting go of the outcomes: "You have the right to work, but never to the fruit of work. You should never engage in action for the sake of rewards, nor should you long for inaction." The Bhagavad Gita, verse 47, translated by Eknath Easwaran, *The End of Sorrow: Bhagavad Gita for Daily Living* (Berkeley, CA: Blue Mountain Center of Meditation, 1975).

281. 18 to 45 percent carry the virus: National AIDS Control Organization, India, "HIV Sentinel Surveillance and HIV Estimation in India 2007: A Technical Brief," 2007, http://www.avert.org/india-hiv-aids-statistics.htm. For a fascinating technical article, please see "Repeated Surveys to Assess Changes in Behaviors and Prevalence of HIV/STIs in Populations at risk of HIV," www.fhi.org, especially p. 100.

285. To break that cycle: For more information on the Self-Employed Workers Association, please see www.sewa.org. For more information on women's credit and lending, please see Darryl Collins, et al., *Portfolios of the Poor: How the World's Poor Live on $2 a Day* (Princeton, NJ: Princeton University Press, 2009), and the website Women in Informal Employment: Globalizing and Organizing, www.wiego.org.

286. Account holders in Kamathipura: For more information, please see http://infochangeindia.org/Agenda/Against-exclusion/Sex-workers-as-economic-agents.html.

286. Seane has a remarkable history: For more information on Seane and her advocacy work, please see www.seanecorn.com, and www.offthematintotheworld.org.

289. Injecting drug users: United Nations Office on Drugs and Crime, *Extent of Injecting Drug Use and HIV/AIDS in India*, Monograph/08, April 9, 2006, www.unodc.org.

292. Falkland Road Clinic was 37 percent: Statistics supplied by PSI India. For a fascinating technical report that showcases how surveys are conducted, data collected, and methodology, see *Integrated Behavioral and Biological Assessment Report, Repeated Surveys to Assess Changes in Behaviors and Prevalence of HIV/STIs in Populations at Risk of HIV 2005–2007, India*, at www.fhi.org

293. She had to let Kim go: Kim has been clean, sober, and abstinent for thirty years. She is a licensed chemical dependency clinician with special expertise in experiential therapy and helping addicted youth. In 2005, she came home to Buffalo Gap from Austin, Texas, because she wanted to work with her mother at Shades of Hope. She regularly says that her parents' detachment during her years of active addiction was the best thing they ever did for her.

Chapter 18

299. Truckers are already living with HIV: Case Study: Transport Corporation of India Limited, September 2006, p. 35. http://siteresources.worldbank.org/SOUTHASIAEXT/Resources/Publications/448813-1183659111676/tci.pdf Please see also www.gatesfoundation.org/avahan/Documents/Avahan_OffTheBeatenTrack.pdf.

Chapter 19

316. Community-based antitrafficking NGO: For more information about Ruchira Gupta and Apne Aap, see www.apneaap.org. Even a figure as brilliant and charismatic as Ruchira Gupta is not immune to controversy. While her intimate knowledge of and vision for ending sex slavery is unassailable, a few individuals have complained that the changes Ms. Gupta and Apne Aap strive for are to slow to come and that certain services rendered to survivors have not in some cases been significant enough. I have personally visited Apne Aap programs and know the extraordinary difficulty of the context in which they work is both impossible to fully describe or be apprehended by outsiders, including me.

321. **What a priceless, indescribable gift:**   This story is an example of the unforeseen complications and unintended consequences that inhere in the well-intentioned yet speculative work of intervening on another person's behalf. Although we much appreciated Vinay Rai's offer of a scholarship, it was ultimately declined in 2007 over a disagreement about publicity efforts for Rai University. PSI India subsequently paid Neelam's monthly stipend toward her education of 5,000 rupees from our own funding. This ended in July 2010, when she was to have finished high school. The Mumbai team recently reestablished contact with her, and Neelam is reportedly in a private computer school, which is funded from the stipend.

321. **A travesty of justice:**   Happily, Naina was released and returned to her mother. An update is available at www.apneaap.org/voices/survivors-conferences. To learn more about her escape from slavery, please see the Sky News report *Saving India's Sex Slaves*, April 10, 2007, www.sky.com.

Chapter 20

327. **Unspeakable genocide in 1994:**   The history and aftermath of genocide in Rwanda has been documented in many books, including Linda Melvern, *Conspiracy to Murder: The Rwandan Genocide* (London: Verso, 2004); Samantha Power, *A Problem from Hell: America and the Age of Genocide* (New York: Basic, 2002); and Mahmood Mamdani, *When Victims Become Killers: Colonialism, Nativism, and the Genocide in Rwanda* (Princeton, NJ: Princeton University Press, 2001).

332. **Kagame himself told me:**   This meeting took place on a subsequent trip to Rwanda, September 1, 2010.

332. **Lack of safe water:**   Figures here were given to me by Rwanda's minister of health.

333. **To meet Zainab Salbi:**   For more information about Women for Women International and how to help women survivors of war and armed conflict, please see www.womenforwomen.org.

336. **Bring back traditional *gacacas*:**   Anne Aghion worked for ten years or more on a *gacaca* documentary trilogy—*Gacaca, Living Together Again in Rwanda; In Rwanda We Say . . . The Family That Does Not Speak Dies*; and *The Notebooks of Memory*—and the feature-length film *My Neighbor My Killer*, which spans the trilogy. See www.anneaghionfilms.com/.

337. **A stunning 60 percent reduction:**   From the PSI publication *Healthy Lives: Winning the Battle Against Malaria in Rwanda*, www.psi.org.

338. **Population growth is reduced:**   See *Return of the Population Growth Factor—Its Impact upon the Millennium Development Goals*, report of hearings by the All Party Parliamentary Group on Population, Development and Reproductive Health, London, January 2007.

Chapter 21

344. **Life-destroying problem:**   For more about fistula, please see www.who.int/making_pregnancy_safer/topics/maternal_mortality/en/index.html and www.endfistula.org.

347. **Our next stop:** For more information about the HEAL Africa program, please see www.healafrica.org/

351. **The insane and diabolical:** For a comprehensive history of the Congo tragedy, please see Adam Hochschild, *King Leopold's Ghost: A Story of Greed, Terror, and Heroism in Colonial Africa* (New York: Houghton Mifflin, 1998).

353. **The violence of poverty:** For more information on alleviating poverty, please see www.thepowerofthepoor.com/concepts/c6.php; http://234next.com/csp/cms/sites/Next/News/5651294-147/nigerian_others_receive_alternative_nobel_prize.csp;andwww.grameenfoundation.org/what-we-do.

357. **A rather forgotten primate:** Special thanks to Vanessa Woods of Duke University for her help in checking the facts about bonobos. Please see her book: *Bonobo Handshake: A Memoir of Love and Adventure in the Congo* (New York: Gotham, 2010). For a discussion of primate behavior as it can shed light on human behavior, see Dale Peterson and Richard Wrangham, *Demonic Males: Apes and the Origins of Human Violence* (New York: Houghton Mifflin,1990); Barbara Smuts, "Male Aggression Against Women: An Evolutionary Perspective," *Human Nature* (1992); Diane L. Rosenfeld, *"Sexual Coercion, Patriarchal Violence, and Law,"* and Richard W. Wrangham and Martin N. Muller, "Sexual Coercion in Humans and Other Primates: The Road Ahead," both in *Sexual Coercion in Primates and Humans: An Evolutionary Perspective on Male Aggression Against Females,* Muller and Wrangham, eds. (Cambridge, MA: Harvard University Press, 2009).

Chapter 22

372. **Carol Lee Flinders, one of my mentors:** My sister gave me a gloriously named book for my thirty-eighth birthday soon after I returned home from Shades of Hope. Reading Carol Lee Flinders's *At the Root of This Longing: Reconciling a Spiritual Hunger and a Feminist Thirst* (New York: HarperCollins, 1998) was a revelation that spoke to my deepest beliefs. Through the wonderful networking that sisterhood intuitively and pragmatically supports, I was able to meet her immediately. "You wrote my book!" I exclaimed. Since then, Carol has become a close friend and adviser. She introduced me to one of my most cherished spiritual practices, passage meditation, which was brought to this country by her spiritual teacher, Eknath Easwaran. I am deeply indebted to Carol for the many gifts she has given me; her willingness to be my friend and share her life experiences with me has powerfully shaped my own.

379. **Diane Rosenfeld, who taught a course:** An impeccable scholar who thinks outside the box, Professor Rosenfeld represents the very best Harvard has to offer. Her classroom is a dynamic space in which sharp analysis meets new ideas, yielding great hope that today's students will be the pioneers who solve great social crises, such as gender violence, in this country and abroad. Given the extraordinarily painful nature of much of the material willingly faced by students and faculty alike, she is to be commended that her classroom is a safe and nurturing place in which the students' thoughts and feelings are equally valued as portals to experiential change. Readers are urged to look in particular at Professor Rosenfeld's articles on intimate partner violence, GPS monitoring for batterers who violate restraining orders, and lethality assessments and on how to bring those tools to their own communities, to help stop the epidemic of intimate partner homicides. Her pioneering work on the relevance of bonobos and female-to-female alliances for upending patriarchy is equally key. Links to her groundbreaking essays can be found at http://dianerosenfeld.org.

382. **I couldn't have guessed that my own story:** Becoming aware of the extraor-

dinary normalization of sexual violence in mainstream pornography is profoundly unpleasant, but breaking this denial is essential. I highly recommend the following material, with the reminder that it is disturbing and traumatizing: "The Cruel Edge: The Painful Truth About Today's Pornography—And What Men Can Do About It," in *Sexual Assault Report,* January–February 2004; Gail Dines, Robert Jensen, and Ann Russo, *Pornography: The Production and Consumption of Inequality* (London: Routledge, 1998); Robert Jensen, *Getting Off: Pornography and the End of Masculinity* (Boston: South End, 2007); "Guilty Pleasures: Pornography, Prostitution, and Stripping," from *The Macho Paradox: Why Some Men Hurt Women, and How All Men Can Help* by Jackson Katz (Chicago: Sourcebooks, 2006); and the documentary film *The Price of Pleasure,* produced, directed, and written by Dr. Chyng Sun, http://thepriceofpleasure.com/.

It has been mentioned in this book that boys and men are equally constrained and damaged by sexist attitudes and practices and that our brothers have an essential role to play in the peaceful transformation of unfair and imbalanced societies into ones where gender equality is the norm. Further discussion of this topic is outside the scope of this book, and the author encourages readers to explore recourses such as the International Center for Research on Women, including its GEMS program (www.icrw.org), and the MVP (Mentoring Violence Prevention) programs here in America, www.jacksonkatz.com.

Epilogue

387. **"Powerfully powerless":** Desmond Tutu and Mpho Tutu, *Made for Goodness,* p. 11.

Acknowledgments

391. **Marshall Ganz (my glorious advisor):** Professor Ganz is a social movements and grassroots organizing pioneer who is a beloved favorite at the Kennedy School, and for ample reason. His generosity with students is legendary, as is his ability to effortlessly infuse academic work with personal meaning and passion. His courses on public narrative and moral leadership (the latter co-taught with Professor Bernard Steinberg) are transformative and unforgettable. For a window into his insights, please see Marshall Ganz, *Why David Sometimes Wins: Leadership, Organization, and Strategy in the California Farm Worker Movement* (Oxford: Oxford University Press, 2009).

ABOUT THE AUTHORS

ASHLEY JUDD is an actor, advocate, and activist. She recently graduated from Harvard Kennedy School and continues to appear in films. She serves on the board of directors of Population Services International, Defenders of Wildlife, Shaker Village of Mt. Pleasant, and the leadership councils of International Center for Research on Women and Apne Aap Worldwide. She has addressed the United Nations, the Senate Foreign Relations committee, and the National Press Club, has served as an expert for the Clinton Global Initiative and the International AIDS conference, and her op-eds have been published in major newspapers. She and her husband, race-car driver Dario Franchitti, live in Tennessee and Scotland with their many beloved animals.

ashleyjudd.com

MARYANNE VOLLERS is the author of *Ghosts of Mississippi*, a finalist for the National Book Award. She has also collaborated on two memoirs: *Living History*, with Hillary Rodham Clinton, and *Ice Bound*, with Jerri Nielsen, both #1 *New York Times* bestsellers.

"I do thank you," she said. "This is wonderful coffee. I feel better."

It is so agreeable to Wolfe to have someone enjoy food that he had almost forgiven her for losing control. He nearly smiled at her.

"You must understand," he said gruffly, "that if you hire me to investigate there are no reservations. I think Mr. Aubry is innocent, but if I find he isn't I am committed to no evasion or concealment. You understand that?"

"Yes. I don't—All right."

"For counsel I suggest Nathaniel Parker. Inquire about him if you wish; if you settle on him we'll arrange an appointment. Now, if Mr. Aubry didn't kill Karnow, who did?"

No reply.

"Well?" Wolfe demanded.

She put the coffee cup down. "Are you asking me?"

"Yes."

"I don't know."

"Then we'll return to that. You said Mr. Aubry has been arrested for murder. Has that charge been entered, or is he being held as a material witness?"

"No, murder. They said I couldn't get bail for him."

"Then they must have cogent evidence, surely something other than the manifest motive. He has talked, of course?"

"He certainly has."

"He has told of his going to the door of Karnow's room yesterday afternoon?"

"Yes."

"Do you know what time that was?"

"Half-past three. Very close to that."

"Then opportunity is established, and motive. As

for the weapon, the published account says it was Karnow's. Has that been challenged?"

"Not that I know of."

"Then the formula is complete; but a man cannot be convicted by a formula and should not be charged by one. Have they got evidence? Do you know?"

"I know one thing." She was frowning at him, concentrated, intent. "They told Paul that one of his business cards was found in Sidney's pocket—the agency name and address, with his name in the corner—and asked him to account for it. He said he and his salesmen hand out dozens of cards every day, and Sidney could have got one many different places. Then they told him this card had his fingerprints on it—clear, fresh ones—and asked him to account for that."

"Could he?"

"He didn't to them, but he did to me later, when they let me see him."

"How did he account for it?"

She hesitated. "I don't like to, but I have to. He had remembered that last Friday afternoon, when he went to a conference at Jim Beebe's office, he had left one of his cards there on Jim's desk."

"Who was at the conference?"

"Besides Paul—and Jim, of course—there were Sidney's Aunt Margaret—Mrs. Savage—and Dick Savage, and Ann and her husband, Norman Horne."

"Were you there?"

"No. I—I didn't want to go. I had had enough of all the talk."

"You say he left one of his cards on Mr. Beebe's desk. Do you mean he remembers that the card was on the desk when he left the conference?"

"Yes, he's pretty sure it was, but anyway, he left first. All the others were still there."

"Has Mr. Aubry now told the police of this?"

"I don't think so. He thought he wouldn't, because he thought it would look as if he were trying to accuse one of Sidney's relatives, and that would hurt more than it would help. That was why I didn't like to tell you about it, but I knew I had to."

Wolfe grunted. "You did indeed, madam. You are in no position to afford the niceties of decent reticence. Since your husband was almost certainly killed by someone who was mortally inconvenienced by his resurrection, and we are excluding you and Mr. Aubry, his other heirs invite scrutiny and will get it. According to what Mr. Aubry told me yesterday, there are three of them: Mrs. Savage, her son, and her daughter. Where is Mr. Savage?"

"He died years ago. Mrs. Savage is Sidney's mother's sister."

"She got, as did her son and her daughter, nearly a third of a million. What did that sum mean to her? What were her circumstances?"

"I guess it meant a great deal. She wasn't well off."

"What was she living on?"

"Well—Sidney had been helping her."

Wolfe tightened his lips and turned a palm up. "My dear madam. Be as delicate as you please about judgments, but I merely want facts. Must I drag them out of you? A plain question: was Mrs. Savage living on Mr. Karnow's bounty?"

She swallowed. "Yes."

"What has she done with her legacy? Has she conserved it? The fact as you know it."

"No, she hasn't." Caroline's chin lifted a little. "You're quite right, I'm being silly—and anyway, lots of people know all about it. Mrs. Savage bought a house in New York, and last winter she bought a villa in southern France, and she wears expensive clothes and gives big parties. I don't know how much she has left. Dick had a job with a downtown broker, but he quit when he got the inheritance from Sidney, and he is still looking for something to do. He is—well, he likes to be with women. It's hard to be fair to Ann because she has wasted herself. She is beautiful and clever, and she's only twenty-six, but there she is, married to Norman Horne, just throwing herself away."

"What does Mr. Horne do?"

"He tells people about the time twelve years ago when he scored four touchdowns for Yale against Princeton."

"Is that lucrative?"

"No. He says he isn't fitted for a commercial society. I can't stand him, and I don't understand how Ann can. They live in an apartment on Park Avenue, and she pays the rent, and as far as I know she pays everything. She must."

"Well." Wolfe sighed. "So that's the job. While Mr. Aubry's motive was admittedly more powerful than theirs, since he stood to lose not only his fortune but also his wife, they were by no means immune to temptation. How much have you been associating with them the past two years?"

"Not much. With Aunt Margaret and Dick almost not at all. I used to see Ann fairly often, but very little since she married Norman Horne."

"When was that marriage?"

"Two years ago. Soon after the estate was distributed." She stopped, and then decided to go on. "That was one of Ann's unpredictable somersaults. She was engaged to Jim Beebe—announced publicly, and the date set—and then, without even bothering to break it off, she married Norman Horne."

"Was Mr. Horne a friend of your husband's?"

"No, they never met. Ann found Norman—I don't know where. They wouldn't have been friends even if they had met, because Sidney wouldn't have liked him. There weren't many people Sidney did like."

"Did he like his relatives?"

"No—if you want facts. He didn't. He saw very little of them."

"I see." Wolfe leaned back and closed his eyes, and his lips began to work, pushing out and then pulling in, out and in, out and in. He only does that when he has something substantial to churn around in his skull. But that time I thought he was being a little premature, since he hadn't even seen them yet, not one. Caroline started to say something, but I shook my head at her, and she subsided.

Finally Wolfe opened his eyes and spoke. "You understand, madam, that the circumstances—particularly the finding of Mr. Aubry's card, bearing his fingerprints, on the body—warrant an explicit assumption: that your husband was killed by one of the six persons present at the conference in Mr. Beebe's office Friday afternoon; and, eliminating Mr. Aubry, five are left. You know them all, if not intimately at least familiarly, and I ask you: is one of them more likely than another? For any reason at all?"

She shook her head. "I don't know. Do we have to —is this the only way?"

"It is. That's our assumption until it's discredited. I want your best answer."

"I don't know," she insisted.

I decided to contribute. "I doubt," I put in, "if this would be a good buy at a nickel, but this morning at the DA's office I met the whole bunch. I had a little chat with Mrs. Horne, who seems to like gags, and when the others appeared she introduced me to them. She told them I was going to give her the third degree, and she added, I quote, 'I expect I'll go to pieces and confess—' Unquote. At that point Horne put his hand on her mouth and told her she talked too much. Mrs. Savage said it was her sense of humor."

"That's like Ann," Caroline said. "Exactly like her, at her worst."

Wolfe grunted. "Mr. Goodwin has a knack for putting women at their worst. He's no help, and neither are you. You seem not to realize that unless I can expose one of those five as the murderer of your husband, Mr. Aubry is almost certainly doomed."

"I do realize it. It's awful, but I do." Her lips tightened. In a moment she spoke. "And I want to help! All night I was trying to think, and one thing I thought of —what Sidney said in his letter about something that would shock me. You said yesterday it's not simple to disinherit a wife, but couldn't he have done it some other way? Couldn't he have signed something that would give someone a claim on the estate, perhaps the whole thing? Isn't there some way he could have arranged for the—shock?"

"Conceivably," Wolfe admitted. "But there would have had to be an authentic transfer of ownership and possession, and there wasn't. Or if he established a trust it would have had to be legally recorded, and the estate would never have been distributed. You'll have to do better than that." He cleared his throat explosively and straightened up. "Very well. I must tackle them. Will you please have them here at six o'clock, madam? All of them?"

Her eyes widened at him. "Me? Bring them here?"

"Certainly."

"But I can't! How? What could I say? I can't tell

them that you think one of them killed Sidney, and you want—No! I can't!" She came forward in the chair. "Don't you see it's just impossible? Anyhow, they wouldn't come!"

Wolfe turned. "Archie. You'll have to get them. I prefer six o'clock, but if that isn't feasible after dinner will do." He glanced up at the wall clock. "Phone Mr. Parker and make an appointment for Mrs. Karnow. Phone Saul and tell him I want him here as soon as possible. Then lunch. After lunch, proceed." He turned to the client. "Will you join us, madam? Fritz's rice-and-mushroom fritters are, if I may say so, palatable."

IV

Since this is a democracy, thank God, please prepare to vote. All those in favor of my describing in full detail my efforts to the utmost, lasting a good five hours, to fill Wolfe's order for three males and two females, say aye. I hear none. Since my eardrums are sensitive I won't ask for the noes.

Then I'll sketch it. James M. Beebe, I found, was not one of the machines in one of the huge legal factories that occupy so many floors in so many of New York's skyscrapers. He was soloing it in a modest space on the tenth floor of a midtown building. The woman in the little anteroom, the only visible or audible employee, with a typewriter on her left and a telephone on her right, said Mr. Beebe would be back soon, and, if you call thirty-five minutes soon, he was.

The inner room he led me to must have been a little cramped with a conference of six people. Its furniture was adequate but by no means ornate. Beebe, who had looked runty alongside Mrs. Savage, could not be called impressive seated at his desk, with a large percentage of the area of his thin face taken up by the black-rimmed glasses. When I showed him my credentials, a note signed by Caroline Karnow saying that Nero Wolfe was acting for her, and told him that Wolfe would like to discuss the situation with those chiefly concerned at his office that afternoon or evening, he said that he understood that the police investigation was making progress, and that he questioned the wisdom of an investigation of a murder by a private detective.

Wise or not, I said, Mrs. Karnow surely had the right to hire Wolfe if she wanted to. He conceded that. Also surely the widow of his former friend and client might reasonably expect him to cooperate in her effort to discover the truth. Wasn't that so?

He looked uncomfortable. He saw that a pencil on his desk was not in its proper place, and moved it, and studied it a while to decide if that was the best spot after all. At length he came back to me.

"It's like this, Mr. Goodwin," he piped. "I sympathize deeply with Mrs. Karnow, of course. But any obligation I am under is not to her, but to my late friend and client, Sidney Karnow. I certainly will do anything I can to help discover the truth, but it is justifiable to suppose that in employing Nero Wolfe Mrs. Karnow's primary purpose, if not her sole purpose, is to save Paul Aubry. As an officer of the law I cannot conscientiously participate in that. I am not Aubry's attorney. I beg you to understand."

I kept after him. He stood pat. Finally, following instructions from Wolfe, I put a question to him.

"I suppose," I said, "you won't mind helping to clear up a detail. At a conference in this room last Friday afternoon Aubry left one of his business cards on your desk. It was there when he left. What happened to it?"

He cocked his head and frowned. "Here on my desk?"

"Right."

The frown deepened. "I'm trying to remember— yes, I do remember. He suggested I might phone him later, and he put it there."

"What happened to it?"

"I don't know."

"Did you phone him?"

"No. As it turned out, there was no occasion to."

"Would you mind seeing if the card is around? It's fairly important."

"Why is it important?"

"That's a long story. But I would like very much to see that card. Will you take a look?"

He wasn't enthusiastic about it, but he obliged. He looked among and under things on top of his desk, including the blotter, in the desk drawers, and around the room some—as, for instance, on top of a filing cabinet. I got down on my knees to see under the desk. No card.

I scrambled to my feet. "May I ask your secretary?"

"What's this all about?" he demanded.

"Nothing you would care to participate in. But the easiest way to get rid of me is to humor me on this one little detail."

He lifted the phone and spoke to it, and in a moment the door opened and the employee entered. He told her I wanted to ask her something, and I did so. She said she knew nothing about any card of Paul Aubry's. She had never seen one, on Beebe's desk or anywhere else, last Friday or any other day. That settled, she backed out, pulling the door with her.

"It's a little discouraging," I told Beebe. "I was counting on collecting that card. Are you sure you don't remember seeing one of the others pick it up?"

"I've told you all I remember—that Aubry put a card on my desk."

"Was there an opportunity for one of them to pick it up without your noticing?"

"There might have been. I don't know what you're trying to establish, Mr. Goodwin, but I will not be led by you to a commitment, even here privately. Probably during the meeting here on Friday I had occasion to leave this chair to get something from my files. I won't say that gave someone an opportunity to remove something from my desk, but I can't prohibit you from saying so." He got to his feet. "I'm sorry I can't be more helpful."

"So am I," I said emphatically.

I arose and turned to go, but halfway to the door his voice came. "Mr. Goodwin."

I turned. He had left his chair and was standing at the end of the desk, stiff and straight. "I'm a lawyer," he said in a different tone, "but I am also a man. Speaking as a man, I ask you to consider my position. My friend and client has been murdered, and the police are apparently convinced that they have the murderer in custody. Nero Wolfe, acting for Mrs. Karnow, wants to prove them wrong. His only hope of success is to fasten the guilt elsewhere. Isn't that the situation?"

"Roughly, yes."

"And you ask me to cooperate. You mentioned a conference in this office last Friday. Besides myself, there were five people here—you know who they were. None of them was, or is, my client. They were all dismayed by the return of Sidney Karnow alive. They were all in dread of personal financial calamity. They all asked me, one way or another, to intercede for them. I have of course given this information to the police, and I see no impropriety in my giving it also to Nero Wolfe. Beyond that I have absolutely no information or evidence that could possibly help him. I tell you frankly, if Paul Aubry is guilty I hope he is convicted and punished; but if one of the others is guilty I hope he—or she—is punished, and if I knew anything operant to that end I certainly would not withhold it."

He lifted a hand and dropped it. "All I'm trying to say—as a lawyer I'm not supposed to be vindictive, but as a man perhaps I am a little. Whoever killed Sidney Karnow should be punished." He turned and went back to his chair.

"A damn fine sentiment," I agreed, and left him.

On the way to the next customer I found a booth and phoned Wolfe a report. All I got in return was a series of grunts.

The house Mrs. Savage had bought was in the Sixties, over east of Lexington Avenue. I am not an expert on Manhattan real estate, but after a look at the narrow gray brick three-layer item my guess was that it had set her back not more than a tenth of her three hundred thousand, not counting the mortgage. When there was no answer to my rings I felt cheated. I hadn't expected anything as lavish as a dolled-up butler, but not even a maid to receive detectives?

It was only a ten-minute walk to the Park Avenue address of Mr. and Mrs. Norman Horne. My luck stayed stubborn. The hallman said they were both out, phoned up at my request, and got no answer.

I like to walk around Manhattan, catching glimpses of its wild life, the pigeons and cats and girls, but that day I overdid it, back and forth between my two objectives. Finally, from an ambush in a hamburger hell on Sixty-eighth Street, where I was sipping a glass of milk, I saw Aunt Margaret navigate the sidewalk across the street and enter the gray brick. I finished the milk, crossed over, and pushed the button.

She opened the door a few inches, thought she saw a journalist, said, "I have nothing to say," and would have closed the door if it hadn't been for my foot.

"Wait a minute," I objected. "We've been introduced—by your daughter, this morning. The name is Archie Goodwin."

She let the door come another inch for a better view of me, and the pressure of my foot kept it going. I crossed the threshold.

"Of course," she said. "We were rude to you, weren't we? The reason I said I have nothing to say, they tell me that's what I must say to everybody, but it's quite true that my daughter introduced you, and we were rude. What do you want?"

She sounded to me like a godsend. If I could kidnap her and get her down to the office, and phone the rest of them that we had her and she was being very helpful, it was a good bet that they would come on the run to yank her out of our clutches.

I gave her a friendly eye and a warm smile. "I'll tell you, Mrs. Savage. As your daughter told you, I work for Nero Wolfe. He thinks there are some aspects of this situation that haven't been sufficiently considered. To mention only one, there's the legal principle that a criminal may not profit by his crime. If it should be proved that Aubry killed your nephew, and that Mrs. Karnow was an accessory, what happens to her half of the estate? Does it go to you and your son and daughter, or what? That's the sort of thing Mr. Wolfe wants to discuss with you. If you'll come on down to his office with me, he's waiting there for you. He wants to know how you feel about it, and he wants your advice. It will only take us—"

A roar came from above. "What's going on, Mumsy?"

Heavy feet were descending stairs behind Mrs. Savage in a hurry. She turned. "Oh, Dickie? I supposed you were asleep."

He was in a silk dressing gown that must have accounted for at least two Cs of Cousin Sidney's dough. I could have choked him. He had been there all the time. After ignoring all my bell ringing for the past two hours, here he was horning in just when I was getting a good start on a snatch.

"You remember Mr. Goodwin," his mother was telling him. "Down at that place this morning? He wants to take me to see Nero Wolfe. Mr. Wolfe wants to ask my advice about a very interesting point. I think I should go, I really do."

"I don't," Dick said bluntly.

"But Dickie," she appealed, "I'm sure you agree that we should do all we can to get this awful business over and done with!"

"Sure I do," he conceded. "God knows I do. But how it could help for you to go and discuss it with a private detective—No, I don't see it."

They looked at each other. The mutual resemblance was so remarkable that you might say they had the same face, allowing for the difference in age; and also they were built alike. Her bulk was more bone and meat than fat, and so was his.

When she spoke I got a suspicion that I had misjudged her. Her tone was new, dry and cool and meaningful. "I think I ought to go," she said.

He appealed now. "Please, Mumsy. At least we can talk it over. You can go later, after dinner." He turned to me. "Could she see Wolfe this evening?"

"She could," I admitted. "Now would be better."

"I really am tired," she told me. Her tone was back to what might have been normal. "All this awful business. After dinner would be better. What is the address?"

I got my wallet, took out a card, and handed it to her. "By the way," I observed, "that reminds me. At that meeting last Friday at Mr. Beebe's office, Aubry put one of his cards on Beebe's desk and left it there. Do you happen to remember what became of it?"

Mrs. Savage said promptly, "I remember he took out a card, but I don't—"

"Hold it," Dick barked at her, gripping her arm so hard that she winced. "Go upstairs."

She tried to twist loose, found it wouldn't work, and leveled her eyes at him to stare him off. That didn't work either. His eyes were as level as hers, and harder and meaner. Four seconds of it was enough for her. When he turned her around she didn't resist, and without a word she walked to the stairs and started up. He faced me and demanded, "What's this about a card?"

"What I said. Aubry put one on Beebe's desk—"

"Who says he did?"

"Aubry."

"Yeah? A guy in for murder? Come again."

"Glad to. Beebe says so too."

Dick snorted. "That little louse? That punk?" He lifted a hand to tap my chest with a finger, but a short backward step took me out of range. "Listen, brother. If you and your boss think you can frame an out for Aubry don't let me stop you, but don't come trying to work my mother in, or me either. Is that plain?"

"I merely want to know—"

"The way out," he said rudely, and strode to the door and opened it. Since I stay where I'm not wanted only when there is a chance of gaining something, I took advantage of his courtesy and passed on through to the sidewalk.

I was getting low on prospects. Back at the Park Avenue address, where the hallman and I were by now on intimate terms, he informed me that Mrs. Horne had come in, and he had told her that Mr. Goodwin had called several times and would return, and she had said to send me up.

At Apartment D on the twelfth floor I was admitted by a maid, properly outfitted, who showed me to a living room where a slice of Karnow's money had been used with no great taste but a keen eye to comfort. I sat down, and almost at once got up again when Ann Horne entered. She met me and let me have a hand.

"We'll have to hurry," she said. "My husband may be home any minute. What do you do first, rubber hose?"

She was wearing a nice simple blue dress that either was silk or wanted to be, and had renovated her make-up since coming in from the street.

"Not here," I told her. "Get the stole. I'm taking you to a dungeon."

She flowed onto a couch. "Sit down and describe it to me. Rats, I hope?"

"No, we can't get rats to stay. Bad air." I sat. "As a matter of fact, I've decided the physical approach wouldn't work with you, and we're going after you mentally. That's Mr. Wolfe's department, and he never leaves the house, so I've come to take you down there. You can leave word for your husband, and he can join us."

"That doesn't appeal to me at all. Mentally I'm a wreck already. What's the matter, are you afraid I can't take it?"

"On the contrary, I'm afraid I can't give it. Nature went to a lot of trouble with you, and I'd hate to spoil it. You'd enjoy a session with Nero Wolfe. He's afraid of women anyhow, and you'd scare him stiff."

She pulled a routine that I approved of. Knowing that if she took a cigarette I'd have to get up to light it, she first picked up a lighter and flicked it on, and then reached to a box for the cigarette. A darned good idea.

"What's the score?" she asked, after inhaling and letting it out.

I told her. "Paul Aubry is charged with murder. Mr. Wolfe can earn a big fee only by clearing him. Mr. Wolfe has never let a big fee get away. So Aubry will be cleared. We'll be glad to let you share the glory, though not the fee. Get the stole, and let's go."

"You're irresistible," she said admiringly. "It's too bad about Paul."

"Not at all. When he gets out he can marry his wife."

"*If* he gets out. Do you remember nursery rhymes?"

"I wrote them."

"Then of course you remember this one:

> "Needles and pins,
> Needles and pins,
> When a man murders
> His trouble begins."

"Sure, that's one of my favorites. Only Aubry didn't murder."

She nodded. "That's your line, of course, and you're

stuck with it." She reached to crush her cigarette in a tray, then suddenly turned to me with her eyes flashing. "All this poppycock! All this twaddle about life being sacred! For everybody there's just one life that's sacred, and everybody knows it! Mine!" She spread her hand on her breast. "Mine! And Sidney's was sacred to him, but he's dead. So it's too bad about Paul."

"If you feel that way about it you ought to be ready to give him a lift."

"I might be if I had anything to lift with."

"Maybe I can furnish something. Last Friday you were at a conference at Jim Beebe's office. Aubry put one of his business cards on Beebe's desk. Why did you pick up that card, and what did you do with it?"

She stared at me a moment. Then she shook her head. "You'll have to get out the rubber hose, or pliers to pull out my nails. Even then I may hold out."

"Didn't you pick up the card?"

"I did not."

"Then who did?"

"I have no idea—if there was a card."

"You don't remember Aubry putting it on the desk? Or seeing it there?"

"No. But this begins to sound like something. You sound as if you're really detecting. Are you?"

I nodded. "This is called the double sly squeeze. First I get you to deny you touched the card, which I have done. Then I display one of Aubry's cards in a cellophane envelope, tell you it has fingerprints on it which I suspect are yours, and dare you to let me take your prints so I can check. You're afraid to refuse—"

"Come and show me how you take my prints. I've never had it done."

I was, I admit it, curious. Was she inviting physical contact because she was like that, or was she expecting to voodoo me, or was she merely passing the time? To find out I got up and went to her, took her offered hand and got it snugly in mine, palm up, and bent over it for a closeup. The hand seemed to be telling me that it didn't mind the operation at all, and with the fingertips of my other hand I spread her fingers apart, bending lower.

Of course I was concentrated on the job. Whether the door from the outside hall to the foyer was opened so quietly that no sound came, or whether my ears caught a sound but I ignored it, what interrupted my investigation was her sudden tight grip on my hand as she straightened up and cried, "Don't! You're hurting me! Norman—thank God!"

My whirl around was checked for a second by her hold on my hand. For her size and sex she had muscle. I suppose to Norman Horne, approaching from behind me, it could have looked as if I were holding her, instead of her me, but even so it must have been obvious that I was turning, and he might have held his fire until I could at least see it coming. As it was, I was off balance when he plugged me on the side of the jaw, and I went clear down, sprawling. Added to the four touchdowns he had scored for Yale against Princeton, that made five.

"He was trying to force me—" Ann was saying with her sense of humor.

Probably I would have scrambled to my feet and departed, since Wolfe wouldn't have appreciated my letting my personal feelings take charge when I was on a job, if it hadn't been for Horne's attitude. He was glaring down at me, with his fists ready, and it was doubtful if he would wait till I got farther up than on my knees. So I did a quick double roll, sprang all the way up, and faced him. He came at me wide open, as if

I had been a dummy, and swung. There wouldn't have been the slightest excuse for my missing the exact spot for a dead kidney punch, and I didn't. Air exploded out of him, and he crumpled, not sprawling, but in a compact heap. Then he sort of settled to get comfortable.

His attractive wife took a couple of steps toward him, stopped to look at me, and said, "I'll be damned."

"You will if they consult me," I told her emphatically, turned, went to the foyer and got my hat, and let myself out. On the way down in the elevator I felt my jaw and took a look at it in the mirror, and decided I would live.

I got home just at the dinner hour, seven-thirty, and since it takes an earthquake to postpone a meal in that house, and no mention of business is permitted at the table, my full report of the afternoon had to wait. If the main dish had been something like goulash or calves' brains probably nothing unusual in my technique would have been apparent, but it was squabs, which of course have to be gnawed off the bones, and while I was working on the second one Wolfe demanded, "What the deuce is the matter with you?"

"Nothing. What?"

"You're not eating, you're nibbling."

"Yeah. Broken jaw. With the compliments of Ann Horne."

He stared. "A *woman* broke your jaw?"

"Sorry, no shoptalk at meals. I'll tell you later."

I did so, in the office, after dinner, and after I had looked into a little matter I was wondering about. I had obeyed the instruction, given me before lunch, to phone Saul Panzer, and Saul had said he would be at the office at two-thirty. By that time I had left. When, on the way from the dining room to the office, I asked

Wolfe if Saul had come, he replied in one word, "Yes,"
indicating that that was all I needed to know about it.
Thinking it wouldn't hurt me any to know more, I went
and opened the safe and got out the little book from
the cash drawer. Sometimes, in addition to the name
and date and amount, Wolfe scribbles something about
the purpose, but that time he hadn't. The latest entry
was merely the date and "SP $1000." All that did was
make me wonder further what Saul was expected to
buy that might cost as much as a grand.

As I reported on my afternoon rounds, giving all
conversations verbatim, which isn't so hard when
you've had plenty of practice and have learned that
nothing less will be acceptable, Wolfe leaned back in
his chair with his eyes closed. He was too damn placid.
Ordinarily, when he sends me out for bacon and I return empty-handed, he makes some pointed cracks, no
matter how hopeless he knows my errand was; but
that time, not a one. That meant either that he didn't
like the job and to hell with it, or that I was just a
sideshow, including my sore jaw, and the main attrac-
tion was elsewhere. When I was through he didn't
open his eyes or ask a single question.

I groaned with pain. "Since it's obvious that I
wasted five hours of your time, and since if I stay here
I may say something that will rile you, I guess I'll go
see Doc Vollmer and have him set my jaw. He'll probably have to wire it."

"No."

"No what?"

He opened his eyes. "I'm expecting a phone call.
Probably not until tomorrow, but it could come this
evening. If it does I'll need you."

"Okay, I'll be upstairs."

I mounted the two flights to my room, turned on

the lights, went to the bathroom mirror to see if there was enough swelling for a compress, decided there wasn't, and settled myself in my easy chair with a collection of magazines.

Nearly two hours had gone by, and I was yawning, when a sound came faintly through the open door—the sound of Wolfe's voice. I went and lifted the phone on my bedside table and put it to my ear. It was dead. I had neglected to plug it in when I left the office. It would have been undignified to go to the hall, to the stair landing, and listen, so I did; but though Wolfe's voice came up at intervals I couldn't get the words. After enough of that I returned to the room and the easy chair, but had barely lowered myself into it when a bellow from below came.

"Archie! *Archie!*"

I did not descend the stairs three steps at a time, but I admit I didn't mosey. Wolfe, at his desk, spoke as I entered the office. "Get Mr. Cramer."

Getting Inspector Cramer of Homicide, day or night, may be very simple or it may be impossible. That time it was in between. He was at his office on Twentieth Street, but in conference and not available, so I had to bear down and make it plain that if he didn't speak with Nero Wolfe immediately God only knew what tomorrow's papers would say.

In a couple of minutes his familiar growl was growling at me. "Goodwin? Is Wolfe on?"

I nodded at Wolfe, and he took up his phone. "Mr. Cramer? I don't know if you know that I'm investigating the Karnow murder. For a client. Mrs. Karnow engaged me at noon today."

"Go ahead and investigate. What do you want?"

"I understand that Mr. Aubry is being held on a murder charge, without bail. That's regrettable, because he's innocent. If you are supporting that charge I advise you to reconsider. On the soundness of that advice I stake my professional reputation."

I would have paid admission to see Cramer's face. He knew Wolfe would rather go without eating a whole day than be caught wrong in a flat statement like that.

"That's all I wanted, your advice." The growl was still a growl, but not the same. "Is it all right if I wait till morning to turn him loose?"

"Formalities may require it. May I ask a question? How many of the others—Mrs. Savage, her son, Mr. and Mrs. Horne, Mr. Beebe—have been eliminated by alibis?"

"Crossed off, no one. But Aubry not only has no alibi, he admits he was there."

"Yes, I know. However, it was one of the others. I must now choose between alternatives. Either I proceed independently to disclose and hand over the culprit, or I invite you to partake. Which would you prefer?"

It was nearly silence, but I thought I could hear Cramer breathe. "Are you saying you've got it?"

"I'm saying I am prepared to expose the murderer. It would be a little simpler if you can spare the time, for I must have them here at my office, and for you that will be no problem. If you care to take part could you get them here in half an hour?"

Cramer cussed. Since it's a misdemeanor to use profanity over the phone, and since I don't want to hang a misdemeanor rap on an inspector, I won't quote it. He added, "I'm coming up there. I'll be there in five minutes."

"You won't get in." Wolfe wasn't nasty, but he was firm. "If you come without those people, or without first assuring me that they will be brought, Mr. Goodwin won't even open the door to the crack the chain bolt will permit. He's in a touchy mood because a man hit him on the jaw and knocked him down. Nor am I in any humor to wrangle with you. I gave you your chance. Do you remember that when you were here this morning I told you that I had the last letter Mrs. Karnow received from her husband, and offered to show it to you?"

"Yes."

"And you said you weren't interested in a letter Karnow wrote nearly three years ago. You were wrong. I now offer again to show it to you before I send it to the District Attorney, but only on the condition as stated. Well?"

I'll say one thing for Cramer, he knew when he was out of choices, and he didn't try to prolong it. He cussed again and then got it out. "They'll be there, and so will I."

Wolfe hung up. I asked him, "What about our client? Hadn't she better be present?"

He made a face. "I suppose so. See if you can get her."

V

It was half-past eleven when I ushered Norman Horne and his attractive wife to the office and to the two vacant seats in the cluster of chairs that had been placed facing Wolfe's desk. At their left was Mrs. Savage; behind them were Dick Savage, James M. Beebe, and Sergeant Purley Stebbins—only not in that order, because Purley was in the middle, behind Ann Horne. There had been another chair in the cluster, for Caroline Karnow, but she had moved it away, over to the side of the room where the bookshelves were, while I was in the hall admitting Mrs. Savage and Dick. That had put her where Purley couldn't see her without turning his head a full quarter-circle, and he hadn't liked it, but I had let him know that it was none of his damn business where our client sat.

The red leather chair was for Cramer, who was in the dining room with Wolfe. After the Hornes had greeted their relatives, including Caroline, and got seated, I crossed to the dining room and told Wolfe we were ready, and he marched to the office and to his desk, and stood.

"Archie?"

"Yes, sir." I was there. "Front row, from the left, Mr. Horne, Mrs. Horne, Mrs. Savage. Rear, from the left, Mr. Savage, Mr. Stebbins you know, and Mr. Beebe."

Wolfe nodded almost perceptibly, sat, and turned his head. "Mr. Cramer?"

Cramer, standing, was surveying them. "I can't say this is unofficial," he conceded, "since I asked you to come here, and I'm here. But anything Mr. Wolfe says to you is solely on his own responsibility, and you're under no obligation to answer any questions he asks if you don't want to. I want that clearly understood."

"Even so," Beebe piped up, "isn't this rather irregular?"

"If you mean unusual, yes. If you mean improper, I don't think so. You weren't ordered to come, you were asked, and you're here. Do you want to leave?"

Apparently they didn't, at least not enough to make an issue of it. They exchanged glances, and someone muttered something. Beebe said, "We certainly reserve the right to leave."

"Nobody will stop you," Cramer assured him, and sat. He looked at Wolfe. "Go ahead."

Wolfe adjusted himself in his chair to achieve the maximum of comfort, and then moved his eyes, left and right, to take them in. He spoke. "Mr. Cramer assured you that you are not obliged to answer my questions. I can relieve your minds of that concern. I doubt if I'll have a single question to put to any of you, though of course an occasion for one may arise. I merely want to describe the situation as it now stands and invite your comment. You may have none."

He interlaced his fingers at the crest of his central bulge. "The news that Mr. Karnow had been murdered was brought here by Mr. Stebbins early last evening, but my interest in it was only casual until Mrs. Karnow came at noon today and aroused it by hiring me. Then I gave it my attention, and it seemed to me that your obvious motive for murder—Mrs. Savage and her son and daughter, and Mr. Horne as the daughter's husband—was not very compelling. From what my client told me of Mr. Karnow's character and temperament, it seemed unlikely that any of you would so fear harsh and exigent demands from him that you would be driven to the dangerous and desperate act of murder. You had received your legacies legally and properly, in good faith, and surely you would at least have first tried an appeal to his reason and his grace. So one of you must have had a stronger motive."

Wolfe cleared his throat. "That derogation of your obvious motives put me up a stump. There were two people with overpowering motives: Mr. Aubry and Mrs. Karnow. Not only did they stand to forfeit a much larger sum than any of you, but also they faced a deprivation even more intolerable. He would lose her, and she would lose him. It is not surprising that Mr.

Cramer and his colleagues were dazzled by the glitter of that powerful motive. I might have been similarly bemused but for two circumstances. The first was that I had concluded that neither Mrs. Karnow nor Mr. Aubry had committed murder. If they had, they had come fresh from that ferocious deed to engage me to negotiate for them with the man one of them had just killed, for the devious purpose of raising the presumption that they didn't know he was dead, and I had sat here and conversed with them for an hour without feeling any twinge of suspicion that they were diddling me. I was compelled either to reject that notion or abandon certain pretensions that feed my ego. The choice wasn't difficult."

"Also Mrs. Karnow was your client," Cramer said pointedly.

Wolfe ignored it, which was just as well. He went on. "The second circumstance was that the possibility of another motive had been suggested to me. It was suggested in a letter which Mrs. Karnow had shown me yesterday—the last letter she had received from her husband, nearly three years ago." He opened a drawer and took out sheets of paper. "Here it is. I'll read only the pertinent excerpt:

"Speaking of death, if he should get me instead of me getting him, something I did before I left New York will give you quite a shock. I wish I could be around to see how you take it. You claim you have never worried about money, that it's not worth it. Also you've told me that I always talk sardonic but haven't got it in me to act sardonic. This will show you. I'll admit I have to die to get the last laugh, but that will be sardonic too. I wonder do I love you or hate you? They're hard to tell apart. Remember me in thy dreams."

He returned the papers to the drawer and closed it. "Mrs. Karnow had the notion that what her husband had done was to make a new will, leaving her out, but that theory was open to two objections. First, a wife cannot be so brusquely disinherited by a man of means; and second, such an act would have been merely malicious, not sardonic. But the phrase 'speaking of death' did imply some connection with his will, and raised the question, how might such a man have so remade his will as to cause such a woman to worry about money? That intention was clearly implied."

Wolfe turned a hand over. "Under the circumstances as I knew them, a plausible conjecture offered itself: that Karnow had made a new will, leaving everything to his wife. That would certainly give her an inescapable worry about money, the same worry he had had—how much should his relatives be pampered? And since it was his money and they were his relatives, for her the worry would be even more bothersome than for him. I would call that sardonic. Also he might have been moved by another consideration, a reluctance to bestow large amounts on them. I had gathered, though Mrs. Karnow didn't make it explicit, that in matters of personal finance and economy Karnow did not regard his relatives as paragons—a judgment that has been verified by their management of their bequests."

Ann Horne's head jerked around, and she told Caroline, "Thank you so much, Lina darling." Caroline made no reply. Judging from her intent face and rigid posture, if she replied to anything it would be an explosion.

"Therefore," Wolfe resumed, "it appeared that the hypothesis that Karnow had made a new will deserved a little exploration. To ask any of you about it would of course have been jackassery. It was reasonable to suppose that for such a chore he would have called upon his friend and attorney, Mr. Beebe, but it seemed impolitic to approach Mr. Beebe on the matter. I don't know whether any of you has ever heard the name Saul Panzer?"

No reply. No shake of a head. They might all have been in a trance.

"I employ Mr. Panzer," Wolfe said, "on important missions for which Mr. Goodwin cannot be spared. He has extraordinary qualities and abilities. I told him that if Mr. Beebe had drafted a new will for Mr. Karnow it had probably been typed by his secretary, and Mr. Panzer undertook to see Mr. Beebe's secretary and try to get on terms with her without arousing her suspicion. I would entrust so ticklish an errand to no other man except Mr. Goodwin. Early this afternoon he called on her in the guise of an invesigator from the Federal Security Agency, wanting to clear up some confusion about her Social Security number."

"Impersonating an officer of the law," Beebe protested.

"Possibly," Wolfe conceded. "If such an investigator is an officer of the law, he is a federal officer, and Mr. Panzer can await his doom. In ten minutes he collected an arsenal of data. Mr. Beebe's secretary, whose name is Vera O'Brien, has been with him two and one-half years. Her predecessor, whose name was Helen Martin, left Mr. Beebe's employ in November nineteen-fifty-one to marry a man named Arthur Rabson, and went to live with her husband in Florence, South Carolina, where he owns a garage. So if Karnow made a new will before he left New York, and if Mr. Beebe drafted it, and if Mr. Beebe's secretary typed it, it was typed by the now Mrs. Arthur Rabson."

"Three ifs," Cramer muttered.

"Yes," Wolfe agreed, "but open for test. I was tempted to get Mrs. Rabson on the phone in South Carolina, but it was too risky, so Mr. Panzer took a plane to Columbia, and I phoned there and chartered a small one to take him on to Florence. An hour ago, or a little more, I got a phone call from him. He has talked with Mrs. Rabson, she has signed a statement, and she is willing to come to New York if necessary. She says that Mr. Beebe dictated to her a new will for Mr. Karnow in the fall of 1951, that she typed it, and that she was one of the witnesses to Karnow's signature. The other witness was a woman named Nora Wayne, from a nearby office. She supposes that Miss Wayne did not know the contents of the will. By it Karnow left everything to his wife, and it contained a request that she use discretion in making provision for Karnow's relatives, who were named. Mrs. Rabson didn't know that—"

"Sidney wouldn't do that!" Aunt Margaret cried. "I don't believe it! Jim, are you going to just sit there and blink?"

All eyes were at Beebe except Wolfe's. His were on the move. "I should explain," he said, "that meanwhile Mr. Goodwin was making himself useful. He learned, for instance, that the only item of tangible evidence against Mr. Aubry, a card of his that was found in Mr. Karnow's pocket, had been accessible to all of you last Friday in Mr. Beebe's office."

"How's that?" Cramer demanded.

"You'll get it," Wolfe assured him, "and you'll like it." He focused on Beebe. "The occasion has arisen, I think, Mr. Beebe, for a question. As Mr. Cramer told you, you're not obliged to answer it. What happened to Mr. Karnow's last will?"

Thinking it over later, I decided that Beebe probably took his best bet. Him being a lawyer, you might suppose that he would simply have clammed up, but, knowing as he did that he was absolutely hooked on the will, he undoubtedly figured, in the short time he had for figuring, that the best way was to go ahead and take the little one so as to dodge the big one.

He addressed Cramer. "I would like to speak to you privately, Inspector—you and Mr. Wolfe, if you want him present."

Cramer glanced at Wolfe. Wolfe said, "No. You may refuse to answer, or you may answer here and now."

"Very well." Beebe straightened his shoulders and lifted his chin. At the angle I had on him I couldn't see his eyes behind the black-rimmed glasses. "This will ruin me professionally, and I bitterly regret the part I have played. It was a month or so before the notice came that Sidney had been killed in action that I told Ann about the new will he had made. That was my first mistake. I did it because I—of the way I felt about her. At that time I would have done just about anything she wanted. When word came that Sidney had been killed she came to my office and insisted on my showing her the will. I was even—"

"Watch it, Jim!" Ann, turned in her chair, called to him. "You dirty little liar! Ad libbing it, you'll get all twisted—"

"Mrs. Horne!" Wolfe said sharply. "Would you rather hear him or be taken from the room?"

She stayed turned to Beebe. "Go on, Jim, but watch it."

Beebe resumed, "I was then even more infatuated

with her than before. I got the will from the safe and showed it to her, and she took it and stuffed it inside her dress. She insisted on taking it to show to her mother. It's easy to say I should have gone to any length to prevent that—it's easy now, but then I was incapable of opposing her. She took the will with her, and I never saw it again. Two weeks later our engagement was publicly announced. I presented Sidney's former will for probate, and that was completely insane, since I only had Ann's word for it that the new will had been destroyed—even though the girl who had typed the new will had got married and gone away."

Beebe lifted a hand to adjust his cheaters. "I won't say what it was that cured me of my infatuation for Ann Savage. It was—a personal thing, and it was enough to cure me good. I only wish to God it had happened sooner. Of course I couldn't stop the probate of the will without ruining myself. In May the estate was distributed, and later that month Ann married Norman Horne. That ended that business, I thought. I had had my lesson, and it had been a tough one."

He pulled his narrow shoulders back. "Then, two years later, this jolt came. Sidney was alive and would soon be in New York. You can imagine how it hit me, or maybe you can't. I finally got it in focus enough to see that I had only two choices: either fall out of my office window or tell Sidney exactly how it had happened. Meanwhile I had to go through all the motions of talking it over with them and listening to all their crazy suggestions. It wasn't until Monday, day before yesterday, that I decided, and I phoned Ann the next morning, yesterday, that I was going to see Sidney that evening and tell him the whole story. Then came the news that Sidney had been murdered. I don't know who killed him. All I know is what I'm telling you, and of course for me that's enough." He stopped for his mouth to do little spasms. He tagged it. "As a counselor-at-law, I'm through."

I was a little disappointed at Norman Horne. Surely he might have been expected to react manfully and promptly to such an indictment of his attractive wife, but he wasn't even looking at Beebe. He was looking at her, there beside him, and it was not a gaze of loyal and trusting faith. It was just as well that she didn't see it.

She didn't see it because her eyes were on Wolfe. "Is he through?" she asked.

"Apparently, madam, yes. At least for the moment. Would you like to comment?"

"I don't want to make a speech. I don't think I need to. Just that he's a liar. Just lies."

Wolfe shook his head. "I doubt if that's adequate. It wasn't all lies, you know. Mr. Karnow did make a new will; you and Mr. Beebe were engaged to marry but didn't; the estate was distributed under the terms of a previous will, with you as a legatee; and Mr. Karnow did return alive and was murdered. I strongly advise you either to keep silent, even though that would expose you to an adverse presumption, or to tell the truth without reservation. You warned Mr. Beebe of the hazard of an improvised complex lie. I urge you to heed your own warning. Now?"

She glanced aside at her husband, but he had focused on Wolfe. Her head swiveled for a glance to her left, at her mother, but that wasn't met either. She looked at Wolfe. "You're quite a performer, aren't you?"

"Yes," he said.

"I believe you already know the truth."

"If so, for you to try to withhold it would be pointless."

"Well, I'd hate to be pointless. You're right, some of what Jim said was true. He did tell me about the new will, but after the news came that Sidney had been killed in action, not before. He did take it from his safe and let me read it. It did leave everything to Caroline. He said that no one knew its contents except his former secretary, and she had got married and gone to some little town in the South, so she was out of the way. He said there was no other copy of it, and that he was sure Caroline didn't know about it because of a letter she had shown him from Sidney. He said he would destroy it, and I and my mother and brother would inherit under the previous will, if I would marry him. Do you want to know everything we said?"

"I think just the essential points."

"Then I don't need to tell how I really felt about marrying him. I didn't tell him. I agreed to it. I suppose you don't care what I thought, but Sidney was dead, and I thought it was only fair for us to get a share. So I agreed, but I never had any intention of marrying Jim Beebe. He wanted an immediate wedding, before he presented the will for probate, but I talked him out of that, and our engagement was announced. When the will had gone through and the estate had been distributed and we had our share, I married Norman Horne. I didn't know whether Jim had destroyed the new will or not, but that didn't matter because he wouldn't dare to produce it then." She fluttered a hand. "That's all."

"Not quite," Wolfe objected. "The sequel. Mr. Karnow's return."

"Oh, yes." Her tone implied that it was careless of her to overlook that little detail. "Of course Jim killed him. If you mean how I felt about Sidney's turning up alive, you may not believe it, but in a way I was glad of it, because I always liked him. I was sorry for Caroline and Paul, because I liked them too, but I knew Sidney wouldn't try to get our share back from us. There was just one person who didn't dare to face him. Of course Jim did face him when he went to his hotel room, but he wasn't facing him when he killed him—he shot him in the back of the head." She turned to Beebe. "Did you tell him about the will, Jim? I'll bet you didn't. I'll bet he never knew." She turned back to Wolfe. "Will that do for the truth?"

"It'll do for a malicious lie," Beebe squeaked.

Wolfe addressed the law. "I would prefer, Mr. Cramer, to turn the issue of veracity over to you. In my opinion, Mr. Beebe fumbled it, and Mrs. Horne didn't."

At a later date, in a courtroom, a jury concurred. Justice is a fine thing, but that night in Wolfe's office it slipped up on one detail. After Cramer and Stebbins had escorted Beebe out, and the others had gone, Caroline Karnow decided that the occasion called for her returning the kiss she had received in that room twelve hours earlier. But she went right past me, around to Wolfe behind his desk, put her arms around his neck, and gave it to him on both cheeks.

"Wrong address," I said bitterly.

Die
Like a Dog

I

I do sometimes treat myself to a walk in the rain, though I prefer sunshine when there's not enough wind to give the dust a whirl. That rainy Wednesday, however, there was a special inducement: I wanted his raincoat to be good and wet when I delivered it. So with it on my back and my old brown felt on my head, I left the house and set out for Arbor Street, some two miles south in the Village.

Halfway there the rain stopped and my blood had pumped me warm, so I took the coat off, folded it wet side in, hung it on my arm, and proceeded. Arbor Street, narrow and only three blocks long, had on either side an assortment of old brick houses, mostly of four stories, which were neither spick nor span. Number 29 would be about the middle of the first block.

I reached it, but I didn't enter it. There was a party going on in the middle of the block. A police car was double-parked in front of the entrance to one of the houses, and a uniformed cop was on the sidewalk in an attitude of authority toward a small gathering of citizens confronting him. As I approached I heard him demanding, "Whose dog is this?"—referring, evidently, to an animal with a wet black coat standing behind him. I heard no one claim the dog, but I wouldn't have anyway, because my attention was diverted. Another police car rolled up and stopped behind the first one, and a man got out, pushed through the crowd to the sidewalk, nodded to the cop without halting, and went in the entrance, above which appeared the number 29.

The trouble was, I knew the man, which is an understatement. I do not begin to tremble at the sight of Sergeant Purley Stebbins of Manhattan Homicide West, which is also an understatement, but his presence and manner made it a cinch that there was a corpse in that house, and if I demanded entry on the ground that I wanted to swap raincoats with a guy who had walked off with mine, there was no question what would happen. My prompt appearance at the scene of a homicide would arouse all of Purley's worst instincts, backed up by reference to various precedents, and I might not get home in time for dinner, which was going to be featured by grilled squab with a brown sauce which Fritz calls *Vénitienne* and is one of his best.

Purley had disappeared within without spotting me. The cop was a complete stranger. As I slowed down to detour past him on the narrow sidewalk he gave me an eye and demanded, "That your dog?"

The dog was nuzzling my knee, and I stooped to give him a pat on his wet black head. Then, telling the cop he wasn't mine, I went on by. At the next corner I turned right, heading back uptown. I kept my eye peeled for a taxi the first couple of blocks, saw none, and decided to finish the walk. A wind had started in from the west, but everything was still damp from the rain.

Marching along, I was well on my way before I saw the dog. Stopping for a light on Ninth Avenue in the Twenties, I felt something at my knee, and there he was. My hand started for his head in reflex, but I pulled it back. I was in a fix. Apparently he had picked me for a pal, and if I just went on he would follow, and you can't chase a dog on Ninth Avenue by throwing rocks. I could have ditched him by taking a taxi the rest of the way, but that would have been pretty rude after the appreciation he had shown of my charm. He had a collar on with a tag, and could be identified, and the station house was only a few blocks away, so the simplest and cheapest way was to convoy him there. I moved to the curb to look for a taxi coming downtown, and as I did so a cyclone sailed around the corner and took my hat with it into the middle of the avenue.

I didn't dash out into the traffic, but you should have seen that dog. He sprang across the bow of a big truck, wiping its left front fender with his tail, braked landing to let a car by, sprang again, and was under another car—or I thought he was—and then I saw him on the opposite sidewalk. He snatched the hat from under the feet of a pedestrian, turned on a dime, and started back. This time his crossing wasn't so spectacular, but he didn't dally. He came to me and stood, lifting his head and wagging his tail. I took the hat. It had skimmed a puddle of water on its trip, but I thought he would be disappointed if I didn't put it on, so I did. Naturally that settled it. I flagged a cab, took the dog in with me, and gave the driver the address of Wolfe's house.

My idea was to take my hat hound upstairs to my room, give him some refreshment, and phone the

ASPCA to send for him. But there was no sense in passing up such an opportunity for a little buzz at Wolfe, so after letting us in and leaving my hat and the raincoat on the rack in the hall, I proceeded to the door to the office and entered.

"Where the devil have you been?" Wolfe asked grumpily. "We were going over some lists at six o'clock, and it's a quarter to seven."

He was in his oversized chair behind his desk with a book, and his eyes hadn't left the page to spare me a glance. I answered him. "Taking that damn raincoat. Only I didn't deliver it, because—"

"What's that?" he snapped. He was glaring at my companion.

"A dog."

"I see it is. I'm in no temper for buffoonery. Get it out of here."

"Yes, sir, right away. I can keep him in my room most of the time, but of course he'll have to come downstairs and through the hall when I take him out. He's a hat hound. There is a sort of a problem. His name is Nero, which, as you know, means 'black,' and of course I'll have to change it. Ebony would do, or Jet, or Inky, or—"

"Bah. Flummery!"

"No, sir. I get pretty darned lonesome around here, especially during the four hours a day you're up in the plant rooms. You have your orchids, and Fritz has his turtle, and Theodore has his parakeets up in the potting room, and why shouldn't I have a dog? I admit I'll have to change his name, though he is registered as Champion Nero Charcoal of Bantyscoot. I have suggested . . ."

I went on talking only because I had to. It was a fizzle. I had expected to induce a major outburst, even possibly something as frantic as Wolfe leaving his chair to evict the beast himself, and there he was gazing at Nero with an expression I had never seen him aim at any human, including me. I went on talking, forcing it.

He broke in. "It's not a hound. It's a Labrador retriever."

That didn't faze me. I'm never surprised at a display of knowledge by a bird who reads as many books as Wolfe does. "Yes, sir," I agreed. "I only said hound because it would be natural for a private detective to have a hound."

"Labradors," he said, "have a wider skull than any other dog, for brain room. A dog I had when I was a boy, in Montenegro, a small brown mongrel, had a rather narrow skull, but I did not regard it as a defect. I do not remember that I considered that dog to have a defect. Today I suppose I would be more critical. When you smuggled that creature in here did you take into account the disruption it would cause in this household?"

It had backfired on me. I had learned something new about the big fat genius: he would enjoy having a dog around, provided he could blame it on me and so be free to beef when he felt like it. As for me, when I retire to the country I'll have a dog, and maybe two, but not in town.

I snapped into reverse. "I guess I didn't," I confessed. "I do feel the need for a personal pet, but what the hell, I can try a canary or a chameleon. Okay, I'll get rid of him. After all, it's your house."

"I do not want to feel responsible," he said stiffly, "for your privation. I would almost rather put up with its presence than with your reproaches."

"Forget it." I waved a hand. "I'll try to. I promise not to rub it in."

"Another thing," he persisted. "I refuse to interfere with any commitment you have made."

"I have made no commitment."

"Then where did you get it?"

"Well, I'll tell you."

I went and sat at my desk and did so. Nero, the four-legged one, came and lay at my feet with his nose just not touching the toe of my shoe. I reported the whole event, with as much detail as if I had been reporting a vital operation in a major case, and, when I had finished, Wolfe was of course quite aware that my presentation of Nero as a permanent addition to the staff had been a plant. Ordinarily he would have made his opinion of my performance clear, but this time he skipped it, and it was easy to see why. The idea of having a dog that he could blame on me had got in and stuck.

When I came to the end and stopped there was a moment's silence, and then he said, "Jet would be an acceptable name for that dog."

"Yeah." I swiveled and reached for the phone. "I'll call the ASPCA to come for him."

"No." He was emphatic.

"Why not?"

"Because there is a better alternative. Call someone you know in the Police Department—anyone. Give him the number on the dog's tag, and ask him to find out who the owner is. Then you can inform the owner directly."

He was playing for time. It could happen that the owner was dead or in jail or didn't want the dog back, and if so Wolfe could take the position that I had committed myself by bringing the dog home in a taxi and that it would be dishonorable to renege. However, I didn't want to argue, so I phoned a precinct sergeant who I knew was disposed to do me small favors. He took Nero's number and said it might take a while at that time of day, and he would call me back. As I hung up, Fritz entered to announce dinner.

The squabs with that sauce were absolutely edible, as they always are, but other phenomena in the next couple of hours were not so pleasing. The table talk in the dining room was mostly one-sided and mostly about dogs. Wolfe kept it on a high level—no maudlin sentiment. He maintained that the basenji was the oldest breed on earth, having originated in Central Africa around 5000 B.C., whereas there was no trace of the Afghan hound earlier than around 4000 B.C. To me all it proved was that he had read a book I hadn't noticed him with.

Nero ate in the kitchen with Fritz and made a hit. Wolfe had told Fritz to call him Jet. When Fritz brought in the salad he announced that Jet had wonderful manners and was very smart.

"Nevertheless," Wolfe asked, "wouldn't you think him an insufferable nuisance as a cohabitant?"

On the contrary, Fritz declared, he would be most welcome.

After dinner, feeling that the newly formed Canine Canonizing League needed slowing down, I first took Nero out for a brief tour and, returning, escorted him up the two flights to my room and left him there. I had to admit he was well behaved. If I had wanted to take on a dog in town it could have been him. In my room I told him to lie down, and he did, and when I went to the door to leave, his eyes, which were the color of caramel, made it plain that he would love to come along, but he didn't get up.

Down in the office Wolfe and I got at the lists. They were special offerings from orchid growers and collectors from all over the world, and it was quite a job to check the thousands of items and pick the few that Wolfe might want to give a try. I sat at his desk, across from him, with trays of cards from our files, and we were in the middle of it, around ten-thirty, when the doorbell rang. I went to the hall and flipped a light switch and saw out on the stoop, through the one-way glass panel in the door, a familiar figure—Inspector Cramer of Homicide.

I went to the door, opened it six inches, and asked politely, "Now what?"

"I want to see Wolfe."

"It's pretty late. What about?"

"About a dog."

It is understood that no visitor, and especially no officer of the law, is to be conducted to the office until Wolfe has been consulted, but this seemed to rate an exception. Wolfe had been known to refuse an audience to people who topped inspectors, and, told that Cramer had come to see him about a dog, there was no telling how he might react in the situation as it had developed.

I considered the matter for about two seconds and then swung the door open and invited cordially, "Step right in."

II

"Properly speaking," Cramer declared as one who wanted above all to be perfectly fair and square, "it's Goodwin I want information from."

He was in the red leather chair at the end of Wolfe's desk, just about filling it. His big round face was no redder than usual, his gray eyes no colder, his voice no gruffer. Merely normal.

Wolfe came at me. "Then why did you bring him in here without even asking?"

Cramer interfered for me. "I asked for you. Of course you're in it. I want to know where the dog fits in. Where is it, Goodwin?"

That set the tone—again normal. He does sometimes call me Archie, after all the years, but it's exceptional. I inquired, "Dog?"

His lips tightened. "All right, I'll spell it. You phoned the precinct and gave them a tag number and wanted to know who owns the dog. When the sergeant learned that the owner was a man named Philip Kampf, who was murdered this afternoon in a house at twenty-nine Arbor Street, he notified Homicide. The officer who had been on post in front of that house had told us that the dog had gone off with a man who had said it wasn't his dog. After we learned of your inquiry about the owner, the officer was shown a picture of you and said it was you who enticed the dog. He's outside in my car. Do you want to bring him in?"

"No, thanks. I didn't entice."

"The dog followed you."

I gestured modestly. "Girls follow me, dogs follow me, sometimes even your own dicks follow me. I can't help—"

"Skip the comedy. The dog belonged to a murder victim, and you removed it from the scene of the murder. Where is it?"

Wolfe butted in. "You persist," he objected, "in imputing an action to Mr. Goodwin without warrant. He did not 'remove' the dog. I advise you to shift your ground if you expect us to listen."

His tone was firm but not hostile. I cocked an eye at

him. He was probably being indulgent because he had learned that Jet's owner was dead.

"I've got another ground," Cramer asserted. "A man who lives in that house, named Richard Meegan, and who was in it at the time Kampf was murdered, has stated that he came here to see you this morning and asked you to do a job for him. He says you refused the job. That's what he says." Cramer jutted his chin. "Now. A man at the scene of a murder admits he consulted you this morning. Goodwin shows up at the scene half an hour after the murder was committed, and he entices—okay, put it that the dog goes away with him, the dog that belonged to the victim and had gone to that house with him. How does that look?" He pulled his chin in. "You know damn well the last thing I want in a homicide is to find you or Goodwin anywhere within ten miles of it, because I know from experience what to expect. But when you're there, there you are, and I want to know how and why and what, and by God I intend to. Where's the dog?"

Wolfe sighed and shook his head. "In this instance," he said, almost genial, "you're wasting your time. As for Mr. Meegan, he phoned this morning to make an appointment and came at eleven. Our conversation was brief. He wanted a man shadowed, but divulged no name or any other specific detail because in his first breath he mentioned his wife—he was overwrought—and I gathered that his difficulty was marital. As you know, I don't touch that kind of work, and I stopped him. My vanity bristles even at an offer of that sort of job. My bluntness enraged him, and he dashed out. On his way he took his hat from the rack in the hall, and he took Mr. Goodwin's raincoat instead of his own. Archie. Proceed."

Cramer's eyes came to me, and I obeyed. "I didn't

find out about the switch in coats until the middle of
the afternoon. His was the same color as mine, but
mine's newer. When he phoned for an appointment this
morning he gave me his name and address, and I
wanted to phone him to tell him to bring my coat back,
but he wasn't listed, and Information said she didn't
have him, so I decided to go get it. I walked, wearing
Meegan's coat. There was a cop and a crowd and a PD
car in front of twenty-nine Arbor Street, and, as I approached, another PD car came, and Purley Stebbins
got out and went in, so I decided to skip it, not wanting
to go through the torture. There was a dog present,
and he nuzzled me, and I patted him. I will admit, if
pressed, that I should not have patted him. The cop
asked me if the dog was mine, and I said no and went
on, and headed for home. I was—"

"Did you call the dog or signal it?"

"No. I was at Twenty-eighth and Ninth Avenue before I knew he was tailing me. I did not entice or remove. If I did, if there's some kind of a dodge about the
dog, please tell me why I phoned the precinct to get
the name of his owner."

"I don't know. With Wolfe and you I never know.
Where is it?"

I blurted it out before Wolfe could stop me. "Upstairs in my room."

"Bring it down here."

"Right."

I was up and going, but Wolfe called me sharply.
"Archie!"

I turned. "Yes, sir."

"There's no frantic urgency." He went to Cramer.
"The animal seems intelligent, but I doubt if it's up to
answering questions. I don't want it capering around
my office."

"Neither do I."

"Then why bring it down?"

"I'm taking it downtown. We want to try something with it."

Wolfe pursed his lips. "I doubt if that's feasible. Sit down, Archie. Mr. Goodwin has assumed an obligation and will have to honor it. The creature has no master, and so, presumably, no home. It will have to be tolerated here until Mr. Goodwin gets satisfactory assurance of its future welfare. Archie?"

If we had been alone I would have made my position clear, but with Cramer there I was stuck. "Absolutely," I agreed.

"You see," he told Cramer. "I'm afraid we can't permit the dog's removal."

"Nuts. I'm taking it."

"Indeed? What writ have you? Replevin? Warrant for arrest as a material witness?"

Cramer opened his mouth and shut it again. He put his elbows on the chair arms, interlaced his fingers, and leaned forward. "Look. You and Meegan check, either because you're both telling it straight, or because you've framed it, I don't know which, and we'll see. But I'm taking the dog. Kampf, the man who was killed, lived on Perry Street, a few blocks away from Arbor Street. He arrived at twenty-nine Arbor Street, with the dog on a leash, about five-twenty this afternoon. The janitor of the house, named Olsen, lives in the basement, and he was sitting at his front window, and he saw Kampf arrive with the dog and turn in at the entrance. About ten minutes later he saw the dog come out, with no leash, and right after the dog a man came out. The man was Victor Talento, a lawyer, the tenant of the ground-floor apartment. Talento says he left his apartment to go to an appointment, saw the dog in the hall, thought it was a stray, and chased it out, and that's all he knows. Anyhow, Olsen says Talento walked off, and the dog stayed there on the sidewalk."

Cramer unlaced his fingers and sat back. "About twenty minutes later, around ten minutes to six, Olsen heard someone yelling his name and went to the rear and up one flight to the ground-floor hall. Two men were there, a live one and a dead one. The live one was Ross Chaffee, a painter, the tenant of the top-floor studio—that's the fourth floor. The dead one was the man that had arrived with the dog. He had been strangled with the dog's leash, and the body was at the bottom of the stairs leading up. Chaffee says he found it when he came down to go to an appointment, and that's all he knows. He stayed there while Olsen went downstairs to phone. A squad car arrived at five-fifty-eight. Sergeant Stebbins arrived at six-ten. Goodwin arrived at six-ten. Excellent timing."

Wolfe merely grunted. Cramer continued, "You can have it all. The dog's leash was in the pocket of Kampf's raincoat, which was on him. The laboratory says it was used to strangle him. The routine is still in process. I'll answer questions within reason. The four tenants of the house were all there when Kampf arrived: Victor Talento, the lawyer, on the ground floor; Richard Meegan, whose job you say you wouldn't take, second floor; Jerome Aland, a night-club performer, third floor; and Ross Chaffee, the painter with the studio. Aland says he was sound asleep until we banged on his door and took him down to look at the corpse. Meegan says he heard nothing and knows nothing."

Cramer sat forward again. "Okay, what happened? Kampf went there to see one of those four men, and had his dog with him. It's possible he took the leash off in the lower hall to leave the dog there, but I doubt it. At least it's just as possible that he took the dog along to the door of one of the apartments, and the dog was wet and the tenant wouldn't let it enter, so Kampf left it outside. Another possibility is that the dog was actually present when Kampf was killed, but we'll know more about that after we see and handle the dog. The particular thing we want—we're going to take the dog in that house and see which door it goes to. We're going to do that now. There's a man out in my car who knows dogs." Cramer stood up.

Wolfe shook his head. "You must be hard put. You say Mr. Kampf lived on Perry Street. With a family?"

"No. Bachelor. Some kind of a writer. He didn't have to make a living; he had means."

"Then the beast is orphaned. He's in your room, Archie?"

"Yes, sir." I got up and started for the door.

Wolfe halted me. "One moment. Go up and in, lock your door, and stay there till I notify you. Go!"

I went. It was either that or quit my job on the spot, and I resign only when we haven't got company. Also, assuming that there was a valid reason for refusing to surrender the dog to the cops, Wolfe was justified. Cramer, needing no warrant to enter the house because he was already in, wouldn't hesitate to mount to my room to do his own fetching, and stopping him physically would have raised some delicate points. Whereas breaking through a locked door would be another matter.

I didn't lock it, because it hadn't been locked for years and I didn't remember which drawer of my chest the key was in, and while I was searching Cramer might conceivably have made it up the carpeted stairs and come right in, so I left it open and stood on the sill to listen. If I heard him coming I would shut it and brace it with my foot. Nero, or Jet, depending on where you stand, came over to me, but I ordered him back, and he went without a murmur. From below came voices, not cordial, but not raised enough for me to get words. Before long there was the sound of Cramer's heavy steps leaving the office and tramping along the hall, and then the slam of the front door.

I called down, "All clear?"

"No!" It was a bellow. "Wait till I bolt it!" And after a moment: "All right!"

I shut my door and went to the stairs and descended. Wolfe was back in his chair behind his desk, sitting straight. As I entered he snapped at me, "A pretty mess! You sneak a dog in here to badger me, and what now?"

I crossed to my desk, sat, and spoke calmly. "We're way beyond that. You will never admit you bollixed it up yourself, so forget it. When you ask me what now, that's easy. I could say I'll take the dog down and deliver him at Homicide, but we're beyond that too. Not only have you learned that he is orphaned, as you put it, which sounds terrible, and therefore adopting him will probably be simple, but also you have taken a stand with Cramer, and of course you won't back up. If we sit tight with the door bolted I suppose I can take the dog out back for his outings, but what if the law shows up tomorrow with a writ?"

He leaned back and shut his eyes. I looked up at the wall clock: two minutes past eleven. I looked at my wristwatch: also two minutes past eleven. They both said six minutes past when Wolfe opened his eyes.

"From Mr. Cramer's information," he said, "I doubt if that case holds any formidable difficulties."

I had no comment.

"If it were speedily solved," he went on, "your commitment to the dog could be honored at leisure. I had thought until now that my disinclination to permit a policeman to storm in here and commandeer any person or object in this house that struck his fancy was shared by you."

"It is. Within reason."

"That's an ambiguous phrase, and I must be allowed my own interpretation short of absurdity. Clearly the simplest way to settle this matter is to find out who killed Mr. Kampf. It may not be much of a job; if it proves otherwise we can reconsider. An immediate exploration is the thing, and luckily we have a pretext for it. You can go there to get your raincoat, taking Mr. Meegan's with you, and proceed as the occasion offers. The best course would be to bring him here, but, as you know, I wholly rely on your discretion and enterprise in such a juncture."

"Thank you very much," I said bitterly. "You mean now."

"Yes."

"They may still have Meegan downtown."

"I doubt if they'll keep him overnight. In the morning they'll probably have him again."

"I'll have to take the dog out first."

"Fritz will take him out back in the court."

"I'll be damned." I arose. "No client, no fee, no nothing except a dog with a wide skull for brain room." I crossed to the door, turned, said distinctly, "I will be damned," went to the rack for my hat and Meegan's coat, and beat it.

III

The rain had ended, and the wind was down. After dismissing the taxi at the end of Arbor Street, I walked to number 29, with the raincoat hung over my arm. There was light behind the curtains of the windows on the ground floor, but none anywhere above, and none in the basement. Entering the vestibule, I inspected the labels in the slots between the mailboxes and the buttons. From the bottom up they read: Talento, Meegan, Aland, and Chaffee. I pushed the button above Meegan, put my hand on the doorknob, and waited. No click. I twisted the knob, and it wouldn't turn. Another long push on the button, and a longer wait. I varied it by trying four short pushes. Nothing doing.

I left the vestibule and was confronted by two couples standing on the sidewalk staring at me, or at the entrance. They exchanged words, decided they didn't care for my returning stare, and passed on. I considered pushing the button of Victor Talento, the lawyer who lived on the ground floor, where light was showing, voted to wait a while for Meegan, with whom I had an in, moved down ten paces to a fire hydrant, and propped myself against it.

I hadn't been there long enough to shift position more than a couple of times when the light disappeared on the ground floor of number 29, and a little later the vestibule door opened and a man came out. He turned toward me, gave me a glance as he passed, and kept going. Thinking it unlikely that any occupant of that house was being extended the freedom of the city that night, I cast my eyes around, and sure enough, when the subject had gone some thirty paces a figure emerged from an areaway across the street and started strolling. I shook my head in disapproval. I would have waited until the guy was ten paces farther. Saul Panzer would have made it ten more than that, but Saul is the best tailer alive.

As I stood deploring that faulty performance, an idea hit me. They might keep Meegan downtown another two hours, or all night, or he might even be up in his bed asleep. This was at least a chance to take a stab at something. I shoved off, in the direction taken by the subject, who was now a block away. Stepping along, I gained on him. A little beyond the corner I was abreast of the city employee, who was keeping to the other side of the street; but I wasn't interested in him. It seemed to me that the subject was upping the stroke a little, so I did too, really marching, and as he reached the next intersection I was beside him. He had looked over his shoulder when he heard me coming up behind, but hadn't slowed. As I reached him I spoke.

"Victor Talento?"

"No comment," he said and kept going. So did I.

"Thanks for the compliment," I said, "but I'm not a reporter. My name's Archie Goodwin, and I work for Nero Wolfe. If you'll stop a second I'll show you my credentials."

"I'm not interested in your credentials."

"Okay. If you just came out for a breath of air you won't be interested in this either. Otherwise you may be. Please don't scream or look around, but you've got a Homicide dick on your tail. Don't look or he'll know I'm telling you. He's across the street, ninety feet back."

"Yes," he conceded, without changing pace, "that's interesting. Is this your good deed for the day?"

"No. I'm out dowsing for Mr. Wolfe. He's investigating a murder just for practice, and I'm looking for a seam. I thought if I gave you a break you might feel like reciprocating. If you're just out for a walk, forget it, and sorry I interrupted. If you're headed for something you'd like to keep private maybe you could use some expert advice. In this part of town at this time of night there are only two approved methods for shaking a tail, and I'd be glad to oblige."

He looked it over for half a block, with me keeping step, and then spoke. "You mentioned credentials."

"Right. We might as well stop under that light. The dick will keep his distance."

We stopped. I got out my wallet and let him have a look at my licenses, detective and driver's. He didn't skimp it, being a lawyer. I put my wallet back.

"Of course," he said, "I was aware that I might be followed."

"Sure."

"I intended to take precautions. But it may not be —I suppose it's not as simple as it seems. I have had no experience at this kind of maneuver. Who hired Wolfe to investigate?"

"I don't know. He says he needs practice."

"All right, if it's qualified." He stood sizing me up by the street light. He was an inch shorter than me, and some older, with his weight starting to collect around the middle. He was dark-skinned, with eyes to match, and his nose hooked to point down. I didn't prod him. My lucky stab had snagged him, and it was his problem. He was working on it.

"I have an appointment," he said.

I waited.

He went on. "A woman phoned me, and I arranged to meet her. My wire could have been tapped."

"I doubt it. They're not that fast."

"I suppose not. The woman had nothing to do with

the murder, and neither had I, but of course anything I do and anyone I see is suspect. I have no right to expose her to possible embarrassment, and I can't be sure of shaking that man off."

I grinned at him. "And me too."

"You mean you would follow me?"

"Certainly, for practice. And I'd like to see how you handle it."

He wasn't returning my grin. "I see you've earned your reputation, Goodwin. You'd be wasting your time, because this woman has no connection with this business, but I should have known better than to make this appointment. I won't keep it. It's only three blocks from here. You might be willing to go and tell her I'm not coming, and I'll get in touch with her tomorrow. Yes?"

"Sure, if it's only three blocks. If you'll return the favor by calling on Nero Wolfe for a little talk. That's what I meant by reciprocating."

He considered it. "Not tonight."

"Tonight would be best."

"No. I'm all in."

"Tomorrow morning at eleven?"

"Yes, I can make it then."

"Okay." I gave him the address. "If you forget it, it's in the book. Now brief me."

He took a respectable roll of bills from his pocket and peeled off a twenty. "Since you're acting as my agent, you have a right to a fee."

I grinned again. "That's a neat idea, you being a lawyer, but I'm not acting as your agent. I'm doing you a favor on request and expecting one in return. Where's the appointment?"

He put the roll back. "Have it your way. The woman's name is Jewel Jones, and she's at the southeast corner of Christopher and Grove Streets, or will be." He looked at his wrist. "We were to meet there at midnight. She's medium height, slender, dark hair and eyes, very goodlooking. Tell her why I'm not coming, and say she'll hear from me tomorrow."

"Right. You'd better take a walk in the other direction to keep the dick occupied, and don't look back."

He wanted to shake hands to show his appreciation, but that would have been just as bad as taking the twenty, since before another midnight Wolfe might be tagging him for murder, so I pretended not to notice. He headed east, and I headed west, moving right along without turning my head for a glimpse of the dick. I had to make sure that he didn't see a vision and switch subjects, but I let that wait until I got to Christopher Street. Reaching it, I turned the corner, went twenty feet to a stoop, slid behind it with only my head out, and counted a slow hundred. There were passers-by, a couple and a guy in a hurry, but no dick. I went on a block to Grove Street, passed the intersection, saw no loitering female, continued for a distance, and turned and backtracked. I was on the fifth lap, and it was eight minutes past twelve, when a taxi stopped at the corner, a woman got out, and the taxi rolled off.

I approached. The light could have been better, but she seemed to meet the specifications. I stopped and asked, "Jones?" She drew herself up. I said, "From Victor."

She tilted her head back to get my face. "Who are you?" She seemed a little out of breath.

"Victor sent me with a message, but naturally I have to be sure it reaches the right party. I've ante'd half of your name and half of his, so it's your turn."

"Who are you?"

I shook my head. "You go first, or no message from Victor."

"Where is he?"

"No. I'll count ten and go. One, two, three, four—"

"My name is Jewel Jones. His is Victor Talento."

"That's the girl. I'll tell you." I did so. Since it was desirable for her to grasp the situation fully, I started with my propping myself on the fire hydrant in front of 29 Arbor Street and went on from there, as it happened, including, of course, my name and status. By the time I finished she had developed a healthy frown.

"Damn it," she said with feeling. She moved and put a hand on my arm. "Come and put me in a taxi."

I stayed planted. "I'll be glad to, and it will be on me. We're going to Nero Wolfe's place."

"We?" She removed the hand. "You're crazy."

"One will get you ten I'm not. Look at it. You and Talento made an appointment at a street corner, so you had some good reason for not wanting to be seen together tonight. It must have been something fairly urgent. I admit the urgency didn't have to be connected with the murder of Philip Kampf, but it could be, and it certainly has to be discussed. I don't want to be arbitrary. I can take you to a Homicide sergeant named Stebbins, and you can discuss it with him; or I'll take you to Mr. Wolfe. I should think you'd prefer Mr. Wolfe, but suit yourself."

She had well-oiled gears. For a second, as I spoke, her eyes flashed like daggers, but then they went soft and appealing. She took my arm again, this time with both hands. "I'll discuss it with you," she said, in a voice she could have used to defrost her refrigerator. "I wouldn't mind that. We'll go somewhere."

I said come on, and we moved, with her maintaining contact with a hand hooked cozily on my arm. We hadn't gone far, toward Seventh Avenue, when a taxi came along and I flagged it and we got in. I told the driver, "Nine-eighteen West Thirty-fifth," and he started.

"What's that?" Miss Jones demanded.

I told her, Nero Wolfe's house. The poor girl didn't know what to do. If she called me a rat that wouldn't help her any. If she kicked and screamed I would merely give the hackie another address. Her best bet was to try to thaw me, and if she had had time for a real campaign, say four or five hours, she might conceivably have made some progress, because she had a knack for it. She didn't coax or argue; she just told me how she knew I was the kind of man she could tell anything to and I would believe her and understand her, and after she had done that she would be willing to go anywhere or do anything I advised, but she was sure I wouldn't want to take advantage . . .

There just wasn't time enough. The taxi rolled to the curb, and I had a bill ready for the driver. I got out, gave her a hand, and escorted her up the seven steps of the stoop, applauding her economy in not wasting breath on protests. My key wouldn't let us in, since the chain bolt would be on, so I pushed the button, and in a moment the stoop light shone on us, and in another the door opened. I motioned her in and followed. Fritz was there.

"Mr. Wolfe up?" I asked.

"In the office." He was giving Miss Jones a look, the look he gives any strange female who enters that house. There is always in his mind the possibility, however remote, that she will bewitch Wolfe into a mania for a mate. After asking him to conduct her to the front room, and putting my hat and the raincoat on the rack, I went on down the hall and entered the office.

Wolfe was at his desk, reading, and curled up in the middle of the room, on the best rug in the house, which was given to Wolfe years ago as a token of gratitude by an Armenian merchant who had got himself in a bad hole, was the dog. The dog greeted me by lifting his head and tapping the rug with his tail. Wolfe greeted me by raising his eyes from the book and grunting.

"I brought company," I told him. "Before I introduce her I should—"

"Her? The tenants of that house are all men! I might have known you'd dig up a woman!"

"I can chase her if you don't want her. This is how I got her." I proceeded, not dragging it out, but including all the essentials. I ended up, "I could have taken her to a spot I know of and grilled her myself, but it would have been risky. Just in a six-minute taxi ride she had me feeling—uh, brotherly. Do you want her or not?"

"Confound it." His eyes went to his book and stayed there long enough to finish a paragraph. He dog-eared it and put it down. "Very well, bring her."

I crossed to the connecting door to the front room, opened it, and requested, "Please come in, Miss Jones." She came, and as she passed through gave me a wistful smile that might have gone straight to my heart if there hadn't been a diversion. As she entered, the dog suddenly sprang to his feet, whirling, and made for her with sounds of unmistakable pleasure. He stopped in front of her, raising his head so she wouldn't have to reach far to pat it, and wagged his tail so fast it was only a blur.

"Indeed," Wolfe said. "How do you do, Miss Jones. I am Nero Wolfe. What's the dog's name?"

I claim she was good. The presence of the dog was a complete surprise to her. But without the slightest sign of fluster she put out a hand to give it a gentle pat, looked around, spotted the red leather chair, went to it, and sat.

"That's a funny question right off," she said, not complaining. "Asking me your dog's name."

"Pfui." Wolfe was disgusted. "I don't know what position you were going to take, but from what Mr. Goodwin tells me I would guess you were going to say that the purpose of your appointment with Mr. Talento was a personal matter that had nothing to do with Mr. Kampf or his death, and that you knew Mr. Kampf either slightly and casually or not at all. Now the dog has made that untenable. Obviously he knows you well, and he belonged to Mr. Kampf. So you knew Mr. Kampf well. If you try to deny that you'll have Mr. Goodwin and other trained men digging all around you, your past and your present, and that will be extremely disagreeable, no matter how innocent you may be of murder or any other wrongdoing. You won't like that. What's the dog's name?"

She looked at me, and I met it. In good light I would have qualified Talento's specification of "very good-looking." Not that she was unsightly, but she caught the eye more by what she looked than how she looked. It wasn't just something she turned on as needed; it was there even now, when she must have been pretty busy deciding how to handle it.

It took her only a few seconds to decide. "His name is Bootsy," she said. The dog, at her feet, lifted his head and wagged his tail.

"Good heavens," Wolfe muttered. "No other name?"

"Not that I know of."

"Your name is Jewel Jones?"

"Yes. I sing in a night club, the Flamingo, but I'm

not working right now." She made a little gesture, very appealing, but it was Wolfe who had to resist it, not me. "Believe me, Mr. Wolfe, I don't know anything about that murder. If I knew anything that could help I'd be perfectly willing to tell you, because I'm sure you're the kind of man that understands and you wouldn't want to hurt me if you didn't have to."

That wasn't what she had fed me verbatim. Not verbatim.

"I try to understand," Wolfe said dryly. "You knew Mr. Kampf intimately?"

"Yes, I guess so." She smiled as one understander to another. "For a while I did. Not lately, not for the past two months."

"You met the dog at his apartment on Perry Street?"

"That's right. For nearly a year I was there quite often."

"You and Mr. Kampf quarreled?"

"Oh no, we didn't quarrel. I just didn't see him any more. I had other—I was very busy."

"When did you see him last?"

"Well—you mean intimately?"

"No. At all."

"About two weeks ago, at the club. He came to the club once or twice and spoke to me there."

"But no quarrel?"

"No, there was nothing to quarrel about."

"You have no idea who killed him, or why?"

"I certainly haven't."

Wolfe leaned back. "Do you know Mr. Talento intimately?"

"No, not if you mean—of course we're friends. I used to live there."

"With Mr. Talento?"

"Not *with* him." She was mildly shocked. "I never live with a man. I had the second-floor apartment."

"At twenty-nine Arbor Street?"

"Yes."

"For how long? When?"

"For nearly a year. I left there—let's see—about three months ago. I have a little apartment on East Forty-ninth Street."

"Then you know the others too? Mr. Meegan and Mr. Chaffee and Mr. Aland?"

"I know Ross Chaffee and Jerry Aland, but no Meegan. Who's he?"

"A tenant at twenty-nine Arbor Street. Second floor."

She nodded. "Well, sure, that's the floor I had." She smiled. "I hope they fixed that damn table for him. That was one reason I left. I hate furnished apartments, don't you?"

Wolfe made a face. "In principle, yes. I take it you now have your own furniture. Supplied by Mr. Kampf?"

She laughed—more of a chuckle—and her eyes danced. "I see you didn't know Phil Kampf."

"Not supplied by him, then?"

"A great big no."

"By Mr. Chaffee? Or Mr. Aland?"

"No and no." She went very earnest. "Look, Mr. Wolfe. A friend of mine was mighty nice about that furniture, and we'll just leave it. Archie told me what you're interested in is the murder, and I'm sure you wouldn't want to drag in a lot of stuff just to hurt me and a friend of mine, so we'll forget the furniture."

Wolfe didn't press it. He took a hop. "Your appointment on a street corner with Mr. Talento—what was that about?"

She nodded. "I've been wondering about that. I mean what I would say when you asked me, because I'd hate to have you think I'm a sap, and I guess it sounds like it. I phoned him when I heard on the radio about Phil and where he was killed, there on Arbor Street, and I knew Vic still lived there and I simply wanted to ask him about it."

"You had him on the phone."

"He didn't seem to want to talk about it on the phone."

"But why a street corner?"

This time it was more like a laugh. "Now, Mr. Wolfe, you're not a sap. You asked about the furniture, didn't you? Well, a girl with furniture shouldn't be seen places with a man like Vic Talento."

"What is he like?"

She fluttered a hand. "Oh, he wants to get close."

Wolfe kept at her until after one o'clock, and I could report it all, but it wouldn't get you any further than it did him. He couldn't trip her or back her into a corner. She hadn't been to Arbor Street for two months. She hadn't seen Chaffee or Aland or Talento for weeks, and of course not Meegan, since she had never heard of him before. She couldn't even try to guess who had killed Kampf. The only thing remotely to be regarded as a return on Wolfe's investment of a full hour was her statement that as far as she knew there was no one who had both an attachment and a claim to Bootsy. If there were heirs she had no idea who they were. When she left the chair to go the dog got up too, and she patted him, and he went with us to the door. I took her to Tenth Avenue and put her in a taxi, and returned.

I got a glass of milk from the kitchen and took it to the office. Wolfe, who was drinking beer, didn't scowl at me. He seldom scowls when he is drinking beer.

"Where's Bootsy?" I inquired.

"No," he said emphatically.

"Okay." I surrendered. "Where's Jet?"

"Down in Fritz's room. He'll sleep there. You don't like him."

"That's not true, but you can have it. It means you can't blame him on me, and that suits me fine." I sipped milk. "Anyhow, that will no longer be an issue after Homicide comes in the morning with a document and takes him away."

"They won't come."

"I offer twenty to one. Before noon."

He nodded. "That was roughly my own estimate of the probability, so while you were out I phoned Mr. Cramer. I suggested an arrangement, and I suppose he inferred that if he declined the arrangement the dog might be beyond his jurisdiction before tomorrow, though I didn't say so. I may have given that impression."

"Yeah. You should be more careful."

"So the arrangement has been made. You are to be at twenty-nine Arbor Street, with the dog, at nine o'clock in the morning. You are to be present throughout the fatuous performance the police have in mind, and keep the dog in view. The dog is to leave the premises with you, before noon, and you are to bring him back here. The police are to make no further effort to constrain the dog for twenty-four hours. While in that house you may find an opportunity to flush something or someone more contributive than that volatile demirep. If you will come to my room before you go in the morning I may have a suggestion."

"I resent that," I said manfully. "When you call her that, smile."

IV

It was a fine bright morning. I didn't take Meegan's raincoat, because I didn't need any pretext and I doubted if the program would offer a likely occasion for the exchange.

The law was there in front, waiting for me. The one who knew dogs was a stocky middle-aged guy who wore rimless glasses. Before he touched the dog he asked me the name, and I told him Bootsy.

"A hell of a name," he observed. "Also that's a hell of a leash you've got."

"I agree. His was on the corpse, so I suppose it's in the lab." I handed him my end of the heavy cord. "If he bites you it's not on me."

"He won't bite me. Would you, Bootsy?" He squatted before the dog and started to get acquainted. Sergeant Purley Stebbins growled, a foot from my ear, "He should have bit you when you kidnapped him."

I turned. Purley was half an inch taller than me and two inches broader. "You've got it twisted," I told him. "It's women that bite me. I've often wondered what would bite you."

We continued exchanging pleasantries while the dog man, whose name was Loftus, made friends with Bootsy. It wasn't long before he announced that he was ready to proceed. He was frowning. "In a way," he said, "it would be better to keep him on leash after I go in, because Kampf probably did. Or did he? Maybe you ought to brief me a little more. How much do we know?"

"To swear to," Purley told him, "damn little. But putting it all together from what we've collected, this is how it looks, and I'll have to be shown different. When Kampf and the dog entered it was raining and the dog was wet. Kampf left the dog in the ground-floor hall. He removed the leash and had it in his hand when he went to the door of one of the apartments. The tenant of the apartment let him in, and they talked. The tenant socked him, probably from behind without warning, and used the leash to finish him. He stuffed the leash in the pocket of the raincoat. It took nerve and muscle both to carry the body out and down the stairs to the lower hall, but he damn well had to get it out of his place and away from his door, and any of those four could have done it in a pinch, and it sure was a pinch. Of course the dog was already outside, out on the sidewalk. While Kampf was in one of the apartments getting killed, Talento had come into the lower hall and seen the dog and chased it out."

"Then," Loftus objected, "Talento's clean."

"No. Nobody's clean. If it was Talento, after he killed Kampf he went out to the hall and put the dog out in the vestibule, went back in his apartment and carried the body out and dumped it at the foot of the stairs, and then left the house, chasing the dog on out to the sidewalk. You're the dog expert. Is there anything wrong with that?"

"Not necessarily. It depends on the dog and how close he was to Kampf. There wasn't any blood."

"Then that's how I'm buying it. If you want it filled in you can spend the rest of the day with the reports of the other experts and the statements of the tenants."

"Some other day. That'll do for now. You're going in first?"

"Yeah. Come on, Goodwin."

Purley started for the door, but I objected. "I'm staying with the dog."

"For God's sake. Then keep behind Loftus."

I changed my mind. It would be interesting to

watch the experiment, and from behind Loftus the view wouldn't be good. So I went into the vestibule with Purley. The inner door was opened by a Homicide colleague, and we crossed the threshold and moved to the far side of the small lobby, which was fairly clean but not ornate. The colleague closed the door and stayed there. In a minute he pulled it open again, and Loftus and the dog entered. Two steps in, Loftus stopped, and so did the dog. No one spoke. The leash hung limp. Bootsy looked around at Loftus. Loftus bent over and untied the cord from the collar, and held it up to show Bootsy he was free. Bootsy came over to me and stood, his head up, wagging his tail.

"Nuts," Purley said, disgusted.

"You know what I really expected," Loftus said. "I never thought he'd show us where Kampf took him when they entered yesterday, but I did think he'd go to the foot of the stairs, where the body was found, and I thought he might go on to where the body came from —Talento's door, or upstairs. Take him by the collar, Goodwin, and ease him over to the foot of the stairs."

I obliged. He came without urging, but gave no sign that the spot held any special interest for him. We all stood and watched him. He opened his mouth wide to yawn.

"Fine," Purley rumbled. "Just fine. You might as well go on with it."

Loftus came and fastened the leash to the collar, led Bootsy across the lobby to a door, and knocked. In a moment the door opened, and there was Victor Talento in a fancy rainbow dressing gown.

"Hello, Bootsy," he said, and reached down to pat.

"Goddamit!" Purley barked. "I told you not to speak!"

Talento straightened up. "So you did." He was apol-

ogetic. "I'm sorry, I forgot. Do you want to try it
again?"

"No. That's all."

Talento backed in and closed the door.

"You must realize," Loftus told Purley, "that a Labrador can't be expected to go for a man's throat.
They're not that kind of dog. The most you could expect would be an attitude, or possibly a growl."

"You can have 'em," Purley growled. "Is it worth
going on?"

"By all means. You'd better go first."

Purley headed for me, and I gave him room and
then followed him up the stairs. The upper hall was
narrow and not very light, with a door at the rear end
and another toward the front. We backed up against
the wall opposite the front door to leave enough space
for Loftus and Bootsy. They came, Bootsy tagging, and
Loftus knocked. Ten seconds passed before footsteps
sounded, and then the door was opened by the speci-
men who had dashed out of Wolfe's place the day before and taken my coat with him. He was in his shirt
sleeves, and he hadn't combed his hair.

"This is Sergeant Loftus, Mr. Meegan," Purley
said. "Take a look at the dog. Have you ever seen it
before? Pat it."

Meegan snorted. "Pat it yourself. Go to hell."

"Have you ever seen it before?"

"No."

"Okay, thanks. Come on, Loftus."

As we started up the next flight the door slammed
behind us, good and loud. Purley asked over his shoulder, "Well?"

"He didn't like him," Loftus replied from the rear,
"but there are lots of people lots of dogs don't like."

The third-floor hall was a duplicate of the one below. Again Purley and I posted ourselves opposite the door, and Loftus came with Bootsy and knocked. Nothing happened. He knocked again, louder, and pretty soon the door opened to a two-inch crack, and a squeaky voice came through.

"You've got the dog."

"Right here," Loftus told him.

"Are you there, Sergeant?"

"Right here," Purley answered.

"I told you that dog don't like me. Once at a party at Phil Kampf's—I told you. I didn't mean to hurt it, but it thought I did. What are you trying to do, frame me?"

"Open the door. The dog's on a leash."

"I won't! I told you I wouldn't!"

Purley moved. His arm, out stiff, went over Loftus's shoulder, and his palm met the door and kept going. The door hesitated an instant and then swung open. Standing there, holding to its edge, was a skinny individual in red-and-green-striped pajamas. The dog let out a low growl and backed up a little.

"We're making the rounds, Mr. Aland," Purley said, "and we couldn't leave you out. Now you can go back to sleep. As for trying to frame you—"

He stopped because the door shut.

"You didn't tell me," Loftus complained, "that Aland had already fixed it for a reaction."

"No, I thought I'd wait and see. One to go." He headed for the stairs.

The top-floor hall had had someone's personal attention. It was no bigger than the others, but it had a nice clean tan-colored runner, and the walls were painted the same shade and sported a few small pictures. Purley went to the rear door instead of the front, and we made room for Loftus and Bootsy by flattening against the wall. When Loftus knocked footsteps responded at once, approaching the door, and it swung wide open. This was the painter, Ross Chaffee, and he was dressed for it, in an old brown smock. He was by far the handsomest of the tenants, tall, erect, with artistic wavy dark hair and features he must have enjoyed looking at.

I had ample time to enjoy them too as he stood smiling at us, completely at ease, obeying Purley's prior instructions not to speak. Bootsy was also at ease. When it became quite clear that no blood was going to be shed, Purley asked, "You know the dog, don't you, Mr. Chaffee?"

"Certainly. He's a beautiful animal."

"Pat him."

"With pleasure." He bent gracefully. "Bootsy, do you know your master's gone?" He scratched behind the black ears. "Gone forever, Bootsy, and that's too bad." He straightened. "Anything else? I'm working. I like the morning light."

"That's all, thanks." Purley turned to go, and I let Loftus and Bootsy by before following. On the way down the three flights no one had any remarks.

As we hit the level of the lower hall Victor Talento's door opened, and he emerged and spoke. "The District Attorney's office phoned. Are you through with me? They want me down there."

"We're through," Purley rumbled. "We can run you down."

Talento said that would be fine and he would be ready in a minute. Purley told Loftus to give me Bootsy, and he handed me the leash.

"I am willing," I said helpfully, "to give you a detailed analysis of the dog's conduct. It will take about a week."

"Go to hell," Purley growled, "and take the goddam dog along."

I departed. Outside the morning was still fine. The presence of two PD cars in front of the scene of a murder had attracted a small gathering, and Bootsy and I were objects of interest as we appeared and started off. We both ignored the stares. We moseyed along, in no hurry, stopping now and then to give Bootsy a chance to inspect something if he felt inclined. At the fourth or fifth stop, more than a block away, I saw the quartet leaving number 29. Stebbins and Talento took one car and Loftus and the colleague the other, and they rolled off.

I shortened up on Bootsy a little, walked him west until an empty taxi appeared, stopped it and got in, took a five-dollar bill from my wallet, and handed it to the hackie.

"Thanks," he said with feeling. "For what, down payment on the cab?"

"You'll earn it, brother," I assured him. "Is there somewhere within a block or so of Arbor and Court where you can park for anywhere from thirty minutes to three hours?"

"Not three hours for a finif."

"Of course not." I got another five and gave it to him. "I doubt if it will be that long."

"There's a parking lot not too far. On the street without a passenger I'll be solicited."

"You'll have a passenger—the dog. I prefer the street. He's a nice dog. When I return I'll be reasonable. Let's see what we can find."

He pulled the lever and we moved. There are darned few legal parking spaces in all Manhattan at that time of day, and we cruised around several corners before we found one, on Court Street two blocks from Arbor. He backed into it and I got out, leaving the windows down three inches. I told him I'd be back when he saw me, and headed south, turning right at the second corner.

There was no police car at 29 Arbor, and no gathering. That was satisfactory. Entering the vestibule, I pushed the button under Meegan and put my hand on the knob. No click. Pushing twice more and still getting no response, I tried Aland's button, and that worked. After a short wait the click came, and I shoved the door open, entered, mounted two flights, went to the door, and knocked with authority.

The squeaky voice came through. "Who is it?"

"Goodwin. I was just here with the others. I haven't got the dog. Open up."

The door swung slowly to a crack, and then wider. Jerome Aland was still in his gaudy pajamas. "For God's sake," he squeaked, "what do you want now? I need some sleep!"

I didn't apologize. "I was going to ask you some questions when I was here before," I told him, "but the dog complicated it. It won't take long." Since he wasn't polite enough to move aside, I had to brush him, skinny as he was, as I went in. "Which way?"

He slid past me, and I followed him across to chairs. They were the kind of chairs that made Jewel Jones hate furnished apartments, and the rest of the furniture didn't help any. He sat on the edge of one and demanded, "All right, what?"

It was a little tricky. Since he was assuming I was one of the Homicide personnel, it wouldn't do for me to know either too much or too little. It would be risky to mention Jewel Jones, because the cops might not have got around to her at all.

"I'm checking some points," I told him. "How long

has Richard Meegan occupied the apartment below you?"

"Hell, I've told you that a dozen times."

"Not me. I said I'm checking. How long?"

"Nine days. He took it a week ago Tuesday."

"Who was the previous tenant? Just before him."

"There wasn't any. It was empty."

"Empty ever since you've been here?"

"No, I've told you, a girl had it, but she moved out about three months ago. Her name is Jewel Jones, and she's a fine artist, and she got me my job at the night club where I work now." His mouth worked. "I know what you're doing, you're trying to make it nasty, and you're trying to catch me getting my facts twisted. Bringing that dog here to growl at me—can I help it if I don't like dogs?"

He ran his fingers, both hands, through his hair. When the hair was messed good he gestured like a night-club performer. "Die like a dog," he said. "That's what Phil did, died like a dog. Poor Phil, I wouldn't want to see that again."

"You said," I ventured, "that you and he were good friends."

His head jerked up. "I did not. Did I say that?"

"More or less. Maybe not in those words. Why, weren't you?"

"We were not. I haven't got any good friends."

"You just said that the girl that used to live here got you a job. That sounds like a good friend. Or did she owe you something?"

"Not a damn thing. Why do you keep bringing her up?"

"I didn't bring her up, you did. I only asked who was the former tenant in the apartment below you. Why, would you rather keep her out of it?"

"I don't have to keep her out. She's not in it."

"Perhaps not. Did she know Philip Kampf?"

"I guess so. Sure she did."

"How well did she know him?"

He shook his head. "Now you're getting personal, and I'm the wrong person. If Phil was alive you could ask him, and he might tell you. Me, I don't know."

I smiled at him. "All that does, Mr. Aland, is make me curious. Somebody in this house murdered Kampf. So we ask you questions, and when we come to one you shy at, naturally we wonder why. If you don't like talking about Kampf and that girl, think what it could mean. For instance, it could mean that the girl was yours, and Kampf took her away from you, and that was why you killed him when he came here yesterday. Or it could—"

"She wasn't mine!"

"Uh-huh. Or it could mean that although she wasn't yours, you were under a deep obligation to her, and Kampf had given her a dirty deal, or he was threatening her with something, and she wanted him disposed of, and you obliged. Or of course it could be merely that Kampf had something on you."

He had his head tilted back so he could look down on me. "You're in the wrong racket," he asserted. "You ought to be writing TV scripts."

I stuck with him only a few more minutes, having got all I could hope for under the circumstances. Since I was letting him assume that I was a city employee, I couldn't very well try to pry him loose for a trip to Wolfe's place. Also I had two more calls to make, and there was no telling when I might be interrupted by a phone call or a courier to one of them from downtown. The only further item I gathered from Jerome Aland was that he wasn't trying to get from under by slipping in any insinuations about his co-tenants. He had no opinions or ideas about who had killed poor Phil. When I left he stood up, but he let me go and open the door for myself.

I went down a flight, to Meegan's door, and knocked and waited. Just as I was raising a fist to make it louder and better there were footsteps inside, and the door opened. Meegan was still in his shirt sleeves and still uncombed.

"Well?" he demanded.

"Back again," I said firmly but not offensively. "With a few questions. If you don't mind?"

"You know damn well I mind."

"Naturally. Mr. Talento has been called down to the District Attorney's office. This might possibly save you another trip there."

He sidestepped, and I went in. The room was the same size and shape as Aland's, above, and the furniture, though different, was no more desirable. The table against a wall was lopsided—probably the one that Jewel Jones hoped they had fixed for him. I took a chair at its end, and he took another and sat frowning at me.

"Haven't I seen you before?" he wanted to know.

"Sure, we were here with the dog."

"I mean before that. Wasn't it you in Nero Wolfe's office yesterday?"

"That's right."

"How come?"

I raised my brows. "Haven't you got the lines crossed, Mr. Meegan? I'm here to ask questions, not to answer them. I was in Wolfe's office on business. I often am. Now—"

"He's a fat, arrogant halfwit!"

"You may be right. He's certainly arrogant. Now,

I'm here on business." I got out my notebook and pencil. "You moved into this place nine days ago. Please tell me exactly how you came to take this apartment."

He glared. "I've told it at least three times."

"I know. This is the way it's done. I'm not trying to catch you in some little discrepancy, but you could have omitted something important. Just assume I haven't heard it before. Go ahead."

"Oh, my God." His head dropped and his lips tightened. Normally he might not have been a bad-looking guy, with blond hair and gray eyes and a long bony face, but now, having spent the night, or most of it, with Homicide and the DA, he looked it, especially his eyes, which were red and puffy.

He lifted his head. "I'm a commercial photographer —in Pittsburgh. Two years ago I married a girl named Margaret Ryan. Seven months later she left me. I didn't know whether she went alone or with somebody. She just left. She left Pittsburgh too, or anyway I couldn't find her there, and her family never saw her or heard from her. About five months later, about a year ago, a man I know, a businessman I do work for, came back from a trip to New York and said he'd seen her in a theater here with a man. He went and spoke to her, but she claimed he was mistaken. He was sure it was her. I came to New York and spent a week looking around but didn't find her. I didn't go to the police because I didn't want to. You want a better reason, but that's mine."

"I'll skip that." I was writing in the notebook. "Go ahead."

"Two weeks ago I went to look at a show of pictures at the Institute in Pittsburgh. There was a painting there, an oil, a big one. It was called 'Three Young Mares at Pasture,' and it was an interior, a room, with three women in it. One of them was on a couch, and two of them were on a rug on the floor. They were eating apples. The one on the couch was my wife. I was sure of it the minute I saw her, and after I stood and studied it I was even surer. There was absolutely no doubt of it."

"We're not challenging that," I assured him. "What did you do?"

"The artist's signature looked like Chapple, but of course the catalogue settled that. It was Ross Chaffee. I went to the Institute office and asked about him. They thought he lived in New York but weren't sure. I had some work on hand I had to finish, and it took a couple of days, and then I came to New York. I had no trouble finding Ross Chaffee; he was in the phone book. I went to see him at his studio—here in this house. First I told him I was interested in that figure in his painting, that I thought she would be just right to model for some photographs I wanted to do, but he said that his opinion of photography as a medium was such that he wouldn't care to supply models for it, and he was bowing me out, so I told him how it was. I told him the whole thing. Then he was different. He sympathized with me and said he would be glad to help me if he could, but he had painted that picture more than a year ago, and he used so many different models for his pictures that it was impossible to remember which was which."

Meegan stopped, and I looked up from the notebook. He said aggressively, "I'm repeating that that sounded phony to me."

"Go right ahead. You're telling it."

"I say it was phony. A photographer might use hundreds of models in a year, and he might forget, but not a painter. Not a picture like that. I got a little tactless with him, and then I apologized. He said he might be able to refresh his memory and asked me to phone him the next day. Instead of phoning I went back the next day to see him, but he said he simply couldn't remember and doubted if he ever could. I didn't get tactless again. Coming in the house, I had noticed a sign that there was a furnished apartment to let, and when I left Chaffee I found the janitor and rented it, and went to my hotel for my bags and moved in. I knew damn well my wife had modeled for that picture, and I knew I could find her. I wanted to be as close as I could to Chaffee and the people who came to see him."

I wanted something too. I wanted to say that he must have had a photograph of his wife along and that I would like to see it, but of course I didn't dare, since it was a cinch that he had already either given it to the cops, or refused to, or claimed he didn't have one. So I merely asked, "What progress did you make?"

"Not much. I tried to get friendly with Chaffee but didn't get very far. I met the other two tenants, Talento and Aland, but that didn't get me anywhere. Finally I decided I would have to get some expert help, and that was why I went to see Nero Wolfe. You were there, you know how that came out—that big blob."

I nodded. "He has dropsy of the ego. What did you want him to do?"

"I've told you."

"Tell it again."

"I was going to have him tap Chaffee's phone."

"That's illegal," I said severely.

"All right, I didn't do it."

I flipped a page of the notebook. "Go back a little.

During that week, besides the tenants here, how many of Chaffee's friends and acquaintances did you meet?"

"Just two, as I've told you. A young woman, a model, in his studio one day, and I don't remember her name, and a man that was there another day, a man that Chaffee said buys his pictures. His name was Braunstein."

"You're leaving out Philip Kampf."

Meegan leaned forward and put a fist on the table. "Yes, and I'm going to leave him out. I never saw him or heard of him."

"What would you say if I said you were seen with him?"

"I'd say you were a dirty liar!" The red eyes looked redder. "As if I wasn't already having enough trouble, now you set on me about a murder of a man I never heard of! You bring a dog here and tell me to pat it, for God's sake!"

I nodded. "That's your hard luck, Mr. Meegan. You're not the first man that's had a murder for company without inviting it." I closed the notebook and put it in my pocket. "You'd better find some way of handling your troubles without having people's phones tapped." I arose. "Stick around, please. You may be wanted downtown anyhow."

He went to open the door for me. I would have liked to get more details of his progress with Ross Chaffee, or lack of it, and his contacts with the other two tenants, but it seemed more important to have some words with Chaffee before I got interrupted. As I mounted the two flights to the top floor my wristwatch said twenty-eight minutes past ten.

V

"I know there's no use complaining," Ross Chaffee said, "about these interruptions to my work. Under the circumstances." He was being very gracious about it.

The top floor was quite different from the others. I don't know what his living quarters in front were like, but the studio, in the rear, was big and high and anything but crummy. There were sculptures around, big and little, and canvases of all sizes were stacked and propped against racks. The walls were covered with drapes, solid gray, with nothing on them. Each of two easels—one much larger than the other—held a canvas that had been worked on. There were several plain chairs and two upholstered ones, and an oversized divan, nearly square. I had been steered to one of the upholstered numbers, and Chaffee, still in his smock, had moved a plain one to sit facing me.

"Only don't prolong it unnecessarily," he requested.

I said I wouldn't. "There are a couple of points," I told him, "that we wonder about a little. Of course it could be merely a coincidence that Richard Meegan came to town looking for his wife, and came to see you, and rented an apartment here just nine days before Kampf was murdered, but a coincidence like that will have to stand some going over. Frankly, Mr. Chaffee, there are those, and I happen to be one of them, who find it hard to believe that you couldn't remember who modeled for an important figure in a picture you painted. I know what you say, but it's still hard to believe."

"My dear sir." Chaffee was smiling. "Then you must think I'm lying."

"I didn't say so."

"But you do, of course." He shrugged. "To what end? What deep design am I cherishing?"

"I wouldn't know. You say you wanted to help Meegan find his wife."

"No, not that I wanted to. I was willing to. He was a horrible nuisance."

"He must have been a first-class pest."

"He was. He is."

"It should have been worth some effort to get rid of him. Did you make any?"

"I have explained what I did—in a statement, and signed it. I have nothing to add. I tried to refresh my memory. One of your colleagues suggested that I might have gone to Pittsburgh to look at the picture. I suppose he was being funny."

A flicker of annoyance in his fine dark eyes, which were as clear and bright as if he had had a good eight hours of innocent slumber, warned me that I was supposed to have read his statement, and if I aroused a suspicion that I hadn't he might get personal.

I gave him an earnest eye. "Look, Mr. Chaffee. This thing is bad for all concerned. It will get worse instead of better until we find out who killed Kampf. You men in this house must know things about one another, and maybe some things connected with Kampf, that you're not telling. I don't expect a man like you to pass out dirt just for the hell of it, but any dirt that's connected with this murder is going to come out, and if you know of any and are keeping it to yourself you're a bigger fool than you look."

"Quite a speech." He was smiling again.

"Thanks. You make one."

"I'm not as eloquent as you are." He shook his head. "No, I don't believe I can help you any. I can't say I'm a total stranger to dirt; that would be smug;

but what you're after—no. You have my opinion of
Kampf, whom I knew quite well; he was in some respects admirable but had his full share of faults. I
would say approximately the same of Talento. I have
known Aland only casually—certainly not intimately. I
know no more of Meegan than you do. I haven't the
slightest notion why any of them might have wanted to
kill Philip Kampf. If you expect—"

A phone rang. Chaffee crossed to a table at the end
of the divan and answered it. He told it yes a couple of
times, and then a few words, and then, "But one of
your men is here now. . . . I don't know his name, I
didn't ask him. . . . He may be, I don't know. . . .
Very well, one-fifty-five Leonard Street. . . . Yes, I
can leave in a few minutes."

He hung up and turned to me. I spoke first, on my
feet. "So they want you at the DA's office. Don't tell
them I said so, but they'd rather keep a murder in the
file till hell freezes over than have the squad crack it. If
they want my name they know where to ask."

I marched to the door, opened it, and was gone.

There were still no PD cars out in front. After turning left on Court Street and continuing two blocks, I
was relieved to find the cab still there, with its passenger perched on the seat looking out at the scenery. If
the hackie had gone off with him to sell him, or if Stebbins had happened by and hijacked him, I wouldn't
have dared to go home at all. He seemed pleased to see
me, as he damned well should have been. During the
drive to Thirty-fifth Street he sat with his rump
braced against me for a buttress. The meter said only
six dollars and something, but I didn't request any
change. If Wolfe wanted to put me to work on a murder merely because he had got infatuated with a dog,
let it cost him something.

I noticed that when we entered the office Jet went over to Wolfe, in place behind his desk, without any sign of bashfulness or uncertainty, proving that the evening before, during my absence, Wolfe had made approaches, probably had fed him something, and possibly had even patted him. Remarks occurred to me, but I saved them. I might be called on before long to spend some valuable time demonstrating that I had not been guilty of impersonating an officer, and that it wasn't my fault if murder suspects mistook me for one.

Wolfe put down his empty beer glass and inquired, "Well?"

I reported. The situation called for a full and detailed account, and I supplied it, with Wolfe leaning back with his eyes closed. When I came to the end he asked no questions. Instead, he opened his eyes, straightened up, and began, "Call the—"

I cut him off. "Wait a minute. After a hard morning's work I claim the satisfaction of suggesting it myself. I thought of it long ago. What's the name of the Institute in Pittsburgh where they have shows of pictures?"

"Indeed. It's a shot at random."

"I know it is, but it's only a buck. I just spent ten on a taxi. What's the name?"

"Pittsburgh Art Institute."

I swiveled for the phone on my desk, got the operator, and put in the call. I got through to the Institute in no time, but it took a quarter of an hour, with relays to three different people, to get what I was after.

I hung up and turned to Wolfe. "The show ended a week ago yesterday. Thank God I won't have to go to Pittsburgh. The picture was lent by Mr. Herman Braunstein of New York, who owns it. It was shipped back to him by express four days ago. He wouldn't give me Braunstein's address."

"The phone book."

I had it and was flipping the pages. "Here we are. Business on Broad Street, residence on Park Avenue. There's only one Herman."

"Get him."

"I don't think so. He may be a poop. It might take all day. Why don't I go to the residence without phoning? It's probably there, and if I can't get in you can fire me. I'm thinking of resigning anyhow."

He had his doubts, since it was my idea, but he bought it. After considering the problem a little, I went to the cabinet beneath the bookshelves, got out the Veblex camera, with accessories, slung the strap of the case over my shoulder, told Wolfe I wouldn't be back until I saw the picture, wherever it was, and beat it. Before going I dialed Talento's number to tell him not to bother to keep his appointment, but there was no answer. Either he was still engaged at the DA's office or he was on his way to Thirty-fifth Street, and if he came during my absence that was all right, since Jet was there to protect Wolfe.

A taxi took me to the end of a sidewalk canopy in front of one of the palace hives on Park Avenue in the Seventies, and I undertook to walk past the doorman without giving him a glance, but he stopped me. I said professionally, "Braunstein, taking pictures, I'm late," and kept going, and got away with it. After crossing the luxurious lobby to the elevator, which luckily was there with the door open, I entered, saying, "Braunstein, please," and the chauffeur shut the door and pulled the lever. We stopped at the twelfth floor, and I stepped out. There was a door to the right and another to the left, and I turned right without asking, on a

fifty-fifty chance, listening for a possible correction
from the elevator man, who was standing by with his
door open.

It was one of the simplest chores I have ever performed. In answer to my ring the door was opened by
a middle-aged female husky, in uniform with apron,
and when I told her I had come to take a picture she
let me in, asked me to wait, and disappeared. In a couple of minutes a tall and dignified dame with white hair
came through an arch and asked what I wanted. I apologized for disturbing her and said I would deeply appreciate it if she would let me take a picture of a
painting which had recently been shown at the Pittsburgh Institute, on loan by Mr. Braunstein. It was
called "Three Young Mares at Pasture." A Pittsburgh
client of mine had admired it, and had intended to go
back and photograph it for his collection, but the picture had gone before he got around to it.

She wanted some information, such as my name
and address and the name of my Pittsburgh client,
which I supplied gladly without a script, and then led
me through the arch into a room not quite as big as
Madison Square Garden. It would have been a pleasure, and also instructive, to do a little glomming at the
rugs and furniture and other miscellaneous objects, especially the dozen or more pictures on the walls, but
that would have to wait. She went across to a picture
near the far end, said, "That's it," and lowered herself
onto a chair.

It was a nice picture. I had half expected the mares
to be without clothes, but they were fully dressed. Re-
marking that I didn't wonder that my client wanted a
photograph of it, I got busy with my equipment, including flash bulbs. She sat and watched. I took four
shots from slightly different angles, acting and looking

professional, I hoped; got my stuff back in the case; thanked her warmly on behalf of my client; promised to send her some prints; and left. That was all there was to it.

Out on the sidewalk again, I walked west to Madison, turned downtown and found a drugstore, went in to the phone booth, and dialed a number.

Wolfe's voice came. "Yes? Whom do you want?"

I've told him a hundred times that's a hell of a way to answer the phone, but he's too damn pigheaded.

I spoke. "I want you. I've seen the picture, and I wouldn't have thought that stallion had it in him. It glows with color and life, and the blood seems to pulsate under the warm skin. The shadows are transparent, with a harmonious blending—"

"Shut up! Yes or no?"

"Yes. You have met Mrs. Meegan. Would you like to meet her again?"

"I would. Get her."

I didn't have to look in the phone book for her address, having already done so. I left the drugstore and flagged a taxi.

There was no doorman problem at the number on East Forty-ninth Street. It was an old brick house that had been painted a bright yellow and modernized, notably with a self-service elevator, though I didn't know that until I got in. Getting in was a little complicated. Pressing the button marked "Jewel Jones" in the vestibule was easy enough, and also unhooking the receiver and putting it to my ear, and placing my mouth close to the grille, but then it got more difficult.

A voice crackled. "Yes?"

"Miss Jones?"

"Yes. Who is it?"

"Archie Goodwin. I want to see you. Not a message from Victor Talento."

"What do you want?"

"Let me in and I'll tell you."

"No. What is it?"

"It's very personal. If you don't want to hear it from me I'll go and bring Richard Meegan, and maybe you'll tell him."

I heard the gasp. She should have known those house phones are sensitive. After a pause. "Why do you say that? I told you I don't know any Meegan."

"You're way behind. I just saw a picture called 'Three Young Mares at Pasture.' Let me in."

Another pause, and the line went dead. I put the receiver on the hook, and turned and placed my hand on the knob. There was a click, and I pushed the door and entered, crossed the little lobby to the elevator, pushed the button and, when the door opened, slid in, pushed the button marked 5, and was ascending. When the elevator stopped I opened the door and emerged into a tiny foyer. A door was standing open, and on the sill was Miss Jones in a blue negligee. She started to say something, but I rudely ignored it.

"Listen," I said, "There's no sense in prolonging this. Last night I gave you your pick between Mr. Wolfe and Sergeant Stebbins; now it's either Mr. Wolfe or Meegan. I should think you'd prefer Mr. Wolfe because he's the kind of man that understands; you said so yourself. I'll wait here while you change, but don't try phoning anybody, because you won't know where you are until you've talked with Mr. Wolfe, and also because their wires are probably tapped. Don't put on anything red. Mr. Wolfe dislikes red. He likes yellow."

She stepped to me and had a hand on my arm. "Archie. Where did you see the picture?"

"I'll tell you on the way down. Let's go."

She gave the arm a gentle tug. "You don't have to wait out here. Come in and sit down." Another tug, just as gentle. "Come on."

I patted her fingers, not wishing to be boorish. "Sorry," I told her, "but I'm afraid of young mares. One kicked me once."

She turned and disappeared into the apartment, leaving the door standing open.

VI

"Don't call me Mrs. Meegan!" Jewel Jones cried.

Wolfe was in as bad a humor as she was. True, she had been hopelessly cornered, with no weapons within reach, but he had been compelled to tell Fritz to postpone lunch until further notice.

"I was only," he said crustily, "stressing the fact that your identity is not a matter for discussion. Legally you are Mrs. Richard Meegan. That understood, I'll call you anything you say. Miss Jones?"

"Yes." She was on the red leather chair, but not in it. Just on its edge, she looked as if she were set to spring up and scoot any second.

"Very well." Wolfe regarded her. "You realize, madam, that everything you say will be received skeptically. You are a competent liar. Your offhand denial of acquaintance with Mr. Meegan last night was better than competent. Now. When did Mr. Chaffee tell you that your husband was in town looking for you?"

"I didn't say Mr. Chaffee told me."

"Someone did. Who and when?"

She was hanging on. "How do you know someone did?"

He wiggled a finger at her. "I beg you, Miss Jones, to realize the pickle you're in. It is not credible that Mr. Chaffee couldn't remember the name of the model for that figure in his picture. The police don't believe it, and they haven't the advantage of knowing, as I do, that it was you and that you lived in that house for a year, and that you still see Mr. Chaffee occasionally. When your husband came and asked Mr. Chaffee for the name, and Mr. Chaffee pleaded a faulty memory, and your husband rented an apartment there and made it plain that he intended to persevere, it is preposterous to suppose that Mr. Chaffee didn't tell you. I don't envy you your tussles with the police after they learn about you."

"They don't have to learn about me, do they?"

"Pfui. I'm surprised they haven't got to you already, though it's been only eighteen hours. They soon will, even if not through me. I know this is no frolic for you, here with me, but they will almost make it seem so."

She was thinking. Her brow was wrinkled and her eyes straight at Wolfe. "Do you know," she asked, "what I think would be the best thing? I don't know why I didn't think of it before. You're a detective, you're an expert at helping people in trouble, and I'm certainly in trouble. I'll pay you to help me. I could pay you a little now."

"Not now or ever, Miss Jones." Wolfe was blunt. "When did Mr. Chaffee tell you that your husband was here looking for you?"

"You won't even listen to me," she complained.

"Talk sense and I will. When?"

She edged back on the chair an inch. "You don't know my husband. He was jealous about me even before we married, and then he was worse. It got so bad

I couldn't stand it, and that was why I left him. I knew if I stayed in Pittsburgh he would find me and kill me, so I came to New York. A friend of mine had come here—I mean, just a friend. I got a job at a modeling agency and made enough to live on, and I met a lot of people. Ross Chaffee was one of them, and he wanted to use me in a picture, and I let him. Of course he paid me, but that wasn't so important, because soon after that I met Phil Kampf, and he got me a tryout at a night club, and I made it. About then I had a scare, though. A man from Pittsburgh saw me at a theater and came and spoke to me, but I told him he was wrong, that I had never been in Pittsburgh."

"That was a year ago," Wolfe muttered.

"Yes. I was a little leery about the night club, in public like that, but months went by and nothing happened, and then all of a sudden this happened. Ross Chaffee phoned me that my husband had come and asked about the picture, and I asked him for God's sake not to tell him who it was, and he promised he wouldn't. You see, you don't know my husband. I knew he was trying to find me so he could kill me."

"You've said that twice. Has he ever killed anybody?"

"I didn't say anybody; I said me. I seem to have an effect on men." She gestured for understanding. "They just go for me. And Dick— Well, I know him, that's all. I left him a year and a half ago, and he's still looking for me, and that's what he's like. When Ross told me he was here I was scared stiff. I quit working at the club because he might happen to go there and see me, and I didn't hardly leave my apartment until last night."

Wolfe nodded. "To meet Mr. Talento. What for?"

"I told you."

"Yes, but then you were merely Miss Jones. Now you are also Mrs. Meegan. What for?"

"That doesn't change it any. I had heard on the radio about Phil being killed, and I wanted to know about it. I rang Ross Chaffee and I rang Jerry Aland, but neither of them answered, so I rang Vic Talento. He wouldn't tell me anything on the phone, but he said he would meet me."

"Did Mr. Aland and Mr. Talento know you had sat for that picture?"

"Sure they did."

"And that Mr. Meegan had seen it and recognized you, and was here looking for you?"

"Yes, they knew all about it. Ross had to tell them, because he thought Dick might ask them if they knew who had modeled for the picture, and he had to warn them not to tell. They said they wouldn't, and they didn't. They're all good friends of mine."

She stopped to do something. She opened her black leather bag on her lap, took out a purse, and fingered its contents, peering into it. She raised her eyes to Wolfe. "I can pay you forty dollars now, to start. I'm not just in trouble, I'm in danger of my life, really I am. I don't see how you can refuse— You're not listening!"

Apparently he wasn't. With his lips pursed, he was watching the tip of his forefinger make little circles on his desk blotter. Her reproach didn't stop him, but after a moment he moved his eyes to me and said abruptly, "Get Mr. Chaffee."

"No!" she cried. "I don't want him to know—"

"Nonsense," he snapped at her. "Everybody will have to know everything, and why drag it out? Get him, Archie. I'll speak to him."

I got at the phone and dialed. I doubted if he would be back from his session with the DA, but he was. His "hello" was enough to recognize his voice by. I pitched mine low so he wouldn't know it, not caring to start a debate as to whether I had or had not impersonated an officer, and merely told him that Nero Wolfe wished to speak to him.

Wolfe took it at his desk. "Mr. Chaffee? This is Nero Wolfe. . . . I've assumed an interest in the murder of Philip Kampf and have done some investigating. . . . Just one moment, please, don't ring off. . . . Sitting here in my office is Mrs. Richard Meegan, alias Miss Jewel Jones. . . . Please let me finish. . . . I shall of course have to detain her and communicate with the police, since they will want her as a material witness in a murder case, but before I do that I would like to discuss the matter with you and the others who live in that house. Will you undertake to bring them here as soon as possible? . . . No, I'll say nothing further on the phone, I want you here, all of you. If Mr. Meegan is balky, you might as well tell him his wife is here. I'll expect—"

She was across to him in a leap that any young mare might have envied, grabbing for the phone and shrieking at it, "Don't tell him, Ross! Don't bring him! Don't—"

My own leap and dash around the end of the desk was fairly good too. Getting her shoulders, I yanked her back, with enough enthusiasm so that I landed in the red leather chair with her on my lap, and since she was by no means through I wrapped my arms around her, pinning her arms to her sides, whereupon she started kicking my shins with her heels. She kept on kicking until Wolfe finished with Chaffee. When he hung up she suddenly relaxed and was limp, and I realized how warm she felt tight against me.

Wolfe scowled at us. "An affecting sight," he snorted.

VII

There were various aspects of the situation. One was lunch. For Wolfe it was unthinkable to have company in the house at mealtime, no matter what his or her status was, without feeding him or her, but he certainly wasn't going to sit at table with a female who had just pounced on him and clawed at him. That problem was simple. She and I were served in the dining room, and Wolfe ate in the kitchen with Fritz. We were served, but she didn't eat much. She kept listening and looking toward the hall, though I assured her that care would be taken to see that her husband didn't kill her on those premises.

A second aspect was the reaction of three of the tenants to their discovery of my identity. I handled that myself. When the doorbell rang and I admitted them, at a quarter past two, I told them I would be glad to discuss my split personality with any or all of them later, if they still wanted to, but they would have to file it until Wolfe was through. Victor Talento had another beef that he wouldn't file, that I had double-crossed him on the message he had asked me to take to Jewel Jones. He wanted to get nasty about it and demanded a private talk with Wolfe, but I told him to go climb a rope.

I also had to handle the third aspect, which had two angles. There was Miss Jones's theory that her husband would kill her on sight, which might or might not be well founded, and there was the fact that one of them had killed Kampf and might go to extremes if pushed. On that I took three precautions: I showed them the Carley .38 I had put in my pocket and told them it was loaded; I insisted on patting them from shoulders to ankles; and I kept Miss Jones in the dining room until I had them seated in the office, on a row of chairs facing Wolfe's desk, and until Wolfe had come in from the kitchen and been told their names. When he was in his chair behind his desk I went across the hall for her and brought her in.

Meegan jumped up and started for us. I stiff-armed him and made it good. She got behind me. Talento and Aland left their chairs, presumably to help protect the mare. Meegan was talking, and so were they. I detoured with her around back of them and got her to a chair at the end of my desk, and when I sat I was in an ideal spot to trip anyone headed for her. Talento and Aland had pulled Meegan down onto a chair between them, and he sat staring at her.

"With that hubbub over," Wolfe said, "I want to be sure I have the names right." His eyes went from left to right. "Talento, Meegan, Aland, Chaffee. Is that correct?

I told him yes.

"Then I'll proceed." He glanced up at the wall clock. "Twenty hours ago Philip Kampf was killed in the house where you gentlemen live. The circumstances indicate that one of you killed him. But I won't rehash the multifarious details which you have already discussed at length with the police; you are familiar with them. I have not been hired to work on this case; the only client I have is a dog, and he came to my office by inadvertence. However, it is—"

The doorbell rang. I asked myself if I had put the chain bolt on, and decided I had. Through the open door to the hall I saw Fritz passing to answer it. Wolfe started to go on, but was annoyed by the sound of voices, Fritz's and another's, coming through, and stopped. The voices continued. Wolfe shut his eyes and compressed his lips. The audience sat and looked at him.

Then Fritz appeared in the doorway and announced, "Inspector Cramer, sir."

Wolfe's eyes opened. "What does he want?"

"I told him you are engaged. He says he knows you are, that the four men were followed to your house and he was notified. He says he expected you to be trying some trick with the dog, and he knows that's what you are doing, and he intends to come in and see what it is. Sergeant Stebbins is with him."

Wolfe grunted. "Archie, tell—No. You'd better stay where you are. Fritz, tell him he may see and hear what I'm doing, provided he gives me thirty minutes without interruptions or demands. If he agrees to that, bring them in."

"Wait!" Ross Chaffee was on his feet. "You said you would discuss it with us before you communicated with the police."

"I haven't communicated with them, they're here."

"You told them to come!"

"No. I would have preferred to deal with you men first and then call them, but here they are and they might as well join us. Bring them, Fritz, on that condition."

"Yes, sir."

Fritz went. Chaffee thought he had something more to say, decided he hadn't, and sat down. Talento said something to him, and he shook his head. Jerry Aland, much more presentable now that he was combed and dressed, kept his eyes fastened on Wolfe.

For Meegan, apparently, there was no one in the room but him and his wife.

Cramer and Stebbins marched in, halted three paces from the door, and took a survey.

"Be seated," Wolfe invited them. "Luckily, Mr. Cramer, your usual chair is unoccupied."

"Where's the dog?" Cramer barked.

"In the kitchen. You had better suspend that prepossession. It's understood that you will be merely a spectator for thirty minutes?"

"That's what I said."

"Then sit down. But you should have one piece of information. You know the gentlemen, of course, but not the lady. Her current name is Miss Jewel Jones. Her legal name is Mrs. Richard Meegan."

"Meegan?" Cramer stared. "The one in the picture Chaffee painted? Meegan's wife?"

"That's right. Please be seated."

"Where did you get her?"

"That can wait. No interruptions and no demands. Confound it, sit down!"

Cramer went and lowered himself onto the red leather chair. Purley Stebbins got one of the yellow ones and planted it behind the row, between Chaffee and Aland.

Wolfe regarded the quartet. "I was about to say, gentlemen, that it was something the dog did that pointed to the murderer for me. But before—"

"What did it do?" Cramer barked.

"You know all about it," Wolfe told him coldly. "Mr. Goodwin related it to you exactly as it happened. If you interrupt again, by heaven, you can take them all down to your quarters, not including the dog, and stew it out yourself."

He went back to the four. "But before I come to

that, another thing or two. I offer no comment on your guile with Mr. Meegan. You were all friends of Miss Jones's, having, I suppose, enjoyed various degrees of intimacy with her, and you refused to disclose her to a husband whom she had abandoned and professed to fear. I will even concede that there was a flavor of gallantry in your conduct. But when Mr. Kampf was murdered and the police swarmed in, it was idiotic to try to keep her out of it. They were sure to get to her. I got to her first only because of Mr. Goodwin's admirable enterprise and characteristic luck."

He shook his head at them. "It was also idiotic of you to assume that Mr. Goodwin was a police officer, and admit him and answer his questions, merely because he had been present during the abortive experiment with the dog. You should have asked to see his credentials. None of you had any idea who he was. Even Mr. Meegan, who had seen him in this office in the morning, was bamboozled. I mention this to anticipate any possible official complaint that Mr. Goodwin impersonated an officer. You know he didn't. He merely took advantage of your unwarranted assumption."

He shifted in his chair. "Another thing. Yesterday morning Mr. Meegan called here by appointment to ask me to do a job for him. With his first words I gathered that it was something about his wife, and I don't take that kind of work, and I was brusque with him. He was offended. He rushed out in a temper, getting his hat and raincoat from the rack in the hall, and he took Mr. Goodwin's coat instead of his own. Late in the afternoon Mr. Goodwin went to Arbor Street, with the coat that had been left in error, to exchange it. He saw that in front of number twenty-nine there were collected two police cars, a policeman on post, some people, and a dog. He decided to postpone his errand and went on by, after a brief halt during which he patted the dog. He walked home, and had gone nearly two miles when he discovered that the dog was following him. He brought the dog in a cab the rest of the way, to this house and this room."

He flattened a palm on his desk. "Now. Why did the dog follow Mr. Goodwin through the turmoil of the city? Mr. Cramer's notion that the dog was enticed is poppycock. Mr. Goodwin is willing to believe, as many men are, that he is irresistible to both dogs and women, and doubtless his vanity impeded his intellect or he would have reached the same conclusion that I did. The dog didn't follow him; it followed the coat. You ask, as I did, how to account for Mr. Kampf's dog following Mr. Meegan's coat. I couldn't. I can't. Then, since it was unquestionably Mr. Kampf's dog, it couldn't have been Mr. Meegan's coat. It is better than a conjecture, it is next thing to a certainty, that it was Mr. Kampf's coat."

His gaze leveled at the husband. "Mr. Meegan. Some two hours ago I learned from Mr. Goodwin that you maintain that you had never seen or heard of Mr. Kampf. That was fairly conclusive, but before sending for you I had to verify my conjecture that the model who had sat for Mr. Chaffee's picture was your wife. I would like to hear it straight from you. Did you ever meet with Philip Kampf alive?"

Meegan was meeting the gaze. "No."

"Don't you want to qualify that?"

"No."

"Then where did you get his raincoat?"

No answer. Meegan's jaw worked. He spoke. "I didn't have his raincoat, or if I did I didn't know it."

"That won't do. I warn you, you are in deadly peril.

The raincoat that you brought into this house and left here is in the hall now, there on the rack. It can easily be established that it belonged to Mr. Kampf and was worn by him. Where did you get it?"

Meegan's jaw worked some more. "I never had it, if it belonged to Kampf. This is a dirty frame. You can't prove that's the coat I left here."

Wolfe's voice sharpened. "One more chance. Have you any explanation of how Kampf's coat came into your possession?"

"No, and I don't need any."

He may not have been pure boob. If he hadn't noticed that he wore the wrong coat home, and he probably didn't, in his state of mind, this had hit him from a clear sky and he had no time to study it.

"Then you're done for," Wolfe told him. "For your own coat must be somewhere, and I think I know where. In the police laboratory. Mr. Kampf was wearing one when you killed him and pushed his body down the stairs—and that explains why, when they were making that experiment this morning, the dog showed no interest in the spot where the body had lain. It had been enveloped, not in his coat but in yours. That can be established too. If you won't explain how you got Mr. Kampf's coat, then explain how he got yours. Is that also a frame?"

Wolfe pointed a finger at him. "I note that flash in your eye, and I think I know what it means. But your brain is lagging. If, after killing him, you took your raincoat off of him and put on him the one that you thought was his, that won't help you any. For in that case the coat that was on the body is Mr. Goodwin's, and certainly that can be established, and how would you explain that? It looks hopeless, and—"

Meegan was springing up, but before he even got

well started Purley's big hands were on his shoulders, pulling him back and down. And a new voice sounded.

"I told you he would kill me! I knew he would! He killed Phil!"

Jewel Jones was looking not at her husband, who was under control, but at Wolfe. He snapped at her, "How do you know he did?"

Judging by her eyes and the way she was shaking, she would be hysterical in another two minutes, and maybe she knew it, for she poured it out. "Because Phil told me—he told me he knew Dick was here looking for me, and he knew how afraid I was of him, and he said if I wouldn't come and be with him again he would tell Dick where I was. I didn't think he really would—I didn't think Phil could be as mean as that, and I wouldn't promise, but yesterday morning he phoned me and told me he had seen Dick and told him he thought he knew who had posed for that picture, and he was going to see him again in the afternoon and tell him about me if I didn't promise, and so I promised. I thought if I promised it would give me time to decide what to do. But Phil must have gone to see Dick again anyway—"

"Where had they met in the morning?"

"At Phil's apartment, he said. And he said—that's why I know Dick killed him—he said Dick had gone off with his raincoat, and he laughed about it and said he was willing for Dick to have his raincoat if he could have Dick's wife." She was shaking harder now. "And I'll bet that's what he told Dick! That was like Phil! I'll bet he told Dick I was coming back to him and he thought that was a good trade, a raincoat for a wife! That was like Phil! You don't—"

She giggled. It started with a giggle, and then the valves busted open and here it came. When something happens in that office to smash a woman's nerves, as it has more than once, it usually falls to me to deal with it, but that time three other guys, led by Ross Chaffee, came to her, and I was glad to leave it to them. As for Wolfe, he skedaddled. If there is one thing on earth he absolutely will not be in a room with it's a woman in eruption. He got up and marched out. As for Meegan, Purley and Cramer had him.

When they left with him, they didn't take the dog. To relieve the minds of any of you who have the notion, which I understand is widespread, that it makes a dog neurotic to change its name, I might add that he responds to Jet now as if his mother had started calling him that before he had his eyes open.

As for the raincoat, Wolfe had been right about the flash in Meegan's eye. Kampf had been wearing Meegan's raincoat when he was killed, and of course that wouldn't do, so after strangling him Meegan had taken it off and put on the one he thought was Kampf's. Only it was mine. As a part of the DA's case I went down to headquarters and identified it. At the trial it helped the jury to decide that Meegan deserved the big one. After that was over I suppose I could have claimed it, but the idea didn't appeal to me. My new one is a different color.

The World of
Rex Stout

Now, for the first time ever, enjoy a peek into the life of Nero Wolfe's creator, Rex Stout, courtesy of the Stout Estate. Pulled from Rex Stout's own archives, here are rarely seen, never-before-published memorabilia. Each title in "The Rex Stout Library" will offer an exclusive look into the life of the man who gave Nero Wolfe life.

Three Witnesses

In 1967 Rex Stout was approached by the school newspaper of Junior High School 115 in New York City and asked the following question: "Which book or books were your favorites as a teenager and why?" Stout's reply is reproduced here.

I was an insatiable book reader from the age of five. The list below of some of my favorites as a teenager may give the impression that I am showing off, but I'm not: it is quite honest.

History of England by Macaulay, _Essays_ by Francis Bacon, _Alice in Wonderland_ by Lewis Carroll, _Vanity Fair_ by Thackeray, _Little Lord Fauntleroy_ by Frances Hodgson Burnett, _Les Miserables_ by Victor Hugo, _Poems_ by John Keats, _Paradise Lost_ by John Milton, the Sherlock Holmes stories by Conan Doyle, _Little Women_ by Louisa May Alcott, _Tom Sawyer_ by Mark Twain, and the novels and stories of Rudyard Kipling.

Thank you for reminding me of those wonderful days when I read so many exciting things the first time.

Sincerely,

Rex Stout